LOTUS SOURCE

BECOMING LOTUS BORN

LOTUS SOURCE

BECOMING LOTUS BORN

C. R. LAMA & JAMES LOW

Published by Simply Being www.simplybeing.co.uk

British Library Cataloguing in Publication Data. A catalogue record for this book is available from the British Library.

ISBN: 978-1-7399381-2-3

Cover image by Sarah Allen

Other images are taken from the *Himalayan Art Resources* (*https://www. himalayanart.org/*) which kindly makes their resources available for personal, educational and non-commercial use.

Layout by Sarah Allen.

Contents

HOMAGE

I thought I saw you
But I merely projected

You saw me
Yet I wasn't rejected

Preface

This is a book about light. Light shines out into space illuminating that vastness and all that arises in it. We see this with the sun and the moon – when their light is unimpeded it flows equally in all directions, free of bias. But when it illuminates things, shadows occur as areas of darkness. The aim of the practices described here is to experience translucence free of impediment and shadow. The absence of inherent existence in objects such as houses, people or bananas is actual, yet is disguised by our own reifying projections.

The root of all suffering for all sentient beings is not disease, war, climate change, the harmful actions of others, or even our own current mistakes and delinquencies. These immediate causes of distress arise from one root – our unawareness of how we actually are. Due to this unawareness we do not see clearly but only through the veils of our imaginings. We imagine that we and all the creatures we meet actually exist as independent entities. Then it is as if each living creature was just itself. For example, we see a cow in a field and we exclaim, "Oh what a beautiful cow!" We tend to ignore the fact that the cow is an enslaved prisoner, a captive who will serve the purposes of its owner. The word 'cow' seems to indicate an autonomous entity – a cow is a cow is a cow. Yet the cow must eat and breathe and is dependent on the farmer for water and salt. The farmer maintains the cow and the cow maintains the farmer. Their functions are mutually confirming. There are no self-existing cows, or self-existing farmers or self-existing humans or anything else 'self-existing'.

The light of our own mind as it is is like that of the sun and the moon, spreading evenly to display the patterns of light which we mistake for entities. When we do not see light as light we imagine entities and these entities become the limit of our world. We are like a lamp in a clay pot illuminating a small universe where we think we know all about what is going on. We know ourselves and the patterns of our life – and so everything seems to be much as we conceive it to be. The function of the practice is to break open or see through the clay pot of contrivance, association, assumption and delusion so that the intrinsic light of our unborn mind shines forth free of limitation and reification.

Light is energy and the energy of the base or ground or source arises as both phenomena and ideas. The interplay between the potential of light as 'physical' illumination and colour and the potential of light as 'mental' illumination and thought, feeling, memory and so on generates all the possibilities we encounter in this life and in all our lives. To see this directly we need to awaken from the sleep wherein we dream the seeming 'reality' of our illusions. We need to see that as openness we are the source of light; and that as presence we are the clarity of light, the brightness or immediacy of this field of display; and that as participation our light activates that of other light forms, leading to freedom to spontaneously respond as light with light.

We are part of a lineage of light. The primordial Buddha, the intrinsic awakening present in all sentient beings, is known as Always Good Unchanging Light *(Tib. Kun-Tu-bZang-Po 'Od-Mi-'Gyur)*. He manifests the triple aspect of Limitless Light Amitabha *(Tib. sNang-Ba mTha'-Yas)*, Measureless Light Odpagme *(Tib. 'Od-dPag-Med)* and Measureless Life Amitayus *(Tib. Tshe-dPag-Med)*. They are the Buddha forms of the Lotus Family and they embody the original unchanging knowing which discerns the unique specificity of each appearance without bias or desire. From the heart of Buddha Amitabha, Limitless Light, a letter HRI radiates light manifesting as the Lotus Born, Padmasambhava *(Tib. Padma 'Byung-gNas)*.

The lotus is the source, open ungraspable emptiness, the mind itself, pure from the very beginning. This source instantly gives rise to the presence of the kindness of all the buddhas, the effortlessly arising multi-form apparition who offers liberation through merging in his heart. He is Guru Rinpoche, the Precious Guru who is both Lotus Source and Lotus Born and all three names will be used in this book. However, although he is known as Lotus Born he has never been born and he will never die for he is the unchanging body of light. This is also who and how we are if we allow our adventitious obscurations to fall away and experience boundless lucidity. The names Amitabha and Amitayus both derive from the Sanskrit word a-mṛta, "immortal". That which is unborn is also undying. The focus of our practice is to find ourselves in this bright intrinsic freedom.

Lotus Source is the inseparability of openness and potentiality. Appearance is light. Light is ungraspable, fresh, uncontrived, immediate. The lineage also flows from Amitabha, Limitless Light, to Avalokitesvara, the Lord who Sees, and then to Padmasambhava, the Lotus Born apparition of light. In Dewachen, Great Happiness, the pure land buddha field of Amitabha, all are born in a lotus. The mantra of Avalokitesvara, Om Mani Padme Hung Hri, reminds us that the jewel of compassion is inseparable from the lotus of ever pure emptiness where it dwells. Padmasambhava the unborn Lotus Born is the vital presence of appearance and emptiness dissolving all reification and its consequent delusion. He is depicted sitting on cushions of the sun and the moon – two great outer sources of light – and they rest on a lotus, the ultimate source.

The prayers and aspirations at the beginning of the book are a means of allowing us to connect with the truth of who we are. Devotion unites where ignoring has divided. The power of devotion can be strengthened by reciting the words of the great yogis of the past, including Padmasambhava. You will find such gems in THE SEVEN CHAPTERS OF PRAYER: AS TAUGHT BY PADMA SAMBHAVA OF URGYEN, KNOWN IN TIBETAN AS LE`U BDUN MA (wandel verlag, Germany 2010) and in LONGING FOR LIMITLESS LIGHT: LETTING IN THE LIGHT OF AMITABHA'S LOVE (Simply Being, UK, 2021).

Then we have practices in the tantric style for merging with Padmasambhava either by dissolving in his light or by being carried instantly by his light into his heart. To gain the full benefit of these practices it is vital to receive the initiation and practise with others in the lineage.

The texts in this book were translated by James Low with the help and blessing of C. R. Lama, Khordong Terchen Tulku Chimed Rigdzin, more than 40 years ago. The translations have been revised by James Low who has written the introduction. The onerous work of typing and inserting corrections was done by Barbara Terris without whose help this book would not have seen the light of day. The individual texts were prepared in book form by Sarah Allen.

May we all live as light in light.

Introduction

WHO ARE YOU? Apart from all the identities you will adopt and discard in this life, you are sentient being. You are sentient, able to sense, to feel, to think, to know. You have a mind, although your 'mind' as you have learned to think of it is not how it actually is. Indeed, your concepts of and thoughts about your body, speech and mind are your great ongoing limitation. Neither you nor the world with all its inhabitants and objects are what you think they are.

WHY IS THIS? Due to reification, attachment and judgement the bright awareness which is your actual basis is hidden from you. Who has caused this? No one. In one suddenly arising moment, the delusion of an entity arose in the vast expanse illuminated by awareness. The excessive insistence of this bright delusion thickened it into a proto-existent. Dulled by the intensity of its own bright energy the moment seemed to linger after it was gone. This trace, shadow, echo, evoked a further insistent moment and gradually their traces thickened like smoke or mist till there was an impenetrable 'something'. This opacity manifested as the bifurcation of light into subject, the seeming illuminator, and object, the seemingly illuminated. From their interaction arose the diversity of imagined entities, all the people, animals, hills, tractors, and so on that form the domain of our lived experience.

Experiencing ourselves as someone somewhere we experience feelings of liking and not liking towards the objects that we encounter. Having desire for the things we like, we seek to gain access to them, and having aversion for the things we do not like, we seek to avoid contact with them. This pulse of attraction and aversion is taken to be a valid response to the actual qualities of these objects. Thus, all that we encounter becomes infected with our mental attributions and our reaction to these invested entities is inflected by our unawareness that they are reflections of our habit formations and by our responsive feelings.

Acting and reacting, our habits and tendencies become potentiated, and this leads to birth in any and all of the six realms of samsara.

Our current virtuous actions give rise later to lifespans in the three upper realms of gods, jealous gods and humans. Our current unvirtuous actions give rise later to lifespans in the three lower realms of animals, hungry ghosts and hells. All of these experiences are patternings of the content of the mind. Although under the deluding power of duality we see seemingly 'real' objects that are quite other than us, this misperception and consequent misapprehension is actually just the diverse dramas of duality enacted in the theatre of unawareness. The characters and props in these dramas manifest from the active influence of the five afflicting poisons: opacity, desire, aversion, pride and jealousy.

Opacity or mental dullness is our inability to see through the veil of reification. We see the unreal as real –just as we can be taken in by a cartoon film. We believe the unbelievable and this prevents our accessing our potential for discerning uncontrived knowing. Desire is the wish for something or someone to complete and fulfil us. It is the expression of a deep-seated sense of lack. Something is missing and we imagine that it is located in this momentarily shining other. Sadly the other fails to fulfil the task assigned to it. Food does not remove hunger forever. Friends and lovers also bring dissatisfaction. The answer does not lie in the other – yet we refuse to accept this. Aversion is the wish to push away the other. It arises from feelings of fear, anxiety and dislike which can mobilise quickly as anger and rage. In this situation, the other is experienced as excess. They are too much, "I can't cope with this. Go away." Yet due to our ego-self being an inhabitant of the domain of duality where subject and object are born together we cannot get rid of the other. The problem does not lie in the other – yet we refused to accept this.

Pride arises as a sense of superiority. It is dignity swelling in excess of itself. I am different from others because I'm special and innately more worthy than they are. This separative move usually requires an audience who will confirm my superiority – and this need for affirmation demonstrates its hollowness. Jealousy arises with the loss of our sense of specialness, for now someone else is the object of the attention and admiration we crave. Our needy lack is exposed as our attempts to hang onto our longed-for centrality prove to be useless. We are cast aside and yet we cannot let go. We cannot exist in isolation from the other, nor can we permanently merge with the other. Try as we might, we cannot find a way to stay in charge and live life on our own terms. Thus we suffer due to getting what we do not want and not getting what we do want.

WHAT ARE THE CONSEQUENCES OF THIS? Birth and death within the matrix of duality. In the upper heavens and in the hells we simply suddenly find ourselves there without any birth process. For humans our entry into life begins with fear and confusion as we rapidly travel in dark constriction. This gives way to the seeming reality of the sexual engagement of the pair who will be our parents. We are drawn into the site of congress and the potential of our subtle consciousness is inflected with desire and aversion. If there is desire for the female and aversion for the male, this tendency will lead to a male body. If there is desire for the male and aversion for the female this tendency it will lead to a female body. The development of the foetus is the unfolding of the interaction between the arriving consciousness and the male and female essences. This releases multiple dynamic processes as the body develops as a complex system of communication both within itself and with the mother's body and through that with the wider world. Life is movement, activity, interaction, the continuous pulse of the heartbeat, and with birth this manifests as the continuous rhythm of breathing. We are movement, co-emergent in posture, gesture, expression and activity with the ever-changing environments we find ourselves engaging with. We are travellers on a journey we do not understand. We have to leave people, places, objects and habits that we may cling to, and we have to join with people, places, objects and habits that we may be wary of.

The years go by as we move along the chain of past, present and future. Sooner or later our journey ends in death. If death is slow, for example due to gradually succumbing to a fatal cancer, then we might have time to prepare. Is it happens suddenly, for example in a car crash, then it occurs before we can reflect on what is happening. In either case, the living system of body-mind is deprived of its life energy. If death occurs slowly, then the consciousnesses of the five senses weaken and merge into our mental consciousness, which is suffused with the consciousnesses of the five afflictions and of the ground potential. All the mental processes that supported our expansion out into the world are now gently fading and merging into a mental self-reflexivity. In parallel with this the five elements, earth, water, fire, wind and space gradually lose their differentiation. The subtle earth element that linked with the gross earth element manifesting as bones and flesh dissolves into the subtle water element, resulting in a heaviness of the body. The subtle water element linked with the gross form of blood, saliva, and so on dissolves into the subtle fire element resulting in dryness in the mouth. The subtle fire element linked with the heat of the liver dissolves into the subtle wind element linked with the flow of the breath. Finally, the subtle wind element dissolves into space and the subtle mental consciousness that was being supported by the breath loses its host in the body.

Now, consciousness is a homeless refugee and must travel forth friendless and alone. Everything that supported one's sense of personal identity is lost. All that remains is the deluding conviction that one exists as something along with one's latent karmic potentials awaiting the right situation in which to ripen. Although access to one's physical body is lost, our consciousness manifests a mental trace body having the form of one's previous body. This is like one's body as it was experienced in a dream. Leaving the bardo or transitional period of death, we enter the bardo of actuality, dharmata. This is the infinite openness of the mind. It is not an object for consciousness and so if we have only accessed our dualistic consciousness in the course of our life we go unconscious. If, through instruction and practice, we have opened to intrinsic awareness, then we remain relaxed and present with this infinite openness free of the opacity of entities. If this occurs, there is liberation in the intrinsic mode, the dharmakaya. This brings us into presence with the presence of our own ground, the ground, source, foundation that the originating moment of unawareness lost sight of. We are returned to the openness we have never actually been apart from. The first thought of a substantial entity and all the subsequent thoughts that led to the arising of samsara were not other than the radiance of the ground. Thus the radiance of the source gave rise to confusion as insubstantial appearance was taken to be the appearances of substances. The intrinsic, the source, gives rise to both awareness and unawareness. It is not made by awareness nor lost by unawareness. in it. To awaken is to re-source in the source and through this to see that all that occurs is the intrinsically pure spontaneity of the source. There is no current error, there has been no error, there never will be any error since all 'errors' are the self-liberating energy of the primordial source. To awaken to this is to be liberated in the deathless.

Having gone unconscious, we are suddenly conscious of bright lights, sweet sounds and smiling deities like Tara and Chenrezi beckoning to us. If we have no experience of such brilliant figures, we become fearful and fall unconscious again. If we have received initiation and teaching and have engaged in the deity practices then we feel that we are among friends and we are finally meeting those we have longed for, the peaceful forms which purify desire. With our joyful opening to them we merge in their heart and find liberation in the enjoyment mode, the sambhogakaya. If we have gone unconscious, we revive to loud, terrifying sounds and the horrifying appearance of fierce creatures with weapons, fangs and staring eyes. These are the wrathful deities who have come to welcome us – but without a previous dharma connection we are likely to collapse in terror and go unconscious. If we have received initiation and have practised then we can open to these wrathful forms that purify aversion and so merge in the enjoyment mode, the sambhogakaya.

When we revive from unconsciousness we find ourselves moving. We travel swiftly passing through hills, walls and so on since we are manifesting as an illusory body which is gradually taking on the shape of our next life embodiment. If we are to be born as human, then we become conscious of two bodies joined in sexual union as previously described. If we have faith, we recognise that they are in fact our guru in yab-yum union. They are the presence of the non-duality of wisdom and compassion, and by freely entering their point of union without the taints of desire and aversion we can be liberated in the apparitional mode, the nirmanakaya.

WHY SHOULD WE PRACTISE INTENTIONAL TRANSFERENCE, PHO-WA? Although there are several opportunities for liberation in the post-death experience as just described, there are also many uncertainties.

When the mind has left its previous embodiment there is usually a feeling of disorientation since the familiar reassuring forms that confirmed our identity are lost to us. Who are we? If I am no longer the person I was used to being and if I have no sense of what I am or what is happening, then it is easy to feel lost, confused and anxious. In order to spare ourselves the dangers and uncertainties of the bardo path we can focus on consciously directing our mind towards a pure land where liberation is facilitated by the presence of a kind and loving teacher such as Dharmakaya Buddha Amitabha, Sambhogakaya Bodhisattva Chenrezi, or Nirmanakaya Guru Padmasambhava.

The practice of intentional transference is quick and direct and so should be the first choice at death. If we are not able to engage with it we can still gain liberation in the several bardo stages because, as a key text says, *"Yet if this (transference) is not possible for us, then when I and all others are leaving this life, immediately may death ripen as the clear light Dharmakaya, with the bardo ripening as the Sambhogakaya, so that birth is as Nirmanakaya benefiting all beings in samsara."*

With the practice of intentional transference we use the power of our devotion to the deity – energised by our intention to gain liberation in order to work for the benefit of all sentient beings – as the means by which we easily let go of all that has bound us to rebirth in samsara. Devotion brings a joyful focus to our life. Whatever happens we have a steady sense of purpose: to awaken in order to help others awaken. As we develop equanimity we are no longer buffeted by the gusts of desire and aversion. Our equanimity is based on not looking for ultimate value in the transient events of this life. The pure land, the buddha field, is near at hand when we allow its value to be revealed. Distraction, dispersal and reactivity keep us on the move, turning this way and that as we try to apprehend the objects that seem to promise us fulfilment. As the years go by we often become disillusioned by the limitations of the people and the objects we had believed in. We become less hopeful and more hopeless and this is a hazardous state to occupy. But with reflection perhaps we can paradoxically allow a deeper disillusionment by seeing that the beguiling forms of this world are illusory and unable to provide what we long for. Letting go of delusion regarding illusion we can reclaim the energy, joy and creativity we have projected into objects and turn these enlivening qualities towards our Dharma path.

The delusion of dualistic separation gives rise to samsara and all its sufferings. The exit from this lies in turning towards the ignored, opening to inclusion and finding union with the Buddha's heart. To merge into the realm of the Buddha, or the body of the Buddha, or the heart of the Buddha, are all ways of awakening to our non-difference with the Buddha. Even in our usual body we are not other than the emanations of the Buddha's mind. However, due to our karmic and cognitive obscurations we can find this difficult to understand, to believe and to manifest. Therefore, in order to facilitate our awakening, the Buddhas have manifested their pure lands, where support is optimal and difficulties minimal. Dewachen, the buddha field of Amitabha, arose from the power of the vow he made when forming his Bodhisattva intention to help all beings. He vowed to accumulate a vast store of merit and wisdom in order to generate a pure land where happiness is all-pervading. This is Dewachen, *(Skt. Sukhavati),* The Happy. His heart emanation Chenrezi, *(Skt. Avalokitesvara),* manifested the pure land of Potala. Chenrezi sees all the suffering in the world and he was so touched and moved by what he saw that he gave rise to Padmasambhava, the Lotus Born, the Lotus Source.

WHO IS PADMASAMBHAVA? Padmasambhava means 'arising from a lotus' and in this book he is referred to as both Lotus Born and Lotus Source. The lotus flower is a symbol of purity and the supreme purity is the intrinsic purity of the open mind untainted from the beginningless beginning. Arising from the purity of the mind itself, the apparitional form of Padmasambhava is pure empty appearance. He is not a person, a sentient being, a substance, an entity. He is the radiance of five-coloured light, the playful connective light of the Buddha's love. As the *DROWA KUNDROL* text says, *"HRI. From Chenrezi's heart centre rays of five-coloured light flow into the ocean, revealing the apparitional Nirmanakaya free of causes and conditions, the amazing one born from a lotus. Padmasambhava, please come here!"*

The letter HRI is the seed syllable of both Amitabha and Chenrezi and it is present in the heart of Chenrezi. Red in colour, it is the creative potential revealed by the purification of desire. As such it is the originating seed of the Lotus Family, one of the five Buddha families. From it rays of light, white, red, blue, yellow and green, shine out and flow in a stream into the Dhanakosha Lake where they manifest a lotus on which is the form of Padmasambhava as an eight-year-old child. No specific causes or conditions have given rise to him for he is the spontaneous display of the non-dual compassion of the Buddha. He is purity born from purity. He is, of course, not actually born since he is without beginning or end. All appearance is unborn, being inseparable from emptiness and thereby free of the taint of the delusion of inherent existence. In order to bring the living truth of this sentence into the hearts of suffering beings, Padma-sambhava manifests as the instant direct presence of appearance and emptiness, sound and emptiness, awareness and emptiness. This unborn purity effortlessly purifies the delusion of birth and death. Padmasambhava is always present everywhere and is free of coming and going. However, for shaded characters like ourselves who are blind to non-dual integrity, he has made his compassionate form available for connection. We can invite him here to merge into us and reveal our non-duality, so the above text says, *"Please come here!"* We can also go to him, travelling on rays of light to meet him in his Palace of Lotus Light. This is a practice of intentional trans-ference that all the texts in this book are leading up to.

The texts begin on page 27 with an introductory PRAYER TO BUDDHA SHAKYAMUNI, the Buddha of our present period, the one whose turning of the wheel of Dharma is still revolving for the sake of sentient beings. The royal sage of the Shakyas, he is the key source of Dharma in our time and so is the focus of our unending gratitude. When there are long periods when even the name of Buddha is not heard, then the darkness of ignorance thickens and beings in their lostness chase after the false light of entities polished by longing. So with this prayer we celebrate our good fortune in still being able to benefit from his teaching and blessing.

This is followed on page 28 by OFFERING SALUTATION AND PRAISE TO PADMASAMBHAVA, who is also known as the second Buddha. When we recite these verses we are actively making connexion with Padmasambhava. We are drawing close to him and inviting him to come near to us. Our prayers are not expressing a vague hope that he will respond but are the tried and tested method of activating his vow that he will never abandon those who call on him. In our beginner's way we take the Boddhisatva Vow and promise that in this and in all our future lives we will help all beings. But we get tired, distracted, forgetful and regress into our habitual self-focusing. Padmasambhava is free of such unreliability. His is the vajra word, the unchanging full-strength bond with all those who turn towards him. We forget him, he does not forget us. We say these words to remind ourselves of his enduring presence and availability. The words are profound, pointing to his three enlightened modes, which are our own potential.

This section ends with the SEVEN LINE PRAYER, the sure and certain evocation of the Lotus Born. Traditionally we recite this three times: the first time to call him, the second time to welcome him, the third time to receive his blessing and to merge with him. He manifests in order to return us to ourselves. The greater our devotion to him, the greater the ease with which obstacles and obscurations dissolve so that by seeing him, we see ourselves.

THE ASPIRATION OF THE VAJRA KNOT on page 34 is a brief summary of the path emphasising our wish never to be separated from the Dharma. The fourth stanza points to the heart of our tantric practice: whatever appears is forever inseparable from the ever-changing net of illusion. All sounds are the ungraspable sound of mantra. The movements of our mind are actually our own uncreated awareness. May we fully open to the infinite happiness which is neither gained nor lost. The more frequently we can recite the precious words of this aspiration written by the great Minling Terchen, the more the mutually collaborative aspects of all our practices will become clear. Through this aspiration the blessing of the path is absorbed through our body, voice and mind preparing us to meet the Lotus Born.

On page 40 we find THE PRAYER OF ASPIRATION WHICH IS A WISH FULFILLING JEWEL. This is a treasure terma text spoken by Padmasambhava, then hidden, and later revealed by Rigdzin Godem. It begins with the confessing of mistakes made during practice. When you recite it you can also add any other errors that you are conscious of in your practice. The root of the many different ways we cannot fulfil our intention to practise correctly is set out in the seventh stanza: *"I and all sentient beings without exception from the beginning of this great aeon until now have been drawn to the karmic activity of grasping at appearances as if they were substantial entities. Due to this we have gone under the power of the five poisons, have broken our vows and insulted the Dharma. We humbly confess these actions which have become obstacles to our liberation."* All merit and demerit arises from the orientation of our mind. Once we turn away from the actual, delusion corrupts our intention like sewage released into a river. Until we are fully enlightened we need to be vigilant in purifying the errors and stains arising from reification and attachment. Then, as Buddhas, the purification of all will be our ceaseless activity. May we gain the merit and wisdom that will let us benefit others by our mere presence, just as Padmasambhava is able to do.

It comes to an end with the aspiration that we will purify the five poisons so that their true qualities of great happiness, great love, benign control, great peace, and helpful activity become effortlessly apparent. By frequently reciting this prayer we immerse ourselves in the tantric Buddhist tradition and thereby soften our self-affirming ego structure so that we become sensitive, pliable, and responsive in the service of others.

THE SUTRA OF THE STORY OF THE LAMP OF KING GOLDEN HAND AND HIS ASPIRATION on page 63 offers an indication of the power of sacrifice. In the present time 'Me first!' is a popular cry, whether it refers to a person, a gender, a country, or a species: if suffering and difficulty has to occur then let it happen to others! This sutra tells of a profound altruistic intention being empowered by an act of self-sacrifice. Many religions have stories demonstrating the cost of putting the other first. These may seem bizarre or even perverse in our egoic self-indulgent cultures. However to take on suffering in order to free others and to give one's merit, pleasure and freedom to others in order that they might thrive, is the key to the practice of exchange. In this way we go beyond empathic attunement to actually, willingly exposing ourselves to the suffering that others are enduring. Taking it on ourselves we find that we must ground ourselves in the presence of emptiness if we are going to live what our words say. The merit generated by the sacrifice in this story shines forth like light from a vast lamp illuminating all the darkest most desolate places where beings dwell.

The sutra is often recited during funeral ceremonies as a way of generating great merit that can be offered for the welfare of the deceased. It is an encouragement to us to never forget or abandoned the needy, the weak, the vulnerable. It is particularly important here if we're going to perform the intentional transference for someone who has just died.

On page 83 we have THE ASPIRATION FOR PURE DISCERNMENT written by the late Dudjom Rinpoche, Jigdral Yeshe Dorje. He transmitted it at a short teaching retreat in France and I translated it at that time. It is very warm and deep and enriching, and it arose, as he tells us in the colophon, from a vision of Padmasambhava. Speaking from the heart he points out in various ways how we deceive ourselves and abandon our highest ideals. Rather than quietly examining our own laziness and avoidance we seek the toxic pleasure of judging others and delighting in exposing their faults. Our pretence, our cover-ups, our dishonesty, are the means by which we cheat others and cheat ourselves. Seeing this, with shame and guilt and fear we need to make confession *"from the depths of our heart."* We need to turn away from reliance on the baubles of the world and then turn towards the light of the Dharma shining in the heart of the guru. We need help for we cannot find the true way on our own so we pray to the Guru in the form of Guru Rinpoche, *"Show us our own mind as it is!"* Stilling the ceaseless flow of distraction with the intensity of our devotion we asked the Guru to bless us so that we never stray from the true Dharma, *"Please bless us so that we enter non-dual original knowing."* Humility is our great friend for it cleans the mirror so that at first our faults are clearly displayed to us. Then the mirror shows us the illusory nature of all reflections, interpretations and constructs. Finally, the mirror shows us that our own awareness is like the mirror, ever-empty, ever-full, ever-bright.

Page 107 offers us an intriguing invitation, IF YOU WISH TO PURIFY YOUR SINS AND OBSCURATIONS. Well, do we? This is a tantric practice of purification whereby incidental obscurations arising from karmic tendencies and erroneous beliefs can be fully cleansed from our mind. The practice hinges on our complete belief in the power of Padmasambhava. He and his consort, the white dakini, are the actual presence of complete purity. Relying on them we activate the heart of the non-dual view: intrinsic purity can never be defiled and all seeming defilements are illusory without the least real existence. By reciting the modified Seven Line Prayer the truth of purity banishes the delusion of defilement. The liberating elixir arising from the dissolution of the demon of ego flows into us from the union of wisdom and compassion and this washes out all faults, stains, habits, limitations and so on. We are set free by the efficacy of the four powers: the pure object; our recognition of our errancy; our regret and repentance; our commitment never to err again. Then the Guru and his consort melt into me and I become inseparable from their unobstructed clarity, the non-duality of awareness and emptiness. Resting in that sky-like openness there is not even an atom of existence around which delusion could form. All that arises is within the infinite mandala of the Guru and so no matter what occurs we do not stray from primordial purity. With this, our confidence that we can transfer our mind into the heart of Padmasambhava is strengthened and simplified by direct experience.

THE PRAYER EFFORTLESSLY FULFILS OUR WISHES on page 113 is a prayer by which the blessing of Padmasambhava is elicited and evoked in order to deal with the many provocations that can arise. It commences with Buddha Amitabha manifesting his blessing in the form of Padmasambhava who, present in this world, acts directly for the benefit of beings. He came with the intention to help, he has vowed to help, and so we should rely on his help without doubt or hesitation. He offers his compassionate assistance freely – it is for us and we do not need to earn it or deserve it. This is amazing. Just because he is, and we turn towards him, all the help we need is freely available. This is due to our intrinsic purity, a purity often hidden from us but obvious to the Great Guru. He is relating to us as we actually are and if we open to him the veil of our delusion will fade like mist in the morning light. Devotion, faith, trust, confidence – as these grow so our allegiance to our limitations loses its power over us.

As the fourth stanza reminds us, Padmasambhava comes each morning and evening *"riding on the radiant rays of the rising and setting sun."* He comes from his pure land of Lotus Light, and he comes as light, to bring us light, and to show us that the actuality of all appearance is light – light and sound, energy as pulsation. The refrain of each verse is, *"Padmasambhava of Urgyen, we pray to you – please bless us that our wishes may be fulfilled without effort."* We express a wish and the returning vibration fulfils it. Our life is conversation. When we converse with the Precious Guru there is the fresh immediacy of resonant to-ing and fro-ing. It is the dreary monologue of the isolated ego that misses the beat, that can't find the rhythm and that just goes on and on playing its sad lonely tune.

With great prescience Padmasambhava predicts the several invasions of Tibet when important Dharma centres will be destroyed. At these times, *"We must pray without doubt or uncertainty."* To give way to hopelessness is self-defeating. To rest in the manic hope that someone will rescue us is disempowering. We must pray, enter the depths of the practice and focus all our attention on liberation from the delusion of reification. Rather than seeking only material science-based antidotes to new diseases, we must also pray and dissolve the misleading nexus of duality which gives rise to all the diverse impediments we encounter. The five elements are linked with the mind through our body – body-mind are not two separate domains. Materiality, primarily the earth element, is not the basis for the mind; rather it is the mind that gives rise to the play of the elements arising as our illusory materiality.

Whatever difficulties and hazards arise, whether as human oppressors, as climate change, as fierce animals and so on, we should focus on the practice and not disperse our energy by searching here and there for antidotes when the one true antidote is already with us – the actual truth of our mind itself. Moreover, as death approaches, if we focus on Padmasambhava we will be guided to Dewachen, Potala or Lotus Light Zangdopalri where we will settle in the heart of one of the inseparable modes of the Lotus Family. Turn to the light! Turn to the light and all else will dissolve like mere shadows pierced by sunlight. This prayer, like the one that follows it, was directly spoken by Padmasambhava to his twenty-five closest disciples in Tibet. He left these prayers as part of his living legacy, his presence in relatable form, his ongoing invitation to us to be with him and to have him always with us. They can be found together with other profoundly connective prayers in the book *THE SEVEN CHAPTERS OF PRAYER BY PADMASAMBHAVA* translated by Chimed Rigdzin Rinpoche and James Low (wandel verlag, Berlin, 2010).

Linked with the previous prayer, on page 134 we find *THE PRAYER WHICH IMMEDIATELY REMOVES ALL OBSTACLES*. Here Padmasambhava appears in semi-wrathful form manifesting the power and authority to stop troublesome demons in their tracks. He summons them towards him in order to tame their wild and disruptive tendencies. It is vital to recall that there are no real or existent demons, there is only energy. This is the energy of the ground source emptiness. If it is seen as such it is quiescent. If it is not clearly seen it absorbs our hopes and fears and this intermingling manifests as the forms and situations which terrify us. Every 'thing', including our 'selves', is within the whole, the infinite play of clarity. If this is disregarded we are at the mercy of the hopes and fears arising from dualistic karmic vision.

Each verse has the same refrain offering us words of connection, faith and comfort. *"With your compassion please bless us! Lead us to salvation with your loving care! Grant us accomplishments with your presence! Remove our obstacles with your power! Resolve outer obstacles where they are! Resolve inner obstacles where they are! Resolve subtle obstacles in emptiness! We prostrate with devotion and take refuge in you! Guru Padmasambhava with indestructible body, speech and mind – please grant us the accomplishment of buddhahood!"* The prayer outlines some of the great activities performed by the Lotus Born. Remembering his great qualities and especially his ability to keep his word and fulfil his commitments, gives us confidence that in this life, and in particular at the time of our transference or our death, he will be with us guiding us to him. As pointed out earlier, the periods just before, during and after death are times of heightened vulnerability. The outer situation changes rapidly and this sets off intense reactions in our mind stream. This outer turbulence and inner agitation is like a magnet for many kinds of demons. They are the unsettled and unsettling patterns of energy which seek out disturbance as their food. Hence this prayer emphasises the importance of not going under the power of agitation and fear. Rather we can turn towards the Precious Guru and hold fast to his securing presence. His power is sufficient so we should avoid dispersal of our focus and unify our mind with his. The key point is undistracted devotion – so even if the prayer is mentioning events we are unfamiliar with we should trust the mood of these sweet words and open to Padmasambhava, the apparition of our own intrinsic purity.

THE PRAYER WHICH QUICKLY FULFILS OUR WISHES on page 166 was written by the late Dudjom Rinpoche. It continues our practice of calling on Padmasambhava to help us. Our power is not sufficient. When we experience ourselves as sentient beings wandering in samsara it seems obvious that we are weak and limited. So if we fall into this deluded identity it is vital to call on the Lotus Born since he is the presence of our true actuality. In our limiting current condition of duality we call on him, yet we have never been truly separate. He invites us to merge in him as the reliable quick way to awaken to our own actual presence.

At the end of the prayer there is a verse honouring the mother of all the Buddhas. This mother manifests in various forms and here she is identified as Prajnaparamita, the presence of the wisdom of emptiness, highlighted as the mother of all the Buddhas of the past. She also manifests as the dakini Vidyadhari, the presence of awareness – as such she is the mother giving rise to Buddhas in the present. She also manifests as Maha Karma Indrani dakini who generates the Buddhas of the future. It was she who swallowed Padmasambhava and gave him initiation as he passed through her body to exit from her vagina. Although Padmasambhava is often depicted on his own he is actually never separate from his female counterpart. Symbolically the female is space while the male is manifestation as awareness, clarity and expression. They are non-dual within the great completion – the inseparability of the implicit and the explicit.

On page 172 we find THE PRAYER OF THE STAINLESS BIOGRAPHY which was written by the Terton Nyima Ozer. It again sets out key events in the story of Padmasambhava, encouraging us to ripen our trust and confidence so that the rainbow bridge between our heart and his will manifest and we can relax in the certainty that our liberation is assured. Padmasambhava is neither one nor many. He is not one, since he cannot be defined by concepts and is beyond summation.

He is not many, since his diverse manifestations all have the same ungraspable actuality. Beyond thought and expression, he is never limited by our thoughts and feelings about him. He is not an object of thought, being himself the ground of thought. Unborn and unstopped, we find him by ceasing to seek. He is all that we see, yet we do not see. Therefore the sole path is trust, infinite trust by which we relax and release and find ourselves where we actually are.

This prayer offers us a pilgrimage to the places made holy by the presence of the Precious Guru. Reciting and believing, we can be touched by these events from long ago which are still resonant. As this story unfolds we can be inspired by it, breathing it in through our recitation. Out of the sky-like space of Padmasambhava's mind, the warm wind of his compassion flows into us revitalising our heart, energy and spirit. Opening, receiving, responding – the interplay of his generosity and our gratitude generates the clarity of our path.

If we live in modern societies there are probably few symbols of the Dharma in our world – no stupas, prayer walls, temples, prayer wheels, sacred sites and so on. Therefore, it is vital that we light our own Dharma lamp from the flame of the tradition so that we will find Dharma illumination with us wherever we go.

Having recited the verses of the prayer, we focus on the visualised and felt presence of the Precious Guru. He is here with us looking at us with kind eyes and smiling at us. We recite his mantra OM AA HUNG BENZA GURU PEMA SIDDHI HUNG as many times as we can, experiencing the dissolving of any obstacles lying between us. Then in the state of open clarity we receive his blessing. From the letters OM at his forehead, AA at his throat and HUNG at his heart, rays of light, white, red and blue, radiate out and merge into our three centres. This empowers us to enter the practice, purifies our obscurations of the afflictions and cognitions so that we become effective vessels for the non-dual practices of the lineage. Due to this our body is simply a radiant body of light free of all substanti-ation. Then I merge into the light body of the Guru so that we are completely inseparable, and all traces of my former limitations are gone. With this I see my own original face, the dharmakaya beyond concepts. This is liberation in and as the intrinsic.

PURE WHITE LOTUS, THE LIFE OF THE LOTUS BORN FROM ODDIYANA on page 197 is a treasure text revealed by Sera Khandro only 100 years ago. It is a very concise charming and lyrical biography of Padmasambhava hidden at the time when he was leaving Tibet. This text provides us with a sense of the impact the Precious Guru had on those he met and we see how he responded to various situations. He was not acting from a fixed template or rule book but responded spontaneously, offering optimal benefit with minimal intervention. He did not settle in one place but travelled widely, learning and teaching and exposing himself to unpredictable situations. Through this he demonstrated his flexibility, curiosity and creativity. He was willing and happy to respond to need but if he encountered a lack of interest in and enthusiasm for the pure Dharma he was unwilling to offer more time and energy to those who preferred to cultivate their obscurations – see Chapter 9 of this biography. Teaching and transmission is a two way street; there has to be a willingness to teach and a willingness to learn. The co-emergence of these factors mirrors the non-duality of the view.

On page 223 we have a prayer by the 5th Dalai Lama, THE GREAT CLOUD OF BLESSINGS, in which we find the many manifestations of Padmasambhava being named and briefly described. He is invoked as the fulfiller of all the hopes of his faithful followers and he is invited to come in person from his pure land of Zangdopalri along with his inner circle of dakinis and heroes. We need you here and now so, *"Show the appearance of your clear and shining body to our eyes! Send the Dharma sound of your sweet speech to our ears! Let the blessing of your relaxed gentle mind melt into our hearts! Touch us with your great blessing! Please grant us the four initiations!"* We then request him to protect us from the ripening of our own bad deeds. This cannot be done by mere intention; the very root of this ripening must be cut in emptiness so that both object and subject forms are self-liberating. So we call upon Padmasambhava to remember his promise and act now when our need is so great.

IMPLORING PADMASAMBHAVA on page 236 is a further prayer by the late Dudjom Rinpoche, one which again is fervent and heartfelt. Due to the ripening of bad actions the demonic forces of bigotry, prejudice, exploitation, cruelty and so on increase and spread everywhere. We need the protection of Padmasambhava and his teachings embodying wisdom and compassion when we encounter the selfish, the shameless, and those who denigrate the true path to liberation and its followers. Moreover we also are caught up in hypocrisy, self-deception and the denial that our problems are due to the ripening of our own negative karma. Our joy is superficial, and we are pervaded by sadness and loss of hope – we need your help! You must act and put all negative forces under your power and dissolve all problems in their own spacious ground. Empower us to act for the benefit of all. How accurately Dudjom Rinpoche gives voice to the troubles in our heart. He wrote this prayer in response to the invasion of Tibet and the consequent loss of freedom for the Tibetan people. Sadly such horrors manifest throughout the world as traditional cultures are uprooted, forests and habitats destroyed, species endangered and weapons ever multiplying in their deadliness and availability. If we see clearly, we will see these mounting waves of disaster rushing towards us. Now is the time for practice and to strengthen our commitment to act for the benefit of all, including those who hurt and harm.

On page 244 we have a brief text offering worship of Padmasambhava entitled *THE PRECIOUS GURU OF ODDIYANA*. With it we move from taking refuge to developing the wish to gain enlightenment in order to help others, and on to accumulating merit through the Seven Branch Practice. Then we directly address Padmasambhava and call on him using the Seven Line Prayer. Having established our certainty at his presence, we recount his qualities as manifest through the signs and symbols he displays. This gives us a richer and deeper sense of how all the Dharma views and paths are present within and as him. This acts as a preparation for the next text which is a brief yet complete tantric sadhana on the Precious Guru.

LOTUS SOURCE PRACTICE on page 259 invites us to open to the brief form of the written practice revealed as a treasure text by the first Khordong Terchen Rinpoche, Nuden Dorje Drophan Lingpa Drolo Tsal. This is a very effective method to find oneself in the actual state of Padmasambhava. It was prepared according to the instructions of the fourth Khordong Terchen, Chimed Rigdzin. The full benefits of the practice will only be revealed if one gains the ripening initiation according to the lineage. However Chimed Rigdzin told me many times that faith was the main element of the initiation and that if people of good heart and clear intention truly wish to practise yet were unable to gain the initiation then their heartfelt practice would still be beneficial, and they should be supported in their desire. It is for this reason that this practice and the intentional transference on page 337 are offered here.

A recording of a full explanation of this text is available on the simply being website www.simplybeing.co.uk. The details are important since we need to absorb the actual practice as revealed and not smother it in our own projections and interpretations. Pure intention, the wish to liberate all beings, is the very heart of the practice and this text shows how to maintain clarity when we arise from the meditation cushion and engage with others in all the complexity of our social life together. There is no event or circumstance which cannot be integrated with the practice. Whatever arises is the path.

ASPIRATION FOR ZANGDOPALRI on page 293 is the first of two texts describing in some detail the Copper-Coloured Mountain (Zangdopalri)where Padmasambhava went when he left Tibet. On this mountain is his mandala palace of Lotus Light where he lives surrounded by the rakshasa cannibals whom he has gradually civilised. According to the tradition, Padmasambhava left Tibet on a magic flying horse and rapidly traversed the distance to Fly Whisk Island (Camaradvipa) whose outer form is that of Sri Lanka. At that time the island was dominated by a vicious king who encouraged his subjects to be selfish and cruel. He has many similarities to Ravana, the demon king of Sri Lanka whose battles with Ram and Lakshman are detailed in the Hindu text, the Ramayana. When Padmasambhava arrived there he secretly entered the palace and with his body of light fused with the sleeping form of the king of the cannibals. He ejected the king's consciousness to a place where he could progress towards enlightenment. In the morning the demon king awoke – a demon king body inhabited by Padmasambhava's pure awareness. The local people did not detect any difference in the king. However, slowly and carefully, Padmasambhava changed the behaviour manifested by this demonic form. The subjects gradually adjusted to the king's behaviour without knowing that they were doing so. By this subtle method Padmasambhava brought peace and prosperity to all the inhabitants of Fly Whisk Island and there he remains to this day, although his many emanations are to be found in every land, carrying out the work of liberation whilst skilfully arousing minimal resistance.

The prayer describes the setting for the palace of the Precious Guru. It is on a round flat island surrounded by islands and lakes. Beautiful in appearance, every plant, every form is pleasing to the senses and a cause for relaxation and delight. The prayer outlines all the pleasing aspects of the palace and its surroundings so clearly that we are bathed in its presence. As we read this prayer we repeat the refrain at the end of each stanza, *"We must take birth in this land of Lotus Light."* The palace is called Lotus Light; Padmasambhava is himself Lotus Light, the radiance of unborn purity; and Lotus Light also describes our actuality, the non-duality of primordial purity and instant presence. Thus, may we awaken through being born there, through being close to and then inseparable from Padmasambhava and through our inclusion in the inseparability of pure openness and ceaseless unborn display. All the factors facilitative of awakening are present there and all impediments have been rendered ineffectual. We are welcomed, included and assisted on our path which is now so easy. That is why at death the option to make an intentional transfer of our awareness to that supreme place is most valuable and its practice will shortly be set out in detail.

This is followed on page 315 by *A DESCRIPTION OF ZANGDOPALRI* which gives a similar description of the palace yet evokes a slightly different mood. It begins by describing how the infinite openness of the source dharmadhatu manifests through the vaginas of the wives of the Five Family Buddhas as the five elements giving rise to Zangdopalri. Thus the dharmakaya awareness reveals the sambhogakaya creativity emanating the nirmanakaya collaboration of the five elements. The Copper-Coloured Mountain is directly manifesting from the mind of the Buddha as an island which is self-existing and all-pervading. Zangdopalri is simultaneously to the south of India and everywhere. How you see it depends on whether you have the eyes of the heart or the eyes of the intellect. The heart of the demonic mother-eating Matram Rudra fell here after he was killed by the energy of Hayagriva whose partner, Vajravarahi, has blessed the island as a happy place for dakinis and mother goddesses. Beautiful to behold, charming in every way, this is the place where awakening is easy. It is not a distant Buddha field like Dewachen but is present here in the dimension of this earth as a nirmanakaya pure place.

Here resides Padmasambhava in the form of the Lotus Born Vajra, splendid and impressive with the power to change appearance according to the needs of those who come to him. Smiling at all, his voice is resonant and welcoming as he manifests many emanations to carry out his compassionate activity. He is surrounded by the mandalas of the deities of the Eight Great Practices along with oceans of deities, dakinis, messengers and so on. Everything that is needed for awakening is easily available here in this land of purification and joy. There is no better place to be and so if we are to practise intentional transference and have full faith in Padmasambhava then we should recite this prayer again and again until we are convinced that this is the only desired destination when our consciousness leaves our body. We pray to Padmasambhava with the Seven Line Prayer repeating it again and again and then we recite verses which invite him to actually come to us, preparing the way for us to go to him. How joyful to be welcomed by this dancing swaying guru with rhythms and melodies that set the world in motion! All fixed beliefs in real entities dissolve as his caravan of light gets closer and closer. We request him to hold us close, remove all obstacles and bless us with freedom from the ocean of samsara. Through the power of this prayer which Padmasambhava gave to his consort Yeshe Tshogyal so that her sadness at his departure would be softened, we also will gain the comfort and confidence that we will never be apart from him. Now we are ready to fly to him....

On page 337 we have the practice of intentional transference entitled *In One's Own Hand: The Profound Instructions for Using Death as the Path*. This text was developed by C. R. Lama from the work of Padma Trinlae. It provides a complete explanation of how to perform the intentional transference of one's own mind into the heart of Padmasambhava. It is unsafe to practise it without the supervision of a meditator experienced in the practice. Moreover, it requires initiation and explanation. It is presented here so that the dynamic of mind-body connectivity can be understood clearly, and to provide encouragement for people to prepare for the time when body and mind separate.

At the beginning of this introduction we looked briefly at the death process as it occurs, with the exhaustion of the karmic factors that sustained life. We noted that the mental body that arises with the final dissolving of the elements into space is able to move rapidly and without impediment through whatever appears to it. This gives us a sense of how the mind, freed of its identifications with the density of the five skandha components, can move faster than the wind. Indeed, as this text will show, it travels on rays of light and arrives instantly in the heart of Padmasambhava. This lightness free of content and substance allows it to travel as light along light. Several of the preceding texts have offered the practice of receiving white, red and blue light from the Guru's centres of body, voice and mind. As we fill with this light our substantial self is washed out, leaving our presence as light while dualistic consciousness resolves into non-dual original knowing. Then we merge with the Guru who has offered his illusory apparitional form as the means for our awakening to our actuality. If we practise this again and again we become able to instantly slough off the accretions of karmic habit and rest in naked awareness. This is the key preparation that enables the practice of intentional transference to be successful.

The text begins with an outline of how death can be used as a path of liberation. This highlights intentional transference as the most profound method in its simplicity and immediacy. Then we have the Refuge and Bodhicitta followed by the prayer requesting help from the Buddhas and Bodhisattvas, which is also important to recite if we are doing the transference for someone else. The prayer highlights just how terrifying it is to leave all that you know and to travel alone in confusion, fear and desolate loneliness. So many outer and inner appearances can preoccupy us leading to a loss of recollection of all the good intentions we have developed in the life we are leaving. We need help. This is why the humility of devotion is our great ally. We are used to being honest about our limitations and are open to receiving help with the genuine gratitude that helps us to make good use of it. Because our body after death is insubstantial, we can easily merge with the Buddhas if we are without doubt or hesitation. The habit of relying on our own thoughts as a guide to situations now becomes a time-consuming obstacle. Faith and devotion prepare us for the quick path of merging into the bright presence of the Buddha. The open empty trusting mind will quickly find non-dual liberation.

Then we offer salutation to the Buddhas of the past, present and future along with the Great Bodhisattvas. This leads into a short lineage prayer commencing with Nuden Dorje and concluding with a reminder that our own Guru is the actual presence of Amitabha, Chenrezi and Padma Thod Treng Tsal. With this as our focus we recite the Seven Line Prayer many, many times in order to separate from all that we are leaving and to unite with all that we are moving towards. With one-pointed focus on Padmasambhava we pray that we will receive the blessing of all the great masters and that they will send their emissaries, the dakinis, to meet us at the point of death and to lead us to the realm of Lotus Light. Then we pray for what we want, focusing on Fly Whisk Island in its outer, inner, secret, and most secret modes of presence. The pure land is not other than the inseparability of the openness, clarity and apparitional formation which is the truth of all the Buddhas and our own truth. With this clarity we pray that all obscurations will be purified so that we see our own true face of primordial purity. Then at death we will be guided to Zangdopalri where we will see Padmasambhava, hear his voice and gain all the teachings we need to become identical with him. Then as an enlightened one may we benefit and guide all beings so that they gain the same awakening!

Then on page 367 we have the first of the intentional transferences, the GENTLE TRANSFERENCE. Resting in the simple trust of the open state we hold the presence of Padmasambhava clearly in our heart-mind so that we are fresh and ready to leave the bondage of samsara. Then in an instant we travel along a path of five-coloured light leading to the Copper-Coloured Mountain. The familiar world fades away and the pure land of Padmasambhava becomes clearer and clearer, brighter and brighter, until we merge into the heart of the Precious Guru and become inseparable. Relaxed and happy, all we see is the bright beauty of this pure land free of the taints of conceptualisation.

On page 369 we commence the ACTIVE INTENTIONAL TRANSFERENCE by reciting the Seven Line Prayer many times. We pray to Padma-sambhava as the presence of the three enlightened modes and then we imagined that in our heart is an eight-petaled lotus with each petal being the site of one of our eight consciousnesses. In the centre of this lotus my essential consciousness, my mind as I know it to be, is moving and vibrating getting ready to leave. Then it shoots upwards on shimmering rays of light and merges into the heart-mind of Padmasambhava. Saying HIK! HIK! HIK! PHAT! PHAT! PHAT! we irreversibly leave the body and vanish into his heart. If this practice is done with devotion and force the mind will separate from the body so it is vital to remember that it should only be done a) when one is dying, b) when one is being tortured, or having a slow painful death, or c) is forced to stop Dharma practice. To fully practise if these conditions are not present is equivalent to suicide if one does it for oneself, or murder if one does it for another. Then we say prayers to strengthen our faith in the pure Buddha Land. Whether we say Dewachen, Potala or Zangdopalri our heart's devotion will take us to our liberation. It is important not to reify the pure deities and take them to be special human beings. There are light forms and their forms shift according to our need.

Then on page 376 we have an active TRANSFERENCE RELYING ON CHENREZI. Unlike the previous two transference practices where we were in our familiar body, in this practice we imagine that we, or the person for whom we are doing the practice, is in the form of Chenrezi. This imagined identity softens our habitual identification with the form we are used to seeing as our own and as definitive of who we are. Then my root Guru manifests as Chenrezi and sits on a lotus on the top of my head blocking the hole my consciousness will exit from. Then as the text describes clearly, our consciousness force-fully exits from the top of our head and merges straight into their heart-mind of Chenrezi. When we practise this it is vital that we also do the long life practise of Chenrezi since the transference practice loosens the mind-body connection. In this practice Amitayus – the aspect of Amitabha which relatively strengthens the life force and ultimately brings us to the deathless – purifies our embodiment and revitalises it. At the end of it we received blessings and attainments from Padmasambhava imagining five-coloured rays of light pouring into us and giving us energy and strength.

Then on page 394 we have the concluding prayers with the dedication of merit. This brings the intentional transference practice to an end. It is the focused essence of all the devotion we have developed in the previous practices. It lessens our concern with the ever-changing issues of this life and lets us see that they are not real events but merely the play of the mind wrongly interpreted.

Finally, on page 398 we have a short *DEDICATION PRAYER* expressing our wish to harness all our merit, skill and commitment to the benefit of all sentient beings. *"By this merit may I become omniscient. Then defeating all troublesome enemies may I liberate all beings from the ocean of samsara where they are tossed and tumbled by the tidal waves of birth, old age, sickness and death."*

Without effort may we all arrive fully, openly,
In the simplicity of how it is and always is!

Prayer to Buddha Shakyamuni

ཐབས་མཁས་ཐུགས་རྗེ་ཤཱཀྱའི་རིགས་སུ་འཁྲུངས།

THAB	KHAE	THU JE	SHA KYAI	RIG	SU	TRUNG
methods, doctrines	*skilled, experienced*	*compassionate*	*Shakya*	*family*	*in*	*born*

Compassionate one born in the Shakya family, skilled in methods,

གཞན་གྱིས་མི་ཐུབ་བདུད་ཀྱི་དཔུང་འཇོམས་པ།

ZHAN	GYI	MI	THUB	DUD	KI	PUNG	JOM PA
others	*by*	*not*	*able to resist*	*maras demons*	*of*	*mass, force*	*defeat*

You are the invincible conqueror of all demons everywhere.

གསེར་རི་ལྷུན་པོ་ལྟ་བུར་བརྗིད་པའི་སྐུ།

SER	RI	LHUN PO	TA BUR	JI PAI	KU
golden	*mountain*	*heap, mass*	*like*	*splendid, shining magnificent*	*body*

Your body shines like a mountain of gold –

ཤཱཀྱའི་རྒྱལ་པོའི་ཞབས་ལ་གསོལ་བ་འདེབས།

SHA KYAI	GYAL POI	ZHAB	LA	SOL WA DE
Shakya's	*king's*	*feet*	*at*	*pray*

King of the Shakyas, I pray at your feet.

Compassionate one born in the Shakya family, skilled in methods, you are the invincible conqueror of all demons everywhere. Your body shines like a mountain of gold – King of the Shakyas, I pray at your feet.

བསྟོད་པ་ནི།
Offering Salutation and Praise

ཧཱུྃ༔ མ་བཅོས་སྤྲོས་བྲལ་བླ་མ་ཆོས་ཀྱི་སྐུ༔

HUNG	MA CHO	TOE TRAL	LA MA	CHO KYI KU
Hung	*unartificial, without artifice*	*free of all dual and relative positions*	*guru, master*	*dharmakaya, intrinsic mode*

Hung. Free of artifice and all relative positions is the dharmakaya guru.

བདེ་ཆེན་ལོངས་སྤྱོད་བླ་མ་ཆོས་ཀྱི་རྗེ༔

DE	CHEN	LONG CHO	LA MA	CHO KYI JE
happiness	*great*	*sambhogakaya, enjoyment mode*	*guru*	*lord of dharma*

The lord of dharma enjoying great happiness is the sambhogakaya guru.

པད་སྡོང་ལས་འཁྲུངས་བླ་མ་སྤྲུལ་པའི་སྐུ༔

PAE	DONG	LAE	TRUNG	LA MA	TRUL PAI KU
lotus (symbol of unchanging purity)	*stem*	*from*	*born*	*guru*	*nirmanakaya, apparitional mode*

Born from a lotus stem is the nirmanakaya guru.

སྐུ་གསུམ་རྡོ་རྗེ་འཆང་ལ་ཕྱག་འཚལ་བསྟོད༔

KU	SUM	DOR JE CHANG	LA	CHA TSAL	TOE
body, mode	*three*	*Vajradhara, the supreme original and eternal Buddha*	*to*	*prostrate, and salute*	*praise*

I salute and praise Vajradhara embodying these three modes.

Hung. Free of artifice and all relative positions is the dharmakaya guru. The lord of dharma enjoying great happiness is the sambhogakaya guru. Born from a lotus stem is the nirmanakaya guru. I salute and praise Vajradhara embodying these three modes.

གསོལ་བ་འདེབས་པ་ནི།

Prayer

ཨེ་མ་ཧོཿ ཕྱོས་བྲལ་ཆོས་ཀྱི་དབྱིངས་ཀྱི་ཞིང་ཁམས་སུཿ

E MA HO	TOE TRAL	CHO KYI YING	KYI	ZHING KHAM	SU
wonderful!	*free from*	*dharmadhatu, all-*	*of*	*pure space*	*in*
(emptiness)	*all relativity*	*encompassing space*			

Wonderful. In the sphere of space free of entities and all relative positions,

ཆོས་ཉིད་དུས་གསུམ་སྐྱེ་འགག་མེད་པའི་ངང་ཿ

CHO NYI	DU	SUM	KYE	GA	ME PAI	NGANG
actuality of	*times*	*three*	*start,*	*stopped*	*without*	*uncontrived*
phenomena	*(past, present, future)*		*born*			

Is the actuality of phenomena, the uncontrived state that is free of the starting and stopping of the three times.

བྱ་བྲལ་ལྷུན་རྫོགས་བདེ་བ་ཆེན་པོའི་སྐུཿ

JA TRAL	LHUN DZO	DE WA	CHEN POI	KU
free of dualistic	*effortlessly*	*bliss*	*great*	*body, mode*
worldly activity	*complete*	*(unchanging happiness free of sorrow)*		

It is the intrinsically complete body of great happiness free of activity,

ནམ་མཁའ་བཞིན་དུ་ཐུགས་རྗེ་ཕྱོགས་རིས་མེདཿ

NAM KHA	ZHIN DU	THU JE	CHO RI ME
space, without	*similar to*	*compassion,*	*impartial, without*
centre or edge		*kindness*	*preference*

With kindness impartial as space.

བླ་མ་ཆོས་ཀྱི་སྐུ་ལ་གསོལ་བ་འདེབསཿ

LA MA	CHO KYI KU	LA	SOL WA DE
Guru	*dharmakaya*	*to*	*make prayer*

We pray to the dharmakaya guru.

ཨོ་རྒྱན་པདྨ་འབྱུང་གནས་ལ་གསོལ་བ་འདེབསཿ

UR GYEN	PAE MA	JUNG NAE	LA	SOL WA DE
Oddiyana	*lotus*	*born*	*to*	*make prayer*

We pray to Padmasambhava from Urgyen.

Wonderful! In the sphere of space free of entities and all relative positions,
is the actuality of phenomena, the uncontrived state that is free of the

starting and stopping of the three times. It is the intrinsically complete body of great happiness free of activity, with kindness impartial as space. We pray to the Dharmakaya Guru. We pray to Padmasambhava from Urgyen.

བདེ་ཆེན་ལྷུན་གྱིས་གྲུབ་པའི་ཞིང་ཁམས་སུ༔

DE	CHEN	LHUN GYI DRU PAI	ZHING KHAM	SU
happiness	*great*	*effortlessly arising*	*sphere, realm*	*in*

In the realm of effortlessly arising great happiness

སྐུ་གསུང་ཐུགས་དང་ཡོན་ཏན་ཕྲིན་ལས་ཀྱི༔

KU	SUNG	THU	DANG	YON TEN	TRIN LAE	KYI
body	*speech*	*mind*	*and*	*good qualities of buddhhood*	*compassionate activity*	*of*

Is the body, speech, mind, good qualities and compassionate activity

ཡེ་ཤེས་ལྔ་ལྡན་བདེ་བར་གཤེགས་པའི་སྐུ༔

YE SHE	NGA	DEN	DE WAR SHE PAI	KU
original knowing	*five*	*having*	*Happily Gone*	*mode*

Of the Happily Gone possessing the five original knowings and

ཐུགས་རྗེས་བྱེ་བྲག་སྣ་ཚོགས་སོ་སོར་སྟོན༔

THU JE	JE TRA	NA TSO	SO SOR	TON
kindness	*particular*	*diverse*	*individually*	*showing*

Showing diverse specific aspects of kindness.

བླ་མ་ལོངས་སྤྱོད་རྫོགས་སྐུ་ལ་གསོལ་བ་འདེབས༔

LA MA	LONG CHO DZO KU	LA	SOL WA DE
guru	*sambhogakaya*	*to*	*make prayer*

We pray to the Sambhogakaya Guru.

ཨུ་རྒྱན་པདྨ་འབྱུང་གནས་ལ་གསོལ་བ་འདེབས༔

UR GYEN	PAE MA	JUNG NAE	LA	SOL WA DE
Oddiyana	*lotus*	*born*	*to*	*make prayer*

We pray to Padmasambhava from Urgyen.

In the realm of effortlessly arising great happiness is the body, speech, mind, good qualities and compassionate activity of the Happily Gone possessing the five original knowings and showing diverse specific aspects of kindness. We pray to the Sambhogakaya Guru. We pray to Padmasambhava from Urgyen.

ཨེ་མ་ཛེད་འཛིག་རྟེན་དག་པའི་ཞིང་ཁམས་སུ༔

MI	JE	JIG TEN	DAG PAI	ZHING KHAM	SU
without	*number*	*worlds*	*pure*	*realm*	*in*

(all worlds everywhere are pure for Padmasambhava)

In the pure realms of numberless worlds

ཐུགས་རྗེ་ཆེན་པོས་འགྲོ་བའི་དོན་ལ་བྱོན༔

THU JE	CHEN POE	DRO WAI	DON	LA	JON
kindness	*with great*	*beings*	*benefit, welfare*	*for*	*come*

They manifest with great kindness in order to benefit beings,

གང་ལ་གང་འདུལ་ཐབས་ཀྱི་འགྲོ་དོན་མཛད༔

GANG LA GANG DUL		THAB	KYI	DRO	DON	DZAE
doing whatever is necessary		*method*	*by*	*beings*	*benefit*	*doing*

Helping them with whatever method is required.

འདས་དང་མ་བྱོན་ད་ལྟ་དུས་གསུམ་གྱི༔

DAE	DANG	MA JON	TAN DA	DU	SUM	GYI
past	*and*	*future*	*present*	*times*	*three*	*of*

Those of the past, the future and the present — to all the

བླ་མ་སྤྲུལ་པའི་སྐུ་ལ་གསོལ་བ་འདེབས༔

LA MA	TRUL PAI KU	LA	SOL WA DE
guru	*nirmanakaya*	*to*	*make prayer*

Nirmanakaya Gurus we pray.

ཨོ་རྒྱན་པདྨ་འབྱུང་གནས་ལ་གསོལ་བ་འདེབས༔

UR GYEN	PAE MA	JUNG NAE	LA	SOL WA DE
Oddiyana	*lotus*	*born*	*to*	*make prayer*

We pray to Padmasambhava from Urgyen.

In the pure realms of numberless worlds they manifest with great kindness in order to benefit beings, helping them with whatever method is required. Those of the past, the future and the present — to all the Nirmanakaya Gurus we pray. We pray to Padmasambhava from Urgyen.

Seven Line Prayer

ཧཱུཾ༔ ཨོ་རྒྱན་ཡུལ་གྱི་ནུབ་བྱང་མཚམས༔

HUNG	UR GYEN YUL	GYI	NUB JANG	TSHAM
vocative, seed letter of Padmasambhava	*Oddiyana, the dakinis' land*	*of*	*north-west*	*border, corner*

Hung. In the land of Urgyen's north-west corner,

བད་མ་གེ་སར་སྡོང་པོ་ལ༔

PAE MA	GE SAR	DONG PO	LA
lotus	*stamen*	*stem*	*on*

Upon a lotus stem and stamen,

ཡ་མཚན་མཆོག་གི་དངོས་གྲུབ་བརྙེས༔

YAM TSHEN	CHO GI	NGO DRU	NYE
marvellous, wonderful	*supreme (i.e. buddhahood)*	*siddhis, attainments*	*has got*

With marvellous and supreme accomplishments,

བད་འབྱུང་གནས་ཞེས་སུ་གྲགས༔

PAE MA JUNG NAE	ZHE SU	DRA
Padmasambhava, Guru Rinpoche	*known as*	*famous (famed as)*

The Lotus Born is your famous name.

འཁོར་དུ་མཁའ་འགྲོ་མང་པོས་བསྐོར༔

KHOR	DU	KHAN DRO	MANG POE	KOR
retinue	*as*	*dakinis, sky-goddesses (here it means all sky travelling deities)*	*many*	*by*	*surrounded*

As retinue many dakinis surround you.

ཁྱེད་ཀྱི་རྗེས་སུ་བདག་སྒྲུབ་ཀྱིས༔

KHYE	KYI JE SU	DA	DRU	KYI
you	*following after, emulating*	*I*	*practice*	*by that*

Following and relying on you, I do your practice, therefore,

བྱིན་གྱིས་བརླབ་ཕྱིར་གཤེགས་སུ་གསོལ༔

JIN GYI LAB	CHIR	SHE SU SOL
blessing	*in order to*	*please come*

In order to bless us, please come here!

 གུ་རུ་པདྨ་སིདྡྷི་ཧཱུྃ༔

GU RU   **PAE MA**   **SID DHI**   **HUNG**
guru, master   *Padmasambhava*   *real attainment*   *give me!*

Guru Padmasambhava grant us the accomplishment of buddhahood!

Hung. In the land of Urgyen's north-west corner, upon a lotus stem and stamen, with marvellous and supreme accomplishments, the Lotus Born is your famous name. As retinue many dakinis surround you. Following and relying on you, I do your practice, therefore, in order to bless us, please come here! Guru Padmasambhava grant us the accomplishment of buddhahood!

ཞེས་ཅི་ནུས་དང་།

[Recite this as many times as you can with true devotion from your heart.]

སྦོན་ལམ་རྡོ་རྗེའི་རྒྱ་མདུད་ནི།

Aspiration of the Vajra Knot

བླ་མ་ཡི་དམ་ལྷ་ཚོགས་དགོངས་སུ་གསོལ།

LA MA	YI DAM LHA	TSHO	GONG SU	SOL
guru, master	path deities	host	pay attention, hear me	please, I pray

All gurus and path deities, please listen to me!

དེང་འདིར་བརྩོན་པས་བསྒྲུབས་པའི་དགེ་བ་དང་།

DENG DIR	TSON PAE		DRU PAI	GE WA	DANG
today, here now	diligence, hard work		practice	virtue	and

The virtue of my diligent practice here today, and

དུས་གསུམ་བསགས་དང་ཡོད་པའི་དགེ་བ་རྣམས།

DU	SUM	SAG	DANG	YOE PAI	GE WA	NAM
times	three	collected	and	have	virtue, merit	all
(past, present, future)				(from the past and present)		

All that I collect in the three times, and the virtue I already have—

བསྡོམས་ཏེ་བླ་མེད་བྱང་ཆུབ་ཆེན་པོར་བསྔོ།

DOM TE	LA ME	JANG CHU	CHEN POR	NGO
all, total	unsurpassed	bodhi, enlightenment	great	give, dedicate

I dedicate all of this towards the unsurpassed great enlightenment of all!

All gurus, and path deities, please listen to me! The virtue of my diligent practice here today and all that I collect in the three times, and the virtue I already have — I dedicate all of this towards the unsurpassed great enlightenment of all!

དེང་ནས་བྱང་ཆུབ་སྙིང་པོར་མཆིས་ཀྱི་བར།

DENG	NAE	JANG CHU	NYING POR	CHI KYI	BAR
this time	from	bodhi, enlightenment	essence	get	until

From this time on until the heart of enlightenment is gained,

རིགས་བཟང་བློ་གསལ་ང་རྒྱལ་མེད་པ་དང་།

RIG	ZANG	LO	SAL	NGA GYAL	ME PA	DANG
family, kula	good	mind, intellect	clear	pride, egoism	without	and

May we be born in good families, have clear intellect free of pride,

སྙིང་རྗེ་ཆེ་ཞིང་བླ་མ་ལ་གུས་ལྡན།

NYING JE	CHE	ZHING	LA MA	LA	GUE	DEN
compassion	*great*	*with*	*guru*	*to*	*devotion*	*having*

Have great compassion, and have devotion to our gurus.

དཔལ་ལྡན་རྡོ་རྗེའི་ཐེག་ལ་ངེས་གནས་ཤོག།

PAL DEN	DOR JEI	THEG	LA	NGE	NAE	SHO
glorious	*vajra* *vajrayana, tantra*	*vehicle*	*in, to*	*really*	*stay*	*we must*

We must truly abide in the glorious Vajrayana.

From this time on until the heart of enlightenment is gained, may we be born in good families, have clear intellects free of pride, have great compassion, and have devotion to our gurus. We must truly abide in the glorious Vajrayana.

དབང་གིས་སྨིན་ཅིང་དམ་ཚིག་སྡོམ་པར་ལྡན།

WANG	GI	MIN CHING	DAM TSHI	DOM PAR	DEN
initiation, *empowerment*	*by*	*ripening,* *making ready*	*tantric vows*	*vows*	*keep*

Being ripened by initiation may we keep our tantric vows, and

རིམ་གཉིས་ལམ་ལ་བསྙེན་སྒྲུབ་མཐར་ཕྱིན་ཏེ།

RIM	NYI	LAM	LA	NYEN DRU	THAR CHIN	TE
system	*two*	*path*	*of*	*recitation sadhana*	*perfecting*	
		(kyerim; the developing system: dzogrim; the perfecting system)				

Complete the practices and mantra recitations of the developing and perfecting systems.

དཀའ་བ་མེད་པར་རིག་འཛིན་གོ་འཕང་བསྒྲོད།

KA WA	ME PAR	RIG DZIN	GO PHANG	DRO
difficulty	*without*	*vidyadharas,* *wise*	*stage, rank,*	*get, go to*

Entering the stages of the wise without difficulty

དངོས་གྲུབ་རྣམ་གཉིས་བདེ་བླག་འགྲུབ་གྱུར་ཅིག།

NGO DRU	NAM	NYI	DE LA	DRU	GYUR CHI
siddhis, *attainments*	*kinds* *(supreme and general)*	*two*	*easily*	*get, attain*	*may we!*

May we easily gain the supreme and general accomplishments.

Being ripened by initiation may we keep our tantric vows, and complete the practices and mantra recitations of the developing and perfecting systems. Entering the stages of the wise without difficulty, may we easily gain the supreme and general accomplishments.

ཆིར་སྣང་སྒྱུ་འཕྲུལ་དྲ་བའི་འཁོར་ལོར་རྫོགས།

CHIR NANG	GYU TRUL	DRA WAI	KHOR LOR	DZO
whatever is seen,	maya, illusion	jala, net	chakra, wheel	complete, get

(according to the Mayajalachakratantra all appearances are empty apparitions)

Whatever appears is forever inseparable from the ever-changing net of illusion.

གྲགས་པ་ཐམས་ཅད་བརྗོད་བྲལ་སྔགས་ཀྱི་སྒྲ།

DRA PA	THAM CHE	JO TRAL	NGA KYI	DRA
sounds, whatever is heard	all	beyond expression, indefinable	mantra's	sound

All sounds are the ungraspable sound of mantra.

སེམས་ཀྱི་འགྱུ་བ་རང་རིག་འདུས་མ་བྱས།

SEM KYI	GYU WA	RANG	RIG	DU MA JE
mind's	movements	own	awareness, vidya	uncompounded, not made by anyone

The movements of our mind are actually our own uncreated awareness.

བདེ་ཆེན་འདུ་འབྲལ་མེད་པ་མངོན་གྱུར་ཤོག

DE	CHEN	DU	TRAL	ME PA	NGON GYUR	SHO
happiness	great, empty	joining	separating	without (i.e. always naturally present)	fully, clearly	must come

May we fully open to the infinite happiness which is neither gained nor lost.

Whatever appears is forever inseparable from the ever-changing net of illusion. All sounds are the ungraspable sound of mantra. The movements of our mind are actually our own uncreated awareness. May we fully open to the infinite happiness which is neither gained nor lost.

ཉམས་ཆགས་རྟོག་སྒྲིབ་མ་སྤངས་གནས་སུ་དག

NYAM CHA	TO	DRIB	MA	PANG	NAE SUE	DA
all lost vows	thoughts	obscurations	not	discarding, pushing away	in their own place, naturally	pure

Lapsed vows, thoughts and obscurations are pure as they are, without need of discarding.

ཕྱི་ནང་གསང་བ་དབྱེར་མེད་རྟོགས་པས་བསྐངས།

CHI	NANG	SANG WA	YER ME	TO PAE	KANG
outer (world)	inner (body)	secret (mind)	inseparable, without difference	actualise	come full

Complete through abiding in the inseparability of outer world, inner body and secret mental events

གང་ཤར་རང་གྲོལ་ཀུན་བཟང་ཀློང་ཡངས་སུ།

GANG	SHAR	RANG DROL	KUN ZANG	LONG YANG	SU
what is,	*arises*	*self-liberating*	*Samantabhadra,*	*expanse, infinitude,*	*in*
whatever			*'All Good',*	*vast space, sunyata*	

Whatever arises is self-liberating in the vast expanse Samantabhadra.

ངན་སོང་དོང་སྤྲུགས་སྲིད་ཞི་མཉམ་གྱུར་ཅིག།

NGAN SONG	DONG TRU	SI	ZHI	NYAM	GYUR CHI
states of woe,	*upturn and empty*	*samsara,*	*nirvana,*	*equal*	*must be*
evil places*		*becoming*	*peace*		

*hells, pretas, animals

The states of woe must be upturned and emptied within the equality of samsara and nirvana.

Lapsed vows, thoughts and obscurations are pure as they are, without need of discarding. Complete through abiding in the inseparability of outer world, inner body and secret mental events, whatever arises is self-liberating in the vast expanse Samantabhadra. The states of woe must be upturned and emptied within the equality of samsara and nirvana.

ཐིག་ལེ་ཆེན་པོ་སྐུ་དང་ཞིང་ཁམས་རྫོགས།

THIG LE	CHEN PO	KU	DANG	ZHING KHAM	DZO
bindu	*great*	*body, three*	*and*	*realm*	*fill, complete*
(sunyata)		*kayas or modes*			

All the modes and realms are intrinsically complete within the great sphere.

སྒྱུ་འཕྲུལ་དྲ་བའི་ལམ་གསང་སེམས་ལ་རྫོགས།

GYU TRUL	DRA WAI	LAM	SANG	SEM	LA	DZO
maya, illusion	*jala, net*	*path*	*secret*	*mind*	*in*	*fill, complete*
(according to the Mayajala Tantra)						

With the secret path of the net of illusion our minds awaken as intrinsically complete.

ཕྲིན་ལས་རྣམ་བཞི་ལྷུན་གྱིས་གྲུབ་པ་ཡིས།

TRIN LE	NAM	ZHI	LHUN GYI DRU PA	YI
activities, deed	*kind*	*four**	*effortlessly arising*	*by*

* pacifying, expanding, overpowering and destructive

By the effortlessly arising four kinds of activity,

 སུ་མཐའ་མེད་པའི་འགྲོ་བ་སྒྲོལ་བར་ཤོག།

MU THA	ME PAI	DRO WA	DROL WAR	SHO
end, limit	*without*	*beings,those movingin samsara*	*freed, liberated*	*must be!*

Limitless beings must be freed!

All the modes and realms are intrinsically complete within the great sphere. With the secret path of the net of illusion our minds awaken as intrinsically complete. By the effortlessly arising four kinds of activity, limitless beings must be freed!

ཞི་ཁྲོ་སྤྲུལ་པའི་འཁོར་ལོས་ལུང་སྟོན་ཞིང་།

ZHI	TRO	TRUL PAI	KHOR LOE	LUNG TON ZHING
peaceful	*wrathful*	*emanations*	*circles, groups*	*predictions, (about our progress on the path)*

With predictions from the peaceful and wrathful emanations, and with

མཁའ་འགྲོ་རྣམས་ཀྱིས་བུ་བཞིན་སྐྱོང་བ་དང་།

KHAN DRO	NAM	KYI	BU	ZHIN	KYONG WA	DANG
dakini	*plural*	*by*	*child, son*	*like, in that way*	*protecting, taking care of*	*and*

The dakinis protecting us as their children, and

ཆོས་སྐྱོང་སྲུང་མས་བར་ཆད་ཀུན་བསལ་ནས།

CHO KYONG	SUNG MAE	BAR CHAE	KUN	SAL	NE
dharma protectors	*guardians*	*obstacles, obstructions*	*all*	*remove, clear away*	*then*

The dharma-protectors and guardians removing all obstacles,

ཡིད་ལ་སྨོན་པ་མཐའ་དག་འགྲུབ་གྱུར་ཅིག།

YI	LA	MON PA	THA DA	DRU GYUR	CHI
mind	*to*	*wishes, desires*	*to the limit*	*accomplished*	*must be!*

All our wishes must be fulfilled!

With predictions from the peaceful and wrathful emanations, and with the dakinis protecting us as their children, and the dharma-protectors and guardians removing all obstacles, all our wishes must be fulfilled!

རྒྱལ་བའི་བསྟན་པ་དར་ཞིང་རྒྱས་པ་དང་།

GYAL WAI	TEN PA	DAR ZHING	GYE PA	DANG
victor, Buddha	*doctrines*	*spreading*	*expanding*	*and*

With the Victor's doctrine spreading widely and

བསྟན་འཛིན་རྣམས་ཀྱི་བཞེད་པའི་དོན་ཀུན་འགྲུབ།

TEN DZIN	NAM KYI	ZHE PAI	DON	KUN	DRU
doctrine holders	*all*	*thinking,*	*meaning*	*all*	*come full,*
(great lamas)		*desiring*			*be accomplished*

All the plans of the doctrine-holders being fulfilled,

མ་ལུས་སྐྱེ་རྒུའི་འགལ་རྐྱེན་ཀུན་ཞི་ཞིང་།

MA LU	KYE GUI	GAL	KYEN	KUN	ZHI ZHING
without	*beings*	*bad, difficult,*	*conditions*	*all*	*pacifying*
exception		*troublesome*			

All the difficulties of all beings without exception must be pacified, and

ཕུན་ཚོགས་མཐའ་དག་ཡིད་བཞིན་འབྱོར་གྱུར་ཅིག། །

PHUN TSHO	THA DA	YI ZHIN	JOR GYUR	CHI
all good things	*to the limit*	*as is desired*	*come full, get*	*must*

Satisfaction gained according to our desires!

With the Buddha's doctrine spreading widely and all the plans of the doctrine-holders being fulfilled, all the difficulties of all beings without exception must be pacified, and satisfaction gained according to our desires!

ཅེས་པའང་འགྱུར་མེད་རྡོ་རྗེས་སྤྲར་བའོ།། །།

This was written by Minling Terchen, Rigdzin Gyurme Dorje Terdag Lingpa.

॥སྨོན་ལམ་ཡིད་བཞིན་ནོར་བུའོ།

The Prayer of Aspiration which is a Wish-Fulfilling Jewel

བྱང་ཆུབ་སེམས་དཔའི་སྤྱོད་དབང་གི༔ དཀྱིལ་འཁོར་བྱ་བ་རྫོགས་པ་དང་༔ བཤགས་པ་བྱ་ཞིང་
སྨོན་ལམ་གདབ༔ ཐམས་ཅད་གུས་པས་ཐལ་མོ་སྦྱར༔

Completing the mandala section of the Byang-Chub-Sems-dPai' sPyod-dBang
practice, offer confession and then make this prayer of aspiration, holding your
hands at your heart in devotion.

ན་མོ་ཕྱོགས་བཅུ་དུས་གསུམ་སངས་རྒྱས་དང་༔

NA MO	CHO	CHU	DU	SUM	SANG GYE	DANG
salutation	direction	ten	times	three	buddhas	and

Salutation. Buddhas of the ten directions and the three times,

བདེ་གཤེགས་རིགས་ལྔ་བྱང་ཆུབ་སེམས་དཔའ་དང་༔

DE SHE	RIG	NGA	JANG CHU SEM PA	DANG
tathagatas Happily Gone	kulas, families	five	bodhisattva	and

Tathagatas of the five families, bodhisattvas, and

གསང་སྔགས་རིག་སྔགས་ལྷ་ཚོགས་ཐམས་ཅད་རྣམས༔

SANG	NGA	RIG	NGA	LHA	TSHO	THAM CHE	NAM
secret	mantra	awareness	mantra	gods	hosts	all	all

All you secret mantra and awareness mantra deities,

བདག་དང་ཡོན་བདག་རྣམས་ལ་དགོངས་སུ་གསོལ༔

DA	DANG	YON DA	NAM	LA	GONG	SU SOL
me	and	patrons (beings)	all	to	pay attention, think of	please do

Please pay heed to me and all beings.

Salutation. Buddhas of the ten directions and the three times, tathagatas of the five families, bodhisattvas, and all you secret mantra and awareness mantra deities, please pay heed to me and all beings.

བདེ་བར་གཤེགས་པ་ཁྱེད་ཀྱི་སྤྱན་སྔ་རུ༔

DE WA SHE PA   KYE   KYI   CHEN NGA RU
sugatas, buddhas*   you   of   in the presence of, before
*those who have passed into nirvana

All Sugatas, before you

བདག་གིས་མི་དགེའི་སྡིག་པ་བགྱིས་པ་རྣམས༔

DA GI   MI GEI   DIG PA   GYI PA   NAM
me*   by   unvirtuous   errors   done   plural
* wherever 'I' occurs in the text we should take this to mean ourselves and all sentient beings.

All of the unvirtuous errors I have made

ཐམས་ཅད་མ་ལུས་སོ་སོར་བཤགས་པར་བགྱི༔

THAM CHE   MA LU   SO SOR   SHA PAR GYI
all   without   each single one   confess[1] and request forgiveness
    exception

I confess each one individually.

All Sugatas, before you I confess each of the unvirtuous errors I have made.

ཡི་དམ་ལྷ་ཡི་ཏིང་འཛིན་བསྒོམས་པའི་ཚེ༔

YI DAM   LHA   YI   TING DZIN   GOM PAI   TSHE
path deity   god   of   absorbed   meditation,   when, time
            contemplation   practice

When practising absorbed contemplation of the path deities

སྣང་སྟོང་འཇའ་ཚོན་ལྟ་བུར་མ་བསྒོམས་པར༔

NANG   TONG   JA TSHON   TA BUR   MA   GOM PAR
appearance   emptiness   rainbow   like, as   not   meditated

I did not imagine them as appearance and emptiness, like a rainbow.

རང་རྒྱུད་དངོས་པོར་བསྒོམས་པ་མཐོལ་ལོ་བཤགས༔

RANG   GYU   NGOE POR   GOM PA   THOL LO SHA
self   flow   substantial   meditate   humbly confess with hands
                held at your heart

I humbly confess that I have meditated as if the flow of experience consisted of entities.

When practising absorbed contemplation of the path deities, I did not imagine them as appearance and emptiness, like a rainbow. I humbly confess that I have meditated as if the flow of experience consisted of entities.

བྱང་ཆུབ་སེམས་དཔའི་སྡོམ་པ་སེམས་བསྐྱེད་དང༔

JANG CHU SEM PAI	DOM PA	SEM KYE	DANG
bodhisattva's	*vows,*	*develop*	*and*
	ordination	*bodhicitta**	

* an inclusive intention towards enlightenment

My bodhisattva vow to develop inclusivity and

ཉན་ཐོས་བསླབ་པ་ཉམས་པ་མཐོལ་ལོ་བཤགས༔

NYAN THO	LA PA	NYAM PA	THOL LO SHA
shravaka	*vows, rules,*	*lost, lapsed*	*humbly confess*
(hinayana)	*training*		

My training in disciplined study and practice – I humbly confess that I have lapsed in these commitments.

I humbly confess that I have lapsed in my bodhisattva vows to develop inclusivity and in my training in disciplined study and practice.

ཐེག་ཆེན་ཆོས་ལ་སྐུར་པ་བཏབ་པ་དང༔

THEG CHEN	CHO	LA	KUR PA	TAB PA	DANG
mahayana	*dharma,*	*towards*	*insult*	*do*	*and*
	doctrines				

Insulting the mahayana doctrines,

ཕ་དང་མ་ལ་ངན་ཚིག་སྨྲས་པ་དང༔

PHA DANG MA	LA	NGEN	TSHI	ME PA	DANG
parents	*to*	*bad,*	*speech,*	*speak*	*and*
		coarse	*words*		

Speaking roughly to my parents,

ཆོས་ཀྱི་གྲོགས་ལ་འགྲན་ཞིང་བཀྱལ་བ་དང༔

CHO KYI DRO	LA	DREN ZHING	GAL WA	DANG
dharma friends	*to*	*challenging, taking*	*dispute,*	*and*
		them to be rivals	*oppose*	

Challenging and disputing with my dharma friends, and

ཚེ་རབས་ཐོག་མེད་དུས་ན་བསགས་པ་ཡི༔

TSHE RAB	THO ME	DU	NA	SAG PA	YI
cycles of rebirth	*beginningless*	*time*	*in*	*accumulated*	*of*

All the bad karma that I have accumulated in all my lives during beginningless time

མི་དགེ་བཅུ་དང་མཚམས་མེད་ལྔ་ཡི་ལས༔

MI GE CHU	DANG	TSHAM ME NGA	YI	LAE
ten unvirtuous	*and*	*five boundless errors*	*of*	*karma, activity*

Arising from the five boundless errors and the ten unvirtuous actions –

བགྱིད་དང་བགྱིད་དུ་སྩལ་དང་ཡི་རང་བགྱིས༔

GYI DANG GYI DU TSAL DANG YI RANG GYI
I did and encouraged others and was happy at that
to do

Whatever errors I have done, encouraged others to do, and rejoiced at the performance of,

དེ་དག་ཐམས་ཅད་མ་ལུས་སོ་སོར་བཤགས༔

DE DA THAM CHE MA LU SO SOR SHA
those all without each single one I confess
exception

I confess them all, each single one without exception.

Insulting the mahayana doctrines, speaking roughly to my parents, challenging and disputing with my dharma friends, and all the bad karma that I have accumulated in all my lives during beginningless time arising from the five boundless errors and the ten unvirtuous actions – whatever errors I have done, encouraged others to do, and rejoiced at the performance of, I confess them all, each single one without exception.

ལེ་ལོ་བག་མེད་དབང་དུ་གྱུར་པ་ཡིས༔

LE LO BA ME WANG DU GYUR PA YI
laziness carelessness power under go by

Due to going under the power of carelessness and laziness

ཚོར་དང་མ་ཚོར་མ་རིག་མུན་པས་བསྒྲིབས༔

TSHOR DANG MA TSHOR MA RIG MUN PAE DRI
perceive and not perceive ignorance darkness covered
(not realise what one is doing)

I have committed sins that I was aware of and that I was not aware of, all while obscured by the darkness of ignorance.

རྩ་བ་ཡན་ལག་དམ་ཚིག་ཉམས་པ་རྣམས༔

TSA WA YEN LA DAM TSHI NYAM PA NAM
root branch tantric vows broken, lost all

All my lapses in my root and branch tantric vows

ཐམས་ཅད་མ་ལུས་སོ་སོར་བཤགས་པར་བགྱི༔

THAM CHE MA LU SO SOR SHA PAR GYI
all without each single confess and request forgiveness
exception one

I confess to you individually without exception and request your forgiveness.

Due to going under the power of laziness and carelessness, I have committed errors that I was aware of and that I was not aware of, all while obscured by the darkness of ignorance. All my lapses in my root and branch tantric vows I confess individually to you without exception and request your forgiveness.

བདག་གིས་དང་པོར་སེམས་བསྐྱེད་རྒྱ་ཆེན་བགྱིས༔

DA GI	DANG POR	SEM KYE	GYA CHEN	GYI
me by	*firstly*	*developing enlightenment mind*	*vast*	*did*

At first I developed a vast inclusive aspiration for enlightenment,

ལེ་ལོ་ཤེས་རབ་དམན་པས་དེ་ལས་ཉམས༔

LE LO	SHE RAB	MEN PAE	DE	LAE	NYAM
laziness	*stupidity*		*that*	*from*	*fall away, lapse*

But then due to laziness and weak understanding I fell away from it.

སེམས་བསྐྱེད་དམ་བཅའ་ཉམས་པ་མཐོལ་ལོ་བཤགས༔

SEM KYE	DAM CHA	NYAM PO	THOL LO SHA
bodhicitta	*vows*	*lost*	*humbly confess*

I humbly confess the lapses in my bodhicitta vow to include all in enlightenment.

At first I developed a vast inclusive aspiration for enlightenment, but then due to laziness and weak understanding I fell away from it. I humbly confess the lapses in my bodhicitta vow to include all in enlightenment.

བདག་དང་སེམས་ཅན་མ་ལུས་ཐམས་ཅད་ཀྱིས༔

DA	DANG	SEM CHEN	MA LU	THAM CHE	KYI
I	*and*	*sentient beings*	*without exception*	*all*	*by*

I and all sentient beings without exception,

བསྐལ་པ་ཆེན་པོའི་གོང་ནས་ད་ལྟའི་བར༔

KAL PA	CHEN POI	GONG	NAE	DA TAI	BAR
kalpa, aeon	*great's*	*beginning*	*from*	*now*	*until*

From the beginning of this great aeon until now,

དངོས་པོར་འཛིན་པའི་ལས་ལ་ཞེན་པ་ཡིས༔

NGO POR	DZIN PAI	LAE	LA	ZHEN PA	YI
things, substantial entities	*grasping at, believing in*	*karmic activity*	*for*	*desire, hope*	*due to*

Have been drawn to the karmic activity of grasping at appearances as if they were substantial entities.

དུག་ལྔའི་དབང་གྱུར་སྡོམ་པ་ཉམས་པ་དང་༔

DU NGAI	WANG	GYUR	DOM PA	NYAM PA	DANG
*five poisons**	*power*	*gone under*	*vow*	*lost, broken*	*and*

*stupidity, anger, desire, pride and jealousy

Due to this we have gone under the power of the five poisons, have broken our vows, and

དམ་པའི་ཆོས་ལ་སྐུར་པ་བཏབ་པ་རྣམས༔

DAM PAI	CHÖ	LA	KUR PA TA PA	NAM
holy, excellent	*dharma*	*to*	*said bad things about*	*all*

Insulted the excellent Dharma.

ཐར་པའི་གེགས་སུ་གྱུར་པ་མཐོལ་ལོ་བཤགས༔

THAR PAI	GE	SU	GYUR PA	THOL LO SHA
mukti, liberation	*obstacle*	*as*	*become*	*humbly confess*

We humbly confess these actions which have become obstacles to our liberation.

From the beginning of this great aeon until now, I and all sentient beings without exception have been drawn to the karmic activity of grasping at appearances as if they were substantial entities. Due to this we have gone under the power of the five poisons, have broken our vows, and insulted the excellent Dharma. We humbly confess these actions which have become obstacles to our liberation.

ཕྱོགས་བཅུ་དུས་གསུམ་བདེ་བར་གཤེགས་པ་རྣམས༔

CHO	CHU	DU	SUM	DE WAR	SHE PA	NAM
directions	*ten*	*times*	*three*	*happily*	*gone (sugatas, buddhas)*	*all*

Happily Gone of the ten directions and the three times

འཇིག་རྟེན་ཁམས་འདིར་རྟག་པར་བཞུགས་ནས་ཀྱང་༔

JIG TEN	KHAM	DIR	TA PAR	ZHU	NAE	KYANG
external world		*here*	*always*	*stay*	*then*	*also*

Please remain always in this world, and

མྱ་ངན་མི་འདའ་འགྲོ་དྲུག་ཐུགས་རྗེས་གཟིགས༔

NYA NGAN	MI DA	DRO DRU	THU JE	ZI
misery	*not go beyond (not die, not pass into nirvana)*	*beings of the six realms*	*with compassion*	*look*

Without passing into nirvana, please look with compassion upon the beings in the six realms of samsara.

ཐེག་ཆེན་ཆོས་ཀྱི་འཁོར་ལོ་བསྐོར་དུ་གསོལ༔

THEG CHEN	CHO	KYI	KHOR LO	KOR	DU SOL
mahayana	*dharma*	*of*	*wheel*	*turn*	*please*
					(i.e. teach)

We request you to teach the mahayana dharma.

Happily Gone of the ten directions and the three times please remain always in this world, and without passing into nirvana please look with compassion upon the beings in the six realms of samsara. We request you to teach the mahayana dharma.

བདག་གིས་བྱང་ཆུབ་མཆོག་ཏུ་སེམས་བསྐྱེད་དེ༔

DA GI	JANG CHU	CHO	TU	SEM	KYE	DE
I	*by*	*enlightenment,*	*excellent,*	*to*	*mind of*	*develop,*	*that*
		inclusion	*supreme*		*enlightenment*	*raise*	

I will develop the mind that includes all in excellent enlightenment and with that

བདེ་བར་གཤེགས་པ་ཁྱེད་ཀྱི་གདུང་གསོབ་ཆིང༔

DE WAR SHE PA	KHYE KYI	DUNG SO CHING
sugatas, buddhas	*your*	*follow you, come into your family or lineage*

I will enter your lineage, you, the Happily Gone.

སེམས་ཅན་བདེ་བའི་དོན་ཆེན་བསྒྲུབ་པའི་ཕྱིར༔

SEM CHEN	DE WAI	DON	CHEN	DRU PAI	CHIR
sentient beings	*happiness*	*benefit*	*great*	*practice*	*in order to*

In order to accomplish the great benefit of happiness for sentient beings

བླ་མེད་བྱང་ཆུབ་མཆོག་ཏུ་སེམས་བསྐྱེད་དོ༔

LA ME	JANG CHU	CHO	TU	SEM	KYE DO
supreme,	*enlightenment*	*excellent*	*to*	*mind of*	*develop,*
unsurpassed				*enlightenment*	*raise*

I will develop the mind that includes all in supreme enlightenment.

I will develop the mind that includes all in excellent enlightenment and with that I will enter your lineage, you, the Happily Gone. In order to accomplish the great benefit of happiness for sentient beings I will develop the mind that includes all in supreme enlightenment.

བདག་གིས་སེམས་བསྐྱེད་རྒྱ་ཆེན་བགྱིས་པ་ཡིས༔

DA GI	SEM KYE	GYA	CHEN	GYI PA	YI
me	*by*	*develop*	*vast*	*great*	*do*	*by that*
		bodhicitta			

By my giving rise to a great vast mind of inclusion

ཁམས་གསུམ་སེམས་ཅན་མ་ལུས་ཐམས་ཅད་ཀུན༔

KHAM SUM	SEM CHEN	MA LU	THAM CHE	KUN
three worlds	*sentient beings*	*without*	*all*	*all*
(desire, form, formless)				

May all sentient beings in the three worlds without exception

མི་ཁོམ་སྡུག་བསྔལ་བརྒྱད་དང་ངན་སོང་གསུམ༔

MI KHOM	DU NGAL	GYAE	DANG	NGEN SONG	SUM
no leisure*	*miseries*	*eight #*	*and*	*lower realms*	*three+*

* not possible to practise Dharma
\# birth in hells, insatiable ghosts, animals, long-living gods, uncivilised tribes, among those with wrong views, barbarian border countries, and as an idiot
+ hells, insatiable ghosts and animals

Be freed from the eight sorrowful conditions of non-leisure and the three lower realms, and

དེ་ལས་ཐར་ནས་བྱང་ཆུབ་ཐོབ་པར་ཤོག༔

DE	LAE	THAR	NAE	JANG CHU	THO PA	SHO
these places	*from*	*liberate*	*then*	*enlightenment inclusivity*	*get*	*must*

May they all gain enlightenment!

By my giving rise to a great vast mind of inclusion, all sentient beings without exception in the three worlds must be freed from the eight sorrowful conditions of non-leisure and the three lower realms and may they all gain enlightenment!

དཀོན་མཆོག་གསུམ་དང་ནམ་ཡང་མི་འབྲལ་ཞིང༔

KON CHO SUM	DANG	NAM YANG MI	TRAL ZHING
triple gem*	*and*	*never*	*separating*

* buddha, dharma, sangha; guru, deva, dakini; dharmakaya, sambhogakaya, nirmanakaya

Never being separated from the Three Jewels, and

ཚེ་རབས་ཀུན་ཏུ་དགེ་བཅུ་སྤྱོད་པ་དང༔

TSHE RAB	KUN	TU	GE	CHU	CHOE PA	DANG
lives	*all*	*in*	*virtues*	*ten**	*practice*	*and*

* the ten virtues are not taking life; not to take what is not given; ethical sexual behaviour; to speak the truth; to speak gently; not to break a promise; not to speak slander; not to covet another's property; not harming others; to respect the dharma.

Practising the ten virtues in all my lives

འགྲོ་བ་དྲུག་ལ་རྒྱུན་དུ་སྙིང་རྗེས་བལྟ༔

DRO WA	DRU		LA	GYUN DU	NYING JE	TA
beings	*of the six realms*		*to*	*always*	*with compassion*	*look*

May I always look with compassion upon those moving in the six realms and

གཞན་དོན་ཕུན་སུམ་ཚོགས་པ་སྒྲུབ་པར་ཤོག༔

ZHEN	DON	PHUN SUM TSHO PA	CHOE PAR	SHO
others	*benefit*	*all good things (grace, glory, wealth)*	*gain the use of*	*must*

Be able to help others and give them access to all that is beneficial.

Never being separated from the Three Jewels and practising the ten virtues in all my lives, may I always look with compassion upon those moving in the six realms and be able to help others and give them access to all that is beneficial.

བདག་དང་དད་ལྡན་གནས་འདིར་ཚོགས་པ་རྣམས༔

DA	DANG	DAE	DEN	NAE	DIR	TSHO PA	NAM
I	*and*	*having*	*faith*	*place*	*here*	*hosts*	*(plural)*

For myself and all those here who have faith,

ཚེ་རིང་ནད་མེད་ལོངས་སྤྱོད་རྒྱས་པ་དང་༔

TSHE RING	NE ME	LONG CHO	GYAE PA	DANG
long life	*good health*	*wealth*	*increase*	*and*

May we have long lives, with our health and wealth increasing, and

མི་མཐུན་གནོད་པའི་རྐྱེན་རྣམས་ཞི་བ་དང་༔

MI THUN	NOE PAI	KYEN NAM	ZHI WA	DANG
inharmonious	*troublesome*	*reasons, conditions*	*pacified*	*and*

With all inharmonious and troublesome conditions being pacified,

བདག་གཞན་ཕུན་སུམ་ཚོགས་པ་སྒྲུབ་པར་ཤོག༔

DA	ZHAN	PHUN SUM TSHO PA	CHOE PAR	SHO
I	*others*	*all good things (grace, glory, wealth)*	*gain the use of*	*must*

May I and all others enjoy all that is beneficial.

For myself and all those here who have faith, may we have long lives, with our health and wealth increasing, and with all inharmonious and troublesome conditions being pacified, may I and all others enjoy all that is beneficial.

ཤེས་རབ་སྤོབས་པ་དྲན་པ་ཏིང་འཛིན་ནི༔

SHE RAB	PO PA	DREN PA	TING DZIN NI
discernment	*confidence*	*remembrance*	*samadhi, absorbed contemplation*

Gaining true discernment, confidence, remembrance, absorbed contemplation, and

བྱང་ཆུབ་སེམས་ལ་མི་བརྗེད་གཟུངས་ཐོབ་ནས༔

JANG	CHU	SEM	LA	MI	JE	ZUNG	THO	NAE
bodhicitta			*to*	*not*	*forget*	*memory,*	*get*	*then*
inclusivity						*holding*	*power*	

Constant remembrance of our inclusivity,

ས་དང་པ་རོལ་ཕྱིན་པའི་ལམ་བགྲོད་དེ༔

SA	DANG	PHA ROL CHIN PAI		LAM	DROE	DE
bhumi,	*and*	*paramita, transcendental*		*way,*	*traverse*	*thus*
ten stages		*virtues*		*path*		

We will move through the ten stages and the path of the transcendent virtues.

བླ་མེད་བྱང་ཆུབ་མྱུར་དུ་ཐོབ་པར་ཤོག༔

LA ME	JANG CHU	NYUR DU	THO PAR	SHO
supreme,	*enlightenment,*	*quickly*	*get*	*must*
unsurpassed	*inclusion*			

May we thus quickly gain supreme enlightenment.

Gaining true discernment, confidence, remembrance, absorbed contemplation, and constant remembrance of our inclusivity, we will move through the ten stages and the path of the transcendent virtues. May we thus quickly gain supreme enlightenment.

བདག་འདྲ་ཆེ་གེ་མོ་ཞེས་བགྱི་བ་ཡིས༔

DA DRA	CHE GE MO		ZHE GYI WA	YI
I	*(say your own name)*		*so called*	*by*

I, (say your own name)

དུས་འདི་ནས་བཟུང་བསྐལ་པ་དཔག་མེད་དུ༔

DU	DI	NAE ZUNG	KAL PA	PA ME	DU
time	*this*	*from now on*	*kalpa*	*measureless*	*in*

Promise that from this time onwards, for measureless aeons,

སེམས་བསྐྱེད་རྒྱ་ཆེན་བགྱིད་པར་དམ་བཅའ་འོ༔

SEM KYE	GYA CHEN	GYI PAR	DAM CHA O
developing	*vast, great*	*do, perform*	*I promise*
bodhicitta			

I will act to generate a vast inclusive mind.

དཀོན་མཆོག་གསུམ་གྱིས་བདག་གི་གྲོགས་མཛོད་ཅིག༔

KON CHO SUM	GYI	DA GI	DRO	DZOE	CHI
triple gem	*by*	*me of*	*helper,*	*do*	*please*
(guru, deva, dakini etc.)			*friend*		

May the Three Jewels assist me in this!

I, (say your own name), promise that from this time onwards, for measureless aeons, I will act to generate a vast inclusive mind. May the Three Jewels assist me in this!

ཚེ་རབས་འདི་དང་བསྐལ་པ་དཔག་མེད་ཀྱི༔

TSHE RAB	DI	DANG	KAL PA	PA ME	KYI
lifetime	*this*	*and*	*kalpa*	*measureless*	*of*

(during this huge period of time all beings in samsara will enter into some kind of relationship with me)

In this lifetime and during measureless aeons,

བདག་གི་ཕ་དང་མ་དང་འཁོར་བྲན་འཁོལ་དང༔

DA GI	PHA	DANG	MA	DANG	DREN KHOL	DANG
my	*father*	*and*	*mother*	*and*	*servants*	*and*

My parents and servants,

བུ་དང་བུ་མོ་མཛའ་བའི་གྲོགས་ལ་སོགས༔

BU	DANG	BU MO	DZA WAI	DRO	LA SO
sons	*and*	*daughters*	*dear, intimate*	*friends*	*and so on*

My sons and daughters, intimate friends and so on –

ཐམས་ཅད་ངན་སོང་གསུམ་གྱི་གནས་ན་འཁོར༔

THAM CHE	NGEN SONG SUM	GYI	NAE	NA	KHOR
all	*lower realms three*	*of*	*place*	*in*	*revolve, dwell*

All will come to dwell in the three lower realms.

དེ་ཕྱིར་བདག་གིས་འགྲོ་དྲུག་སེམས་ཅན་རྣམས༔

DE CHIR	DA GI	DRO DRU	SEM CHEN	NAM
therefore,	*I*	*by*	*beings (in the*	*sentient being*	*(plural)*
			six realms)		

Since all sentient beings in the six realms

ཉེ་རིང་བྱས་ནས་སྤང་བླང་ཇི་ལྟར་བྱེད༔

NYE RING	JAE	NAE	PANG	LANG	JI TAR	JE
*near and far**	*do*	*then*	*abandon,*	*help,*	*like that*	*do*
			forsake	*adopt*		

* my people and other people

Discriminate between intimates and strangers, and then help or abandon them accordingly, these actions

འགྲོ་བ་དྲུག་གི་གནས་འདི་མ་སྟོངས་པར༔

DRO WA	DRU	GI	NAE	DI	MA	TONG PAR
beings	*six realms*	*of*	*places*	*these*	*not*	*empty*

(because beings act wrongly towards each other and do not practise unbiased openness, samsara goes on and on)

Ensure that the six realms will not be emptied of beings.

བདག་གི་སེམས་བསྐྱེད་ཉམས་པར་མ་གྱུར་ཅིག༔

DA GI	SEM KYE	NYAM PAR	MA	GYUR	CHI
I	*developing bodhicitta*	*weak, lapsed*	*not*	*grow, become*	*must*

Therefore, I must not allow my inclusion of all to weaken.

In this lifetime and during measureless aeons, my parents and servants, my sons and daughters, intimate friends and so on – all will come to dwell in the three lower realms. Since all sentient beings in the six realms discriminate between intimates and strangers, and then help or abandon them accordingly, these actions ensure that the six realms will not be emptied of beings. Therefore, I must not allow my inclusion of all to weaken.

བདག་ནི་དུས་འདིར་ནུས་པ་མཆོག་ཐོབ་ནས༔

DA NI	DU	DIR	NU PA	CHO	THO	NAE
I	*time*	*here*	*power, opportunity*	*supreme, very good*	*get*	*then*

Now, when I have gained the most excellent power of inclusivity,

རིགས་དྲུག་སེམས་ཅན་མ་ལུས་ཐམས་ཅད་ཀྱི༔

RIG	DRU	SEM CHEN	MA LU	THAM CHE	KYI
classes	*six*	*sentient beings*	*without*	*all*	*of*
	(sentient beings in the six realms)				

May I destroy all the karma and karmic results of

ལས་དང་ལས་ཀྱི་རྣམ་སྨིན་འཇོམས་པར་ཤོག༔

LAE	DANG	LAE	KYI	NAM MIN	JOM PAR	SHO
karma	*and*	*karma*	*of*	*fully ripening result*	*subdue*	*must do*

All sentient beings in the six realms without exception.

བདག་ནི་ཡིད་བཞིན་ནོར་བུ་ལྟར་གྱུར་ཏེ༔

DA NI	YI ZHIN NOR BU	TAR	GYUR	TE
I	*wish-fulfilling gem*	*like*	*become*	*this*

Becoming like the wish-fulfilling gem,

ཡིད་ལ་ཅི་བསམས་མ་ལུས་འགྲུབ་པར་ཤོག༔

YI	LA	CHI	SAM	MA LU	DRU PAR	SHO
mind	*in*	*every*	*thought*	*without*	*accomplish*	*must*

May I accomplish every ethical wish that arises in the minds of all beings.

Now, when I have gained the most excellent power of inclusivity, may

I destroy all the karma and karmic results of all sentient beings without exception in the six realms. Becoming like the wish-fulfilling gem, may I accomplish every ethical wish that arises in the minds of all beings.

དམྱལ་བ་ཡི་དགས་བྱོལ་སོང་ངན་སོང་གསུམ༔

NYAL WA	YI DA	JOL SONG	NGEN SONG	SUM
hell	*insatiable ghosts*	*animal*	*lower realms*	*three*

All the three lower realms of hells, insatiable ghosts and animals,

བདག་གིས་སྙིང་རྗེའི་ཡུལ་དུ་དྲན་པ་ཡིས༔

DA GI	NYING JEI	YUL	DU	DREN PA	YI
I	*by compassion*	*object*	*as*	*remember*	*by*

I will recollect as my objects of kindness, and

ཚ་གྲང་བཀྲེས་སྐོམ་གཏི་མུག་ལས་ངན་བྱང༔

TSHA	DRANG	TRE KOM	TI MU	LAE NGEN	JANG
hot	*cold*	*hunger and thirst*	*stupidity*	*bad karma*	*purify*
(hot hells)	*(cold hells)*	*(insatiable ghosts)*	*(animals)*		

I will purify the bad karma which leads to great heat and cold, hunger and thirst, and dull stupidity.

བདག་གི་འཁོར་དང་གདུལ་བྱར་སྐྱེ་བར་ཤོག༔

DA GI	KHOR	DANG	DUL JAR	KYE WA	SHO
my	*circle*	*and*	*disciples*	*born as*	*must be*

May all these beings be born as my associates and disciples.

All the three lower realms of hells, insatiable ghosts and animals, I will recollect as my objects of kindness, and I will purify the bad karma which leads to great heat and cold, hunger and thirst, and dull stupidity. May all these beings be born as my associates and disciples.

ལྷ་དང་ལྷ་མིན་མི་ཡི་རིགས་རྣམས་ཀུན༔

LHA	DANG	LHA MIN	MI	YI	RIG NAM	KUN
gods	*and*	*asuras*	*human*	*of*	*classes*	*all*

With all those in the realms of gods, demi-gods, and humans,

བདག་གིས་ཡིད་ཀྱི་ཡུལ་དུ་དྲན་པ་ཡིས༔

DA GI	YI	KYI	YUL	DU	DREN PA	YI
I	*by*	*mind*	*of*	*object*	*as*	*think of, remember*	*by*

Being remembered and held in mind,

ཆགས་སྡང་འཐབ་རྩོད་ལེ་ལོའི་སྡུག་བསྔལ་བྱང་༔

CHA	DANG	THAB TSOE	LE LOI	DU NGAL	JANG
desire	anger	disputing	laziness	suffering	purify
(humans)	(asuras)	(gods)			

May all their sufferings of desire, anger, strife and laziness be purified, and

ཐམས་ཅད་བྱང་ཆུབ་སེམས་དང་ལྡན་པར་ཤོག༔

THAM CHE	JANG CHU SEM	DANG DEN PAR	SHO
all	bodhicitta	have	must

May they find the mind of inclusivity.

With all those in the realms of gods, demi-gods, and humans, being remembered and held in mind, may all their sufferings of desire, anger, strife and laziness be purified, and may they find the mind of inclusivity.

བདག་གི་དགྲ་བགེགས་རྣམས་ཀྱིས་བདག་མཐོང་ན༔

DA GI	DRA	GEG	NAM	KYI	DA	THONG	NA
my	enemies	obstructors		by	me	see	if, when

When my enemies and opponents see me

ཞེ་སྡང་གནོད་སེམས་སྙིང་རྗེའི་སེམས་སུ་བགྱུར༔

ZHE DANG	NOE SEM	NYING JEI	SEM	SU	GYUR
anger	ill will	compassionate	mind	to	change

May their anger and ill will change into a compassionate attitude.

བདག་གི་གཉེན་དང་འཁོར་གྱིས་བདག་མཐོང་ན༔

DA GI	NYEN	DANG	KHOR	GYI	DA	THONG	NA
my	relatives	and	people of my circle	by	me	look, see	if, when

And when my relatives and associates see me

འཁོར་བ་སྤོང་བའི་བློ་དང་ལྡན་པར་ཤོག༔

KHOR WA	PONG WAI	LO	DANG	DEN PAR	SHO
samsara	renounce, stop	mind, thought	with	have	must get

May they gain the intention to renounce samsara.

When my enemies and opponents see me may their anger and ill will change into a compassionate attitude. When my relatives and associates see me may they gain the intention to renounce samsara.

ཆེ་བཙན་རྒྱལ་པོ་རྣམས་ཀྱིས་བདག་མཐོང་ན༔

CHE TSEN	GYAL PO	NAM	KYI	DA	THONG	NA
great and strong, powerful	*king*	*(plural)*	*by*	*me*	*look, see*	*if, when*

When great and powerful kings see me

ཁེངས་དྲེགས་ངམ་སེམས་ཐུལ་ནས་ཆོས་སྤྱོད་ཤོག༔

KHENG DRE	NGAM SEM	THUL	NAE	CHO	CHOE	SHO
egoism, arrogance, strong pride	*violent mind*	*restrain, stop*	*then*	*dharma*	*practise*	*must*

May their haughty arrogance and rough violent minds be restrained and may they practise the Dharma.

When great and powerful kings see me may their haughty arrogance and rough violent minds be restrained and may they practise the Dharma.

གཞན་ཡང་ནད་དང་སྡུག་བསྔལ་དྲག་པོས་གཟིར༔

ZHEN YANG	NE	DANG	DU NGAL	DRA POE	ZIR
moreover	*disease*	*and*	*misery*	*terrible*	*troubled, tortured pierced*

Moreover, when beings have diseases and are pierced by terrible sufferings,

འཆི་ཁ་དང་ནི་བར་དོའི་སེམས་ཅན་གྱིས༔

CHI KHA	DANG NI	BAR DO	SEM CHEN	GYI
just at the time of dying	*and*	*intermediate periods*	*sentient beings*	*by*

When they are on the point of death and in the subsequent periods,

བདག་ཉིད་མཐོང་བ་དང་ནི་དྲན་པ་ཡིས༔

DA NYI	THONG WA	DANG NI	DREN PA	YI
me, myself	*look, see*	*and*	*remember*	*by*

By seeing and remembering me

རང་རང་ལས་ཀྱི་སྡུག་བསྔལ་ཞི་བར་ཤོག༔

RANG RANG	LAE	KYI	DU NGAL	ZHI WAR	SHO
each separate	*karma*	*of*	*suffering*	*pacified*	*must*

May each have their own karmic sufferings pacified.

Moreover, when beings have diseases and are pierced by terrible sufferings, when they are on the point of death and in the subsequent periods, by seeing and remembering me, may each have their own karmic sufferings pacified.

སེམས་ཅན་དབུལ་ཕོངས་བཀྲེས་སྐོམ་ཉེན་པ་རྣམས༔

SEM CHEN	WUL PHONG	TRE	KOM	NYEN PA	NAM
sentient beings	*poor*	*hunger*	*thirst*	*troubled, in danger*	*those who are*

May all sentient beings who are troubled by poverty, hunger and thirst,

བདག་ཉིད་མཐོང་ངམ་དྲན་པས་འབྱོར་པ་རྒྱས༔

DA NYI	THONG	NGAM	DREN	PAE	JOR PA	GYE
me	*look, see*	*or*	*remember*	*by*	*fortune,*	*increase wealth*

By seeing or remembering me, have their fortune increase and

ལོངས་སྤྱོད་ཕུན་སུམ་ཚོགས་པ་ཐོབ་པར་ཤོག༔

LONG CHOE	PHUN SUM TSHO PA	THO PAR	SHO
useful things	*all good things*	*get*	*must*

Gain enjoyment and fulfilment.

By seeing or remembering me, may all sentient beings who are troubled by poverty, hunger, and thirst, have their fortune increase and gain enjoyment and fulfilment.

སེམས་ཅན་གཤེད་མའི་ལག་ཏུ་བཟུང་བ་ཡི༔

SEM CHEN	SHE MAI	LAG	TU	ZUNG WA	YI
sentient beings	*executioner, killer*	*hand*	*in*	*held*	*of*

When sentient beings are caught by a killer,

མི་དང་དུད་འགྲོ་སེམས་ཅན་ཐམས་ཅད་ཀྱི༔

MI	DANG	DUN DRO	SEM CHEN	THAM CHE	KYI
human being	*and*	*animals*	*sentient beings*	*all*	*of*

For all beings, whether they be human or animal,

ཚེ་སྲོག་བདག་གིས་བླུ་ཞིང་སྐྱོབ་པར་ཤོག༔

TSHE	SO	DA GI	LU ZHING	KYO PAR	SHO
life	*force*	*me by*	*ransom*	*save*	*must*

May I ransom their lives and protect them.

When sentient beings, be they human or animal, are caught by a killer, may I ransom their lives and protect them.

སྐྱེ་བོ་སྡིག་ཅན་རྣམས་ཀྱིས་བདག་མཐོང་ན༔

KYE WO	DIG CHEN	NAM	KYI	DA	THONG	NA
human being	*sinful*	*those who are*	*by*	*me*	*see*	*if, when*

When sinful humans see me,

ཞེ་སྡང་རྔམ་སེམས་ལོག་པའི་སེམས་ཞི་ནས༔

ZHE DANG	NGAM SEM	LOG PAI SEM	ZHI	NAE
anger	*violent*	*wrong ideas*	*pacify*	*then*

May their anger, violent thoughts and wrong views be pacified and then

ཞི་དུལ་སྙིང་རྗེའི་སེམས་དང་ལྡན་པར་ཤོག༔

ZHI DUL	NYING JEI	SEM	DANG DEN PAR	SHO
peaceful	*compassionate*	*mind*	*have*	*must*

May they gain calm and compassionate minds.

When sinful humans see me, may their anger, violent thoughts and wrong views be pacified, and may they gain calm and compassionate minds.

བུད་མེད་སྐྱེ་དམན་རྣམས་ཀྱིས་བདག་མཐོང་ན༔

BU ME	KYE MEN	NAM	KYI	DA	THONG	NA
woman	*female*	*(plural)*	*by*	*me*	*look at*	*if, when*

When women see me,

འདོད་ཆགས་ཞེན་པའི་བསམ་པ་དག་གྱུར་ནས༔

DOE CHA	ZHEN PAI	SAM PA	DA	GYUR	NAE
desire, lust	*hopeful*	*thoughts*	*pure*	*become*	*then*

May their desireful thoughts and hopeful attachments be purified, and then

དྲན་རིག་བདེ་བ་ཆེན་པོ་རྟོགས་པར་ཤོག༔

DREN RIG	DE WA	CHEN PO	TO PAR	SHO
mindfulness, awareness	*happiness*	*great*	*realise*	*must*

May they realise the great happiness of mindfulness.

When women see me, may their desireful thoughts and hopeful attachments be purified, and then may they realise the great happiness of mindfulness.

རབ་བྱུང་བཙུན་པ་རྣམས་ཀྱིས་བདག་མཐོང་ན༔

RAB JUNG	TSUN PA	NAM	KYI	DA	THONG	NA
bhikshus, renunciates	*saintly beings*	*(plural)*	*by*	*me*	*look at, see*	*if, when*

When monks and nuns of all classes see me,

ཚུལ་ཁྲིམས་སྡོམ་པ་གཙང་ཞིང་བདེན་པ་དང་ཿ

TSHUL TRIM   DOM PA   TSANG ZHING   DEN PA   DANG
morality   vows   purity   keep   and

May they keep their vows and morality pure and

ཕ་རོལ་ཕྱིན་པ་དྲུག་ལ་སློང་པར་ཤོག་ཿ

PHA ROL CHIN PA   DRU   LA   CHOE PAR   SHO
paramitas, transcendent   six   in   practise   must do*

* Generosity, morality, endurance, diligence, absorbed contemplation and wisdom. It is their inseparability from emptiness which makes them transcendent.

Practise the six aspects of transcendence.

When monks and nuns of all classes see me, may they keep their vows and morality pure and practise the six aspects of transcendence.

གསང་སྔགས་རྣལ་འབྱོར་རྣམས་ཀྱིས་བདག་མཐོང་ནཿ

SANG NGA   NAL JOR   NAM   KYI   DA   THONG   NA
tantra   yogi   (plural)   by   me   see   if, when

When tantric yogis see me,

དམ་ཚིག་ཉམས་ཆགས་ཐམས་ཅད་སྐོང་གྱུར་ནསཿ

DAM TSHI   NYAM   CHA   THAM CHE   KONG   GYUR   NAE
vows   lapsed   lost   all   full   become   and then

May all their lost and lapsed vows be restored and

བདག་གཞན་གཉིས་སུ་མེད་པའི་དོན་རྟོགས་ཤོག་ཿ

DA ZHAN   NYI SU ME PAI   DON   TO   SHO
I   others   not different   meaning   actualise   must

May they actualise the non-duality of self and others.

When tantric yogis see me, may all their lost and lapsed vows be restored and may they actualise the non-duality of self and others.

བླ་མེད་རྣལ་འབྱོར་སྒྲུབ་པས་བདག་མཐོང་ནཿ

LA ME   NAL JOR   DRU PAE   DA   THONG   NA
supreme   yoga   practitioners   me   see   if, when

When practitioners of the highest tantric yoga see me,

སྣང་སྲིད་འཁོར་འདས་སེམས་སུ་ཐག་ཆོད་ནསཿ

NANG SI   KHOR   DAE   SEM   SU   THA CHO   NAE
all possible   samsara   nirvana   mind   as   decide, resolve   then
appearances

May they be confident that all the possible appearances of samsara and nirvana are the play of the mind, and then

 མ་བཅོས་རང་བྱུང་ཡེ་ཤེས་དོན་ཏོ་ཤོག༔

MA CHOE	RANG JUNG	YE SHE	DON	TO	SHO
non-artificial	*spontaneous*	*original knowing*	*nature*	*actualise*	*must*

Actualise uncontrived, uncreated original knowing.

When practitioners of the highest tantric yoga see me, may they be confident that all the possible appearances of samsara and nirvana are the play of the mind, and then actualise uncontrived, uncreated original knowing.

སྲིད་པའི་རྩེ་ནས་དམྱལ་བའི་གནས་ཡན་ཆད༔

SI PAI	TSE	NAE	NYAL WAI	NAE	YAN CHE
world	*top point*	*from*	*hell's*	*place*	*from up to down*

From the highest levels of this world down to the realms of hell, and

ཚངས་པའི་ལྷ་དང་འཛག་མའི་སྲིན་བུའི་བར༔

TSHANG PAI LHA	DANG	JAG MAI	SIN BUI	BAR
brahma gods	*from*	*grass*	*insect*	*until, including*

From the brahma gods to the tiniest insects in the grass,

རིགས་དྲུག་སེམས་ཅན་གཟུགས་ལྡན་གཟུགས་མེད་ཀུན༔

RIG DRU	SEM CHEN	ZUG DEN	ZUG ME	KUN
six realms of samsara	*sentient beings*	*with body, form*	*without form, body*	*all*

For all sentient beings in the six realms, whether with form or without,

བདག་ཉིད་མཐོང་དང་ཐོས་དང་རེག་པ་དང༔

DA NYI	THONG	DANG	THOE	DANG	REG PA	DANG
me	*see (me or my name)*	*and*	*hear*	*and*	*come in contact*	*and*

By merely seeing, hearing, touching or thinking of me,

བདག་ཉིད་བསམས་པ་ཙམ་གྱིས་སྒྲིབ་པ་སྦྱང༔

DA NYI	SAM PA	TSAM	GYI	DRI PA	JANG
me	*think*	*only*	*by*	*obscurations*	*cleansed*

May all their obscurations be removed.

ཐམས་ཅད་བདག་གི་ཆོས་ལ་སྤྱོད་པར་ཤོག༔

THAM CHE	DA GI	CHO	LA	CHOE PAR	SHO
all of them	*my*	*dharma*	*to*	*practise*	*must*

May they practise my Dharma.

From the highest levels of this world down to the realms of hell, and

from the brahma gods to the tiniest insects in the grass, for all sentient beings in the six realms, whether with form or without, by merely seeing, hearing, touching or thinking of me, may all their obscurations be removed. May they practise my Dharma.

བདག་ནི་རང་བྱུང་ཡེ་ཤེས་ཆེན་པོ་སྟེ༔

DA NI	RANG JUNG	YE SHE	CHEN PO	TE
I	*spontaneous*	*original knowing*	*great*	*thus*

With uncreated great original knowing

ཉོན་མོངས་དུག་ལྔ་ཡེ་ཤེས་ལྔ་རུ་ཤེས༔

NYON MONG	DU	NGA	YE SHE	NGA	RU	SHE
afflictions	*poisons*	*five**	*original knowing*	*five#*	*as*	*know*

* stupidity, anger, desire, pride, jealousy   # these are listed in the following verses

We know the five afflicting poisons to be the five original knowings.

With the uncreated great original knowing we know the five afflicting poisons to be he five original knowings.

འདོད་ཆགས་བདེ་བ་ཆེན་པོའི་ངོ་བོར་ཤར༔

DOE CHA	DE WA CHEN POI	NGO WOR	SHAR
desire	*great happiness, bliss*	*essence*	*arises*

The essence of desire arises as great happiness.

གཉིས་སུ་མེད་པར་ཚིམ་པར་སྦྱར་བ་ཡིས༔

NYI SU ME PAR	TSHIM PAR	JAR WA	YI
non-duality	*happily satisfied*	*joining**	*by*

*subject and object having the same ground and being interpenetrating

With satisfying union in non-duality

སོ་སོར་རྟོག་པའི་ཡེ་ཤེས་རྟོགས་པར་ཤོག༔

SO SOR TO PAI	YE SHE	TO PAR	SHO
clearly discerning	*original knowing*	*actualise*	*must*

May we all actualise the knowing that sees each precise detail.

The essence of desire arises as great happiness. With satisfying union in non-duality, may we all actualise the knowing that sees each precise detail.

ཞེ་སྡང་བྱམས་པ་ཆེན་པོའི་ངོ་བོར་ཤར༔

ZHE DANG	JAM PA	CHEN POI	NGO WOR	SHAR
anger, hate	kindness, love	great	essence	rise, understand

The essence of anger arises as great love.

བསད་བཅད་ཚར་གཅོད་དྲག་པོས་བསྒྲལ་བ་ཡིས༔

SAE	CHE	TSAR CHOE	DRA POE	DRAL PA	YI
kill	cut	annihilate	strongly	kill, liberate	by

(i.e. killing ignorance and the seeming substantiality of appearances)

By liberating with powerful killing, cutting and annihilation

སྟོང་པ་ཉིད་ཀྱི་ཡེ་ཤེས་ཐོབ་པར་ཤོག༔

TONG PA NYI		KYI	YE SHE	THO PAR	SHO
sunyata, dharmadhatu, infinite hospitality		of	original knowing	actualise	must

May we all actualise the original knowing of infinite hospitality.

The essence of anger arises as great love. By liberating with powerful killing, cutting, and annihilation may we all actualise the original knowing of infinite hospitality.

ང་རྒྱལ་འགྲོ་བ་དབང་བསྡུས་དངོས་སུ་ཤར༔

NGA GYAL	DRO WA	WANG DU	NGO	SU	SHAR
arrogance, pride	sentient beings	power over	truth	as	arise

The essence of pride arises as the benign control of sentient beings.

དྲག་པོ་ཟིལ་གནོན་འགགས་མེད་སྒྲ་བསྒྲགས་པས༔

DRA PO	ZIL NON	GAG ME	DRA	DRA PAE
fierce, strong	overpowering personality	without stopping	sound	roaring by

By the ceaseless roaring sound of a powerful, awesome personality

མཉམ་པ་ཉིད་ཀྱི་ཡེ་ཤེས་ཐོབ་པར་ཤོག༔

NYAM PA NYI	KYI	YE SHE	THO PAR	SHO
perfect equality*	of	original knowing	actualise	must

*purifying pride by seeing the actual equality of all phenomena

May we all actualise the original knowing of equality.

The essence of pride arises as the benign control of sentient beings.By the ceaseless roaring sound of a powerful, awesome personality may we all actualise the original knowing of equality.

གཏི་མུག་ཞི་བ་ཆེན་པོའི་ངང་དུ་ཤར༔

TI MU		ZHI WA	CHEN POI	NGANG	DU	SHAR
mental opacity		*peace*	*great*	*state*	*as*	*arise*

The essence of mental opacity arises as the presence of great peace.

མ་བཅོས་རང་གསལ་ཆེན་པོའི་མདངས་ཤར་ནས༔

MA CHO	RANG SAL		CHEN POI	DANG	SHAR	NAE
natural	*inherent clarity*		*great*	*radiance*	*rises*	*then*

With the arising of the radiance of uncontrived inherent clarity,

མེ་ལོང་ལྟ་བུའི་ཡེ་ཤེས་ཐོབ་པར་ཤོག༔

ME LONG	TA BUI	YE SHE	THO PAR	SHO
mirror	*like*	*original knowing*	*actualise*	*must*

May we all actualise the mirror-like original knowing.

The essence of mental opacity arises as the state of great peace. With the arising of the radiance of uncontrived inherent clarity, may we all actualise the mirror-like original knowing.

ཕྲག་དོག་འཕྲིན་ལས་ལམ་གྱི་གྲོགས་སུ་ཤར༔

TRA DO	TRIN LAE	LAM	GYI	DRO	SU	SHAR
jealousy	*activity*	*way*	*of*	*assistance, support*	*as*	*arise*

The essence of jealousy arises as a support on the path of activity.

དམིགས་བྱ་ཡུལ་གྱི་བསམས་པའི་དོན་གྲུབ་ནས༔

MIG JA		YUL	GYI	SAM PAI	DON	DRU	NAE
conceptualised		*place, object*	*of*	*thoughts*	*meaning, nature*	*understanding*	*then*

With effective understanding of the thoughts that underlie reified objects,

བྱ་བ་གྲུབ་པའི་ཡེ་ཤེས་ཐོབ་པར་ཤོག༔

JA WA	DRU PAI	YE SHE	THO PAR	SHO
deed	*accomplish*	*original knowing*	*actualise*	*must*

May we all actualise the original knowing that accomplishes everything.

The essence of jealousy arises as a support on the path of activity. With effective understanding of the thoughts that underlie reified objects, may we all actualise the original knowing that accomplishes everything.

ཨེ་མ་ཧོ་ལྟ་བཀུ་སྟེགས་མའི་དུས༔ ལས་ཅན་སྐྱེས་པའི་རྣལ་འབྱོར་བ༔ ང་ཡི་གཏེར་དང་
འཕྲད་པར་འགྱུར༔ དུས་གསུམ་བདེ་གཤེགས་དཔང་དུ་བཟུག༔ གྲུ་རུ་སེམས་དཔའི་ཚ་
ལུགས་ཅན༔ གིང་དང་མཁའ་འགྲོ་མང་པོས་བསྐོར༔ ལས་རྣམས་གང་བྱེད་གྲོགས་སུ་
བསམ༔ སྨོན་ལམ་རྣམ་དག་འདི་བཏབ་ན༔ འགྲོ་དོན་རྒྱ་ཆེན་འགྲུབ་པར་འགྱུར༔ ཞེས་
གསུངས་སོ༔ ཆོས་ཀྱི་འཁོར་ལོ་གསུམ་པའི༔ དེའི་དུས་སུ་བོད་ཀྱི་རྗེ་འབངས་བསམ་པའི་
དོན་གྲུབ་ནས༔ ལྷ་སྲས་མུ་ཁྲི་བཙན་པོས་དཀར་ཆག་ཡི་གེར་བཀོད་ནས་བསེ་སྒྲོམ་སྨུག་པོར་
སྦས་སོ༔ རིག་འཛིན་རྒོད་ཀྱི་ལྡེམ་འཕྲུ་ཅན་གྱིས་ལྷོ་གསེར་མཛོད་སེར་པོ་ནས་སྤྱན་དྲངས་
པའི༔ ས་མ་ཡ་རྒྱ་རྒྱ་རྒྱ༔

*"Wonderful! In the debased times of the final five hundred year period, a
fortunate secret yogi (Rig-'Dzin rGod-lDem) will meet with my treasure. The
Happily Gone Buddhas of the three times will be his witness and will help him.*

*See the guru in the form of Vajrasattva surrounded by many agents and dakinis.
They act as his helpers in whatever activities he performs.*

*If you recite this very pure prayer of aspiration you will accomplish a great
benefit for sentient beings. "* Thus it was said (by Padmasambhava).

At the time of the third dharmachakra the wishes of the Tibetan king and the
other twenty-five disciples were fulfilled. Prince Lha Sras Mu-Khri bTsan-Po
wrote this prayer down and then it was hidden in the maroon leather casket.
Rig-'Dzin rGod-Kyi lDem 'Phru-Chan took it out from the yellow coloured
golden treasury on the south side of the container.

Vows.   Seal.   Seal.   Seal.

Notes

1. The confession must be made honestly with sincere regret as if one
    had swallowed poison, and with a firm intention never to make
    such errors again. If done like this then the confession will be a
    truly effective purification because the buddhas will send their
    healing light revealing the intrinsic emptiness of all phenomena
    which has been obscured by the attachment to the idea of entities
    which leads to error.

རྒྱལ་པོ་གསེར་གྱི་ལག་པའི་མར་མེའི་ལོ་རྒྱུས་དང་སྨོན་ལམ་གྱི་མདོ་བཞུགས་སོ།།

The Sutra of the Story of the Lamp of King Golden Hand and His Aspiration

༈ རྒྱ་གར་སྐད་དུ། རཱཛཀཉྩུ་བྷུ་ཏི་པ་སྱ་པྲ་ཀྲི་ཡ་ཙ་ཏྲ་སཱུ་ཏྲ། བོད་སྐད་དུ། རྒྱལ་པོ་གསེར་གྱི་ལག་པའི་མར་མེའི་ལོ་རྒྱུས་དང་སྨོན་ལམ་གྱི་མདོ། དཀོན་མཆོག་གསུམ་ལ་ཕྱག་འཚལ་ལོ། སྔོན་སངས་རྒྱས་མར་མེ་མཛད་ཀྱིས་སྟོན་པ་མཛད་པའི་དུས་ན། རྒྱལ་པོ་གསེར་གྱི་ལག་པ་ཞེས་བྱ་བས། བཅོམ་ལྡན་འདས་མར་མེ་མཛད་ལ་འདི་སྐད་ཅེས་གསོལ་ཏེ། བཅོམ་པ་ཁྱོད་སྟོན་གྱི་དུས་ན་དགེ་བའི་རྩ་བ་ཅི་ཞིག་སྤྱད་ན། དཔེར་མཚོན་དང་དཔེ་བྱད་དུ་ལྡན་ཏེ། སྐུ་ལས་འོད་ཟེར་མཐའ་ཡས་པ་འབྱུང་བའི་རྒྱ་གར་ལགས། རྒྱན་གར་ལགས། བཅོམ་ལྡན་འདས་ཀྱིས་བཀའ་སྩལ་པ། རྒྱལ་པོ་ཆེན་པོ་ཉོན་ཅིག །ངས་སྔོན་གྱི་སྐྱེ་བོའི་དུས་ན། ཕྱོགས་བཅུའི་སངས་རྒྱས་ཐམས་ཅད་ལ་བྱང་ཆུབ་ཏུ་སེམས་བསྐྱེད་ནས། ལུས་ལ་རས་བལ་གྱི་ཡེའུ་ཏིལ་མར་གྱི་ནང་དུ་བཅོས་པ་སྟོང་བཞུགས་ཏེ། ཕྱོགས་བཅུ་དུས་གསུམ་གྱི་སངས་རྒྱས་ཐམས་ཅད་ལ། གདན་པ་མེད་པའི་མཆོད་པར་ཕུལ་བས། དཔེར་ན་ཉིད་སངས་རྒྱས་མར་མེ་མཛད་ཅེས་བྱ་བར་གྱུར་པ་ཡིན་ནོ་ཞེས་གསུངས་པ་དང་། དེའི་རྒྱལ་པོ་ཆེན་པོ་ཉིན་ཏུ་ཡི་རངས་ཏེ། དེ་ནས་རྒྱལ་པོ་དེས་རང་གི་ལག་པ་གཡས་པ་རས་བལ་མར་གྱིས་བཅོས་ནས་དགུས་ཏེ་མེ་བཏང་ནས། ལག་པ་གཡོན་པ་བར་སྤུར་ལ་བཀུང་སྟེ། ཕྱོགས་བཅུའི་སངས་རྒྱས་ཐམས་ཅད་དང་། བདག་གི་སྟོན་པ་བཅོམ་ལྡན་འདས་མར་མེ་མཛད་དགོངས་སུ་གསོལ་ལོ། འགྲོད་པ་མེད་པའི་སེམས་ཀྱིས། ཕྱོགས་བཅུའི་སངས་རྒྱས་ཐམས་ཅད་ཡིད་ཀྱིས་མཆོད་སྐུམ་དུ་དམིགས་ཏེ། གདན་པ་མེད་པའི་མཆོད་པར་བསྔོས་ནས་སྨོན་ལམ་འདེབས་ཏེ། འདི་སྐད་དོ།

Sanskrit: *rajakancanabahudipasyaprakriyapranidhana sutra*

Tibetan: *rGyal-Po gSer-Gyi Lag-Pa'i Mar-Me'i Lo-rGyus Dang sMon-Lam-Gyi mDo*

Salutation to the Three Jewels.

When Dipamkara, the Buddha of the earlier period before the time of Buddha Shakyamuni, was teaching, King Golden Hand asked him, *"Venerable One, what was the basis of the virtue that you created in former times resulting in you now displaying the major and minor signs of a Buddha and radiating infinite light from your body?"*

Buddha Dipamkara replied, *"Listen, great king! When I was an ordinary being, in front of all the Buddhas of the ten directions I developed altruistic bodhicitta. Then I dipped one thousand cotton wicks in clarified butter and placed them on my body. Without hope or expectation I lit them as an offering to all the Buddhas of the ten directions and the three times. That is why I am now known as Buddha Dipamkara, 'the one who made the butterlamp'."*

The great king rejoiced at this. He wrapped his own right hand in cotton wool, dipped it in clarified butter and lit it. He raised his left hand to the sky and said, *"Buddhas of the ten directions and Buddha Dipamkara, my teacher, please think of me."*

With a mind free of regret he clearly visualised all the buddhas of the ten directions. He dedicated the merit of this offering given without expectation, and made this prayer of aspiration:

[Firstly, light a butterlamp or candle. If you are reciting this to generate merit for one who is dying or who has died, then say their name and holding them in mind, recite the sutra with your hands raised, palms facing the sky.]

མར་མེའི་སྣོད་ནི་སྟོང་གསུམ་གྱི་སྟོང་ཆེན་པོའི

MAR MEI	NOE	NI	TONG	SUM	GYI	TONG	CHEN POI
butterlamp	*pot*	*this*	*thousand (infinite)*	*three*	*of*	*thousand*	*great*

May the pot of this lamp become as vast as the infinity

འཇིག་རྟེན་གྱི་ཁམས་ཚམ་དུ་གྱུར་ཅིག

JIG TEN	GYI	KHAMS	TSAM DU	GYUR CHI
worlds	*of*	*realms*	*as much as*	*become*

Of all the countless worlds.

སྙིང་པོ་ནི་རིའི་རྒྱལ་པོ་རི་རབ་ཚམ་དུ་གྱུར་ཅིག

NYING PO	NI	RI	GYAL PO	RI RAB	TSAM DU	GYUR CHI
wick	*this*	*mountains*	*king*	*Mt. Meru**	*like*	*become*

*Mount Meru, in traditional Buddhist cosmology, is the mountain at the centre of our world system. It is so high that night appears when the sun disappears behind it in the evening.

May the wick become as big as Mount Meru, the king of mountains.

འོད་ཀྱིས་ནི་སྲིད་པའི་རྩེ་མོ་མན་ཆད་ནས།

WOE	**KYI**	**NI**	**SI PAI**	**TSE MO**	**MEN CHAE**	**NAE**
light	*by*	*this*	*world*	*top*	*down*	*from*

May the rays of its light reach from the top of this world

མནར་མེད་པའི་སེམས་ཅན་དམྱལ་བ་ཡན་ཆད་ནས།

NAR ME PAI	**SEM CHEN**	**NYAL WA**	**YAN CHAE**	**NAE**
name of the lowest hell	*sentient beings*	*hell*	*above*	*also*

Down to the beings in the lowest Avici hell.

May the pot of this lamp become as vast as the infinity of all the countless worlds. May the wick become as big as Mount Meru, the king of mountains. May the rays of its light reach from the top of this world down to the beings in the lowest Avici hell.

གཞན་ཡང་ལྕགས་རི་ཆེན་པོའི་ཕྱི་རྒྱབ་ན།

ZHAN YANG	**CHA**	**RI**	**CHEN POI**	**CHI GYAB**	**NA**
moreover	*iron*	*mountain*	*great*	*behind, beyond*	*at*

May the rays of light reach beyond the iron mountains ringing our world system

སེམས་ཅན་རང་གི་ལས་ཀྱིས་སྒྲིབ་པས་

SEM CHEN	**RANG GI**	**LAE**	**KYI**	**DRI PAE**
sentient beings	*own*	*actions*	*by*	*obscuring*

To reach the people who are living in the enveloping gloom of

བསྒྲིབས་པའི་མུན་ནག་ཆེན་པོའི་ནང་ན།

DRI PAI	**MU**	**NA**	**CHEN POI**	**NANG NA**
covering	*darkness*	*black*	*great*	*in*

The darkness created by their own bad actions and

རང་གི་ལག་པ་བརྐྱང་བསྐུམ་ཡང་མི་མཐོང་བའི་གནས་

RANG GI	**LA PA**	**KYANG KUM**	**YANG**	**MI**	**THONG PAI**	**NAE**
own	*hand*	*moving, waving*	*also*	*not*	*see*	*place*

Who cannot even see the movements of their own hands.

ཚུན་ཆད་སྣང་ཞིང་གསལ་བར་གྱུར་ཅིག།

TSHUN CHAE	**NANG ZHING**	**SAL WAR**	**CHI**
as far as	*light*	*illuminate*	*become*

May this light spread illumination there.

May the rays of its light reach beyond the iron mountains ringing our

world system to reach the people who are living in the enveloping gloom of the darkness created by their own bad actions and who cannot even see the movements of their own hands. May this light spread illumination there.

ཡུན་ནི་དུས་གསུམ་གྱི་སངས་རྒྱས་ཇི་སྲིད་བཞུགས་པ་

YUN NI	DUE	SUM	GYI	SANG GYE	JI SI	ZHU PA
duration	times	three	of	buddhas	as long	staying as that

May this light remain for the duration of all the periods of all the Buddhas

དེ་སྲིད་དུ་གནས་པར་གྱུར་ཅིག།

DE SI	DU	NAE PAR	GYUR CHI
as much	for	stay	make, may

Of the past, present and future.

གྲངས་ནི་ཕྱོགས་བཅུ་འཇིག་རྟེན་གྱི་ཁམས་མཐའ་ཡས་པ་ན་

DRANG NI	CHO	CHU	JIG TEN	GYI	KHAM	THA YAE PA	NA
enumeration	directions	ten*	world	of	realms	limitless	in

*ten direction, i.e. everywhere

May this light shine before the eyes

བཞུགས་པའི་སངས་རྒྱས་གྲངས་མེད་པར་

ZHU PAI	SANG GYE	DRANG ME PAR
staying	buddhas	countless

Of all the numberless Buddhas

རེ་རེའི་སྤྱན་ལམ་དུ་གསལ་བར་གྱུར་ཅིག།

RE REI	CHEN	LAM DU	SAL WAR	GYUR CHI
each	eye	in front of	shine	make

In the countless worlds which pervade the ten directions.

May this light remain for the duration of all the periods of all the Buddhas of the past, present and future. May this light shine before the eyes of all the numberless Buddhas in the countless worlds which pervade the ten directions.

མར་མེ་འདི་གཟུགས་མེད་པའི་གནས་སུ་སྣང་ཞིང་

MAR ME	DI	ZUG ME PAI	NAE	SU	NANG ZHING
butterlamp	this	formless	place	in	appearing

May the light from this lamp illuminate

གསལ་བར་གྱུར་ཅིག།   དེ་ལྟར་གསལ་བའི་མོད་ལ།

SAL WAR   **GYUR CHI**   **DE TAR**   **SAL WAI**   **MOE LA**
illuminating   *make, may*   *in that way*   *shining*   *immediately*

The formless realms.   With this illumination,

གཟུགས་མེད་པའི་ལྷ་རྣམས་མར་མེའི་འོད་ཀྱིས་བསྐུལ་མ་ཐག་ཏུ།

ZUG ME PAI   **LHA**   **NAM**   **MAR MEI**   **OE**   **KYI**   **KUL**   **MA TAG TU**
formless   *gods*   *all*   *butterlamp*   *light*   *by*   *arouse*   *as soon as*

As soon as the gods of these realms are aroused

མཚན་དང་དཔེ་བྱད་དུ་ལྡན་ནས་

TSHAN   **DANG**   **PE JE**   **DU DEN**   **NE**
major signs   *and*   *minor signs*   *gain*   *then*
       (of a buddha's body)

May they gain the major and minor signs of enlightenment and

སྙོམས་པར་འཇུག་པའི་སྐྱེམ་ཆེད་བཞི་ལས་གྲོལ་ཏེ།

NYOM PAR JU PAI   **KYEM CHE**   **ZHI**   **LAE**   **DROL**   **TE**
mental absorption   *sensory supports*   *four**   *from*   *freed*   *then*
*these are the four formless levels, the highest in samsara

Be freed from the mental absorptions of the four levels of subtle sensory
support.

དེ་བཞིན་གཤེགས་པའི་བསམ་གཏན་ལ་སོགས་པར་

DE ZHIN SHE PAI   **SAM TAN**   **LA**   **SO PAR**
Buddha, Tathagata,   *stable forms*   *of*   *different*

May entry to the various meditative states of the Tathagata

སྙོམས་པར་འཇུག་པའི་སྐལ་པ་དང་ལྡན་པར་གྱུར་ཅིག།

NYOM PAR JU PAI   **KAL PA**   **DANG DEN PAR**   **GYUR CHI**
contemplation   *fortunate*   *have*   *make, may*

Be available to these fortunate ones.

*May the light from this lamp illuminate the formless realms. With this
illumination, as soon as the gods of these realms are aroused, may they
gain the major and minor signs of enlightenment and be freed from the
mental absorptions of the four levels of subtle sensory support. May
entry to the various meditative states of the Tathagata be available to
these fortunate ones.*

མར་མེ་འདི་གཟུགས་ན་སྤྱོད་པའི་ལྷ་རྣམས་ཀྱི་

MAR ME   **DI**   **ZUG**   **NA**   **CHOE PAI**   **LHA NAM**   **KYI**
butterlamp   *this*   *form*   *with*   *acting*   *gods*   *of*

May the light from this lamp illuminate

གནས་སུ་གསལ་བར་གྱུར་ཅིག།

NAE   SU   SAL WAR   GYUR CHI
place   to   illuminate   make, may

The realm of the gods with form.

གཟུགས་ན་སྤྱོད་པའི་ལྷ་རྣམས་ཏིང་ངེ་འཛིན་གྱི་

ZUG   NA   CHOE PAI   LHA NAM   TING NGE DZIN   GYI
form   in, with   acting   gods   undisturbed contemplation   of

May these gods enter undisturbed contemplation and

དགའ་བདེ་རྩེ་གཅིག་ལ་ཉམས་སུ་མྱོང་ནས།

GA   DE   TSE   CHI   LA   NYAM SU NYONG   NAE
happy   joy   pointed   one   in   experience   then

Experience unwavering happiness and

ཕྱིར་མི་ལྡོག་པའི་ས་ཐོབ་པར་གྱུར་ཅིག།

CHIR MI DO PAI   SA   THO PAR   GYUR CHI
irreversible   stage   get   make, may*
*state of non return, Anagami, one who does not return to this world again

Gain the state of non-return.

May the light from this lamp illuminate the realm of the gods with form. May these gods enter undisturbed contemplation and experience unwavering happiness and gain the stage of non-return.

མར་མེ་འདི་འདོད་ཁམས་ཀྱི་ལྷ་རྣམས་ཀྱི་གནས་སུ་

MAR ME   DI   DOE   KHAM   KYI   LHA NAM   KYI   NAE   SU
butterlamp   this   desire   realm   of   gods   of   place   to

May the light from this lamp illuminate the environment

སྣང་ཞིང་གསལ་བར་གྱུར་ཅིག།

NANG ZHING   SAL WAR   GYUR CHI
showing   illuminating   make, may

Of the gods of the realm of desire.

འདོད་ཁམས་ཀྱི་ལྷ་རྣམས་ཀྱང་།

DOE   KHAM   KYI   LHA NAM   KYANG
desire   realm   of   gods   also

May these gods

ལྷའི་འདོད་པའི་ལོངས་སྤྱོད་ལ་སེམས་མ་ཆགས་ཤིང་།

LHAI   DOE PAI   LONG CHO   LA   SEM   MA   CHA SHING
god's   desirable   wealth   to   mind   not   attaching

Be free of attachment to the riches of their realm.

རང་གི་སེམས་ལ་ལྟ་ཞིང་།

RANG GI   SEM   LA   TA ZHING
own   mind   to   look, see

May they look at their own minds and

བསམ་གཏན་བཞི་ལ་རིམ་གྱིས་སྙོམས་པར་འཇུག་པའི་

SAM TEN   ZHI   LA   RIM   GYI   NYOM PAR JU PAI
meditative   four   on   in sequence   by   enter that state,*
absorption   settle into stability

*four concentrations: 1. with concepts and investigation, 2.with investigation but no concepts, 3.with mentation free of concepts and investigation, 4. with mentation linked with delight.

Enter each of the four meditative absorptions in turn.

སྐལ་པ་དང་ལྡན་པར་གྱུར་ཅིག།

KAL PA   DANG DAN PAR   GYUR CHI
fortunate   have   make, may
opportunity

May they have the opportunity to experience that.

May the light from this lamp illuminate the environment of the gods of the realm of desire. May these gods be free of attachment to the riches of their realm. May they look at their own minds and enter each of the four meditative absorptions in turn. May they have the opportunity to experience that.

མར་མེ་འདི་ལྷ་མ་ཡིན་རྣམས་ཀྱི་གནས་སུ་

MAR ME   DI   LHA MA YIN   NAM   KYI   NAE   SU
butterlamp   this   demi-gods, asuras   (plural)   of   place   to

May the light from this lamp illuminate

སྣང་ཞིང་གསལ་བར་གྱུར་ཅིག།

NANG ZHING   SAL WAR   GYUR CHI
showing   illuminate   make, may

The realm of the demi-gods.

ལྷ་མ་ཡིན་གྱི་ང་རྒྱལ་དང་ཁྲོ་གཏུམ་དང་།

LHA MA YIN   GYI   NGA GYAL   DANG   TRO TUM   DANG
asuras, jealous   of   pride   and   fury, rage   and
demi-gods

May they be freed from their pride, fury, rage and crudity,

སེམས་ཀྱི་གདུག་པ་ཞི་ནས་ཚད་མེད་པ་བཞི་དང་ལྡན་ནས།

SEM KYI DUG PA ZHI NE TSAE ME PA ZHI DANG DEN NE

crudity, roughness of attitude / pacify / then / immeasurables / four / gain / then*

* love, compassion, joy, equanimity

And develop love, compassion, joyfulness and equanimity.

ཞི་གནས་ཀྱི་སེམས་ཡིད་ལ་བྱེད་པ་དང་ལྡན་པར་གྱུར་ཅིག།

ZHI NE KYI SEM YI LA JE PA DANG DEN PAR GYUR CHI

calm, peaceful / of / mind / practice / gain, have / make, may

May they develop minds that are calm.

May the light from this lamp illuminate the realm of the demi-gods. May they be freed from their pride, fury, and crudity, and develop love, compassion, joyfulness and equanimity. May they develop minds that are calm.

མར་མེ་འདི་གླིང་བཞིའི་མི་རྣམས་ཀྱི་གནས་སུ་

MAR ME DI LING ZHI MI NAM KYI NAE SU

butterlamp / this / continents / four / inhabitants / of / place / to*

*the four islands around Mt. Meru

May the light from this lamp illuminate

སྣང་ཞིང་གསལ་བར་གྱུར་ཅིག།

NANG ZHING SAL WAR GYUR CHI

showing / illuminate / make, may

All who live in the four continents.

གླིང་བཞིའི་མི་རྣམས་ཀྱང་སྡུག་བསྔལ་བརྒྱད་ལས་ཐར་ནས།

LING ZHI MI NAM KYANG DU NGAL GYAE LAE THAR NE

continents / four / inhabitants / also / sufferings / eight / from / free / then*

*birth, aging, illness, death, separation from loved ones, being with the despised, not getting what one wants, the flourishing of the .five skandhas.

May they be freed from the eight sufferings.

བརྩོན་འགྲུས་ཀྱི་ཕ་རོལ་ཏུ་ཕྱིན་པ་དང་ལྡན་པར་གྱུར་ཅིག།

TSON DRUE KYI PA ROL TU JIN PA DANG DAN PAR GYUR CHI

diligence / of / transcendental qualities / gain / make, must*

*transcendental diligence: one of the six paramitas or transcendental qualities of a bodhisattva

May they gain transcendental diligence.

May the light from this lamp illuminate the beings who inhabit the four continents. May they be freed from the eight sufferings. May they gain transcendental diligence.

 མར་མེ་འདི་ཕྱོལ་སོང་རྣམས་ཀྱི་གནས་སུ་

MAR ME	DI	JOL SONG NAM		KYI	NAE	SU
butterlamp	*this*	*animals*		*of*	*place*	*to*

May the light from this lamp illuminate

སྣང་ཞིང་གསལ་བར་གྱུར་ཅིག

NANG ZHING	SAL WAR	GYUR CHI
showing, light up	*illuminate*	*make, may*

All who live in the animal realm.

ཕྱོལ་སོང་དེ་དག་གཅིག་ལ་གཅིག་ཟ་བ་དང་།

JOL SONG	DE DA	CHI LA CHI	ZA WA	DANG
animals	*these*	*one to one (i.e. each other)*	*eat*	*and*

May they stop eating each other, and

བརྫེག་བཏུང་དང་།   གསད་པ་དང་།

DE DUNG	DANG	SAE PA	DANG
fighting	*and*	*killing*	*and*

Be freed from the suffering of fighting, killing,

བཀོལ་བའི་སྡུག་བསྔལ་དང་།   བླུན་རྨོངས་ལས་ཐར་ནས།

KOL WAI	DU NGAL	DANG	LUN MONG	LAE	THAR	NE
enslaved, captured, domesticated	*suffering*	*and*	*stupidity, mental dullness*	*from*	*freed*	*then*

Being enslaved, and being dull and stupid.

ཤེས་རབ་རྣམ་པ་གསུམ་དང་ལྡན་པར་གྱུར་ཅིག།

SHE RAB	NAM PA	SUM	DANG DAN PAR	GYUR CHI
wisdom	*kinds*	*three**	*gain*	*make, may*

* hearing, reflecting on, meditating on dharma teaching

May they gain the wisdom of hearing, thinking about and meditating on the dharma.

May the light from this lamp illuminate all who live in the animal realm. May they stop eating each other and be freed from the suffering of fighting, killing, being enslaved, and being dull and stupid. May they gain the wisdom of hearing, thinking about and meditating on the dharma.

མར་མེ་འདི་གཤིན་རྗེའི་འཇིག་རྟེན་དུ་སྣང་ཞིང་

MAR ME	DI	SHIN JEI	JIG TEN	DU	NANG ZHING
butterlamp	*this*	*lord of death**	*realm, world*	*to*	*show*

*Yama, the one who judges us at death and whose minions punish the guilty.

May the light from this lamp illuminate

གསལ་བར་གྱུར་ཅིག །

SAL WAR   GYUR CHI
illuminate   make, may

The realm of the lord of death.

གཤིན་རྗེ་རྣམས་གསོད་གཅོད་བྱེད་པ་དང་

SHIN JE NAM   SOE CHOE   JE PA   DANG
Yama gods   killing   cutting   and

May these cruel ones cease from

བརྡེག་བཙོང་གི་ལས་ཐར་ནས།

DEG DUN   GI   LE   THAR   NE
beating   of   activity freed   then

killing, cutting and beating.

དེ་བཞིན་གཤེགས་པ་ཐམས་ཅད་ཀྱིས་ཕ་རོལ་ཏུ་ཕྱིན་པ་བསྟན་པས།

DE ZHIN SHE PA   THAM CHE   KYI   PHA ROL TU CHIN PA   DRA PAE
tathagata, buddha   all   by   paramitas, transcendent teach, hear*

* the qualities of generosity; morality; patience; diligence; concentration and wisdom

May they be taught the six transcendental qualities by the Tathagatas, and

སེམས་ཅན་ཐམས་ཅད་གཏོང་བའི་སེམས་འབྱུང་བར་གྱུར་ཅིག །

SEM CHEN   THAM CHE   TONG WAI   SEM   JUNG WAR   GYUR CHI
sentient beings all   generous,   mind,   arise, gain   make, may
                                giving   attitude

By this may they develop attitudes of generosity towards all beings.

*May the light from this lamp illuminate the realm of the lord of death.
May these cruel ones cease from killing, cutting and beating. May they
be taught the six transcendental qualities by the Tathagatas and by this
may they develop attitudes of generosity towards all beings.*

མར་མེ་འདི་ཡི་ཕྲེ་ཏའི་གནས་སུ་གསལ་བར་གྱུར་ཅིག །

MAR ME   DI   PRE TAI   NAE   SU   SAL WAR   GYUR CHI
butterlamp   this   hungry ghost place   to   illuminate   make, may

May the light from this lamp illuminate the realms of the hungry ghosts.

ཕྲེ་ཏ་རྣམས་ཀྱང་བཀྲེས་སྐོམ་གྱི་སྡུག་བསྔལ་ལས་ཐར་ནས།

PRE TA NAM   KYANG   TRE   KOM   GYI   DU NGAL   LE   THAR   NE
hungry ghosts   also   hunger   thirst   of   suffering   from   free   then

May they be freed from the misery of thirst and hunger.

 བྱང་ཆུབ་སེམས་དཔའ་ནམ་མཁའ་མཛོད་ཀྱི་

JANG CHUB SEM PA   **NAM KHA DZOE**   **KYI**
bodhisattva   *sky treasure, akashagarbha*   *of*

By the blessings of the great compassion

ཐུགས་རྗེ་ཆེན་པོའི་བྱིན་གྱི་རླབས་ཀྱིས།

THU JE   **CHEN POI**   **JIN GYI LAB**   **KYI**
compassion   *great*   *blessing*   *by*

Of Bodhisattva Akashagarbha

ཟས་དང་སྐོམ་གྱིས་མི་འཕོངས་པའི་ལོངས་སྤྱོད་

ZAE   **DANG**   **KOM**   **GYI**   **MI PHONG PAI**   **LONG CHO**
food   *and*   *drink*   *by*   *luxurious,*   *supplies, resources*

May they have an inexhaustible supply

ཟད་མི་ཤེས་པ་དང་ལྡན་ཞིང་།

ZAE PA MI SHE PA   **DANG DEN ZHING**
inexhaustible   *have*

Of easily available food and drink.

སྦྱིན་པའི་ཕ་རོལ་ཏུ་ཕྱིན་པའི་དབང་དང་ལྡན་པར་གྱུར་ཅིག།

JIN PAI   **PHA ROL TU CHIN PAI**   **WANG**   **DANG DEN PAR**   **GYUR CHI**
generosity   *paramitas, transcendent*   *power*   *have, gain*   *must, make*

May they gain the power of transcendental generosity.

May the light from this lamp illuminate the realms of the hungry ghosts. May they be freed from the misery of thirst and hunger. By the blessings of the great compassion of Bodhisattva Akashagarbha may they have an inexhaustible supply of easily available food and drink. May they gain the power of transcendental generosity.

མར་མེ་འདི་ན་རག་རྣམས་ཀྱི་གནས་སུ་གསལ་བར་གྱུར་ཅིག།

MAR ME   **DI**   **NA RAG NAM**   **KYI**   **NAE**   **SU**   **SAL WAR**   **GYUR CHI**
butterlamp   *this*   *hells*   *of*   *places*   *to*   *illuminate*   *make, may*

May the light from this lamp illuminate the hell realms.

ན་རག་ནི་སྔོན་གྱི་ལས་ངན་པའི་རྣམ་པར་སྨིན་པས་

NA RAG NI   **NYON GYI**   **LAE**   **NGAN**   **PAI**   **NAM PAR MIN PAE**
hells   *former*   *actions*   *bad*   *by*   *ripening*

Beings suffer there according to the ripening of their previous bad actions,

ཚ་གྲང་གི་སྡུག་བསྔལ་བཟོད་པར་

TSHA DRANG GI DU NGAL ZOE PAR
heat cold of suffering bear, endure

Experiencing intolerable

དཀའ་བ་ཉམས་སུ་མྱོང་པ་ལས།

KA WA NYAM SU NYONG PA LE
difficult experience then

Heat and cold.

འཕགས་པ་སྤྱན་རས་གཟིགས་དབང་ཕྱུག་གི་ཐུགས་རྗེའི་བྱིན་གྱི་རླབས་ཀྱིས།

PHA PA CHEN RE ZI WANG CHU GI THU JEI JIN GYI LAB KYI
arya, noble Avalokitesvara of compassion blessing by

By the blessings of the compassion of the Bodhisattva Arya Avalokitesvara

དམྱལ་བའི་སྡུག་བསྔལ་ཚད་མེད་པ་ལས་ཐར་ནས།

NYAL WAI DU NGAL TSHE ME PE LE THAR NE
hell's suffering limitless from freed then

May they be freed from the limitless sufferings of hell.

བཟོད་པའི་ཕ་རོལ་ཏུ་ཕྱིན་པ་དང་ལྡན་པར་གྱུར་ཅིག།

ZOE PAI PHA ROL TU CHIN PA DANG DEN PAR GYUR CHI
patience paramita gain make, may

May they realise the transcendent quality of patience.

May the light from this lamp illuminate the hell realms. Beings suffer there according to the ripening of their previous bad actions, experiencing intolerable heat and cold. By the blessings of the compassion of the Bodhisattva Arya Avalokitesvara may they be freed from the limitless sufferings of hell. May they realise the transcendent quality of patience.

མར་མེ་འདིས་འཛམ་བུ་གླིང་གི་ཕྱི་རོལ་ན་མུན་ནག་གི་

MAR ME DI DZAM BU LING GI CHI ROL NA MUN NA GI
butterlamp this Jambudvipa, of outside, beyond profound of our world darkness

May the light of this lamp illuminate the realms beyond this world system where,

ནང་ན་འཐོམས་པའི་

NANG NA THOM PAI
in there benighted, dulled

In the darkness, benighted people cannot

སེམས་ཅན་རང་གི་ལག་པ་གཡས་པ་བཀྱང་བ་ཡང་

SEM CHEN	RANG GI	LA PA	YAE PA	KYANG WA	YANG
beings	*own*	*hand*	*right*	*held up in front of them*	*yet*

Even see their own right hand

མི་མཐོང་བའི་གནས་སུ་གསལ་བར་གྱུར་ཅིག །

MI	THONG WAI	NAE	SU	SAL WAR	GYUR CHI
not	*see*	*place*	*to*	*illuminate*	*make, may*

Held up in front of them.

དེ་དག་སྔོན་གྱི་ལས་ངན་པའི་རྣམ་པར་སྨིན་པས་

DE DA	NGON GYI	LAE	NGAN PAI	NAM PAR MIN PAE
they	*former*	*actions*	*bad by*	*ripening*

Due to the ripening of their previous bad actions

ཟས་དང་སྐོམ་འདོད་པ་ལས།

ZAE	DANG	KOM	DOE PA	LAE
food	*and*	*drink*	*desire*	*yet*

They crave food and drink

ནམ་མཁའ་ལ་རང་གི་ལྕགས་ཀྱི་སེན་མོ་ཡོད་པས་

NAM KHA	LA	RANG GI	CHA	KYI	SEN MO	YOE PAE
sky	*to*	*own*	*iron*	*of*	*claws*	*that they have*

But scratch themselves with their iron claws

བསྐྱོགས་བས་ཟས་དང་སྐོམ་མ་རྙེད་ནས།

NYOG WAE	ZAE	DANG	KOM	MA	NYE	NE
scratch, tear	*food*	*and*	*drink*	*not*	*get*	*then*

As they reach out to the sky and so are unsatisfied.

རང་གི་ལུས་ཟིན་པ་དང་ཤ་བཅད་ཅིང་བཟའ་པ་

RANG GI	LU	ZIN PA	DANG	SHA	CHE CHING	ZAE PA
own	*body*	*exhausted*	*and*	*flesh*	*cutting*	*eat*

They are exhausted and cut their own flesh and eat it.

དེ་དག་དེ་བཞིན་གཤེགས་པ་འོད་དཔག་མེད་ཀྱི་

DE DA	DE ZHIN SHE PA	OE PA ME	KYI
these beings	*tathagata, buddha*	*Amitabha*	*of*

By the blessing of the compassion

ཕྲགས་རྗེའི་བྱིན་གྱི་རླབས་ཀྱིས།

THU JEI   JIN GYI LAB   KYI
compassion   blessing   by

Of Buddha Amitabha

མུན་ནག་ཆེན་པོའི་རྨོམས་པ་ལས་ཐར་ནས།

MUN NA   CHEN POI   THOM PA   LAE   THAR   NE
profound   great   dazed,   from   freed   then
darkness   stunned

May they be freed from the bewilderment of that great darkness and

བདེ་བ་ཅན་གྱི་ཞིང་ཁམས་སུ་སྐྱེ་བར་གྱུར་ཅིག།

DE WA CHEN   GYI   ZHING KHAM   SU   KYE WA   GYUR CHI
Sukhavati   of   realm   in   born   make, may*
*or Dewachen, the buddha realm where Amitabha resides

Be reborn in the pure realm of Great Happiness.

May the light of this lamp illuminate the realms beyond this world system where, in the darkness, benighted people cannot even see their own right hand held up in front of them. Due to the ripening of their previous bad actions they crave food and drink but scratch themselves with their iron claws as they reach out to the sky and so are unsatisfied. They are exhausted and cut their own flesh and eat it. By the blessing of the compassion of Buddha Amitabha may they be freed from the bewilderment of that great darkness and be reborn in the pure realm of Great Happiness.

གཞན་ཡང་མར་མེ་འདི་ཀླུའི་གནས་སུ་སྣང་ཞིང་

ZHAN YANG   MAR ME   DI   LUI   NAE   SU   NANG ZHING
moreover   butterlamp this   nagas place   to   showing*
*snake gods who protect the treasures of the earth and guard its resource

May the light of this lamp illuminate

གསལ་བར་གྱུར་ཅིག།

SAL WAR   GYUR CHI
illuminating make, may

The realm of the nagas.

དེ་རྣམས་གཏི་མུག་དང་སེར་སྣའི་མདུད་པ་ལས་བཀྲོལ་ཏེ།

DE NAM   TI MU   DANG   SER NAI   DUE PA   LAE   TROL   TE
they   stupidity   and   envy   snare,   from   freed,   then
                                               knot   untied

May they be freed from the snares of stupidity and envy, and then

གཏོང་བའི་བློ་དང་ལྡན་ཞིང་།

TONG WAI LO DANG DEN ZHING
generosity   attitude   having

With a generosity of spirit

ནམ་མཁའ་ལྡིང་གི་འཇིགས་པ་དང་།

NAM KHA DING GI JIG PA DANG
predatory birds,   of   fear   and
garudas, eagles etc.

May they be freed from the fear of predatory birds,

མེ་ཚན་ཕྱི་ཚན་ལ་སོགས་ཏེ།

ME TSHAN CHE TSHAN LA SO TE
hot air   dry sand   and so on

Heat, dry sand, and

འཇིགས་པ་ཆེན་པོ་བརྒྱད་ལས་ཐར་ནས།

JIG PA CHEN PO GYE LAE THAR NE
fears   great   eight   from   freed   then*
* eight great fears: fear of fire, water, earth, air, elephants, snakes, thieves and kings

The rest of the eight great fears.

སངས་རྒྱས་དང་།   ཆོས་དང་།

SANG GYE DANG   CHO DANG
buddha   and   dharma   and

May they take refuge

དགེ་འདུན་ལ་སྐྱབས་སུ་འགྲོ་ཞིང་།

GEN DUN LA KYAB SU DRO ZHING
sangha   to   refuge   in   go for

In Buddha, Dharma and Sangha

སྲོག་འཚོ་བའི་ཞི་གནས་ཀྱི་ཆུའི་ཐིག་ལེ་སྙིང་ལ་གནས་ནས་

SO TSHO WAI ZHI NAE KYI CHUI THIG LE NYING LA NAE NE
life   sustaining,   calm   of   water-drop (cooling   heart   in   stay   then
       nourishing   abiding   and purifying)

So that the life sustaining waterdrop of calm abiding rests in their hearts and

ཀླུ་རྣམས་འདོད་པའི་ཡོན་ཏན་དང་ལྡན་པར་གྱུར་ཅིག།

LU NAM DOE PAI YON TAN DANG DEN PAR GYUR CHI
nagas   desirable   good   gain   make, may
       qualities

All nagas gain everything they desire.

May the light of this lamp illuminate the realm of the nagas. May they be freed from the snares of stupidity and envy and then with a generosity of spirit may they be freed from the fear of predatory birds, heat, dry sand and the rest of the eight great fears. May they take refuge in Buddha, Dharma and Sangha so that the life sustaining waterdrop of calm abiding rests in their hearts and all nagas gain everything they desire.

 མར་མེ་འདི་སྒྲོ་འཕྱེ་ཆེན་པོའི་གནས་སུ་སྣང་ཞིང་

MAR ME	DI	TO CHE	CHEN POI	NAE	SU	NANG ZHING
butterlamp	this	reptiles	great	place	to	showing

May the light of this lamp illuminate

གསལ་བར་གྱུར་ཅིག།

SAL WAR	GYUR CHI
illuminate	make, may

The realm of the giant reptiles.

དེས་སྒྲོ་འཕྱེ་ཆེན་པོའི་སྡུག་བསྔལ་ཞི་ནས་

DE	TO CHE	CHEN POI	DU NGAL	ZHI	NE
by this	reptiles	great, big	suffering	pacify	then

May their sufferings be removed.

དགའ་བ་རྒྱ་མཚོ་རྣམས་པར་འཕྲུལ་པའི་ཤུགས་

GA WA	GYAM TSO	NAM PAR	TRUL PAI	SHU
happiness	ocean	form	magical	power

May they gain the magical power to abide

དང་ལྡན་པར་གྱུར་ཅིག།

DANG DEN PAR	GYUR CHI
possess	make, may

In oceans of happiness.

May the light of this lamp illuminate the realm of the giant reptiles. May their sufferings be removed. May they gain the magical power to abide in oceans of happiness.

མར་མེ་འདི་འཛམ་བུ་གླིང་གི་ཕྱིར་གནས་པའི་

MAR ME	DI	DZAM BU LING	GI	CHIR	NAE PAI
butterlamp	this	this world	of	beyond	staying

May the light from this lamp illuminate the areas beyond the continent of Jambudvipa that are inhabited

ས་བདག་དང་། ལྷ་དང་། ཀླུ་དང་།

SA DA	DANG		LHA	DANG		LU	DANG
land gods,	*and*		*local gods*	*and*		*nagas*	*and*
protectors of place							

By land gods, local gods, nagas,

ས་བདག་གི་རྒྱལ་པོ་པ་ཏི་ལི་དང་།

SA DA	GI	GYAL PO	PA TI LI	DANG
land gods	*of*	*king*	*his name*	*and*

Patili the king of the land gods,

སའི་རྒྱལ་མོ་ཆེན་པོ་དང་།རྒྱ་མཚོ་ཆེན་པོ་དང་།

SAI GYAL MO	CHEN PO	DANG	GYAM TSHO	CHEN PO	DANG
land queen	*great*	*and*	*(the gods of) oceans*	*great*	*and*

The great queen of the land, and the gods of oceans, and those who live in

མཚོ་བྲན་དང་། རྫིང་དང་། ཁྲོན་པ་ལ་གནས་པ་དང་།

TSHO TRAN	DANG	DZING	DANG	TRON PA	LA	NAE PA	DANG
seas	*and*	*ponds*	*and*	*wells*	*at*	*staying*	*and*

Seas, ponds and wells,

ཀླུང་ཆེན་པོ་དང་། ཀླུང་ཕྲ་མོ་དང་།

LUNG	CHEN PO	DANG	LUNG	TRA MO	DANG
rivers	*big*	*and*	*rivers*	*small*	*and*

Big rivers, small rivers,

ཆུ་མིག་དང་། ལུ་མ་ལ་གནས་པ་དང་།

CHU MI	DANG	LU MA	LA	NAE PA	DANG
springs	*and*	*seasonal ponds*	*at*	*staying*	*and*

Springs, seasonal ponds, and

གངས་རི་མཐོན་མོའི་རྒྱུད་ལ་གནས་པ་དང་།

GANG RI	THON MOI	GYU	LA	NAE PA	DANG
snow mountain	*high*	*flow*	*at*	*stay*	*and*
(glacial stream)					

Those who stay at the high glacial streams, and

རི་ནག་པོ་དང་། གཡའ་དང་། ཤ་སྲང་དང་།

RI	NAG PO	DANG	YA	DANG	SHA SANG	DANG
mountain	*black*	*and*	*slate*	*and*	*water meadows*	*and*

Black mountains, slate hills, water meadows,

སྤང་རི་དང་།　　　ནགས་ཆེན་པོ་དང་།　　　ཤིང་གཅིག་པ་དང་།

PANG RI	DANG	NAG	CHEN PO	DANG	SHING	CHI PA	DANG
hill fields	*and*	*forest*	*big*	*and*	*tree*	*solitary*	*and*

Hill fields, big forests and solitary trees,

གཙུག་ལག་ཁང་དང་།　　　མཆོད་རྟེན་དང་།　　　གྲོང་ཁྱེར་དང་།

TSUG LA KHANG	DANG	CHO TEN	DANG	DRONG KHYER	DANG
temples	*and*	*stupas*	*and*	*cities*	*and*

Temples, stupas, cities and

གྲོངས་ན་གནས་པའི་གནས་སུ་སྣང་ཞིང་གསལ་བར་གྱུར་ཅིག །

JONG	NA	NAE PAI	NAE	SU	NANG ZHING	SAL WAR	GYUR CHI
villages	*in*	*staying*	*places*	*in*	*showing*	*illuminating*	*make, may*

Villages. May all those who stay in these places be illuminated.

དེ་དག་སོ་སོའི་འཁྲུལ་པའི་རྟོག་པ་ཐམས་ཅད་བྱང་ནས།ཐམས་ཅད་བྱང་ནས།

DE DA	SO SOI	TRUL PAI	TOE PA	THAM CHE	JANG	NE
they	*each, individual*	*confusion, delusion*	*thoughts*	*all*	*clear, remove*	*then*

May each of these beings have their own particular confusions removed.

དཀོན་མཆོག་གསུམ་ལ་མི་ཕྱེད་པའི་དད་པ་དང་ལྡན་ཏེ།

KON CHO	SUM	LA	MI CHE PAI	DAE PA	DANG DEN	TE
jewels	*three*	*to*	*unchanging*	*faith*	*gain*	*then, thus*

May they have unchanging faith in the Three Jewels.

བྱང་ཆུབ་ཀྱི་སེམས་དང་ལྡན་ནས་ཐར་པ་

JANG CHU KYI SEM	DANG DEN	NE	THAR PA
bodhisattva's altruistic intention	*gain, have*	*then*	*liberation*

May they gain an altruistic intention towards enlightenment and

ཐོབ་པའི་རྒྱུ་རུ་གྱུར་ཅིག །

THO PAI	GYU	RU	GYUR CHI
gain	*cause*	*as*	*develop, establish*

Establish the cause of liberation.

May the light from this lamp illuminate the areas beyond the continent of Jambudvipa inhabited by land gods, local gods, nagas, Patili the king of the land gods, the great queen of the land, and the gods and denizens of oceans, seas, ponds and wells, big rivers, small rivers, springs, seasonal ponds and those who stay at the high glacial streams, black mountains, slate hills, water meadows, hill fields, big forests, solitary trees, temples, stupas, cities and villages. May all those who stay in these places be illuminated. May each of these beings have their own particular confusions removed. May they have unchanging faith in the Three Jewels. May they gain an altruistic intention towards enlightenment and establish the cause of liberation.

རྒྱལ་པོ་གསེར་གྱི་ལག་པའི་སྨོན་ལམ་གྱི་སྨོན་ལམ་གྱི་མདོ་རྫོགས་སོ།

This concludes The Aspiration of King Golden Hand.

དེ་ལྟར་དེང་མར་མེ་འདིའི་ཡོན་བདག་ཀྱིས་ཀྱང་། གཏན་པ་མེད་པའི་མཆོད་པའི་དེ་ཕུལ་བས་བདག་དང་མཐའ་ཡས་པའི་སེམས་ཅན་རྣམས་དེ་བཞིན་ག་ག་ཤེགས་པ་མར་མེ་མཛད་ཀྱི་ཞབས་དྲུང་དུ་སྐྱེས་ཏེ། མཆོད་པར་རྫོགས་པར་སངས་རྒྱས་ནས། སེམས་ཅན་ཐམས་ཅད་ཀྱི་དཔལ་མགོན་དུ་གྱུར་ཅིག།།

By the sponsoring of these lamps and the offering of this transient display may I and all the infinite sentient beings be reborn at the feet of Buddha Dipamkara. May we gain perfect Buddhahood and become benefactors of all beings.

Translated by C R Lama and James Low, 1985

༄༅། རང་སྐྱོན་རྟོགས་ཤེས་སྐྱབས་ཡུལ་རྗེས་དྲན་གྱི་གསོལ་འདེབས་ནོངས་བཤགས་སྤྱིན་ལམ་ཡང་དག་
སྣང་དོར་གསལ་འདེབས་ཡོད།

The Aspiration for Pure Discernment

The Prayer by which One Recognises One's Own Faults

and

Remembers One's Refuge

together with

A Repentant Confession and Rectification

and

A Very Pure Aspiration to Be Absolutely Clear About
What Is to Be Adopted and What Is to Be Abandoned

by
Dudjom Rinpoche, Jigdral Yeshe Dorje

༄༅། ། ན་མོ་གུ་རུ་བྷེ།

NA MO GU RU BE
homage   master   prostrate

Homage. We bow to the master.

བསྐལ་བཟང་ཞིང་གི་འདྲེན་མཆོག་ཤཱཀྱའི་རྒྱལ།

KAL	ZANG	ZHING	GI	DREN	CHO	SHA KYAI	GYAL
kalpa,	*good*	*realm, sphere*	*of*	*guide,*	*supreme*	*Shakya clan*	*king*
aeon				*leader*		*(i.e. Buddha Shakyamuni)*	
(one in which dharma is taught)							

Buddha Shakyamuni the supreme guide for the universe during this good kalpa,

རྒྱལ་སྲས་བྱང་སེམས་འགྲོ་འདུལ་འཕགས་པའི་ཚོགས།

GYAL	SAE	JANG SEM	DRO	DUL	PHA PAI	TSHO
Victor,	*sons*	*bodhisattvas*	*beings*	*control,*	*arya, noble*	*host, assembly*
Buddha				*educate*		

Noble bodhisattvas, you assembled sons of the Victor who educate beings,

སྙིགས་འགྲོའི་སྐྱོབ་པ་མཚུངས་མེད་གུ་རུ་རྗེ།

NYIG	DROI	KYO PA	TSHUNG ME	GU RU	JE
debased period	*beings*	*protector,*	*unequalled,*	*master*	*noble, superior*
		refuge	*unsurpassed*		

Precious guru, the unsurpassed protector of beings in this debased age,

རྩ་གསུམ་ཆོས་སྐྱོང་དམ་ཅན་ཚོགས་བཅས་ལ།

TSA	SUM	CHO KYONG	DAM CHEN	TSHO	CHE	LA
roots	*three*	*dharma-protectors*	*vow-keepers*	*host*	*together*	*to*
(guru, deva, dakini)						

Together with the Three Roots and the hosts of dharma-protectors and vow-keepers—

རྩེ་གཅིག་སྙིང་ནས་དྲན་པའི་གདུང་ཡུས་ཀྱིས།

TSE CHI		NYING	NE	DRAN PAI	DUNG YUE	KYI
one-pointed, total		*heart*	*from*	*recollection*	*longing, yearning*	*by*
					devotion	

With the yearning devotion of one-pointedly remembering you from the depths of our heart

ཡང་ཡང་གསོལ་འདེབས་ཐུགས་དམ་བསྐུལ་ལགས་ན།

YANG YANG	SON DE	THU DAM KUL		LA	NA
again and again	*pray, solicit*	*invoke, arouse his attention*		*do*	*if, when*

We pray again and again to arouse your attention.

བརྩེ་བས་རྗེས་བཟུང་ཐོགས་མེད་ཐུགས་རྗེའི་མཐུས།

TSE WAE	JE ZUNG	THO ME	THU JEI	THU
with compassion, kindness	followers	unobstructed	compassion's	by that power

Due to your kindness, by the power of your unobstructed compassion for your followers,

བསམ་དོན་ཆོས་བཞིན་འགྲུབ་པར་བྱིན་གྱིས་རློབས།

SAM	DON	CHO	ZHIN	DRU PAR	JIN GYI LO
thoughts	intention, value	dharma	like	accomplish, do	bless us (and all sentient beings)

Please bless us that our thoughts and intentions may be in accord with the dharma.

Buddha Shakyamuni the supreme guide for the universe during this good kalpa, Noble bodhisattvas, you assembled sons of the Victor who educate beings, Precious guru, the unsurpassed protector of beings in this debased age, together with the Three Roots and the hosts of dharma-protectors and vow-keepers – with the yearning devotion of one-pointedly remembering you from the depths of our heart we pray again and again to arouse your attention. Due to your kindness, by the power of your unobstructed compassion for your followers, please bless us that our thoughts and intentions may be in accord with the dharma.

སྔོན་ལས་མ་ཞན་མི་ལུས་རིན་ཆེན་ཐོབ།

NGON	LAE	MA ZHAN	MI LU	RIN CHEN	THO
former	actions, karma	free of grasping (i.e. good)	human existence	precious	gained

Due to former actions performed without grasping we have gained this precious human existence.

བསོད་ནམས་མ་ཆུང་དམ་པའི་ཆོས་དང་མཇལ།

SO NAM	MA CHUNG	DAM PAI	CHO	DANG JAL
merit	not small	holy, excellent	dharma	met

Due to our merit that is by no means small we have met with the holy dharma.

བླ་མས་རྗེས་བཟུང་དབང་བྱིན་གདམས་ངག་ཐོབ།

LA MAE	JE ZUNG	WONG	JIN	DAM NGA	THO
by guru	followers	initiation	blessing	instructions	gain

Our guru has permitted us, his followers, to gain initiation, blessings and instructions.

ནོར་བུ་རང་ལག་རྙེད་པའི་དུས་བྱུང་ཡང་།

NOR BU   **RANG**   **LA**   **NYE PAI**   **DUE**   **JUNG**   **YANG**
jewel   *own*   *hand*   *got*   *time, occasion*   *has occurred*   *yet*
(i.e. precious human body, with the opportunity to practise)

This is the time when we have the jewel right in our own hand, and yet,

ཚུལ་ཆུང་སྤྲེའུ་འདྲ་བའི་རང་སེམས་འདི།

CHOL CHUNG   **TRE U**   **DRA WAI**   **RANG**   **SEM**   **DI**
frivolous, silly actions   *monkey*   *like*   *my*   *mind*   *thus*

Our minds, like frivolous monkeys,

རྣམ་གཡེང་བསྒྱུ་བྱེད་འགོང་པོའི་དབང་སོང་ནས།

NAM YENG   **LU**   **TRI GONG POI**   **WONG SONG**   **NE**
always changing,   *deceived*   *demons,*   *gone under the power of them*
very unstable   *negative forces*

Are completely unstable, and so we go under the power of the misleading negative forces and demons.

རང་ནོར་རང་བདག་ཉམས་ལེན་མ་ནུས་ཏེ།

RANG NOR   **RANG DA**   **NYAM LEN**   **MA**   **NU**   **TE**
my jewel (precious   *what I am master of*   *practice,*   *no*   *power*   *thus here*
human body)   *familiarisation*

We have no power to utilise this jewel which is our very own, and

དལ་འབྱོར་གདམས་ངག་ཆབ་ཅིག་ཆུད་ཟོས་ཤོར།

DAL JOR   **DAM NGA**   **CHAB CHI**   **CHU ZOE SHOR**
the 8 freedoms and 10   *instruction*   *all*   *gone to waste*
opportunities of a precious
human birth

So the instructions we received on the freedoms and opportunities are just thrown away.

Due to former actions performed without grasping we have gained this precious human existence. Due to our merit that is by no means small we have met with the holy dharma. Our guru has permitted us, his followers, to gain initiation, blessings and instructions. This is the time when we have the jewel right in our own hand, and yet, our minds, like frivolous monkeys, are completely unstable and so we go under the power of the misleading negative forces and demons. We have no power to utilise this jewel which is our very own, so the instructions we received on the freedoms and opportunities are just thrown away.

ད་ལྟ་དོན་ཆེན་འགག་ལ་ཐུག་ཉེ་དུས།

DAN TA	DON		CHEN	GA	LA	THU NYE		DU
now	*meaning, value*		*great*	*crux*	*to*	*arrived, met with*		*time*

We are now at a real turning point in our lives.

ཞུས་ཚད་ཐོབ་ཚད་གནའ་བོའི་སྒྲུང་གཏམ་འདྲ།

ZHU	THO	THO	TSHAE		NA WOI DRUNG TAM	DRA
asked	*whatever amount*	*received*	*whatever amount*		*meaningless stories, just an interesting idea*	*like*

Whatever we've requested, whatever we've received, it all seems just like some kind of story.

ལུས་འདི་ཆོས་གཟུགས་ཆོས་པ་ཡིན་རྫུམ་ཡང་།

LU	DI	CHO	ZUG	CHO PA	YIN	LOM	YANG
body, life	*this*	*dharma*	*form*	*dharma person*	*be*	*like, want (and imagine that we are)*	*yet*

We want to live in accordance with the dharma and be real dharma practitioners, yet

སེམས་འདིས་ཡང་དག་ཆོས་པའི་རྗེས་མ་ཟིན།

SEM	DI	YANG DA	CHO PAI	JE MA ZIN
mind	*my, this*	*pure, perfect*	*dharma practitioner*	*not remember to be*

Our own minds forget what it means to be a pure dharma person.

ལྷ་ཆོས་ལྟ་ཅི་མི་ཆོས་རྡིས་མ་གོས།

LHA CHO	TA	CHI	MI CHO	DRI	MA	GO
dharma of deities (i.e. pure buddhadharma)	*view*	*what*	*human dharma (i.e. ideas and concepts)*	*ask*	*not*	*understand*

We don't know how to learn about ordinary human values, let alone the view of the buddhadharma, and

མི་ཆོས་གཙང་མ་བཅུ་དྲུག་གོ་ཡུལ་ཙམ།

MI CHO	TSANG MA CHU DRU	GO YUL	TSAM
human dharma, notion	*pure sixteen (16 rules of good conduct given by King Trisong Deutsen)*	*have heard of vaguely but not really know about*	*only*

We have only a vague notion of the sixteen rules[1] of proper human conduct.

རང་ཕྱོས་སྐྱོན་དན་སྤྱོད་ལ་ངོ་ཚ་བྲལ།

RANG	TOE	CHO	NGAN	CHAE	LA	NGO TSHA	DRAL
self	observe, examine	conduct	bad	done	to	shame	without

We feel no shame when we observe the bad things we have done, yet

གཞན་ཕྱོས་ཁྲེལ་གཞུང་ཕྱི་ཐག་ལྟ་བའི་མཐུད།

ZHAN	TOE	TREL ZHUNG	CHI THA	TRA WAI	JU
others	observe	moral indignation	tie rope, like the rope round an animal's neck	like	hold on to

We're hooked on moral indignation when we observe the conduct of others.

We are now at a real turning point in our lives. Whatever we've requested, whatever we've received, it all seems just like some kind of story. We want to live in accordance with the dharma and be real dharma practitioners, yet our own minds forget what it means to be a pure dharma person. We don't know how to learn about ordinary human values, let alone the view of the buddhadharma, and we have only a vague notion of the sixteen rules of proper human conduct. We feel no shame when we observe the bad things we have done, yet we're hooked on moral indignation when we observe the conduct of others.

ལྷ་ཆོས་དགེ་བཅུ་ཡང་དག་རྟོ་མ་ཐོགས།

LHA CHO	GE	CHU	YANG DA	NGO MA THO
buddhadharma	virtues	ten	very pure, perfect	not recognise or understand

We don't have a really pure understanding of the ten[2] virtues according to the buddhadharma.

སྟོན་པ་གཅིག་གི་བསྟན་ལ་ཕྱོགས་ཞེན་གྱིས།

TON PA	CHI	GI	TAN	LA	CHO ZHEN	GYI
teacher*	one	of	teaching, doctrines	to	partiality	due to

*i.e. the Buddha, the source of all the lineages and teachings

Because of partiality in our attitudes towards the doctrines of the one Teacher who taught them all

ཆོས་དང་དམ་པར་སྐུར་འདེབས་ལས་ངན་བསགས།

CHO	DANG	DAM PAR	KUR DE	LAE	NGAN	SA
dharma	and	holy people (i.e. other sects, lineages and teachers)	insult, disparage	action, karma	bad	accumulate

We disparage the dharma and the saintly ones and so accumulate bad karma.

ཆོས་ལ་བརྟེན་ནས་སྡིག་པའི་ཁུར་ཆེན་ཁྱེར།

CHO	LA	TEN	NE	DIG PAI	KHUR	CHEN	KHYER
dharma	*to*	*rely on*	*then, yet*	*sinful*	*load, burden*	*great*	*carry*

Thus through seemingly relying on the dharma we gain only a great burden of sin to carry.

ཐོས་པ་ཆེ་བཞིན་རང་མཐོང་ང་རྒྱལ་ཆེ།

THO PA	CHE	ZHIN	RANG THONG	NGA GYAL	CHE
listen	*great, much*	*as*	*see oneself*	*pride*	*great*

We've heard a lot of teachings so we look on ourselves with great pride, yet

བསམ་པས་དཔྱད་དོན་གོ་བའི་གཏིང་མ་དཔོགས།

SAM PAE	CHE	DON	GO WAI	TING	MA	PO
by thinking, considering	*analysis, precise definition*	*meaning*	*understand*	*depth*	*not*	*touch, reach*

When we contemplate them, we do not reach a deep understanding of the meaning that is analysed.

སོ་ཐར་ཚུལ་ཁྲིམས་བསྲུང་བར་རྩོམ་ན་ཡང་།

SO THAR		TSHUL TRIM	SUNG WAR	LOM	NA YANG
the hinayana pratimoksa vows of moral discipline		*morality*	*protect*	*wish*	*yet*

We would like to adhere to the moral conduct of the hinayana ordinations,

དགེ་སྦྱོང་ཆོས་བཞི་གར་སོང་ཆ་མེད་སྟོར།

GE JONG	CHO	ZHI	GAR SONG	CHA ME	TOR
virtuous practice, pure layman's conduct	*dharmas, points*	*four[3]*	*go against*	*without trace*	*discard, away*

Yet we act against the four basic points of virtuous practice and totally discard them.

We don't have a really pure understanding of the ten virtues according to the buddhadharma. Because of partiality in our attitudes towards the doctrines of the one Teacher who taught them all we disparage the dharma and the saintly ones and so accumulate bad karma. Thus through seemingly relying on the dharma we gain only a great burden of sin to carry. We've heard a lot of teachings so we look on ourselves with great pride, yet when we contemplate them, we do not reach a deep understanding of the meaning that is analysed. We would like to adhere to the moral conduct of the hinayana ordinations, yet we act against the four basic points of virtuous practice and totally discard them.

ཇྱང་སེམས་བསླབ་ནོར་ལྡན་པར་ལོམ་ན་ཡང་།

JANG SEM **LAB** **NOR** **DEN PAR** **LOM** **NA YANG**
bodhisattva *learning, training* *wealth* *have* *wish, desire* *yet*

We would like to possess the riches of the bodhisattva training,

ཚད་མེད་རྣམ་བཞི་རི་མོའི་མར་མེ་འདྲ།

TSHAE ME **NAM** **ZHI** **RI MOI** **MAR ME** **DRA**
immeasurable *kind* *four* *drawing* *butter-lamp* *as*
(love, compassion, rejoicing, and equanimity) *(i.e. way beyond our grasp)*

Yet the four immeasurable attitudes remain unattainable like a picture seen in a flame.

གསང་སྔགས་དམ་ཚིག་བསྲུང་བར་ལོམ་ན་ཡང་།

SANG NGA **DAM TSHI** **SUNG WAR** **LOM** **NA YANG**
secret mantra, *samaya,* *protect, keep* *wish* *yet*
vajrayana, tantra *sacred vows*

We would like to maintain the tantric samaya vows,

རྩ་ལྟུང་དང་པོར་རྩི་མེད་སྣང་ཆུང་ཤོར།

TSA **TUNG** **DANG POR** **TSI ME** **NANG CHUNG** **SHOR**
root *downfall* *first* *not consider* *of little importance* *put down, discard*

Yet we don't pay attention to even the first root downfall and discard them all as of little importance.

བློ་ལྡོག་རྣམ་བཞི་ཁ་ནས་བཤད་ཤེས་ཀྱང་།

LO **DO** **NAM** **ZHI** **KHA** **NE** **SHE** **SHE** **KYANG**
attitude *change, revise* *plural* *four** *mouth* *from* *explain* *know how to* *yet*

*precious human birth, karma, impermanence and death, suffering in the six realms

We know how to give verbal explanations of the four attitude changers,

དོན་ལ་ལྡོག་མིན་འདིར་སྣང་ཞེན་པས་སྟོན།

DON **LA** **DOG MIN** **DIR** **NANG** **ZHEN PAE** **TON**
values *to* *not reverse* *this life* *appearances, occurances* *wish, attachment* *show, expose*

Yet our attachment to the events of this life expose our continuing involvement with worldly values.

བླ་མ་བསྟེན་བཞིན་མོས་གུས་རིམ་གྱིས་བྲི།

LA MA **TEN** **ZHIN** **MOE** **GUE** **RIM GYI** **TRI**
guru, master *serve* *as* *devotion* *respect* *gradually* *decreases*

We serve the guru yet our respect and devotion gradually decreases.

དག་སྣང་ཚབས་སུ་མཉམ་འགྲོགས་ལོག་པར་མཐོང་།

DA NANG	TSHAB SU	NYAM	DRO	LO PAR	THONG
pure view of teacher's action	*instead of*	*equally*	*as friend*	*wrongly*	*see, interpret*

Instead of having pure vision we mistakenly see the Guru as an equal and a friend.

We would like to possess the riches of the bodhisattva training, yet the four immeasurable attitudes remain unattainable like a picture seen in a flame. We would like to maintain the tantric samaya vows, yet we don't pay attention to even the first root downfall and discard them all as of little importance. We know how to give verbal explanations of the four attitude changers, yet our attachment to the events of this life expose our continuing involvement with worldly values. We serve the guru yet our respect and devotion gradually decreases. Instead of having pure vision we mistakenly see the Guru as an equal and a friend.

རྡོ་རྗེ་སྤུན་ལ་བརྩེ་གདུང་བཀུར་སེམས་ཞན།

DOR JE	PUN	LA	TSE	DUNG	KUR SEM	ZHAN
dorje	*brothers*	*to*	*kindness*	*love*	*insulting attitude*	*keep*

We insult and disparage our vajra brothers and sisters instead of showing them love and kindness.

ཚིག་ངན་ཙམ་ཡང་མི་བཟོད་དམོད་ཆར་འབེབས།

TSI	NGAN	TSAM	YANG	MI ZOE	MOE	CHAR	BE
words	*bad*	*merely*	*yet*	*without forebearance*	*curse*	*rain*	*fall*

When others say a few bad words to us, instead of showing forbearance, we send them a torrent of curses.

འགྲོ་དྲུག་ཕ་མར་ཤེས་པའི་བྱམས་སྙིང་རྗེ།

DRO	DRU	PHA MAR	SHE PAI	JAM	NYING JE
sentient beings	*six (realms)*	*as parents*	*know, recognise*	*love*	*compassion*

The love and compassion of recognising all beings in the six realms to be our own parents

བྱང་སེམས་གཏིང་ནས་མ་འབྱོངས་ན་བུན་བཞིན།

JANG SEM	TING	NE	MA	JONG	NA BUN	ZHIN
bodhisattva, altruistic attitude	*depth*	*from*	*not*	*practise*	*mist*	*as*

Vanishes like mist as we do not practise it from the depth of true bodhicitta.

བསྐྱེད་རྫོགས་ལམ་ལ་ཉམས་ལེན་བྱས་ཁུལ་ཀྱང་།

KYE	DZO	LAM	LA	NYAM LEN	JAE	KHUL	KYANG
developing system	completing system	path	on	practice, familiarisation	do	pretend, no real interest	yet

We force ourselves to do the practices of the developing and completing systems, but

ཐ་མལ་འཁྲུལ་འབྱམས་འདི་ལ་སྒྲགས་མ་རྙེད།

THA MAL	TRUL	JAM	DI	LA	LAG	MA	NYE
ordinary	confusion, bewilderment	submerged	this	to	alternative	not	get

Can't use them as as alternative to being submerged in everyday confusion.

མདོ་སྔགས་ཆོས་ཕུག་སྟོང་ཉིད་ངོ་ཤེས་ཀྱང་།

DO	NGA	CHO	PHU	TONG NYI	NGO SHE	KYANG
sutra	tantra	dharma	depth, interior	emptiness	recognise	yet

We know that emptiness is the essence of the dharma in both sutra and tantra, yet,

སྟོང་གོ་མ་ཆོད་རང་རྒྱུད་ར་ལྟར་གྱོང་།

TONG	GO	MA CHO	RANG GYU	RA	TAR	GYONG
emptiness	understanding	not get	mental flow, personality	horn	as	hard, solid

Not gaining a proper understanding of it, our minds become as stiff and hard as horn.

We insult and disparage our vajra brothers and sisters instead of showing them love and kindness. When others say a few bad words to us, instead of showing forbearance, we send them a torrent of curses. The love and compassion of recognising all beings in the six realms to be our own parents vanishes like mist as we do not practise it from the depth of true bodhicitta. We force ourselves to do the practices of the developing and completing systems, but we can't use them as an alternative to being submerged in everyday confusion. We know that emptiness is the essence of the dharma in both sutra and tantra, yet, not gaining a proper understanding of it, our minds become as stiff and hard as horn.

གནས་ལུགས་སྒོམ་གྱི་རང་ཚུད་མ་ཟིན་པར།

NAE LU	GOM	GYI	RANG TSHU	MA	ZIN PAR
original nature	practice	of	balance	not	keep

Not maintaining the relaxed confidence of abiding in our original nature,

ཁ་ཁྱེར་ལྟ་བས་རྒྱུ་འབྲས་རླུང་ལ་བསྐུར།

KHA KHYER	TA WAE	GYU DRE	LUNG	LA	KUR
lip-service	*with that view*	*karma, cause and effect*	*wind*	*in*	*scatter*
		(i.e. abandon all care regarding activity)			

We pay only lip-service to that view and throw cause and effect to the wind.

ཕྱི་ལྟར་ཚུལ་འཆོས་སྤྱོད་ལམ་བཟང་ན་ཡང་།

CHI TAR	TSHUL CHO	CHOE LAM	ZANG	NA YANG
outwardly	*disciplined behaviour*	*pattern of behaviour*	*good*	*yet*

Outwardly we appear disciplined with very good behaviour,

ནང་དུ་ཆགས་སྲེད་འདོད་རྔམས་མེ་ལྟར་འབར།

NANG DU	CHA	SE	DOE	NGAM	ME	TAR	BAR
inwardly	*attachment*	*craving*	*desire*	*greed*	*fire*	*like*	*blazing*

Yet within, our attachment, craving, desire and greed blaze like fire.

ལུས་འདི་དབེན་པའི་རི་ལ་གནས་ཁུལ་ཀྱང་།

LU	DI	WEN PAI	RI	LA	NAE	KHUL	KYANG
body	*this*	*isolated*	*mountain*	*in*	*stay*	*show, pretend*	*yet*

Though we place our bodies in the solitude of the mountains,

སེམས་འདིས་ཉིན་མཚན་བར་མེད་གྲོང་ཡུལ་འགྲིམས།

SEM	DI	NYIN	TSHAN	BAR ME	DRONG YUL	DRIM
mind	*by this*	*day*	*night*	*constantly*	*towns*	*visit*

Our minds ceaselessly stray to the town by day and by night.

རང་མགོ་ཐོན་པའི་གདིང་ཚེ་མ་ལོངས་བཞིན།

RANG	GO	THON PAI	DING TSHE	MA LONG	ZHIN
own	*head*	*experience*	*confidence*	*not have*	*as*

We don't trust our own experience and practice,

གཞན་མགོ་འདོན་པའི་བསླབ་སྦྱོར་བྱིས་པའི་སྒྲུང་།

ZHAN	GO	DON PAI	SAM JOR	JI PAI	DRUNG
others	*head*	*advice, direction*		*child's*	*story*

Yet we give advice to others like a child telling a story.

Not maintaining the relaxed confidence of abiding in our original nature, we pay only lip-service to that view and throw cause and effect to the wind. Outwardly we appear disciplined with very good behaviour, yet within, our attachment, craving, desire and greed blaze like fire. Though we place our bodies in the solitude of the mountains, our minds ceaselessly stray to the town by day and by night. We don't trust our own experience and practice, yet we give advice to others like a child telling a story.

དཀོན་མཆོག་ཐུགས་རྗེ་བསླུ་བ་མི་སྲིད་ཀྱང་།

KON CHO	THU JE	LU WA	MI SI	KYANG
three jewels	*compassion*	*cheating*	*not possible*	*yet*

It is impossible to be cheated by the compassion of the Three Jewels,

མོས་གུས་ཞན་པས་རང་གིས་རང་བསླུས་དོགས།

MOE	GUE	ZHAN PA	RANG	GI	RANG	LUE	DO
devotion	*respect*	*declining*	*self*	*by*	*self*	*cheated*	*obstructed*

Yet due to our failing devotion we cheat and harm ourselves.

འདི་ལྟར་དམ་པའི་ཆོས་དང་བླ་མ་ལ།

DI TAR	DAM PAI		CHO	DANG	LA MA	LA
in this way	*holy, sacred, excellent*		*dharma*	*and*	*guru*	*to*

Thus, although we are free of the wrong views arising from lack of faith

ཡིད་མ་ཆེས་པའི་ལོག་ལྟ་མེད་མོད་ཀྱང་།

YI MA CHE PAI		LOG TA	ME	MOE	KYANG
without faith, no trusting open mind		*wrong view*	*without*	*are*	*yet*

In the guru and the holy dharma,

དུས་ངན་སེམས་ཅན་ལས་ངན་ཁ་མ་གང་།

DUE	NGAN	SEM CHAN	LAE NGAN	KHA MA GANG
times	*bad, difficult*	*sentient beings*	*bad actions*	*not fulfilled*

Due to these bad times we sentient beings perform bad actions and remain unsatisfied.

གོ་བཞིན་ཤེས་བཞིན་བག་མེད་དབང་དུ་ཤོར།

GO ZHIN	SHE ZHIN	BA ME	WANG	DUE	SHOR
understanding	*realising*	*careless*	*power*	*under*	*gone, fallen*

Our understanding and clarity have gone under the power of carelessness.

དྲན་ཤེས་བྱ་རམ་ཐོང་གྱོང་ཆེན་བརྫབ།

DRAN SHE	JA RA	MA THONG	GYONG	CHEN	DA
mindfulness	*look after*	*not do well*	*loss, trouble*	*great*	*brings*

Not protecting our mindfulness we suffer great loss.

དལྟ་རང་བློས་རང་ལ་དཔྱད་ཉིན་མོ།

DAN TA	RANG	LOE	RANG	LA	CHE	NYIN MO
now	*own*	*by intellect*	*self*	*to*	*examine*	*have time to*

We must now take the time to examine ourselves very carefully.

It is impossible to be cheated by the compassion of the Three Jewels, yet due to our failing devotion we cheat and harm ourselves. Thus, although we are free of the wrong views arising from lack of faith in the guru and the holy dharma, due to these bad times we sentient beings perform bad actions and remain unsatisfied. Our understanding and clarity have gone under the power of carelessness. Not protecting our mindfulness we suffer great loss. We must now take the time to examine ourselves very carefully.

བྱས་ཚད་ཐམས་ཅད་འཁྲུལ་པའི་ཁ་སྟོན་སོང་།

JAE	TSHAE		THAM CHE	TRUL PAI	KHA NON SONG
done	*whatever, as much as*		*all*	*confusion*	*adds further to*

All that we have done has merely added to our confusion.

བསམ་ཚད་ཐམས་ཅད་ཉིན་མོངས་འཛིན་པར་སོང་།

SAM	TSHAE	THAM CHE	NYON MONG		DZIN PAR	SONG
thought, concept	*as much as*	*all*	*affliction (attachment, aversion etc)*		*grasping, mixed with*	*gone*

All our thoughts are suffused with the afflictions and grasping.

དགེ་བའང་སྡིག་པས་མ་བསྲེད་མེད་མཐོང་བས།

GE	WANG	DIG PAE	MA	LE	ME	THONG	WAE
virtue	*also*	*by error*	*not*	*mixed*	*without*	*see*	*by*

The virtue we do is always mixed with error, and though we see this we do nothing about it,

མཐར་ཐུག་འགྲོ་ས་ངན་སོང་ལས་གཞན་ཅི།

THAR THU	DRO SA	NGAN SONG	LAE ZHAN CHI
ultimate	*destination*	*three lower realms**	*where else but these?*
**animal, hungry ghost and hells*

So where else can our final destination be but the three lower realms?

དེ་ལྟར་རང་གི་སྤྱོད་ཚུལ་བྱ་བཞག་རྣམས།

DE TAR	RANG GI	CHO	TSHUL	JA ZHA NAM
in that way	*my*	*action, conduct*	*way, system*	*all actions*

Then, when we look at all our actions and patterns of behaviour,

 དྲན་ནས་རང་གིས་རང་ལ་ཡི་ཆད་ཅིང་།

DRAN	NE	RANG	GI	RANG	LA	YI CHE CHING
remember	*then*	*self*	*by*	*self*	*to*	*lose confidence, remorse*

We lose trust in ourselves, and

གཞན་ལ་བལྟས་ཀྱང་ཡི་མུག་ཁ་སྟོན་ལས།

ZHAN	LA	TAE	KYANG	YI MU	KHA NON	LAE
other	*to*	*look at*	*also*	*dissapointed*	*critical*	*then*

When we consider others we are dissapointed and critical, and then

ཕན་གྲོགས་བློ་བཏག་ཕབ་མཁན་སུ་མ་བྱུང་།

PHEN	DRO	LO BA	PHAB KHAN	SU	MA	JUNG
beneficial	*friend, helper*	*trusting mind*	*reliable helper*	*as*	*not*	*arise*

We find no-one reliable to reassure and help us.

All that we have done has merely added to our confusion. All our thoughts are suffused with the afflictions and grasping. The virtue we do is always mixed with error, and though we see this we do nothing about it, so where else can our final destination be but the three lower realms? Then, when we look at all our actions and patterns of behaviour, we lose trust in ourselves, and when we consider others we are disappointed and critical, and then find no-one reliable to reassure and help us.

དའི་རང་མགོ་རང་གིས་མ་བཏོན་ན།

DA NI	RANG	GO	RANG	GI	MA	TON	NA
now	*own*	*head*	*self*	*by*	*not*	*show*	*if*

If we do not make things clear for ourselves now,

གཤིན་རྗེའི་ཕོ་ཉའི་ལག་ཏུ་ཚུད་ཟིན་དུས།

SHIN JEI	PHO NYAI	LAG	TU	TSHU ZIN	DUE
Lord Yama of death	*messengers'*	*hand*	*in*	*caught*	*when*

Then, when we are caught by the hands of Yama's messengers,

གཞན་པ་སུས་ཀྱང་སློབ་པའི་རེ་བ་ཟད།

ZHAN PA	SUE	KYANG	LO PAI	RE WA	ZAE
other person	*by whom*	*also*	*teachers'*	*hope[4]*	*finish, destroy*

Which of us will not see our teachers' hopes destroyed?

རེ་སྟོང་བསྒུག་པས་བསླུས་ལ་མ་ཚོར་རམ།

RE	TONG	GU PAE	LUE PA	MA	TSHOR	RAM
hopes	*empty*	*wait*	*cheated*	*not*	*feel*	*or*

When we wait then with all our hopes unfulfilled, will we not feel cheated?

དེས་ན་རང་སྐྱོན་ཐོས་ཤིན་གནོང་འགྱོད་ཀྱིས།

DE NA	RANG	KYONG	NGOE ZIN	NONG	GYOE	KYI
thus	*own*	*faults*	*recognise*	*repent, guilt*	*remorse*	*by*

Therefore, with guilt and remorse arising from recognising our own faults,

ཆོས་འགལ་ཉེས་ལྟུང་ཉམས་ཆག་ཅི་མཆིས་པ།

CHO	GAL	NYE	TUNG	NYAM CHA	CHI	CHI PA
dharma	*error*	*fault*	*fall*	*lapses*	*whatever*	*done*

For whatever errors in the dharma, whatever faults, falls and lapses we have made,

མི་འཆབ་མི་སྐྱེད་ཡེ་ཤེས་སྤྱན་ལྡན་དྲུང༌།

MI	CHA	MI	BE	YE SHE	CHAN	DEN	DRUNG
not	*repeat*	*not*	*do*	*original knowing (i.e. Buddha)*	*eye*	*having*	*before, in front of*

Determined never to repeat them again, before those who have the eye of original knowing

སྙིང་ནས་བཤགས་སོ་བརྩེ་བས་བཟོད་བཞེས་ལ།

NYING	NE	SHA SO	TSE WAE	ZOE ZHE	LA
heart	*from*	*confess*	*by compassion*	*forgive*	*then*

We make confession from the depths of our hearts. With your compassion please forgive us.

ལམ་ལོག་གཡང་སའི་འཇིགས་ལས་བསྐྱབ་ནས་ཀྱང༌།

LAM	LO	YANG SAI	JIG	LAE	KYAB	NE	KYANG
path	*wrong, reverse*	*precipice*	*fear*	*from*	*protected*	*then*	*also*

Please protect us from the terror of the chasms of the wrong path and

ཡང་དག་ཐར་ལམ་ཟིན་པར་དབུགས་དབྱུང་གསོལ།

YANG DA	THAR	LAM	ZIN PAR	WUG JUNG	SOL
very pure, perfect	*liberation*	*path*	*hold*	*inspiration, reassurance*	*request*

Sustain us so that we may keep on the pure path to liberation.

If we do not make things clear for ourselves now, then, when we are caught by the hands of Yama's messengers, which of us will not see our teachers' hopes destroyed? Then, when, we wait with all our hopes unfulfilled will we not feel cheated? Therefore, with guilt and remorse arising from recognising our own faults, in front of those who have the eye of wisdom, from the depths of our heart we confess all our dharma errors, faults, falls and lapses and vow never to repeat them. Please forgive us with your compassion. Please protect us from the terror of the chasms of the wrong path and sustain us so that we may keep on the pure path to liberation.

བྱས་བྱས་བསྒྲུབ་བསྒྲུབ་མི་ཚེ་བསྐྱལ་ན་ཡང་།

JE	JE	DRU	DRU		MI	TSHE	KYAL NA	YANG
doing	*doing*	*practising*	*accomplishing*		*human*	*life*	*spend*	*also*

We spend our lives busy, so busy, doing this and that, and yet

དོན་སྙིང་ལག་ཏུ་ལོན་པ་གཅིག་མ་བྱུང་།

DON		NYING	LAG	TU	LON PA	CHI	MA	JUNG
meaning, value		*essential*	*hand*	*in*	*empty*	*one*	*not*	*become*

We are empty-handed without even an atom of the essential truth.

ད་ནི་ཀུན་ཤེས་གཅིག་སྡུག་ལམ་བོར་ནས།

DA NI	KUN	SHE	CHI	DUG	LAM	BOR	NE
now	*all*	*know*	*one*	*suffering*	*path*	*discard*	*ten*

Now, abandoning the path of knowing many things yet experiencing only suffering,

གཅིག་ཤེས་ཀུན་གྲོལ་ལམ་ལ་ཅིས་མི་འཇུག

CHIG	SHE	KUN	DROL	LAM	LA	CHI MI JU
one	*know*	*all*	*free*	*path*	*on*	*why not enter*

Why should we not enter the path of knowing one thing and being free of all?

མི་བསྐུ་རེས་པའི་རེ་ལྟོས་གཅིག་ཆོག་མགོན།

MI	LU		NGE PAI	RE	TOE	CHI CHO	GON
not	*cheat, deceive*		*certain*	*hope*	*reliance*	*sole*	*benefactor*

Unfailing true benefactor, our sole hope and reliance,

རྩ་བའི་བླ་མ་སྐྱབས་གནས་ཀུན་འདུས་ལ།

TSA WAI	LA MA	KYAB NAE		KUN	DUE	LA
root	*guru*	*refuge, place of protection*		*all*	*encompass, embody*	*to*

Root guru who encompasses all the sites of refuge,

རྩེ་གཅིག་གུས་པས་གསོལ་བ་འདེབས་ལགས་ན།

TSE CHI	GUE PAE	SOL WA DE	LA	NA
one-pointed	*by devotion*	*pray, request*	*do*	*if, when*

When we pray to you with one-pointed devotion,

ཕྱགས་རྗེ་གཟིགས་ཤིག་སྐྱབས་མཆོག་དྲིན་ཅན་རྗེ།

THU JE		ZI SHI	KYAB	CHO	DRIN CHEN	JE
with compassion		*look at us!*	*refuge*	*supreme*	*most kind*	*noble one*

Please look on us with compassion, our supreme refuge, most kind lord!

We spend our lives busy, so busy, doing this and that, and yet we are empty-handed without even an atom of the essential truth. Now, abandoning the path of knowing many things yet experiencing only suffering, why should we not enter the path of knowing one thing and being free of all? Unfailing true benefactor, our sole hope and reliance, root guru who encompasses all the sites of refuge, when we pray to you with one-pointed devotion, please look on us with compassion, our supreme refuge, most kind lord!

རང་སྐྱོན་རང་གིས་མཐོང་བར་བྱིན་གྱིས་རློབས།

RANG	KYON	RANG	GI	THONG WAR		JIN GYI LO
my	*faults*	*self*	*by*	*see*		*please bless me*

Please bless us so we see our own faults.

གཞན་སྐྱོན་བལྟ་འདོད་མེད་པར་བྱིན་གྱིས་རློབས།

ZHAN	KYON	TA	DOE ME PAR		JIN GYI LO
others	*faults*	*examine*	*without desire*		*please bless me*

Please bless us so we have no desire to examine the faults of others.

བསམ་ངན་གདུག་རྩུབ་ཞི་བར་བྱིན་གྱིས་རློབས།

SAM	NGAN	DU		TSUB	ZHI WAR	JIN GYI LO
thoughts	*bad*	*disturbance*		*rough*	*pacify*	*please bless me*

Please bless us with the removal of all our disturbing bad thoughts.

བསམ་བཟང་ཁོངས་ནས་འཆར་བར་བྱིན་གྱིས་རློབས།

SAM	ZANG	KHONG	NE	CHAR WAR		JIN GYI LO
thoughts	*good*	*deep inside*	*from*	*arise*		*please bless me*

Please bless us so that good thoughts arise from deep within.

འདོད་ཆུང་ཆོག་ཤེས་ལྡན་པར་བྱིན་གྱིས་རློབས།

DOE	CHUNG	CHO		SHE	DAN PAR	JIN GYI LO
desire	*little*	*limit, capacity*		*know*	*have*	*please bless me*

Please bless us so we have little desire and know our limits.

ནམ་འཆི་ཆ་མེད་དྲན་པར་བྱིན་གྱིས་རློབས།

NAM **CHI** **CHA ME** **DRAN PAR** **JIN GYI LO**
when *die* *uncertain* *remember* *please bless me*

Please bless us so we remember the time of death to be uncertain.

འཆི་དུས་བློ་ལྷག་མེད་པར་བྱིན་གྱིས་རློབས།

CHI **DUE** **LO** **LHAG ME PAR** **JIN GYI LO**
die *when* *likes, intentions* *without remainder* *please bless me*

Please bless us so we are free of worldly intentions when we die.

ཆོས་ལ་ཡིད་ཆེས་སྐྱེ་བར་བྱིན་གྱིས་རློབས།

CHO **LA** **YI CHE** **KYE WAR** **JIN GYI LO**
dharma *to* *believe* *arise, be born* *please bless me*

Please bless us so true trust in the dharma is born in us.

Please bless us so we see our own faults. Please bless us so we have no desire to examine the faults of others. Please bless us with the removal of all our disturbing bad thoughts. Please bless us so that good thoughts may arise from deep within. Please bless us so we have little desire and know our limits. Please bless us so we remember the time of death to be uncertain. Please bless us so we are free of worldly intentions when we die. Please bless us so true trust in the dharma is born in us.

དག་སྣང་ཕྱོགས་མེད་འབྱོངས་པར་བྱིན་གྱིས་རློབས།

DA NANG **CHO ME** **JONG PAR** **JIN GYI LO**
pure vision *partiality, taking sides* *practice* *please bless us*

Please bless us so we practise pure vision free of bias.

བཅོས་མིན་མོས་གུས་སྐྱེ་བར་བྱིན་གྱིས་རློབས།

CHO MIN **MOE** **GUE** **KYE WAR** **JIN GYI LO**
non-artificial, uncontrived *devotion* *respect* *arise* *please bless me*

Please bless us so we feel real genuine respect and devotion.

ལོངས་མེད་བློ་སྣ་ཐུང་བར་བྱིན་གྱིས་རློབས།

LONG ME **LO NA** **THUNG WAR** **JIN GYI LO**
unobtainable *desires, ideas* *diminish* *please bless me*

Please bless us so we reduce our craving for what is unobtainable.

བློ་ཕུག་ཆོས་ལ་གཏད་ནུས་བྱིན་གྱིས་རློབས།

LO **PHU** **CHO** **LA** **TAE** **NU** **JIN GYI LO**
mind, *in depth,* *dharma* *as* *fix,* *power* *please bless me*
intellect *experience* *establish*

Please bless us with the power to establish dharma in the depth of our mind.

ཆོས་ཕུག་སྒྲུབ་ལ་བརྩོན་ནུས་བྱིན་གྱིས་རློབས།

CHO	PHU	DRU	LA	TSON	NU	JIN GYI LO
dharma	*depth*	*practise*	*to*	*diligence*	*power*	*please bless me*

Please bless us with the power of diligence to practise within the depth of dharma.

སྒྲུབ་ཕུག་རང་རྒྱུད་གྲོལ་བར་བྱིན་གྱིས་རློབས།

DRU	PHU	RANG GYU		DROL WAR	JIN GYI LO
practice	*depth*	*own mental capacity, personality*		*liberate*	*please bless me*

Please bless us so we liberate all our experience in the depth of practice.

སྒྲུབ་ལ་བར་ཆད་མེད་པར་བྱིན་གྱིས་རློབས།

DRU	LA	BAR CHE	ME PAR	JIN GYI LO
practise	*to*	*obstacles*	*without*	*please bless me*

Please bless us so our practice is free of obstacles.

སྒྲུབ་འབྲས་མྱུར་དུ་སྨིན་པར་བྱིན་གྱིས་རློབས།

DRU	DRAE	NYUR DU	MIN PAR	JIN GYI LO
practice	*result*	*quickly*	*ripen*	*please bless me*

Please bless us so the results of practice ripen quickly!

Please bless us so we practise pure vision free of bias. Please bless us so we feel real genuine respect and devotion. Please bless us so we reduce our craving for what is unobtainable. Please bless us with the power to establish dharma in the depth of our mind. Please bless us with the power of diligence to practise within the depth of dharma. Please bless us so we liberate all our experience in the depth of practice. Please bless us so our practice is free of obstacles. Please bless us so the results of practice ripen quickly!

འབྲེལ་ཆད་དོན་དང་ལྡན་པར་བྱིན་གྱིས་རློབས།

TREL TSHE		DON DANG DAN PAR	JIN GYI LO
those I have connection with		*meaningful*	*please bless me*

Please bless us so we bring meaning and benefit to all with whom we are connected.

རེ་དོགས་གཉིས་འཛིན་ཞིག་པར་བྱིན་གྱིས་རློབས།

RE	DO	NYI DZIN	ZHIG PAR	JIN GYI LO
hope	*doubts*	*dualism*	*destroy*	*please bless me*

Please bless us with the destruction of duality and its hopes and fears.

གཉིས་མེད་ཡེ་ཤེས་མཐོང་བར་བྱིན་གྱིས་རློབས།

NYI ME	YE SHE	THONG WAR	JIN GYI LO
non-dual	*original knowing*	*see, experience*	*please bless me*

Please bless us so we enter non-dual original knowing.

ཡེ་ཤེས་རང་ངོ་ཤེས་པར་བྱིན་གྱིས་རློབས།

YE SHE	RANG NGO	SHE PAR	JIN GYI LO
original knowing	*own essence*	*know, recognise*	*please bless me*

Please bless us so we actualise the original knowing of our own essence.

རང་ཐོག་བཙན་ས་ཟིན་པར་བྱིན་གྱིས་རློབས།

RANG	THOG	TSAN	SA	ZIN PAR	JIN GYI LO
self	*on*	*secure*	*place**	*hold, abide in*	*please bless me*
	*unborn freedom				

Please bless us so we abide in the secure place right where we are.

རྩོལ་མེད་གདིང་ཆེན་ཐོབ་པར་བྱིན་གྱིས་རློབས།

TSOL ME	DING CHEN	THO PAR	JIN GYI LO
without dualistic effort	*great confidence*	*gain*	*please bless me*

Please bless us so we gain great confidence in non- effort.

Please bless us so we bring meaning and benefit to all with whom we are connected. Please bless us with the destruction of duality and its hopes and fears. Please bless us so we enter non-dual original knowing. Please bless us so we actualise the original knowing of our own essence. Please bless us so we abide in the secure place right where we are. Please bless us so we gain great confidence in non-effort.

ཡེ་གནས་ཡེ་ཤེས་རྡོ་རྗེའི་མཚོན་ཆེན་གྱིས།

YE	NAE	YE SHE	DOR JEI	TSHON	CHEN	GYI
from very beginning	*present*	*original knowing*	*vajra, indestructible*	*weapon*	*great*	*by*

With the great indestructible weapon of original knowing which is always already present,

འཁོར་འདས་སྟོང་སྒྲོག་དུས་གཅིག་བཅད་ནས་ཀྱང་།

KHOR	DAE	TONG	SO	DUE	CHI	CHE	NE	KYANG
samsara	*nirvana*	*thousand things*	*life- force*	*time*	*one*	*cut*	*then*	*also*
						(in the manner of Vajrasattva)		

May the entire diversity of samsara and nirvana be cut off in one instant.

 མ་འགགས་བདེ་ཆེན་སྙེམས་མའི་དགའ་སྟོན་ལ།

MA GA	DE CHEN	NYEM MAI	GA TON	LA
unceasing	*great happiness*	*name of the consort of Vajrasattva*	*festival celebration*	*at, in*

In the ceaseless great happiness of Nyema's celebration

འདུ་འབྲལ་མེད་པར་སྤྱོད་པས་རྟག་བརྟེན་ཤོག

DU	TRAL	ME PAR	CHO PAE	TAG	TSEN	SHO
joining	*separating (i.e.unchanging)*	*without*	*by conduct*	*permanent*	*secure*	*may there be*

May we all find permanent security in the conduct free of all change.

མཉམ་བརྡལ་ཀློང་ན་སྡུག་བསྔལ་མིང་ཙམ་མེད།

NYAM	DAL	LONG	NA	DU NGAL	MING	TSAM	ME
even, equal	*spread, pervade*	*vastness and depth (non-duality of emptiness and awareness)*	*in*	*suffering*	*name*	*even*	*without*

In the infinity which is the same everywhere there is not even the name
of suffering —

དེས་ན་བདེ་བ་འཚོལ་མཁན་སུ་ཞིག་མཆིས།

DE NA	DE WA	TSHOL KHAN	SU ZHI CHI
when there is that	*happiness*	*person who looks for*	*who could there be*

So who could one find there still looking for happiness?

བདེ་སྡུག་རོ་མཉམ་འཛིན་མེད་རང་གྲོལ་གྱི།

DE	DU	RO	NYAM	DZIN ME	RANG DROL	GYI
happiness	*sorrow*	*flavour*	*equal*	*free of grasping*	*self-liberating*	*of*

The self-liberating state free of grasping where happiness and sorrow
taste the same —

ཀུན་བཟང་རྒྱལ་སྲིད་ཚེ་འདིར་ཐོབ་པར་ཤོག

KUN ZANG	GYAL SI	TSHE	DIR	THO PAR	SHO
Samantabhadra, 'always good'	*kingdom*	*life*	*this*	*gain*	*may there be*

In this very life may we gain this kingdom of Samantabhadra.

*With the great indestructible weapon of original knowing which
is always already present, may the entire diversity of samsara and
nirvana be cut off in one instant. In the ceaseless great happiness of
Nyema's celebration may we all find permanent security in the conduct
free of all change. In the infinity which is the same everywhere there
is not even the name of suffering — so who could one find there still
looking for happiness? In this very life may we gain this kingdom
of Samantabhadra, the self-liberating state free of grasping where
happiness and sorrow taste the same.*

COLOPHON

Regarding this work, which is a combination of prayer, repentant confession, and aspiration, one night during the waxing moon of the tenth month of the water-pig year, my wife, Shes-Rab-Ma Rig-'Dzin dBang-Mo, had a dream in which there appeared a lady who had been in her dreams before. This lady said, *"You should now ask Rinpoche to write a prayer."* and then departed.

Moreover, later, on the night of the tenth day of the same month the same lady appeared and told her, *"You must immediately help to request the writing of a prayer."* and then she vanished.

I was informed of the dream the next morning but I said, *"Not many people are ready to recite the prayers that already exist, so it's not that there are no prayers at the present time."* My wife then requested me to quickly write a prayer without being concerned about the length. So then I had the idea to write a prayer since there seemed to be a need for one to request protection from the fears of sickness, famine, weapons and fighting that are prevalent at this time. But it remained only an intention as other things occurred and it seemed less pressing.

However, later on, in the evening of the 10th day of the 11th month, the lady appeared again in my wife's dream and said, *"My request for that prayer is not something of little importance. It is a great necessity."* So then, on the basis of hearing of that dream, on the morning of the 15th day of that month I had the idea to write something.

Then in the evening of the 14th day of the next month I prayed one-pointedly to Guru Rinpoche and made an aspiration for a very meaningful blessing.

At cock-crow the following morning I had a dream in which I was sitting inside a large building that resembled my temple. Suddenly a white man appeared, young, dressed in white, and with long, flowing ringlets. He was playing cymbals very softly and dancing in the clockwise spiralling steps of the Ging as he came through the door and approached closer and closer to me while chanting these words:

If you want to establish the dharma then plant it in your heart.
When it is in the depth of your heart you will get buddhahood.
If you want to reach the buddhaland then purify your attachment to ordinary confusion.
Happily, the pure buddhaland is right beside you.
Develop diligence in the practice of the essence.
If you do not practise then who will gain the attainments?
It is difficult to look at one's own bad faults.
To really see one's own faults is the one essential point of the dharma instructions.
Gradually purify the errors you have and increase and develop the good qualities you have.

At the end of each line he increased the volume of the cymbals and at the end he departed while playing them very loudly—and due to this I woke up. Immediately on awakening I remembered his words and knew that their meaning concerned the difficulty of training in 'rejecting and accepting'. Then, with the regret of having seen my sole father, Guru Padmasambhava, directly in front of me and not recognising him, with longing devotion this old father of the rNying-Ma, Jigtral Yeshe Dorje, wrote this in accordance with my vision. May it be beneficial.

Benefit to All

Notes

1. The Short Chapter on Discrimination (*'byd-pa le'u chung*) lists them as follows: 1. Develop faith in the Three Precious Jewels without sorrow or weariness; 2. Search ultimately for the true doctrine; 3. Skilfully study the excellent sciences; 4. First recollect and then appraise anything that is to be undertaken; 5. Do not hanker after unassigned work; 6. Look to a higher level and emulate the ancients and those of superior conduct; 7. Repay kindness to one's parents of the past, present and future; 8. Be broad-minded and hospitable

in one's dealings with elder and younger siblings and paternal relatives; 9. Ensure that the young respect their elders by degrees; 10. Show loving kindness to one's neighbours; 11. Arduously assist one's acquaintances who are spiritual benefactors; 12. Perfectly fulfil the needs of those nearby who are connected through the worldly round; 13. Help others through one's skill in science and the arts; 14. Provide a refuge with kindness to those who depend upon it; 15. Resist bad advice and establish advice which will increase the happiness of the country; and 16. Entrusting one's deeds to the doctrine, one should bring one's spouse to obtain the ground of enlightenment in future lives. [From THE NYINGMA SCHOOL OF TIBETAN BUDDHISM BY DUDJOM RINPOCHE]

2. 1. Not killing beings, but ransoming them and protecting them. 2. Not taking what is not given, but giving what one has to others. 3.Not indulging in sexual behaviour, but keeping within morality. 4. Not telling lies, but speaking the pure and straightforward truth. 5. Not using disharmonious speech, but endeavouring to reconcile those who are at odds with each other. 6. Not speaking rough words, but speaking sweetly and calmly. 7. Not idly gossiping, but refraining from speech or spending one's time reading religious books or reciting mantras. 8. Not being avaricious, but knowing one's own wealth to be sufficient and meditating on the lack of need for more. 9. Not bearing ill will, but concerning oneself with the benefit of others. 10. Not holding wrong views, but having faith in the Three Jewels of Buddha Dharma and Sangha and in the karmic relation of cause and effect.

3. 1. Not to hate others despite being the object of their hatred. 2. Not to retaliate in anger even when angry. 3. Not to injure others even when injured. 4. Not to beat others even when one is beaten by them.

4. Although we have received many instructions from our kind teachers we have not applied them and so the hopes our teachers placed in us come to naught.

ཕྱག་སྐྱབ་དག་པར་འདོད་ནঃ

If You Wish to Purify Your Sins and Obscurations

རང་གི་སྤྱི་གཙུག་སྟེང་གི་ནམ་མཁའ་ལ་

RANG GI   CHI TSU   TENG GI   NAM KHA   LA
my   crown of head on top of   sky   in

In the sky above the top of my head

ཨོ་རྒྱན་རིན་པོ་ཆེ་སྐུ་མདོག་དཀར་པོ་

OR GYAN   RIN PO CHE   KU   DO   KAR PO
Oddiyana   precious one   body colour white
(Padmasambhava)

Is the Precious One from Urgyen, white in colour and

དར་དང་རིན་པོ་ཆེའི་རྒྱན་ཅནঃ

DAR   DANG   RIN PO CHEI   GYAN   CHAN
cloth   and   jewel,   ornaments   having, wearing
(many different robes) precious substances

Wearing robes and jewel ornaments.

ཕྱག་གཡས་རྡོ་རྗེ་དང་གཡོན་དྲིལ་བུ་འཛིན་པঃ

CHA   YAE   DOR JE   DANG   YON   DRIL BU   DZIN PA
hand   right vajra   and   left   bell   holding

He holds a vajra in his right hand and a bell in his left.

ཡུམ་ཌཱ་ཀི་མ་དཀར་མོས་འཁྱུད་པঃ

YUM   DAK KI MA   KAR MOE   KHYU PA
consort dakini, goddess white   embraced

He is embraced in sexual union by his consort the white dakini.

འཁོར་སློབ་དཔོན་ཆེན་པོ་དྲུག

KHOR   LO PON   CHEN PO   DRU
circle,   acharyas, entourage great teachers   six

The six great acharyas

གིས་བསྐོར་བར་བསམ་ལ༔

GI KOR WAR SAM LA
by surrounded thinking this, believing this

Surround him as his circle. Imagine this.

I imagine that in the sky above the top of my head is the Precious One from Urgyen, white in colour and wearing robes and jewel ornaments. He holds a vajra in his right hand and a bell in his left. He is embraced in sexual union by his consort the white dakini and is surrounded by his circle of the six great acharyas.

ཧཱུྃ༔ ཨོ་རྒྱན་ཡུལ་གྱི་ནུབ་བྱང་མཚམས༔

HUNG UR GYEN YUL GYI NUB JANG TSHAM
vocative, seed letter Oddiyana of north west border, corner
of Padmasambhava

Hung. In the north-west corner of the land of Urgyen,

པདྨ་གེ་སར་སྡོང་པོ་ལ༔

PE MA GE SAR DONG PO LA
lotus stamen stem on

Upon the stem and stamen of a lotus,

ཡ་མཚན་མཆོག་གི་དངོས་གྲུབ་བརྙེས༔

YAM TSHEN CHO GI NGO DRU NYE
marvellous, supreme siddhis, has got
wonderful attainment (i.e. buddhahood)

Are you who have the marvellous and supreme accomplishments,

པདྨ་འབྱུང་གནས་ཞེས་སུ་གྲགས༔

PE MA JUNG NAE ZHE SU DRA
lotus source famous as
Padmasambhava

Padmasambhava of great renown,

འཁོར་དུ་མཁའ་འགྲོ་མང་པོས་བསྐོར༔

KHOR DU KHAN DRO MANG POE KOR
retinue as dakinis, all sky many by surrounded
travelling deities

With a retinue of many dakinis around you.

ཁྱེད་ཀྱི་རྗེས་སུ་བདག་སྒྲུབ་ཀྱིས༔

KHYE KYI JE SU DA DRU KYI
you following after, I practice by that
emulating

Following and relying on you, I do your practice, therefore,

ཕྲིན་གྱིས་བརླབ་ཕྱིར་གཤེགས་སུ་གསོལ༔

JIN GYI LAB   **CHIR**   **SHE SU**   **SOL**
blessing   *in order to*   *come*   *please*

In order to grant your blessings, please come here!

གུ་རུ་པདྨ་སིདྡྷི་ཧཱུྃ༔

GU RU   **PE MA**   **SID DHI**   **HUNG**
guru, master   *Padmasambhava*   *true attainment*   *give me!*

Guru Padmasambhava grant me the accomplishment of buddhahood!

བདག་གི་ཚེ་རབས་བསགས་བྱས་པའི༔

DA GI   **TSE RAB**   **SAG**   **JAE PAI**
my   *lives**   *collected,*   *done*
               accumulated
*past and present

All that I have collected in all my lives of

ཉམས་དང་སྡིག་སྒྲིབ་ཀུན་བྱང་མཛོད༔

NYAM   **DANG**   **DIG**   **DRIB**   **KUN**   **JANG**   **DZOE**
lapses*   *and*   *sins*   *obscurations***   *all*   *cleanse,*   *please do,*
                                          purify   *you must do*
*broken vows and promises   ** of karma and its subtle traces)

Lapses, sins and obscurations must be purified!

Hung. In the north-west corner of the land of Urgyen, upon the stem and stamen of a lotus, are you who have the marvellous and supreme attainments, Padmasambhava of great renown, with a retinue of many dakinis around you. Following and relying on you I do your practice, therefore, in order to grant your blessing, please come here! Guru Padmasambhava, grant me the accomplishment of buddhahood! Please purify all the lapses, sins and obscurations that I have accumulated in my many lives!

ཅེས་གསོལ་ནས་སྟོབས་བཞི་དང་ལྡན་པས་འགྱོད་བཤགས་བྱ༔

[Recite this prayer and make repentant confession via the Four Powers. These are:

1.   Relying on a pure object such as Vajrasattva or an image or a stupa.
2.   Recognising that one has sinned and feeling shame.
3.   Feeling intense regret and repentance as if one has eaten poison.
4.   Promising never to sin again even if one's life is at stake.]

ཨུ་རྒྱན་རིན་པོ་ཆེ་ཡབ་ཡུམ་གྱི་ཐུགས་ཀའི་

UR GYAN RIN PO CHE	YAB YUM	GYI	THU KAI
Padmasambhava	with his consort	of	hearts'

In the hearts of the Precious One from Urgyen and his consort are the
seed syllables Hung.

ས་བོན་དང་སྦྱོར་མཚམས་ནས་བདུད་རྩིའི་རྒྱུན་

SA BON	DANG	JOR TSHAM	NE	DU TSI	GYUN
seed letter* (*Hung)	and	their place of union	from	amrita, liberating elixir	flow, stream

From these Hungs and from their place of union flows a stream of
liberating elixir which

བབས་པས་སྤྱི་གཙུག་ཚངས་བུག་ནས་ཞུགས་

BAB PAE	CHI TSU	TSHANG BU	NE	ZHU
by descending	crown of my head	hole of Brahma*	via	enters me

*the area within a circle drawn four inches in from one's hairline

Descends and enters through the opening in the crown of my head.

ཏེ་ལུས་ཀྱི་ནང་ཡོངས་སུ་གང་སྟེ་

TE	LU	KYI	NANG	YONG SU	GANG	TE
then	body	of	interior	fully	fill	then

It completely fills the inside of my body.

ནད་རྣམས་རྣག་ཁྲག་དང༔   གདོན་འབུ་སྲིན་

NAE	NAM	NAG	TRAG	DANG	DON	BU	SIN
diseases, sickness	(pl)	puss	blood	and	demons, trouble-makers	insects, worms	reptiles, crocodiles

By this all my diseases are expelled in the form of puss and blood. The
demons who trouble me are expelled in the form of insects and reptiles,
and

སྡིག་སྒྲིབ་དུད་སོལ་གྱི་ཁུ་བའི་རྣམ་པར་ཐོན་

DIG	DRIB	DUD	SOL	GYI	KHU WAI	NAM PAR	THON
sins	obscurations	soot	clearing	of	liquid	form	depart

All my sins and obscurations leave me in the form of black sooty liquid.

ནས་ལུས་ཤེལ་གོང་དཀར་པོ་

NE	LU	SHEL	GONG	KAR PO
then	body	crystal	ball	white

I believe that my body has become like a shining ball of white crystal

རྡུལ་ཕྱིས་པ་ལྟར་གྱུར་པར་བསམ༔

DUL	CHI PA		TAR	GYUR PAR SAM
dust	*cleansed, wiped off*		*as*	*become believe*

Wiped free of dust.

In the hearts of the Precious One from Urgyen and his consort are the seed syllables Hung. From these Hungs and from their place of union flows a stream of liberating elixir which descends and enters through the opening in the crown of my head. It completely fills the inside of my body. By this all my diseases are expelled in the form of puss and blood. The demons who trouble me are expelled in the form of insects and reptiles, and all my sins and obscurations leave me in the form of black sooty liquid. I believe that my body has become like a shining ball of white crystal wiped free of dust.

སླར་བླ་མ་ཡབ་ཡུམ་འོད་དུ་ཞུ་ནས་

LAR	LA MA	YAB YUM	WOE	DU	ZHU	NE
again,	*Guru,*	*consort*	*light*	*in, as*	*melt*	*then*
furthermore	*Padmasambhava*					

Then the Guru and his consort dissolve in light and melt into me without difference.

རིག་སྟོང་འོད་གསལ་བའི་ཡེ་ཤེས་དང་

RIG	TONG	WOE	SAL WAI	YE SHE	DANG
awareness	*emptiness*	*light*	*clear*	*original knowing*	*and*

Original knowing of the clear light of awareness and emptiness and

རོ་གཅིག་ཏུ་མཉམ་པར་བཞག་ན༔

RO	CHI	TU	NYAM PAR	ZHA	NA
taste	*one*	*as,*	*equalness*	*maintain*	*if, when*
(emptiness)		*in*	*(undisturbed awareness)*		

My mind have one single taste. Resting in that evenness,

མཚམས་མེད་པ་ལྔ་བྱས་ན་ཡང་

TSHAM ME PA	NGA	JAE	NA	YANG
boundless sins	*five**	*done*	*if*	*also*

*The five boundless sins are: patricide; matricide; killing an arhat; wilfully causing a Tathagata to bleed; causing a schism in the sangha

Even if I have committed the five boundless sins,

བྱང་ཞིང་དག་པར་འགྱུར་རོ༔

JANG ZHING	DAG PAR	GYUR RO
cleansing, washing	*purified*	*become*

All is cleansed and purified.

Then the Guru and his consort dissolve in light and melt into me without difference. Original knowing of the clear light of awareness and emptiness and my mind have one single taste. Resting in that evenness, even if I have committed the five boundless sins, all is cleansed and purified.

ས་མ་ཡཿ   རྒྱ་རྒྱ་རྒྱཿ

Vows.   Seal. Seal. Seal.

གསོལ་འདེབས་བསམ་པ་ལྷུན་གྲུབ།

The Prayer Which Effortlessly Fulfils Our Wishes

ཨེ་མ་ཧོཿ   ནུབ་ཕྱོགས་བདེ་བ་ཅན་གྱི་ཞིང་ཁམས་སུཿ

E MA HO	NUB	CHO	DE WA CHEN	GYI	ZHING KHAM	SU
wonderful	*western*	*direction*	*Sukhavati, 'happy'*	*of*	*realm*	*in*

Wonderful! In the realm of Dewachen that lies to the west,

སྣང་བ་མཐའ་ཡས་ཐུགས་རྗེའི་བྱིན་རླབས་གཡོས༵ཿ

NANG WA THA YAE	THU JEI	JIN LAB	YOE
by Amitabha	*compassion's*	*blessing*	*moved (i.e. emerged in this world as Padma Sambha*

Amitabha released his compassionate blessing and

སྤྲུལ་སྐུ་པདྨ་འབྱུང་གནས་བྱིན་བརླབས་པས༵ཿ

TRUL KU	PAE MA JUNG NAE	JIN LAB PAE
incarnation, emanation	*Padmasambhava*	*by blessing*

You, Padmasambhava, emanated and blessed

འཛམ་གླིང་བོད་ཀྱི་སེམས་ཅན་དོན་ལ་དགོངས༵ཿ

DZAM LING	BOE KYI	SEM CHAN	DON	LA	GONG
world	*Tibetan*	*beings*	*benefit*	*for*	*consider*

The beings of Tibet with your intention for their welfare[1]

འགྲོ་དོན་རྒྱུན་ཆད་མེད་པའི་ཐུགས་རྗེ་ཅན༵ཿ

DRO	DON	GYUN CHA ME PAI	THU JE CHAN
beings	*benefit*	*ceaselessly*	*compassionate one*

You are the compassionate one who acts ceaselessly for the benefit of beings.

ཨོ་རྒྱན་པདྨ་འབྱུང་གནས་ལ་གསོལ་བ་འདེབས༵ཿ

UR GYAN	PAE MA JUNG NAE	LA	SOL WA DE
Oddiyana	*Padmasambhava*	*to*	*pray*

Padmasambhava of Urgyan, we pray to you —

བསམ་པ་ལྷུན་གྱིས་གྲུབ་པར་བྱིན་གྱིས་རློབས༔

SAM PA   **LHUN GYI DRU PAR**   **JIN GYI LO**
wishes   *effortlessly arising*   *bless*

Please bless us that our wishes may be fulfilled without effort!

Wonderful! In the realm of Dewachen that lies to the west, Amitabha released his compassionate blessing and you, Padmasambhava, emanated and blessed the beings of Tibet with your intention for their welfare. You are the compassionate one who acts ceaselessly for the benefit of beings. Padmasambhava of Urgyan, we pray to you – please bless us that our wishes may be fulfilled without effort!

རྒྱལ་པོ་ཁྲི་སྲོང་ལྡེའུ་བཙན་མན་ཆད་ནས༔

GYAL PO   **TRI SONG DEU TSAN**   **MAN CHAE**   **NE**
king   *(name)*   *after, below*   *from*

King Trisong Deutsan and

ཆོས་རྒྱལ་གདུང་བརྒྱུད་མཐའ་ནས་མ་སྟོངས་བར༔

CHO   **GYAL**   **DUNG GYU**   **THA NE**   **MA TONG**   **BAR**
dharma   *king*   *descendants*   *finally*   *not finish*   *until*

All his royal descendants until the end of his line

དུས་གསུམ་རྒྱུན་ཆད་མེད་པར་བྱིན་གྱིས་རློབས༔

DU   **SUM**   **GYUN CHA ME PAR**   **JIN GYI LO**
times   *three*   *continuously*   *bless*

Will be continuously blessed in all the three times

བོད་ཀྱི་ཆོས་སྐྱོང་རྒྱལ་པོའི་གཉེན་གཅིག་པུ༔

BOE   **KYI**   **CHO**   **KYONG**   **GYAL POI**   **NYEN**   **CHI PU**
Tibet   *of*   *dharma*   *protecting*   *king*   *friend*   *only*

By you, the sole friend of the king who protects the dharma in Tibet

རྒྱལ་པོ་ཆོས་སྤྱོད་སྐྱོབ་པའི་ཐུགས་རྗེ་ཅན༔

GYAL PO   **CHO**   **CHO**   **KYO PAI**   **THU JE CHEN**
king   *dharma*   *doing*   *protecting*   *compassionate one*

You are the compassionate one who protects the king who practises the dharma.[2]

ཨོ་རྒྱན་པདྨ་འབྱུང་གནས་ལ་གསོལ་བ་འདེབས༔

UR GYAN   **PAE MA**   **JUNG NAE**   **LA**   **SOL WA DE**

We pray to Padmasambhava of Urgyan.

བསམ་པ་ལྷུན་གྱིས་གྲུབ་པར་བྱིན་གྱིས་རློབས༔

SAM PA   LHUN GYI   DRU PAR   JIN GYI LO

Please bless us that our wishes may be fulfilled without effort!

King Trison Deutsan and all his royal descendants until the end of his line will be continuously blessed in all the three times by you, the sole friend of the king who practises the dharma in Tibet. You are the compassionate one who protects the king who practises the dharma. Padmasambhava of Urgyan, we pray to you – please bless us that our wishes may be fulfilled without effort!

སྐུ་ནི་ལྷོ་ནུབ་སྲིན་པོའི་ཁ་གནོན་མཛད༔

KU NI   LHO NUB   SIN POI   KHA NON   DZAE
body   *south-west*   *rakshashas,*   *supress*   *doing*
(i.e. Ngayabling)   *cannibal demons*

Your body is in the south-west suppressing the cannibal demons

ཐུགས་རྗེས་བོད་ཀྱི་སེམས་ཅན་དོན་ལ་དགོངས༔

THU JE   BOE KYI   SEM CHAN   DON LA   GONG
with compassion   *Tibetan*   *beings*   *benefit*   *consider*

Yet with your compassion you attend to the welfare of the beings of Tibet.[3]

མ་རིག་ལོག་པའི་སེམས་ཅན་འདྲེན་པའི་དཔལ༔

MA RIG   LO PAI   SEM CHAN   DREN PAI   PAL
ignorant   *wrong views, erring*   *sentient beings*   *leading out*   *glory, great one*

As the glorious guide of all those holding the wrong views arising from ignorance

ཉོན་མོངས་གདུལ་དཀའི་སེམས་ཅན་ཐབས་ཀྱིས་གདུལ༔

NYON MONG   DUL KAI   SEM CHAN   THAB   KYI   DUL
afflictions (anger,   *difficult to*   *sentient beings*   *suitable*   *by*   *control,*
desire etc.)   *educate, rough*   *methods*   *educate*

You control the unruly afflicted beings with suitable methods.

བརྩེ་གདུང་རྒྱུན་ཆད་མེད་པའི་ཐུགས་རྗེ་ཅན༔

TSE   DUNG   GYUN CHAE ME PAI   THU JE CHAN
compassion   *love, warm feeling*   *ceaseless, continuous*   *compassionate one*

You are the compassionate one whose tender love and care flows ceaselessly.

ཨུ་རྒྱན་པདྨ་འབྱུང་གནས་ལ་གསོལ་བ་འདེབས༔

UR GYAN   PAE MA   JUNG NAE   LA   SOL WA DE

We pray to Padmasambhava of Urgyan.

བསམ་པ་ལྷུན་གྱིས་འགྲུབ་པར་བྱིན་གྱིས་རློབས༔

SAM PA   LHUN GYI   DRU PAR   JIN GYI LO

Please bless us that our wishes may be fulfilled without effort!

Your body is in the south-west suppressing the cannibal demons yet with your compassion you attend to the welfare of the beings of Tibet. As the glorious guide of all those holding the wrong views arising from ignorance you control the unruly afflicted beings with suitable methods. You are the compassionate one whose tender love and care flows ceaselessly. Padmasambhava of Urgyan, we pray to you — please bless us that our wishes may be fulfilled without effort!

དུས་ངན་སྙིགས་མའི་མཐའ་ལ་ཐུག་པའི་ཚེ༔

DU		NGAN	NYIG MAI	THA	LA	THUG PAI	TSHE
time, period (i.e. the present age)		bad, evil	degenerate, dregs	end	at	reach, come	time, when

During this evil time at the end of the degenerate period

ནང་རེ་དགོངས་རེ་བོད་ཀྱི་དོན་ལ་བྱོན༔

NANG	RE	GONG	RE	BOE	KYI	DON	LA	JON
morning	each	evening	each	Tibet	of	benefit	for	coming

You come each morning and evening in order to benefit the beings of Tibet.[4]

ཉི་ཟེར་འཆར་སྡུད་མདངས་ལ་བཅིབས་ཏེ་འབྱོན༔

NYI	ZER	CHAR	DU	DANG	LA	CHIB	TE	JON
sun	rays	rising	setting	radiance	on	riding	thus	come

You come riding on the radiant rays of the rising and setting sun, and

ཡར་ངོའི་ཚེས་བཅུའི་དུས་སུ་དངོས་སུ་འབྱོན༔

YAR NGOI	TSHE CHUI	DU	SU	NGO SU	JON
waxing	tenth day	time	at	really, actually	come

On the tenth day of the waxing moon you show your actual presence.

འགྲོ་དོན་སྟོབས་ཆེན་མཛད་པའི་ཐུགས་རྗེ་ཅན༔

DRO	DON	TOB	CHEN	DZAE PAI	THU JE CHAN
beings	benefit	power, force	great	doing	compassionate one

You are the compassionate one who acts most strongly for the benefit of beings.

ཨོ་རྒྱན་པདྨ་འབྱུང་གནས་ལ་གསོལ་བ་འདེབས༔

UR GYAN   PAE MA   JUNG NAE   LA   SOL WA DE

We pray to Padmasambhava of Urgyan.

བསམ་པ་ལྷུན་གྱིས་འགྲུབ་པར་བྱིན་གྱིས་རློབས༔

SAM PA   LHUN GYI   DRU PAR   JIN GYI LO

Please bless us that our wishes may be fulfilled without effort!

During this evil time at the end of the degenerate period you come each morning and evening for the sake of those who have faith. You come riding on the radiant rays of the rising and setting sun and, on the tenth day of the waxing moon you show your presence. You are the compassionate one who acts most strongly for the benefit of beings. Padmasambhava of Urgyan, we pray to you — please bless us that our wishes may be easily fulfilled without effort!

ལྔ་བརྒྱ་ཐ་མ་རྩོད་དུས་སྙིགས་མ་ལ༔

NGAB GYA	THA MA		TSO	DU	NYIG MA	LA
five hundred	*final*		*fighting,*	*time*	*degenerate,*	*at*
(the final period of Buddha			*dispute*		*dregs, remnants*	
Shakyamuni's doctrines in this world)						

During the degenerate period of strife in the final five hundred years

སེམས་ཅན་ཐམས་ཅད་ཉོན་མོངས་དུག་ལྔ་རྟགས༔

SEM CHAN	THAM CHE	NYON MONG	DU	NGA	HRAG
sentient beings	*all*	*afflictions*	*poisons*	*five**	*hard, rough, tough*

**stupidity, anger, desire, jealousy and pride*

The five afflicting poisons will be very strong in all sentient beings.

ཉོན་མོངས་འཇོལ་ཉག་དུག་ལྔ་རང་རྒྱུད་སྤྱོད༔

NYON MONG	JOL NYA		DU	NGA	RANG GYU	CHO
afflictions	*mixed, compounded*		*poisons*	*five*	*own mind,*	*doing*
(each affliction being mixed with aspects of the others)					*character*	

These five poisons will work in many permutations within their minds, and

དེ་འདྲའི་དུས་ན་ཁྱེད་ཀྱི་ཐུགས་རྗེ་བསྐྱེད༔

DEN DRAI	DU	NA	KHYE KYI	THU JE	KYE
like that	*time*	*in, at*	*your*	*compassion*	*arise, develop, come out*

At such times your compassion will manifest.

དད་ལྡན་མཐོ་རིས་འདྲེན་པའི་ཕྱགས་རྗེ་ཅན༔

DAE DAN **THO RI** **DREN PAI** **THU JE CHAN**
faithful *heaven, three upper* *leading, guiding to* *compassionate one*
 (higher) realms

You are the compassionate one who leads the faithful to the upper realms.

ཨུ་རྒྱན་པདྨ་འབྱུང་གནས་ལ་གསོལ་བ་འདེབས༔

UR GYAN **PAE MA JUNG NAE** **LA** **SOL WA DE**

Padmasambhava of Urgyan we pray to you —

བསམ་པ་ལྷུན་གྱིས་གྲུབ་པར་བྱིན་གྱིས་རློབས༔

SAM PA **LHUN GYI DRU PAR** **JIN GYI LO**

Please bless us that our wishes may be fulfilled without effort!

During the degenerate period of strife in the final five hundred years, the five afflicting poisons will be very strong in all sentient beings. These five poisons will work in many permutations within their minds and, at such times, your compassion will manifest. You are the compassionate one who leads the faithful to the upper realms. Padmasambhava of Urgyan we pray to you — please bless us that our wishes may be fulfilled without effort!

ཧོར་དང་འཇིགས་པའི་དམག་གིས་མཐའ་བསྐོར་ནས༔

HOR **DANG** **JI PAI** **MA** **GI** **THA** **KOR** **NE**
Mongolian, *and* *frightful* *armies* *by* *border* *surround* *then*
barbarian,
anti-dharma

When the borders are surrounded by terrible and anti-dharma armies, and

ཆོས་འཁོར་གཉན་པོ་འཇིག་ལ་ཐུག་པའི་ཚེ༔

CHO KHOR **NYAN PO** **JI** **LA** **THUG PAI** **TSHE**
dharma teaching *important* *destroy,* *to* *reach, arrive* *time, when*
centres *disintegrate*

The important dharma centres are about to be destroyed

ཡིད་གཉིས་ཐེ་ཚོམ་མེད་པར་གསོལ་བ་ཐོབ༔

YI NYI **THE TSHOM** **ME PAR** **SOL WA THO**
two-minds, indecisive *doubt* *without* *must pray!*

We must pray without doubt or uncertainty!

ཨོ་རྒྱན་ལྷ་སྲིན་སྡེ་བརྒྱད་འཁོར་དང་བཅས༔

UR GYAN	LHA SIN	DE	GYE	KHOR	DANG CHE
Padmasambhava	*local gods and spirits*	*groups*	*eight*	*circle, retinue*	*together with*

For then you, Padmasambhava, will come with your circle of the eight groups of local spirits, and

དམག་དཔུང་ཧུར་ཐུམས་བ་ཟློག་པར་ཐེ་ཚོམ་མེད༔

MA	PUNG	HUR THUM	DOG PAR	THE TSHOM ME
army	*mass*	*quickly destroy, annihilate*	*repel, repulse*	*undoubtedly*

Definitely repulse and quickly destroy these warring hordes.

ཨོ་རྒྱན་པདྨ་འབྱུང་གནས་ལ་གསོལ་བ་འདེབས༔

UR GYAN	PAE MA JUNG NAE	LA	SOL WA DE

Padmasambhava of Urgyan we pray to you —

བསམ་པ་ལྷུན་གྱིས་གྲུབ་པར་བྱིན་གྱིས་རློབས༔

SAM PA	LHUN GYI DRU PAR	JIN GYI LO

Please bless us that our wishes may be fulfilled without effort!

When the borders are surrounded by terrible and anti-dharma armies and the important dharma centres are destroyed we must pray without doubt or uncertainty! For then you, Padmasambhava, will come with your circle of the eight groups of local spirits and definitely repulse and quickly destroy these warring hordes. Padmasambhava of Urgyan we pray to you — please bless us that our wishes may be fulfilled without effort!

སེམས་ཅན་སྒྱུ་ལུས་འཇིག་པའི་ནད་བྱུང་ནས༔

SEM CHAN	GYU LU	JI PAI	NAE	JUNG	NE
sentient beings	*temporary, insubstantial bodies*	*destroying*	*diseases, sickness*	*arise, appear*	*then*

When diseases arise which destroy the insubstantial bodies of sentient beings and

མི་བཟད་སྡུག་བསྔལ་ཆེན་པོས་ནོན་པའི་ཚེ༔

MI DZAE	DU NGAL	CHEN POE	NON POI	TSHE
unbearable	*misery*	*by great*	*oppressed, coerced*	*when*

We are oppressed by unbearable great misery

ཡིད་གཉིས་ཐེ་ཚོམ་མེད་པར་གསོལ་བ་ཐོབ༔

YI NYI THE TSHOM ME PAR SOL WA THO
We must pray without doubt or uncertainty!

ཨུ་རྒྱན་སྨན་གྱི་བླ་དང་དབྱེར་མེད་པས༔

UR GYAN	MEN GYI LA		DANG	YER ME	PAE
Padma Sambhava	Bhaishajya Guru, the Buddha who presides over medicines and healing		and	not different	therefore

For then you, Padmasambhava who are one with the Buddha of Medicine,

ཚེ་ཟད་མ་ཡིན་བར་ཆད་ངེས་པར་སེལ༔

TSHE	ZAE	MA YIN	BAR CHAE	NGE PAR	SEL
life	finished (i.e. before the maximum span possible for one's karma)	not	obstacles (murder, accident, plague etc.)	certainly, really	dispel, remove

Will most certainly dispel all the obstacles that create untimely death.

ཨུ་རྒྱན་པད་འབྱུང་གནས་ལ་གསོལ་བ་འདེབས༔

UR GYAN PAE MA JUNG NAE LA SOL WA DE
Padmasambhava of Urgyan we pray to you —

བསམ་པ་ལྷུན་གྱིས་གྲུབ་པར་བྱིན་གྱིས་རློབས༔

SAM PA LHUN GYI DRU PAR JIN GYI LO
Please bless us that our wishes may be fulfilled without effort!

When diseases arise which destroy our insubstantial bodies and we sentient beings are oppressed by unbearable great misery we must pray without doubt or uncertainty! For then you, Padmasambhava who are one with the Buddha of Medicine, will most certainly dispel all the obstacles that create untimely death. Padmasambhava of Urgyan we pray to you — please bless us that our wishes may be fulfilled without effort!

འབྱུང་བ་དགྲར་ལངས་ས་བཅུད་ཉམས་པའི་ཚེ༔

JUNG WA	DRAR	LANG	SA	CHU	NYAM PAI	TSHE
elements*	as enemies#	arise	land, earth	essence, nutritive power	losing, declining	when

*earth, water, fire, air and space
i.e. acting against the interests of beings

When the elements behave as enemies and the land loses its fertility

སེམས་ཅན་མུ་གེའི་ནད་ཀྱིས་གཟིར་བ་ན༔

SEM CHAN   **MU GEI**   **NAE**   **KYI**   **ZIR WA**   **NA**
sentient beings   *famine's*   *diseases*   *by*   *oppressed,*   *if, when*
                             (hunger and the diseases   *tormented*
                             consequent upon it)

Sentient beings are tormented by the diseases of famine so

ཡིད་གཉིས་ཐེ་ཚོམ་མེད་པར་གསོལ་བ་ཐོབ༔

YI NYI   **THE TSHOM**   **ME PAR**   **SOL WA THO**

We must pray without doubt or uncertainty!

ཨུ་རྒྱན་མཁའ་འགྲོ་ནོར་ལྷའི་ཚོགས་དང་བཅས༔

UR GYAN   **KHAN DRO**   **NOR LHAI**   **TSHO**   **DANG CHE**
Padmasambhava   *dakini*   *wealth gods*   *hosts*   *together with*

For the you, Padmasambhava, will come with your hosts of dakinis and wealth gods and

དབུལ་ཕོངས་བཀྲེས་སྐོམ་སེལ་བར་ཐེ་ཚོམ་མེད༔

UL PHONG   **TRE**   **KOM**   **SEL WAR**   **THE TSHOM ME**
poverty   *hunger*   *thirst*   *dispel*   *undoubtedly*

Most certainly remove all poverty, hunger and thirst.

ཨུ་རྒྱན་པདྨ་འབྱུང་གནས་ལ་གསོལ་བ་འདེབས༔

UR GYAN   **PAE MA JUNG NAE**   **LA**   **SOL WA DE**

Padmasambhava of Urgyan we pray to you —

བསམ་པ་ལྷུན་གྱིས་གྲུབ་པར་བྱིན་གྱིས་རློབས༔

SAM PA   **LHUN GYI DRU PAR**   **JIN GYI LO**

Please bless us that our wishes may be fulfilled without effort!

Sentient beings are tormented by the diseases of famine so when the elements behave as enemies and the land loses its fertility we must pray without doubt or uncertainty! For then you, Padmasambhava, will come with your hosts of dakinis and wealth gods and most certainly remove all poverty, hunger and thirst. Padmasambhava of Urgyan, we pray to you — please bless us that our wishes may be fulfilled without effort!

ལས་ཅན་འགྲོ་བའི་དོན་དུ་གཏེར་འདོན་ན༔

LAE CHAN	DRO WAI	DON DU	TER	DON	NA
fortunate (those having the good karma necessary for following the dharma)	beings	for the sake of	treasure (gTer-Chos doctrines etc.)	take out	when

When we fortunate ones reveal treasures for the sake of beings,

དམ་ཚིག་ཟོལ་ཟོག་མེད་པའི་དཔའ་གདེང་གིས༔

DAM TSHI	ZOL ZO	ME PAI	PA	DENG	GI
tantric vows	break, deceive, cheat	without	energy (i.e. happy and diligent)	confidence	therefore

We need the energy and confidence of having never cheated in our tantric vows, so

ཡིད་གཉིས་ཐེ་ཚོམ་མེད་པར་གསོལ་བ་ཐོབ༔

YI NYI   THE TSHOM   ME PAR   SOL WA THO

We must pray without doubt of uncertainty!

ཨུ་རྒྱན་ཡི་དམ་ལྷ་ཡི་ཚོགས་དང་བཅས༔

UR GYAN	YI DAM	LHA	YI	TSHO	DANG CHE
Padmasambhava	transforming gods	of		hosts	together with

Then you, Padmasambhava, will come with your hosts of transforming gods and

ཕ་ནོར་བུ་ཡི་ལོན་པར་ཐེ་ཚོམ་མེད༔

PHA	NOR	BU	YI	LON PAR	THE TSHOM ME
father (Guru Padmasambhava)	wealth*	son, disciples	by	get	undoubtedly

*i.e the treasure doctrines

We, your disciples, will most certainly gain your wealth.

ཨུ་རྒྱན་པདྨ་འབྱུང་གནས་ལ་གསོལ་བ་འདེབས༔

UR GYAN   PAE MA JUNG NAE   LA   SOL WA DE

Padmasambhava of Urgyan we pray to you —

བསམ་པ་ལྷུན་གྱིས་གྲུབ་པར་བྱིན་གྱིས་རློབས༔

SAM PA   LHUN GYI DRU PAR   JIN GYI LO

Please bless us that our wishes may be fulfilled without effort!

When we fortunate ones reveal treasures for the sake of beings we need the energy and confidence of never having cheated in our tantric vows, so we must pray without doubt or uncertainty! Then you, Padmasambhava, will come with your hosts of transforming gods and we, your disciples, will most certainly gain your wealth. Padmasambhava of Urgyan, we pray to you — please bless us that our wishes may be fulfilled without effort!

སྦས་ཡུལ་ནགས་རོང་དབེན་ས་སྒྲུག་པའི་ཚེ༔

BAE YUL	NAG RONG	WEN SA	NYOG PAI	TSHE
secret land (*uninhabited valleys etc.*)	*forests*	*isolated, quiet place for meditation*	*going there, travelling in*	*when*

When we travel in secret lands and forests to practise in isolation

ཁ་བ་བུ་ཡུག་འཚུབས་ཤིང་ལམ་འགགས་ན༔

KHA WA	BU YU	TSHUB SHING	LAM	GAG	NA
snow	*snow storm, blizzard*	*trapped, smothered blinded*	*path, road*	*blocked, closed*	*when, if*

If our way is blocked and we are trapped by snow and blizzards

ཡི་གཉིས་ཐེ་ཚོམ་མེད་པར་གསོལ་བ་ཐོབ༔

YI NYI	THE TSHOM	ME PAR	SOL WA THO

We must pray without doubt or uncertainty!

ཨུ་རྒྱན་གཞི་བདག་གཉན་པོའི་འཁོར་བཅས་ནས༔

UR GYAN	ZHI DA	NYAN POI	KHOR	CHE	NE
Padmasambhava	*local 'earth-lord' gods*	*important, powerful*	*circle*	*together*	*then*
	(*the gods and spirits presiding over the locality*)				

For then you, Padmasambhava, will come with your circle of powerful lords of the land and

ཆོས་མཛད་ལམ་སྣ་འདྲེན་པར་ཐེ་ཚོམ་མེད༔

CHO	DZAE	LAM	NA DREN PAR	THE TSHOM ME
dharma	*practitioners*	*path*	*leader, guide*	*undoubtedly*

We dharma followers w ill most certainly be led on to the right path.

ཨུ་རྒྱན་པདྨ་འབྱུང་གནས་ལ་གསོལ་བ་འདེབས༔

UR GYAN	PAE MA JUNG NAE	LA	SOL WA DE

Padmasambhava of Urgyan we pray to you —

བསམ་པ་ལྷུན་གྱིས་གྲུབ་པར་བྱིན་གྱིས་རློབས༔

SAM PA	LHUN GYI DRU PAR	JIN GYI LO

Please bless us that our wishes may be fulfilled without effort!

When we travel in secret lands and forests to practise in isolation, if our way is blocked and we are trapped by snow and blizzards, we must pray without doubt or uncertainty! For then you, Padmasambhava,

*will come with your circle of powerful lords of the land and we dharma
followers will most certainly be led on to the right path. Padmasambhava
of Urgyan, we pray to you — please bless us that our wishes may be
fulfilled without effort!*

སྟག་གཟིག་དོམ་དྲེད་དུག་སྦྲུལ་མཆེ་བ་ཅན༔

TA	ZI	DOM	DRE		DU DRUL	CHE WA CHAN
tiger	*leopard*	*bear*	*Tibetan snow bear*		*poisonous snakes*	*animals with fangs*

When tigers, leopards, bears, snow-bears, poisonous snakes and other
dangerous animals surround us

འབྲོག་ཆེན་འཇིགས་པའི་འཕྲང་ལ་འགྲིམས་པའི་ཚེ༔

DRO	CHEN	JI PAI	TRANG	LA	DRIM PAI	TSHE
wilderness, wild solitude	*great*	*frightening*	*narrow passage, difficult path*	*in*	*travelling, passing through*	*when*

As we travel in the great wildernesses and on frightening, perilous
trails

ཡིད་གཉིས་ཐེ་ཚོམ་མེད་པར་གསོལ་བ་ཐོབ༔

YI NYI   THE TSHOM   ME PAR   SOL WA THO

We must pray without doubt or uncertainty!

ཨུ་རྒྱན་དཔའ་བོ་གིང་དང་སྲུང་མར་བཅས༔

UR GYAN	PA WO	GING	DANG	SUNG MAR	CHE
Padmasambhava	*viras, heroes*	*agents*	*and*	*dharma guardians*	*with*

For then you, Padmasambhava, will come with the pawo, ging and
dharma-guardians and

གདུག་པའི་སེམས་ཅན་སྐྲོད་པར་ཐེ་ཚོམ་མེད༔

DU PAI	SEM CHAN	TROE PAR	THE TSHOM ME
evil, harmful	*beings*	*expel, drive out*	*undoubtedly*

Most certainly drive off all harmful creatures.

ཨུ་རྒྱན་པདྨ་འབྱུང་གནས་ལ་གསོལ་བ་འདེབས༔

UR GYAN   PAE MA JUNG NAE   LA   SOL WA DE

Padmasambhava of Urgyan we pray to you —

བསམ་པ་ལྷུན་གྱིས་གྲུབ་པར་བྱིན་གྱིས་རློབས༔

SAM PA   LHUN GYI DRU PAR   JIN GYI LO

Please bless us that our wishes may be fulfilled without effort!

When tigers, leopards, bears, snow-bears, poisonous snakes and other dangerous animals surround us as we travel in the great wildernesses and on frightening, perilous trails, we must pray without doubt or uncertainty! For then you, Padmasambhava, will come with pawo, ging and dharma-guardians and most certainly drive off all harmful creatures. Padmasambhava of Urgyan, we pray to you — please bless us that our wishes may be fulfilled without effort!

ས་ཆུ་མེ་རླུང་འབྱུང་བའི་བར་ཆད་ཀྱིས༔

SA **CHU** **ME** **LUNG** **JUNG WAI** **BAR CHAE** **KYI**
earth *water* *fire* *wind* *elements* *obstacles, troubles* *by*

When the elements, earth, water, fire and air create obstacles

སྒྱུ་ལུས་ཉེན་ཞིང་འཇིག་པའི་དུས་བྱུང་ན༔

GYU LU **NYEN ZHING** **JI PAI** **DU** **JUNG** **NA**
temporary body *dangerous for* *destroying* *time* *arising* *if, when*

That are dangerous for our insubstantial bodies and threaten to destroy them

ཡིད་གཉིས་ཐེ་ཚོམ་མེད་པར་གསོལ་བ་ཐོབ༔

YI NYI **THE TSHOM** **ME PAR** **SOL WA THO**

We must pray without doubt or uncertainty!

ཨུ་རྒྱན་དཔའ་བོ་གྱད་དང་ལྷན་པ་ཡིས༔

UR GYAN **PA WO** **GYAE DANG DAN PA** **YI**
Padmasambhava *viras, heroes* *powerful fighters, champions* *by*

For then you, Padmasambhava, with your champion heroes

འབྱུང་བ་རང་སར་ཞི་བར་ཐེ་ཚོམ་མེད༔

JUNG WA **RANG SAR** **ZHI WAR** **THE TSHOM ME**
elements *in own place* *pacified* *undoubtedly*

Will most certainly cause the elements to be pacified where they are.

ཨུ་རྒྱན་པདྨ་འབྱུང་གནས་ལ་གསོལ་བ་འདེབས༔

UR GYAN **PAE MA JUNG NAE** **LA** **SOL WA DE**

Padmasambhava of Urgyan we pray to you —

བསམ་པ་ལྷུན་གྱིས་འགྲུབ་པར་བྱིན་གྱིས་རློབས༔

SAM PA **LHUN GYI DRU PAR** **JIN GYI LO**

Please bless us that our wishes may be fulfilled without effort!

When the elements, earth, water, fire and air, create obstacles that are

dangerous for our insubstantial bodies and threaten to destroy them, we must pray without doubt or uncertainty! For then you, Padmasambhava, with your champion heroes will most certainly cause the elements to be pacified where they are. Padmasambhava of Urgyan, we pray to you — please bless us that our wishes may be fulfilled without effort!

ལམ་སྲང་འཇིགས་པའི་འཕྲང་ལ་འགྲིམ་པའི་ཚེ༔

LAM SANG	JI PAI	TRANG		LA	DRIM PAI	TSHE
dangerous	*frightening*	*narrow passage, defile*		*on*	*travelling*	*when*

When we travel on dangerous tracks and frightening perilous trails

བསད་ཁྱེར་རྐག་པ་ཆོམས་པོས་ཉེན་པ་ན༔

SAE	KHYER	JAG PAI	CHOM POE		NYEN PA	NA
killed	*steal*	*robber*	*theft*		*troubled by*	*if, when*

If we are in danger from murderers, robbers and thieves

ཡིད་གཉིས་ཐེ་ཚོམ་མེད་པར་གསོལ་བ་ཐོབ༔

YI NYI	THE TSHOM	ME PAR	SOL WA THO

We must pray without doubt or uncertainty!

ཨུ་རྒྱན་ཕྱག་རྒྱ་བཞི་ཡི་དགོངས་པར་ལྡན༔

UR GYAN		CHA GYA	ZHI	YI		GONG PAR	DAN
Padmasambhava		*mudras*	*four*	*of*		*vision,*	*have*
			(to bring the trouble-makers under his power)			*wisdom*	

For then you, Padmasambhava, with the wisdom of the four mudras

ཙོར་མི་རྐོད་རྫས་སེམས་བརྩག་པར་བྱེད༔

TSO RA	MI GOE		NGAM SEM	LAG PAR	JE
thief	*yeti, wild people*		*bad, rough mind*	*destroy*	*do*

Will destroy the thieves, yeti and bad-minded people.

ཨུ་རྒྱན་པདྨ་འབྱུང་གནས་ལ་གསོལ་བ་འདེབས༔

UR GYAN	PAE MA JUNG NAE	LA	SOL WA DE

Padmasambhava of Urgyan we pray to you —

བསམ་པ་ལྷུན་གྱིས་གྲུབ་པར་བྱིན་གྱིས་རློབས༔

SAM PA	LHUN GYI DRU PAR	JIN GYI LO

Please bless us that our wishes may be fulfilled without effort!

When we travel on dangerous tracks and frightening perilous trails, if we are in danger from murderers, robbers and thieves, we must pray without doubt or uncertainty! For then you, Padmasambhava, will destroy the thieves, yeti and bad-minded people with the wisdom of the

four mudras. Padmasambhava of Urgyan, we pray to you — please bless us that our wishes may be fulfilled without effort!

གང་ཞིག་གཤེད་མའི་དམག་གིས་མཐའ་བསྐོར་ནས༔

GANG ZHI	SHE MAI	MA	GI	THA KOR	NE
somebody, whoever	*thugs, dangerous killers*	*armies*	*by*	*surrounded*	*then*

If we are surrounded by armies of dangerous killers and

མཚོན་ཆ་རྣོན་པོས་འདེབས་ཤིང་ཉེན་པ་ན༔

TSHON CHA	NON POE	DE SHING	NYEN PA	NA
weapons	*sharp*	*beating, hit*	*danger*	*if, when*

We are in danger of being beaten with sharp weapons

ཡིད་གཉིས་ཐེ་ཚོམ་མེད་པར་གསོལ་བ་ཐོབ༔

YI NYI	THE TSHOM	ME PAR	SOL WA THO

We must pray without doubt or uncertainty!

ཨུ་རྒྱན་རྡོ་རྗེའི་གུར་དང་ལྡན་པ་ཡིས༔

UR GYAN		DOR JEI	GUR	DANG DAN PA	YI
Padmasambhava		*vajra*	*tent*	*having*	*by*

For then you, Padmasambhava, with your vajra tent

གཤེད་མ་བྲེད་ཅིང་མཚོན་ཆ་འཐོར་པར་འགྱུར༔

SHE MA	DRE CHING		TSHON CHA	THOR PAR	GYUR
thugs	*frightened, alarmed, depressed*		*weapon*	*throw away, abandon*	*become*

Will frighten the thugs and make them throw down their weapons.

ཨུ་རྒྱན་པདྨ་འབྱུང་གནས་ལ་གསོལ་བ་འདེབས༔

UR GYAN	PAE MA JUNG NAE	LA	SOL WA DE

Padmasambhava of Urgyan we pray to you —

བསམ་པ་ལྷུན་གྱིས་གྲུབ་པར་བྱིན་གྱིས་རློབས༔

SAM PA	LHUN GYI DRU PAR	JIN GYI LO

Please bless us that our wishes may be fulfilled without effort!

If we are surrounded by dangerous killers and we are in danger of being beaten by sharp weapons, we must pray without doubt or uncertainty! For then you, Padmasambhava, will frighten the thugs and make them throw down their weapons with your vajra tent. Padmasambhava of Urgyan, we pray to you — please bless us that our wishes may be fulfilled without effort!!

ནམ་ཞིག་ཚེ་ཟད་འཆི་བའི་དུས་བྱུང་ཚེ༔

NAM ZHI   TSHE   ZAE   CHI WAI   DU   JUNG   TSHE
when   life   finish   dying   time   comes   when

When our lives are ending and the time of death approaches

གནད་གཅོད་སྡུག་བསྔལ་དྲག་པོས་ཉེན་པ་ན༔

NAE CHO   DU NGAL   DRA POE   NYEN PA   NA
fatal illness   misery   by terrible   troubled   if, when
(doctors cannot cure it)

If we are troubled by the terrible sufferings of a fatal illness

ཡིད་གཉིས་ཐེ་ཚོམ་མེད་པར་གསོལ་བ་འདེབས༔

YI NYI   THE TSHOM   ME PAR   SOL WA THO

We must pray without doubt or uncertainty!

ཨོ་རྒྱན་སྣང་བ་མཐའ་ཡས་སྤྲུལ་པ་སྟེ༔

UR GYAN   NANG WA THA YAE   TRUL PA   TE
Padmasambhava   Amitabha   emanation   so

For you, Padmasambhava, are Amitabha's emanation and so

བདེ་བ་ཅན་གྱི་ཞིང་དུ་ངེས་པར་སྐྱེ༔

DE WA CHAN   GYI   ZHING   DU   NGE PAR   KYE
Sukhavati, 'happy'   of   realm   in   certainly, definitely   born

We will certainly be born in the realm of Dewachen.

ཨོ་རྒྱན་པདྨ་འབྱུང་གནས་ལ་གསོལ་བ་འདེབས༔

UR GYAN   PAE MA JUNG NAE   LA   SOL WA DE

Padmasambhava of Urgyan we pray to you —

བསམ་པ་ལྷུན་གྱིས་གྲུབ་པར་བྱིན་གྱིས་རློབས༔

SAM PA   LHUN GYI DRU PAR   JIN GYI LO

Please bless us that our wishes may be fulfilled without effort!

If, when our lives are ending and the tine of death approaches, we are troubled by the terrible sufferings of a fatal illness, we must pray without doubt and uncertainty! For you, Padmasambhava, are Amitabha's emanation, and so we will certainly be born in the realm of Dewachen. Padmasambhava of Urgyan, we pray to you — please bless us that our wishes may be fulfilled without effort!

སྒྱུ་ལུས་གཡར་པོ་ཞིག་པའི་བར་དོ་རུཿ

GYU LU	YAR PO	ZHIG PAI	BAR DO	RU
temporary body, mortal form	borrowed (from 4 elements)	destroyed	intermediate period between death and rebirth	in

When we enter the bardo after the destruction of our borrowed mortal form

འཁྲུལ་སྣང་ཉིང་འཁྲུལ་ཆེན་པོས་ཉེན་པ་ནཿ

TRUL NANG	NYING TRUL	CHEN PO	NYEN PA	NA
deceptive, confusing appearances	more deceptive, extra bewildering*	by great	troubled	if, when

*i.e. worse than when we were alive

If we are troubled by the most bewildering deceptive appearances

ཡིད་གཉིས་ཐེ་ཚོམ་མེད་པར་གསོལ་བ་ཐོབཿ

YI NYI	THE TSHOM	ME PAR	SOL WA THO

We must pray without doubt or uncertainty!

ཨུ་རྒྱན་དུས་གསུམ་མཁྱེན་པའི་ཐུགས་རྗེ་ཡིསཿ

UR GYAN	DU	SUM	KHYEN PAI	THU JE	YI
Padmasambhava	times	three	knowing	compassion	by

For then you, Padmasambhava omniscient in the three times, with your compassion

འཁྲུལ་སྣང་རང་སར་གྲོལ་བར་ཐེ་ཚོམ་མེདཿ

TRUL NANG	RANG	SAR	DROL WA	THE TSHOM ME
confusing appearances (of bardo)	own	place	liberate	undoubtedly

Will most definitely cause all confusing appearances to be liberated in their own place.

ཨུ་རྒྱན་པདྨ་འབྱུང་གནས་ལ་གསོལ་བ་འདེབསཿ

UR GYAN	PAE MA JUNG NAE	LA	SOL WA DE

Padmasambhava of Urgyan we pray to you —

བསམ་པ་ལྷུན་གྱིས་འགྲུབ་པར་བྱིན་གྱིས་རློབསཿ

SAM PA	LHUN GYI DRU PAR	JIN GYI LO

Please bless us that our wishes may be fulfilled without effort!

If we are troubled by the most bewildering forms of deceptive appearances when we enter the bardo after the destruction of our borrowed mortal form, we must pray without doubt or uncertainty! For then you,

Padmasambhava, omniscient in the three times, with your compassion will most definitely cause all confusing appearances to be liberated in their own place. Padmasambhava of Urgyan, we pray to you — please bless us that our wishes may be fulfilled without effort!

གཞན་ཡང་ལས་དང་རྐྱེན་གྱི་དབང་གྱུར་ཏེ༔

ZHAN YANG	LAE	DANG	KYEN	GYI	WANG	GYUR TE
moreover	*actions*	*and*	*situations, conditions*	*of*	*power*	*due to, developing*
			(having gone under the power of)			

Moreover, if due to the power of karma and conditions

འཁྲུལ་སྣང་དངོས་པོར་ཞེན་ཅིང་སྡུག་བསྔལ་ན༔

TRUL NANG		NGO POR	ZHEN CHING	DU NGAL	NA
confusing appearances, the false experiences of ignorance		*as entities*	*desiring, wanting attachment*	*misery*	*if*

We suffer because of taking the confusing appearances we project to be real

ཡིད་གཉིས་ཐེ་ཚོམ་མེད་པར་གསོལ་བ་ཐོབ༔

YI NYI	THE TSHOM	ME PAR	SOL WA THO

We must pray without doubt or uncertainty!

ཨུ་རྒྱན་བདེ་ཆེན་རྒྱལ་པོའི་ངོ་བོ་སྟེ༔

UR GYAN	DE CHEN	GYAL POI	NGO WO	TE
Padmasambhava	*very happy*	*king*	*nature*	*thus, then*
		(he is free of all the ignorant confusion that creates sorrow)		

For you, Padmasambhava, have the nature of the king of great happiness and

འཁྲུལ་སྣང་སྡུག་བསྔལ་རྩད་ནས་བཤིག་པར་བྱེད༔

TRUL	NANG	DU NGAL	TSAE	NE	SHIG PAR	JE
confusing	*appearances*	*misery*	*root*	*from*	*destroy*	*do*
			(i.e.totally)			

Will totally destroy the misery of confusing appearances.

ཨུ་རྒྱན་པདྨ་འབྱུང་གནས་ལ་གསོལ་བ་འདེབས༔

UR GYAN	PAE MA JUNG NAE	LA	SOL WA DE

Padmasambhava of Urgyan we pray to you —

བསམ་པ་ལྷུན་གྱིས་འགྲུབ་པར་བྱིན་གྱིས་རློབས༔

SAM PA	LHUN GYI DRU PAR	JIN GYI LO

Please bless us that our wishes may be fulfilled without effort!

Moreover, if due to the power of karma and conditions we suffer because of taking the confusing appearances we project to be real, we must pray without doubt or uncertainty! For you, Padmasambhava, have the nature of the king of great happiness and will totally destroy the misery of confusing appearances. Padmasambhava of Urgyan, we pray to you — please bless us that our wishes may be fulfilled without effort!

འགྲོ་དྲུག་སྡུག་བསྔལ་ཆེན་པོས་ཉེན་པ་དང་༔

DRO DRU		DU NGAL	CHEN POE	NYEN PA	DANG
beings in six realms		*misery*	*by great*	*troubled*	*and*

When the beings in the six realms are troubled by great misery and

ཁྱད་པར་བོད་ཀྱི་རྗེ་འབངས་སྡུག་བསྔལ་ན༔

KHYE PAR	BOE	KYI	JE	BANG	DU NGAL	NA
especially	*Tibet*	*of*	*king*	*subjects*	*misery*	*when*

Especially when the king and people of Tibet are suffering[5]

ཡིད་གཉིས་ཐེ་ཚོམ་མེད་པར་གསོལ་བ་ཐོབ༔

YI NYI	THE TSHOM	ME PAR	SOL WA THO

We must pray without doubt and uncertainty!

དད་གུས་མོས་པས་གདུང་བས་གསོལ་འདེབས་ན༔

DAE	GU	MOE PAE	DUNG WAE	SOL DE	NA
faith	*respect*	*with devotion*	*with real love and deep feeling*	*pray*	*if, when*

For if we pray with genuine loving faith and devotion

ཨུ་རྒྱན་ཐུགས་རྗེས་འཕོ་འགྱུར་མེད་པར་གཟིགས༔

UR GYAN		THU JE	PHO GYUR ME PAR	ZI
Padmasambhava		*compassion*	*unchanging, constant*	*looks, sees and acts*

You, Padmasambhava, will look on us all with your constant compassion.

ཨུ་རྒྱན་པདྨ་འབྱུང་གནས་ལ་གསོལ་བ་འདེབས༔

UR GYAN	PAE MA JUNG NAE	LA	SOL WA DE

Padmasambhava of Urgyan we pray to you —

བསམ་པ་ལྷུན་གྱིས་གྲུབ་པར་བྱིན་གྱིས་རློབས༔

SAM PA	LHUN GYI DRU PAR	JIN GYI LO

Please bless us that our wishes may be fulfilled without effort!

When the beings in the six realms are troubled by great misery and especially when the king and people of Tibet are suffering, we must pray without doubt or uncertainty! For if we pray with genuine loving

faith and devotion you, Padmasambhava, will look on us all with your constant compassion. Padmasambhava or Urgyan, we pray to you — please bless us that our wishes may be fulfilled without effort!

Notes

1.   Alternative readings for non-Tibetans by C. R. Lama:

Page 113 Line 4

འཛམ་གླིང་འགྲོ་དྲུག་སེམས་ཅན་དོན་ལ་དགོངས༔

DZAM LING	DRO	DRU	SEM CHAN	DON	LA	GONG
world	beings	six (realms)	sentient beings	benefit	for	thought, consideration

All the beings in the six realms of the world with your intention for their welfare.

2.   Page 114 line 5 and 6

བོད་སོགས་ཆོས་སྒྲུད་ཡུལ་གྱི་གཉེན་གཅིག་པོ༔

BOE SOE	CHO	CHO	YUL	GYI	NYEN	CHI PO
Tibet etc.	dharma	practising	country	of	friend	only, sole

By you, the sole friend of Tibet and all the other countries where dharma is practised.

ཡུལ་ཁམས་ཆོས་སྒྲུད་སྐྱོབ་པའི་ཐུགས་རྗེ་ཅན༔

YUL KHAM	CHO	CHO	KYO PAI	THU JE CHAN
country	dharma	doing	protecting	compassionate one

You are the compassionate one who protects the lands where dharma is practised.

3.   Page 115 Line 3

ཐུགས་རྗེས་འགྲོ་དྲུག་སེམས་ཅན་དོན་ལ་དགོངས༔

THU JE	DRO	DRU	SEM CHAN	DON	LA	GONG
with compassion	beings	six realms	beings	benefit	to, for	intend

Yet with your compassion you attend to the welfare of all sentient beings.

4.   Page 116 Line 4

ནང་རེ་དགོངས་རེ་དད་ལྡན་དོན་ལ་བྱོན༔

NANG	RE	GONG	RE	DAE DAN	DON	LA	JON
morning	*each*	*evening*	*each*	*faithful*	*benefit*	*thus*	*come*

You come each morning and evening for the sake of those who have faith.

5.   Page 131 Line 2

ཁྱད་པར་བདག་སོགས་རྗེ་འབངས་སྡུག་བསྔལ་ན༔

KHYAE PAR	DA SO	JE	BANG	DU NGAL	NA
especially	*we*	*king*	*subject*	*misery*	*if, when*

Especially when our own rulers and people are suffering

གསོལ་འདེབས་བར་ཆད་ལམ་སེལ་ནི།

The Prayer Which Removes Obstacles From the Path

ༀ་ཨཱ༔ཧཱུྃ༔   བླ་མ་ལ་གསོལ་བ་འདེབས༔

OM   **Aa**   **HUNG**   **LA MA**   **LA**   **SOL WA DE**
body,   *speech,*   *mind,*   *Guru*   *to*   *pray*
nirmanakaya   *sambhogakaya*   *dharmakaya*

Om. Aa. Hung. Guru, we pray to you.

བླ་མ་ཆོས་ཀྱི་སྐུ་ལ་གསོལ་བ་འདེབས༔

LA MA   **CHO KYI KU**   **LA**   **SOL WA DE**
Guru   *dharmakaya*   *to*   *pray*

Dharmakaya Guru, we pray to you.

བླ་མ་ལ་གསོལ་བ་འདེབས༔

LA MA   **LA**   **SOL WA DE**
Guru   *to*   *pray*

Guru, we pray to you.

བླ་མ་ལོངས་སྤྱོད་རྫོགས་པའི་སྐུ་ལ་གསོལ་བ་འདེབས༔

LA MA   **LONG CHO DZO PAI KU**   **LA**   **SOL WA DE**
Guru   *sambhogakaya*   *to*   *pray*

Sambhogakaya Guru, we pray to you.

བླ་མ་ལ་གསོལ་བ་འདེབས༔

LA MA   **LA**   **SOL WA DE**
Guru   *to*   *pray*

Guru, we pray to you.

བླ་མ་སྤྲུལ་པའི་སྐུ་ལ་གསོལ་བ་འདེབས༔

LA MA   **TRUL PAI KU**   **LA**   **SOL WA DE**
Guru   *nirmanakaya*   *to*   *pray*

Nirmanakaya Guru, we pray to you.

བླ་མ་ལ་གསོལ་བ་འདེབས༔

LA MA   **LA**   **SOL WA DE**
Guru   *to*   *pray*

Guru, we pray to you.

མི་མཐུན་རྐྱེན་དང་བར་ཆད་སོལ༔

MI THUN	KYEN	DANG	BAR CHAE	SOL
difficult	*situations,*	*and*	*obstacles,*	*clear*
	circumstances		*interruptions*	

Please clear away all obstacles and difficult circumstances.

བླ་མ་ལ་གསོལ་བ་འདེབས༔

LA MA	LA	SOL WA DE
Guru	*to*	*pray*

Guru, we pray to you.

མཆོག་ཐུན་མོང་གཉིས་ཀྱི་དངོས་གྲུབ་སྩལ་དུ་གསོལ༔

CHO	THUN MONG	NYI	KYI	NGO DRU	TSAL	DU SOL
supreme	*general*	*both*	*of*	*attainments*	*grant*	*please*

Please grant us both supreme and general accomplishments.

Om. Aa. Hung. Guru, we pray to you. Dharmakaya Guru, we pray to you. Guru, we pray to you. Sambhogakaya Guru, we pray to you. Guru, we pray to you. Nirmanakaya Guru, we pray to you. Guru, we pray to you. Please clear away all obstacles and difficult circumstances. Guru, we pray to you. Please grant us both supreme and general accomplishments.

བླ་མ་གསང་འདུས་ལས་སོ།།

(These first lines given above come from the bLa-Ma gSang-'Dus.)

ༀ་ཨཱཿ་ཧཱུྃ༔

OM	Aa	HUNG
body,	*speech,*	*mind,*
nirmanakaya	*sambhogakaya*	*dharmakaya*

Om. Aa. Hung.

ཆོས་སྐུ་སྣང་བ་མཐའ་ཡས་ལ་གསོལ་བ་འདེབས༔

CHO KU	NANG WA THA YAE	LA	SOL WA DE
dharmakaya	*Amitabha,*	*to*	*pray*
	Limitless Light		

Dharmakaya Amitabha, we pray to you.

ལོངས་སྐུ་ཐུགས་རྗེ་ཆེན་པོ་ལ་གསོལ་བ་འདེབས༔

LONG KU	THU JE CHEN PO	LA	SOL WA DE
sambhogakaya	*Avalokitesvara, Chenrezi,*	*to*	*pray*
	Great Compasssion		

Sambhogakaya Avalokitesvara, we pray to you.

སྤྲུལ་སྐུ་པདྨ་འབྱུང་གནས་ལ་གསོལ་བ་འདེབས༔

TRUL KU   **PAE MA**   **JUNG NAE**   **LA**   **SOL WA DE**
nirmanakaya   *Padmasambhava*   *to*   *pray*

Nirmanakaya Padmasambhava, we pray to you.

བདག་གི་བླ་མ་ངོ་མཚར་སྤྲུལ་པའི་སྐུ༔

DA GI   **LA MA**   **NGO TSHAR**   **TRUL PAI KU**
my   *Guru*   *wonderful*   *nirmanakaya, emanation*
(Padmasambhava)

You, my Guru, are the wonderful emanation.

རྒྱ་གར་ཡུལ་དུ་སྐུ་འཁྲུངས་ཐོས་བསམ་མཛད༔

GYA GAR   **YUL**   **DU**   **KU TRUNG**   **THO**   **SAM**   **DZAE**
India   *country*   *in*   *born*   *hearing*   *reflecting*   *did*
(i.e.Oddiyana)   *(i.e. studied and practised)*

Born in the land of India, you studied and practised there, then

བོད་ཡུལ་དབུས་སུ་ཞལ་བྱོན་དྲེགས་པ་བཏུལ༔

BOE YUL   **WU**   **SU**   **ZHAL JON**   **DRE PA**   **TUL**
Tibet   *centre*   *in*   *came*   *rough local gods*   *tamed*

Came to the centre of Tibet and tamed the arrogant local gods.

ཨུ་རྒྱན་ཡུལ་དུ་སྐུ་བཞུགས་འགྲོ་དོན་མཛད༔

UR GYAN   **YUL**   **DU**   **KU ZHU**   **DRO**   **DON**   **DZAE**
Oddiyana   *country*   *in*   *stayed*   *being*   *benefit*   *did, made*

You stayed in the land of Urgyan and acted for the sake of beings.

Om. Aa. Hung. Dharmakaya Amitabha, we pray to you. Sambhogakaya Avalokitesvara, we pray to you. Nirmanakaya Padmasambhava, we pray to you. You, my Guru, are the wonderful emanation. Born in the land of India you studied and practised there, then came to the centre of Tibet and tamed the arrogant local gods. You stayed in the land of Urgyan and acted for the sake of beings.

སྐུ་ཡི་ངོ་མཚར་མཐོང་བའི་ཚེ༔

KU YI   **NGO TSHAR**   **THONG WAI**   **TSHE**
body   *wonderful*   *see*   *when*

When we see your wonderful form

གཡས་པས་རལ་གྲིའི་ཕྱག་རྒྱ་མཛད༔

YAE PAE   **RAL TRI**   **CHA GYA**   **DZAE**
right hand   *sword*   *mudra*   *doing*

Your right hand shows the sword mudra and

གཡོན་པས་འགུགས་པའི་ཕྱག་རྒྱ་མཛད༔

YON PA   **GUG PAI**   **CHA GYA**   **DZAE**
left   *summoning*   *mudra*   *doing*

Your left hand shows the summoning mudra.

ཞལ་བགྲད་མཆེ་གཙིགས་གྱེན་ལ་གཟིགས༔

ZHAL   **DRE**   **CHE**   **TSI**   **GYEN**   **LA**   **ZI**
face   *open*   *teeth*   *bared, showing*   *up*   *to*   *look (at sky)*

Your gaping mouth bares your teeth and you gaze upwards,

རྒྱལ་བའི་གདུང་འཛིན་འགྲོ་བའི་མགོན༔

GYAL WAI   **DUNG**   **DZIN**   **DRO WAI**   **GON**
victors'   *lineage*   *holder*   *beings*   *lord, benefactor*

You, the benefactor of beings who holds the Victors' lineage.

When we see your wonderful form your right hand shows the sword mudra and your left hand shows the summoning mudra. Your smiling face displays your teeth and you gaze upwards, you, the benefactor of beings who holds the Victors' lineage.

ཐུགས་རྗེས་བདག་ལ་བྱིན་གྱིས་རློབས༔

THU JE   **DA**   **LA**   **JIN GYI LO**
with compassion   *me*   *to*   *bless!*

With your compassion please bless us!

བརྩེ་བས་བདག་སོགས་ལམ་སྣ་དྲོངས༔

TSE WAE   **DA SO**   **LAM NA DRONG**
with love and compassion   *we*   *lead out (from samsara)*

Lead us to salvation with your loving care!

དགོངས་པས་བདག་ལ་དངོས་གྲུབ་སྩོལ༔

GONG PAE   **DA**   **LA**   **NGO DRUB**   **TSOL**
by your acuity, presence   *me*   *to*   *attainments*   *grant*

Grant us accomplishments with your presence!

ནུས་པས་བདག་སོགས་བར་ཆད་སོལ༔

NU PAE   **DA SO**   **BAR CHE**   **SOL**
by your power   *our*   *obstacles*   *remove, dispel*

Remove our obstacles with your power!

ཕྱི་ཡི་བར་ཆད་ཕྱི་རུ་སོལ༔

CHI YI	**BAR CHE**	**CHI RU**	**SOL**
outer	*obstacles*	*outside*	*clear*

Resolve outer obstacles where they are!

ནང་གི་བར་ཆད་ནང་དུ་སོལ༔

NANG GI	**BAR CHE**	**NANG DU**	**SOL**
inner	*obstacles*	*inside*	*clear*

Resolve inner obstacles where they are!

གསང་བའི་བར་ཆད་དབྱིངས་སུ་སོལ༔

SANG WAI	**BAR CHE**	**YING**	**SU**	**SOL**
secret, subtle	*obstacles*	*space*	*in*	*clear*

Resolve subtle obstacles in emptiness!

གུས་པས་ཕྱག་འཚལ་སྐྱབས་སུ་མཆི༔

GU PAE	**CHA TSHAL**	**KYAB**	**SU**	**CHI**
with devotion	*prostrate*	*refuge*	*for*	*go*

We prostrate with devotion and take refuge in you!

ཨོཾ་ཨཱཿཧཱུྃ་བཛྲ་གུ་རུ་པདྨ་སིདྡྷི་ཧཱུྃ༔

OM	**Aa**	**HUNG**	**BEN ZA**	**GU RU**	**PE MA**	**SID DHI**	**HUNG**
*body**	*speech#*	*mind+*	*vajra, indestructible*	*master*	*Padma Sambhava*	*attainments*	*give*

*nirmanakaya #sambhogakaya +dharmakaya

Guru Padmasambhava with the indestructible body, speech and mind — please grant us the accomplishment of buddhahood.

With your compassion please bless us! Lead us to salvation with your loving care! Grant us accomplishments with your presence! Remove our obstacles with your power! Resolve outer obstacles where they are! Resolve inner obstacles where they are! Resolve subtle obstacles in emptiness! We prostrate with devotion and take refuge in you. Guru Padmasambhava with the indestructible body, speech and mind – please grant us the accomplishment of buddhahood.

དམ་ཆོས་རིན་ཆེན་གསན་པའི་ཚེ༔

DAM	**CHO**	**RIN CHEN**	**SAN PAI**	**TSHE**
holy, sacred	*dharma*	*precious*	*heard, studied*	*when*

When you studied the precious holy dharma

སྐུ་གསལ་འོད་ཟེར་མདངས་དང་ལྡན༔

KU   SAL   WOE ZER   DANG   DANG DAN
body   shining   light rays   radiance   having

Your body was shining and radiant with rays of light.

ཕྱག་གཡས་སྡེ་སྣོད་གླེགས་བམ་བསྣམས༔

CHA   YAE   DE NOE   LEG BAM   NAM
hand   right   pitaka (chatur pitaka)   volumes   holding

Your right hand held the volumes of the Buddha's teachings

གཡོན་པས་ཕུར་པས་པུ་ཏི་བསྣམས༔

YON PAE   PHUR PAE   PU TI   NAM
left   Vajrakila   book   holding

Your left hand held the text of Vajrakila.

ཟབ་མོའི་ཆོས་རྣམས་ཐུགས་སུ་ཆུད༔

ZAB MOI   CHO NAM   THUG   SU   CHU
profound   doctrines   mind   in   put

You fully comprehended the profound doctrines,

ཡང་ལེ་ཤོད་ཀྱི་པཎྜི་ཏ༔

YANG LE SHO   KYI   PAN DI TA
name of a cave in Nepal   of   pandit, scholar.

You the scholar of Yangle Sho.

When you studied the precious holy dharma your body was shining and radiant with rays of light. Your right hand held the volumes of the Buddha's teachings and your left hand held the text of Vajrakila. You fully comprehended the profound doctrines, you, the scholar of Yangle Sho.

ཐུགས་རྗེས་བདག་ལ་བྱིན་གྱིས་རློབས༔

THU JE   DA   LA   JIN GYI LO

With your compassion please bless us!

བརྩེ་བས་བདག་སོགས་ལམ་སྣ་དྲོངས༔

TSE WAE   DA SO   LAM NA DRONG

Lead us to salvation with your loving care!

དགོངས་པས་བདག་ལ་དངོས་གྲུབ་སྩོལ༔

GONG PAE   DA LA   NGO DRUB   TSOL

Grant us accomplishments with your presence!

ནུས་པས་བདག་སོགས་བར་ཆད་སོལ༔

NU PAE   DA SO   BAR CHE   SOL

Remove our obstacles with your power!

ཕྱི་ཡི་བར་ཆད་ཕྱི་རུ་སོལ༔

CHI YI   BAR CHE   CHI RU   SOL

Resolve outer obstacles where they are!

ནང་གི་བར་ཆད་ནང་དུ་སོལ༔

NANG GI   BAR CHE   NANG DU   SOL

Resolve inner obstacles where they are!

གསང་བའི་བར་ཆད་དབྱིངས་སུ་སོལ༔

SANG WAI   BAR CHE   YING   SU   SOL

Resolve subtle obstacles in emptiness!

གུས་པས་ཕྱག་འཚལ་སྐྱབས་སུ་མཆི༔

GU PAE   CHA TSHAL   KYAB   SU   CHI

We prostrate with devotion and take refuge in you.

ཨོཾ་ཨཱཿཧཱུྃ་བཛྲ་གུ་རུ་པདྨ་སིདྡྷི་ཧཱུྃ༔

OM   Aa   HUNG   BEN ZA   GU RU   PE MA   SID DHI   HUNG

Guru Padmasambhava with the indestructible body, speech and mind
— please grant us the accomplishment of buddhahood.

With your compassion please bless us! Lead us to salvation with your loving care! Grant us accomplishments with your presence! Remove our obstacles with your power! Resolve outer obstacles where they are! Resolve inner obstacles where they are! Resolve subtle obstacles in emptiness! We prostrate with devotion and take refuge in you. Guru Padmasambhava with the indestructible body, speech and mind — please grant us the accomplishment of buddhahood.

དམ་ཅན་དམ་ལ་བཏགས་པའི་ཚེ༔

DAM CHAN   DAM   LA   TAG PAI   TSHE
vow-keepers   vows   in, under   put   when

When you put the local gods under vow

 དྲི་མེད་གནས་མཆོག་ཉམས་རེ་དགའ༔

DRI ME	NAE	CHO	NYAM	RE GA
stainless	*place*	*holy, excellent*	*feeling*	*very happy*

You were at the joyous stainless holy place

རྒྱ་གར་བོད་ཡུལ་ས་མཚམས་སུ༔

GYA GAR	BOE	YUL	SA TSHAM	SU
India	*Tibet*	*country (i.e. Nepal)*	*border*	*at*

On the border of India and Tibet

བྱིན་གྱིས་བརླབས་ནས་བྱོན་པའི་ཚེ༔

JIN GYI LAB	NE	JON PAI	TSHE
blessed	*then*	*come (to Tibet)*	*when*

Which you blessed before coming north.

When you put the local gods under vow you were at the joyous stainless holy place on the border of India and Tibet which you blessed before coming north.

དྲི་བསུང་སྤོས་དད་ལྡན་པའི་རི༔

DRI	SUNG	POE NGAE	DAN PAI	RI
smell	*good fragrance*	*powerful scent*	*having*	*hill*

At that hill fragrant with sweet scents

མེ་ཏོག་པད་མ་དགུན་ཡང་སྐྱེ༔

ME TOG	PAE ME	GUN	YANG	KYE
flower	*lotus*	*winter*	*also*	*blossom*

The lotus flowers blossom even in winter, there at

ཆུ་མིག་བྱང་ཆུབ་བདུད་རྩིའི་ཆུ༔

CHU MI	JANG CHU	DU TSI	CHU
spring	*bodhi, enlightenment (name of the spring)*	*amrita, liberating elixir*	*water*

That spring with the elixir water of enlightenment, the

བདེ་ལྡན་དེ་ཡི་གནས་མཆོག་ཏུ༔

DE DAN	DE YI	NAE	CHO	TU
happiness	*that*	*place*	*excellent*	*at*

Most excellent place of happiness.

On that hill fragrant with sweet scents the lotus flowers blossom even in winter at the spring with the elixir water of enlightenment, most excellent place of happiness.

སྐྱེས་མཆོག་ཚུལ་བཟང་ཆོས་གོས་གསོལ༔

KYE CHO	TSHUL	ZANG	CHO	GO	SOL
superior being, exalted one	system	good	dharma (i.e. bhikshu form)	robes	wearing

There you appeared in the pure style of a superior one wearing the dharma robes.

ཕྱག་གཡས་རྡོ་རྗེ་རྩེ་དགུ་བསྣམས༔

CHA	YAE	DOR JE	TSE	GU	NAM
hand	right	vajra	points	nine	holding

In your right hand you held a nine-pointed vajra and

གཡོན་པས་རིན་ཆེན་ཟ་མ་ཏོག༔

YON PAE	RIN CHEN	ZA MA TO
left	jewel, precious	casket for dharma implements

In your left a precious casket

རཀྟ་བདུད་རྩིས་ནང་དུ་གཏམས༔

RAK TA	DU TSI	NANG DU	TAM
blood	liberating elixir	inside	holding

Containing rakta and liberating elixir.

མཁའ་འགྲོ་དམ་ཅན་དམ་ལ་བཏགས༔

KHAN DRO	DAM CHAN	DAM	LA	TA
dakinis	vow-keepers (formerly wild local gods)	vows	in	put

You put the dakinis and local gods under vow, and

ཡི་དམ་ཞལ་གཟིགས་དངོས་གྲུབ་བརྙེས༔

YI DAM	ZHAL	ZI	NGO DRUB	NYE
path deity	face	saw	attainments	gained

Seeing the face of your path deity, you gained accomplishment.

There you appeared in the pure style of a superior one wearing the dharma robes. In your right hand you held a nine-pointed vajra and in your left a precious casket containing rakta and liberating elixir. You put the dakinis and local gods under vow, and seeing the face of your path deity, you gained accomplishment.

ཐུགས་རྗེས་བདག་ལ་བྱིན་གྱིས་རློབས༔

THU JE	DA	LA	JIN GYI LO

With your compassion please bless us!

བརྩེ་བས་བདག་སོགས་ལམ་སྣ་དྲོངས༔

TSE WAE   DA SO   LAM NA DRONG

Lead us to salvation with your loving care!

དགོངས་པས་བདག་ལ་དངོས་གྲུབ་སྩོལ༔

GONG PAE   DA LA   NGO DRUB   TSOL

Grant us accomplishments with your presence!

ནུས་པས་བདག་སོགས་བར་ཆད་སོལ༔

NU PAE   DA SO   BAR CHE   SOL

Remove our obstacles with your power!

ཕྱི་ཡི་བར་ཆད་ཕྱི་རུ་སོལ༔

CHI YI   BAR CHE   CHI RU   SOL

Resolve outer obstacles where they are!

ནང་གི་བར་ཆད་ནང་དུ་སོལ༔

NANG GI   BAR CHE   NANG DU   SOL

Resolve inner obstacles where they are!

གསང་བའི་བར་ཆད་དབྱིངས་སུ་སོལ༔

SANG WAI   BAR CHE   YING   SU   SOL

Resolve subtle obstacles in emptiness!

གུས་པས་ཕྱག་འཚལ་སྐྱབས་སུ་མཆི༔

GU PAE   CHA TSHAL   KYAB   SU   CHI

We prostrate with devotion and take refuge in you.

ཨོཾ་ཨཱཿཧཱུྃ་བཛྲ་གུ་རུ་པདྨ་སིདྡྷི་ཧཱུྃ༔

OM   Aa   HUNG   BEN ZA   GU RU   PE MA   SID DHI   HUNG

Guru Padmasambhava with the indestructible body, speech and mind
— please grant us the accomplishment of buddhahood.

With your compassion please bless us! Lead us to salvation with your loving care! Grant us accomplishments with your presence! Remove our obstacles with your power! Resolve outer obstacles where they are! Resolve inner obstacles where they are! Resolve subtle obstacles in emptiness! We prostrate with devotion and take refuge in you. Guru Padmasambhava with the indestructible body, speech and mind — please grant us the accomplishment of buddhahood.

ক্রুল་བའི་བསྟན་པ་བཙུགས་པའི་ཚེ༔

GYAL WAI	TAN PA	TSUG PAI	TSHE
jina, victor	*doctrines*	*plant (in Tibet)*	*time*

When you were establishing the jina's doctrines

གཡའ་རིའི་ནགས་ལ་སྒྲུབ་པ་མཛད

YA RI	NAG	LA	DRU PA	DZAE
(Yama Long)	*forest*	*in*	*practice*	*did*

You performed practice in the forest of Ya Ri, and

བསྙེན་ཕུར་ནམ་མཁའི་མཐོངས་སུ་འཕངས༔

NYEN	PHUR	NAM KHAI	THONG	SU	PHANG
recitation	*kila, spike*	*sky*	*expanse*	*in*	*throw*

Throwing your mantra nail into the open sky

རྡོ་རྗེའི་ཕྱག་རྒྱས་བླངས་ཞིང་བསྒྲིལ༔

DOR JEI	CHA GYAE	LANG SHING	DRIL
vajra	*mudra*	*caught again*	*rolled back and forth*

You caught it with the vajra mudra and rolled it between your hands.

When you were establishing the jina's doctrines, you performed practice in the forest of Ya Ri, and throwing your mantra nail into the open sky you caught it with the vajra mudra and rolled it between your hands.

བསྒྲིལ་ཞིང་ཙན་དན་ནགས་སུ་འཕངས༔

DRIL ZHING	TSAN DAN	NAG	SU	PHANG
rolling	*a kind of red sandalwood*	*forest*	*into*	*throw*

You rolled the phurpa and threw it into the forest of sandalwood

མེ་འབར་འཁྲུག་ཅིང་མཚོ་ཡང་སྐེམ༔

ME	BAR	TRU CHING	TSHO	YANG	KEM
fire	*blazing*	*wildly*	*lake*	*also*	*dried*

Which burned like an inferno so that even the lake nearby dried up.

སྲིབས་ཀྱི་མུ་སྟེགས་ས་གང་བསྲེགས༔

SIB	KYI	MU TEG	SA	GANG	SE
shadow side	*of*	*tirthikas, anti-buddhists*	*places where their gods stayed*	*fully*	*burnt*

The abodes of the tirthika gods on the dark side of the mountains were burnt right out, and

ཡ་ཀྵ་ནག་པོ་དྲུལ་དུ་བརླག༔

YAK SHA NAG PO   **DUL DU LA**
leader of the anti-dharma forces   *annihilate*

Yaksha Nagpo was annihilated.

འགྲན་གྱི་དོ་མེད་བདུད་ཀྱི་གཤེད༔

DRAN GYI DO ME   **DU**   **KYI**   **SHE**
supreme, incomparable   *demons*   *of*   *destroyer, controller*

You are the supreme destroyer of demons.

You rolled the phurpa and threw it into the forest of sandalwood which burned like an inferno so that even the lake nearby dried up. The abodes of the tirthika gods on the dark side of the mountains were burnt right out and Yaksha Nagpo was annihilated. You are the supreme destroyer of demons.

ཐུགས་རྗེས་བདག་ལ་བྱིན་གྱིས་རློབས༔

THU JE   **DA**   **LA**   **JIN GYI LO**

With your compassion please bless us!

བརྩེ་བས་བདག་སོགས་ལམ་སྣ་དྲོངས༔

TSE WAE   **DA SO**   **LAM NA DRONG**

Lead us to salvation with your loving care!

དགོངས་པས་བདག་ལ་དངོས་གྲུབ་སྩོལ༔

GONG PAE   **DA LA**   **NGO DRUB**   **TSOL**

Grant us accomplishments with your presence!

ནུས་པས་བདག་སོགས་བར་ཆད་སོལ༔

NU PAE   **DA SO**   **BAR CHE**   **SOL**

Remove our obstacles with your power!

ཕྱི་ཡི་བར་ཆད་ཕྱི་རུ་སོལ༔

CHI YI   **BAR CHE**   **CHI RU**   **SOL**

Resolve outer obstacles where they are!

ནང་གི་བར་ཆད་ནང་དུ་སོལ༔

NANG GI   **BAR CHE**   **NANG DU**   **SOL**

Resolve inner obstacles where they are!

གསང་བའི་བར་ཆད་དབྱིངས་སུ་སོལ༔

SANG WAI　　BAR CHE　YING　SU　SOL

Resolve subtle obstacles in emptiness!

གུས་པས་ཕྱག་འཚལ་སྐྱབས་སུ་མཆི༔

GU PAE　　CHA TSHAL　KYAB　SU　CHI

We prostrate with devotion and take refuge in you.

ༀ་ཨཱཿཧཱུྃ་བཛྲ་གུ་རུ་པདྨ་སིདྡྷི་ཧཱུྃ༔

OM　Aa　HUNG　BEN ZA　GU RU　PE MA　SID DHI　HUNG

Guru Padmasambhava with the indestructible body, speech and mind — please grant us the accomplishment of buddhahood.

With your compassion please bless us! Lead us to salvation with your loving care! Grant us accomplishments with your presence! Remove our obstacles with your power! Resolve outer obstacles where they are! Resolve inner obstacles where they are! Resolve subtle obstacles in emptiness! We prostrate with devotion and take refuge in you. Guru Padmasambhava with the indestructible body, speech and mind — please grant us the accomplishment of buddhahood.

སྲིན་པོའི་ཁ་གནོན་མཛད་པའི་ཚེ༔

SIN POI　　　　　　KHA NON　　　　　DZAE PAI　TSE
rakshasas, cannibal demons　controlling, subduing　doing　when

When you were subduing the cannibal demons

ཁྱེའུ་ཆུང་སྤྲུལ་སྐུའི་ཆ་ལུགས་ཅན༔

KHYEU CHUNG　TRUL KUI　CHA LU　　CHAN
young child　　　emanation　form, dress, style　having

You appeared in the form of a youthful emanation.

ཡ་མཚན་གཟུགས་བཟང་ཁ་དོག་ལེགས༔

YAM TSHAN　ZUG　　　　ZANG　KHA DO　LE
wonderful　form, shape　good　colour　　good

Your physique was absolutely wonderful with an excellent colour,

ཚེམས་འགྲིག་དབུ་སྐྲ་སེར་ལ་འཚེར༔

TSHEM　TRI　　　　　　WU TRA　　　SER　LA TSHER
teeth　evenly arranged　hair on his head　yellow　shining

Perfect teeth and shining golden hair.

When you were subduing the cannibal demons you appeared in the

form of a youthful emanation. Your physique was absolutely wonderful with an excellent colour, perfect teeth and shining, golden hair.

དགུང་ལོ་བཅུ་དྲུག་ལོན་པའི་ཚུལ༔

GUNG LO	CHU DRU	LON PAI	TSHUL
age	*sixteen*	*age*	*manner*

You appeared as a sixteen-year old

རིན་ཆེན་རྒྱན་ཆ་སྣ་ཚོགས་གསོལ༔

RIN CHEN	GYAN CHA	NA TSHO	SOL
jewel	*ornaments*	*various*	*wearing*

Adorned with various jewel ornaments.

ཕྱག་གཡས་འཁར་བའི་ཕུར་པ་བསྣམས༔

CHA	YAE	KHAR WAI	PHUR PA	NAM
hand	*right*	*bell metal*	*kila, spike*	*holding*

Your right hand held a phurpa of bell-metal

བདུད་དང་སྲིན་པོའི་ཁ་གནོན་མཛད༔

DU	DANG	SIN POI	KHA NON	DZAE
mara, demons	*and*	*rakshasas, cannibal demons*	*subdue*	*did*

With which you subdued the maras and rakshasas.

You appeared as a sixteen year-old adorned with various jewel ornaments. Your right hand held a phurpa of bell-metal with which you subdued the maras and rakshasas.

གཡོན་པ་སེང་ལྡེང་ཕུར་པ་བསྣམས༔

YON PA	SENG DENG	PHUR PA	NAM
left	*red acacia wood*	*nail*	*holding*

Your left hand held a phurpa of red acacia

མོས་པའི་བུ་ལ་བསྲུང་སྐྱོབ་མཛད༔

MOE PAI	BU	LA	SUNG	KYOB	DZAE
devoted	*sons, disciples*	*to*	*guarding*	*protecting*	*doing*

With which you protected your devoted disciples.

མགུལ་ལ་ལྕགས་ཀྱི་ཕུར་པ་བསྣམས༔

GUL	LA	CHA KYI	PHUR PA	NAM
neck	*at*	*iron*	*nail*	*holding, wearing*

You wore an iron phurpa at your neck,

ཡི་དམ་ལྷ་དང་གཉིས་སུ་མེད༔

YI DAM LHA   DANG   NYI SU ME
path deity   and   not different

You who are not different from the path deity.

གཉིས་མེད་སྤྲུལ་སྐུ་འཛམ་གླིང་རྒྱན༔

NYI ME   TRUL KU   DZAM LING   GYAN
non-dual   emanation   world   ornament

You the non-dual emanation, the ornament of the world.

Your left hand held a phurpa of red acacia with which you protected your devoted disciples. You wore an iron phurpa at your neck, you who are not different from the path deity. You are the non-dual emanation, the ornament of the world.

ཐུགས་རྗེས་བདག་ལ་བྱིན་གྱིས་རློབས༔

THU JE   DA   LA   JIN GYI LO

With your compassion please bless us!

བརྩེ་བས་བདག་སོགས་ལམ་སྣ་དྲོངས༔

TSE WAE   DA SO   LAM NA DRONG

Lead us to salvation with your loving care!

དགོངས་པས་བདག་ལ་དངོས་གྲུབ་སྩོལ༔

GONG PAE   DA LA   NGO DRUB   TSOL

Grant us accomplishments with your presence!

ནུས་པས་བདག་སོགས་བར་ཆད་སོལ༔

NU PAE   DA SO   BAR CHE   SOL

Remove our obstacles with your power!

ཕྱི་ཡི་བར་ཆད་ཕྱི་རུ་སོལ༔

CHI YI   BAR CHE   CHI RU   SOL

Resolve outer obstacles where they are!

ནང་གི་བར་ཆད་ནང་དུ་སོལ༔

NANG GI   BAR CHE   NANG DU   SOL

Resolve inner obstacles where they are!

གསང་བའི་བར་ཆད་དབྱིངས་སུ་སོལ༔

SANG WAI   BAR CHE   YING   SU   SOL

Resolve subtle obstacles in emptiness!

གུས་པས་ཕྱག་འཚལ་སྐྱབས་སུ་མཆི༔

GU PAE   CHA TSHAL   KYAB   SU   CHI

We prostrate with devotion and take refuge in you.

ༀ་ཨཱཿཧཱུྃ་བཛྲ་གུ་རུ་པདྨ་སིདྡྷི་ཧཱུྃ༔

OM   Aa   HUNG   BEN ZA   GU RU   PE MA   SID DHI   HUNG

Guru Padmasambhava with the indestructible body, speech and mind
— please grant us the accomplishment of buddhahood.

*With your compassion please bless us! Lead us to salvation with your
loving care! Grant us accomplishments with your presence! Remove
our obstacles with your power! Resolve outer obstacles where they are!
Resolve inner obstacles where they are! Resolve subtle obstacles in
emptiness! We prostrate with devotion and take refuge in you. Guru
Padmasambhava with the indestructible body, speech and mind —
please grant us the accomplishment of buddhahood.*

འདྲེ་ཡི་ཡུལ་དུ་དགོངས་པའི་ཚེ༔

DRE YI   YUL   DU   GONG PAI   TSHE
evil spirits   country   to   consider   when

When you turned your attention to the land of evil spirits

མེ་དཔུང་ཤོད་ཀྱི་ས་གཞི་ལ༔

ME   PUNG   SHO   KYI   SA ZHI   LA
fire   mass   inside   of   place   to

You entered a place of raging fire

མདའ་རྒྱང་གང་གི་མཚོ་ནང་ན༔

DA   GYANG   GANG   GI   TSHO   NANG NA
arrow   distance   full   of   lake   inside

Which you transformed into a lake an arrow flight wide, and

པདྨའི་སྟེང་ན་བསིལ་བསིལ་འདྲ༔

PAE MAI   TENG NA   SIL SIL   DRA
lotus   on top of   very cool   as

There on top of a lotus you sat very coolly

པདྨའི་ནང་ནས་དགོངས་པ་མཛད༔

PAE MAI   NANG NE   GONG PA   DZAE
lotus   inside   meditation   did

Practising meditation within the lotus.

When you turned your attention to the land of evil spirits you entered a place of raging fire. You transformed it into a lake an arrow-flight wide and there, on top of a lotus, you sat very coolly practising meditation within the lotus.

མཚན་ཡང་པདྨ་འབྱུང་གནས་ཞེས༔

TSHAN   YANG   PE MA JUNG NAE   ZHE
name   also   Padmasambhava   called

Your name then was Padma Jungnae and

རྫོགས་པའི་སངས་རྒྱས་དངོས་སུ་བྱོན༔

DZO PAI   SANG GYE   NGO SU   JON
perfect   Buddha   truly   went to, gained

You truly gained perfect buddhahood,

དེ་འདྲའི་སྤྲུལ་སྐུ་ཡ་མཚན་ཅན༔

DEN DRAI   TRUL KU   YAM TSHAN CHAN
like that   emanation   wonderful

You, the wonderful emanation.

Your name then was Padma Jungnae and you really gained perfect buddhahood — you, the wonderful emanation.

ཐུགས་རྗེས་བདག་ལ་བྱིན་གྱིས་རློབས༔

THU JE   DA   LA   JIN GYI LO

With your compassion please bless us!

བརྩེ་བས་བདག་སོགས་ལམ་སྣ་དྲོངས༔

TSE WAE   DA SO   LAM NA DRONG

Lead us to salvation with your loving care!

དགོངས་པས་བདག་ལ་དངོས་གྲུབ་སྩོལ༔

GONG PAE   DA LA   NGO DRUB   TSOL

Grant us accomplishments with your presence!

ནུས་པས་བདག་སོགས་བར་ཆད་སོལ༔

NU PAE   DA SO   BAR CHE   SOL

Remove our obstacles with your power!

ཕྱི་ཡི་བར་ཆད་ཕྱི་རུ་སོལ༔

CHI YI   BAR CHE   CHI RU   SOL
Resolve outer obstacles where they are!

ནང་གི་བར་ཆད་ནང་དུ་སོལ༔

NANG GI   BAR CHE   NANG DU   SOL
Resolve inner obstacles where they are!

གསང་བའི་བར་ཆད་དབྱིངས་སུ་སོལ༔

SANG WAI   BAR CHE   YING   SU   SOL
Resolve subtle obstacles in emptiness!

གུས་པས་ཕྱག་འཚལ་སྐྱབས་སུ་མཆི༔

GU PAE   CHA TSHAL   KYAB   SU   CHI
We prostrate with devotion and take refuge in you.

ཨོྃ་ཨཱཿཧཱུྃ་བཛྲ་གུ་རུ་པདྨ་སིདྡྷི་ཧཱུྃ༔

OM Aa HUNG BEN ZA GU RU PE MA SID DHI HUNG
Guru Padmasambhava with the indestructible body, speech and mind
— please grant us the accomplishment of buddhahood.

With your compassion please bless us! Lead us to salvation with your loving care! Grant us accomplishments with your presence! Remove our obstacles with your power! Resolve outer obstacles where they are! Resolve inner obstacles where they are! Resolve subtle obstacles in emptiness! We prostrate with devotion and take refuge in you. Guru Padmasambhava with the indestructible body, speech and mind — please grant us the accomplishment of buddhahood.

བོད་ཀྱི་ཉི་མ་མཛད་པའི་ཚེ༔

BOE   KYI   NYI MA   DZAE PAI   TSHE
Tibet   of   sun   doing   when
(i.e. spreading the light of dharma everywhere)
When like the sun you brought light to the land of Tibet

དད་ལྡན་འགྲོ་བ་འདྲེན་པའི་དཔལ༔

DAE DAN   DRO WA   DREN PAI   PAL
faithful   beings   guiding, leading out   glory, best one
You were the supreme guide for faithful beings and

གང་ལ་གང་འདུལ་སྐུར་བསྟན་ནས༔

GANG LA GANG   DUL   KUR   TAN   NE
according to need   taming   form   show   then

Showed whatever form was necessary to tame and educate them.

གཙང་ཁ་ལ་ཡི་ལ་ཐོག་ཏུ༔

TSANG KHA   LA   YI LA THO TU
(place name)   pass   on top of

On the pass of Tsang Kha

དྲ་ལྷའི་དགེ་བསྙེན་དམ་ལ་བཏགས༔

DRA LHAI GE NYEN   DAM   LA   TA
name of an old local god in Tibet   vows   in   put, fixed

You put Dralha Genyen under vow.

When like the sun you brought light to the land of Tibet you were the supreme guide for faithful beings and showed whatever form was necessary to tame and educate them. On the pass of Tsang Kha you put Dralha Genyen under vow.

ཡུལ་ནི་ཚ་བའི་ཚ་ཤོད་དུ༔

YUL NI   TSHA WAI TSHA SHO   DU
country   (a land on the border Tibet and Nepal)   of, in

In the country of Tshawai Tshasho

ལྷ་ཡི་དགེ་བསྙེན་དྲེགས་པ་ཅན༔

LHA YI GE NYEN DRE PA CHAN
(name of some local gods)

You put the twenty-one

ཉི་ཤུ་རྩ་གཅིག་དམ་ལ་བཏགས༔

NYI SHU TSA CHI   DAM   LA   TA
twenty-one   vows   in   put

Lhayi Genyen Dregpachan under vow.

མང་ཡུལ་དེ་ཡི་བྱམས་སྤྲིན་དུ༔

MANG YUL   DE   YE   JAM TRIN   DU
(district)   that   of   (place)   at

At Jamtrin in Mangyul

དགེ་སློང་བཞི་ལ་དངོས་གྲུབ་གནང་༔

GE LONG ZHI   LA   NGO DRU   NANG
(four local gods)   to   samanasiddhi, attainments   gave

You gave general attainments to the Gelong Zhi,

ཁྱད་པར་འཕགས་པའི་རིག་འཛིན་མཆོག༔

KHYAE PAR   **PHA PAI**   **RIG DZIN**   **CHO**
especially   *arya, noble, saintly*   *vidyadhara*   *supreme*

You are the especially exalted supreme vidhyadhara.

In the country of Tshawai Tshashod you put the twenty-one Lhayi Genyen Dregpachan under vow. At Jamtrin in Mangyul you gave general attainments to the Gelong Zhi, you the especially exalted supreme vidhadhara.

ཐུགས་རྗེས་བདག་ལ་བྱིན་གྱིས་རློབས༔

THU JE   **DA**   **LA**   **JIN GYI LO**

With your compassion please bless us!

བརྩེ་བས་བདག་སོགས་ལམ་སྣ་དྲོངས༔

TSE WAE   **DA SO**   **LAM NA DRONG**

Lead us to salvation with your loving care!

དགོངས་པས་བདག་ལ་དངོས་གྲུབ་སྩོལ༔

GONG PAE   **DA LA**   **NGO DRUB**   **TSOL**

Grant us accomplishments with your presence!

ནུས་པས་བདག་སོགས་བར་ཆད་སོལ༔

NU PAE   **DA SO**   **BAR CHE**   **SOL**

Remove our obstacles with your power!

ཕྱི་ཡི་བར་ཆད་ཕྱི་རུ་སོལ༔

CHI YI   **BAR CHE**   **CHI RU**   **SOL**

Resolve outer obstacles where they are!

ནང་གི་བར་ཆད་ནང་དུ་སོལ༔

NANG GI   **BAR CHE**   **NANG DU**   **SOL**

Resolve inner obstacles where they are!

གསང་བའི་བར་ཆད་དབྱིངས་སུ་སོལ༔

SANG WAI   **BAR CHE**   **YING**   **SU**   **SOL**

Resolve subtle obstacles in emptiness!

གུས་པས་ཕྱག་འཚལ་སྐྱབས་སུ་མཆི༔

GU PAE   **CHA TSHAL**   **KYAB**   **SU**   **CHI**

We prostrate with devotion and take refuge in you.

ༀ་ཨཱཿཧཱུྃ་བཛྲ་གུ་རུ་པདྨ་སིདྡྷི་ཧཱུྃ༔

OM   Aa   HUNG   BEN ZA   GU RU   PE MA   SID DHI   HUNG

Guru Padmasambhava with the indestructible body, speech and mind
— please grant us the accomplishment of buddhahood.

*With your compassion please bless us! Lead us to salvation with your
loving care! Grant us accomplishments with your presence! Remove
our obstacles with your power! Resolve outer obstacles where they are!
Resolve inner obstacles where they are! Resolve subtle obstacles in
emptiness! We prostrate with devotion and take refuge in you. Guru
Padmasambhava with the indestructible body, speech and mind —
please grant us the accomplishment of buddhahood.*

དཔལ་མོ་ཐང་གི་དཔལ་ཐང་དུ༔

PA MO   THANG   GI   PA THANG   DU
(name)   plain   of   (village)   at

At Palmo Thang village on the plain of Palmo

བརྟན་མ་བཅུ་གཉིས་དམ་ལ་བཏགས༔

TAN MA CHU NYI   DAM   LA   TA
(twelve local goddesses)   vows   in   put

You put the Tanma Chunyi under vow.

བོད་ཡུལ་ཁ་ལའི་ལ་ཐོག་ཏུ༔

BOE YUL   KHA LAI   LA THOG TU
Tibet   (mountain)   on

On the mountain of Khala in the land of Tibet

གངས་དཀར་ཤ་མེད་དམ་ལ་བཏགས༔

GANG KAR SHA ME   DAM   LA   TA
(local demon)   vow   in   put

You put Gangkar Shame under vow.

འདམ་ཤོད་ལྷ་བུའི་སྙིང་དྲུང་དུ༔

DAM SHO   LHA BUI NYING   DRUNG DU
(village)   (mountain)   beside

At the village of Damsho near Mount Lhabui Nying

ཐང་ལྷ་ཡ་ཞུར་དམ་ལ་བཏགས༔

THANG LHA YA ZHUR   DAM   LA   TA
(local mountain god)   vows   in   put

You put Thanglha Yazhur under vow.

At Palmo Thang village on the plain of Palmo you put the Tanma Chunyi under vow. On the mountain of Khala in the land of Tibet you put Gangkar Shame under vow. At the village of Damsho near Mount Lhabui Nying you put Thanglha Yazhur under vow.

ཆེ་བའི་ལྷ་འདྲེ་ཐམས་ཅད་ཀྱིས༔

CHE WAI	LHA	DRE	THAM CHE	KYI
great	*local gods*	*demons*	*all*	*of*

Among all the great local gods and demons

ལ་ལས་སྲོག་གི་སྙིང་པོ་ཕུལ༔

LA LAE	SO GI	NYING PO	PHUL
by some	*life*	*essence*	*offered*

Some offered their life essence.

ལ་ལས་བསྟན་པ་བསྲུང་བར་བྱས༔

LA LAE	TAN PA	SUNG WAR	JAE
by some	*doctrine*	*guard*	*did (i.e. promised to)*

Some agreed to guard the doctrine and

ལ་ལས་བྲན་དུ་ཁས་ལེན་བྱས༔

LA LAE	DRAN	DU	KHAE LANG	JAE
by some	*servant*	*as*	*promise*	*did*
	(to serve the dharma)			

Some promised to be your servants,

མཐུ་དང་རྫུ་འཕྲུལ་སྟོབས་པོ་ཆེ༔

THU	DANG	DZUN TRUL	TO PO	CHE
power, force	*and*	*miracles*	*strength*	*great*

For your power and miracles are very strong.

Among all the great local gods and demons some offered their life essence, some agreed to guard the doctrine and some promised to be your servants, for your power and miracles are very strong.

ཐུགས་རྗེས་བདག་ལ་བྱིན་གྱིས་རློབས༔

THU JE	DA	LA	JIN GYI LO

With your compassion please bless us!

བརྩེ་བས་བདག་སོགས་ལམ་སྣ་དྲོངས༔

TSE WAE	DA SO	LAM NA DRONG

Lead us to salvation with your loving care!

དགོངས་པས་བདག་ལ་དངོས་གྲུབ་སྩོལ༔

GONG PAE   DA LA   NGO DRUB   TSOL

Grant us accomplishments with your presence!

ནུས་པས་བདག་སོགས་བར་ཆད་སོལ༔

NU PAE   DA SO   BAR CHE   SOL

Remove our obstacles with your power!

ཕྱི་ཡི་བར་ཆད་ཕྱི་རུ་སོལ༔

CHI YI   BAR CHE   CHI RU   SOL

Resolve outer obstacles where they are!

ནང་གི་བར་ཆད་ནང་དུ་སོལ༔

NANG GI   BAR CHE   NANG DU   SOL

Resolve inner obstacles where they are!

གསང་བའི་བར་ཆད་དབྱིངས་སུ་སོལ༔

SANG WAI   BAR CHE   YING   SU   SOL

Resolve subtle obstacles in emptiness!

གུས་པས་ཕྱག་འཚལ་སྐྱབས་སུ་མཆི༔

GU PAE   CHA TSHAL   KYAB   SU   CHI

We prostrate with devotion and take refuge in you.

ཨོཾ་ཨཱཿཧཱུྃ་བཛྲ་གུ་རུ་པདྨ་སིདྡྷི་ཧཱུྃ༔

OM   Aa   HUNG   BEN ZA   GU RU   PE MA   SID DHI   HUNG

Guru Padmasambhava with the indestructible body, speech and mind — please grant us the accomplishment of buddhahood.

With your compassion please bless us! Lead us to salvation with your loving care! Grant us accomplishments with your presence! Remove our obstacles with your power! Resolve outer obstacles where they are! Resolve inner obstacles where they are! Resolve subtle obstacles in emptiness! We prostrate with devotion and take refuge in you. Guru Padmasambhava with the indestructible body, speech and mind — please grant us the accomplishment of buddhahood.

དམ་པའི་ཆོས་ཀྱི་བསྟན་པ་ནི༔

DAM PAI   CHO   KYI   TAN PA NI
holy   *dharma*   *of*   *doctrines*

When you raised the victory banner

རྒྱལ་མཚན་ལྟ་བུར་བཙུགས་པའི་ཚེ༔

GYAL TSHAN   **TA BUR**   **TSU PAI**   **TSHE**
victory banner   *as*   *put up*   *when*

Of the doctrines of the holy dharma

བསམ་ཡས་མ་བཞེངས་ལྷུན་གྱིས་གྲུབ༔

SAM YAE   **MA ZHENG**   **LHUN GYI DRU**
Samye Monastery   *not built*   *effortlessly arising*
                                              (i.e. the construction was miraculous)

You caused Samyae Monastery to arise without laborious construction and

རྒྱལ་པོའི་དགོངས་པ་མཐར་ཕྱིན་མཛད༔

GYAL POI   **GONG PA**   **THAR CHIN DZAE**
king's (Trisong Deutsan)   *wishes, intentions*   *fulfilled*

You fulfilled all the king's wishes.

When you raised the victory banner of the doctrines of the holy dharma you caused Samyae Monastery to arise effortlessly without laborious construction and you fulfilled all the king's wishes.

སྐྱེས་མཆོག་གསུམ་གྱི་མཚན་ཡང་གསོལ༔

KYE CHO   **SUM**   **GYI**   **TSHAN**   **YANG**   **SOL**
superior being   *three*   *of*   *names*   *also*   *used, had*

You were known by the names of your three excellent manifestations:

གཅིག་ནི་པད་འབྱུང་གནས་ཞེས༔

CHI NI   **PAE MA JUNG NAE**   **ZHE**
one   *Padmakara*   *called*

One was Padma Jungnae,

གཅིག་ནི་པད་མ་སམྦྷ༔

CHI NI   **PAD MA SAM BHA VA**
one   *Padmasambhava*

One was Padmasambhava, and

གཅིག་ནི་མཚོ་སྐྱེས་རྡོ་རྗེ་ཞེས༔

CHI NI   **TSHO KYE DOR JE**   **ZHE**
one   *Sororavajra*   *called*

One was Tshokye Dorje.

གསང་མཚན་རྡོ་རྗེ་དྲག་པོ་རྩལ༔

SANG TSHAN DOR JE DRAG PO TSAL
secret name Vajrarudra

Your secret name was Dorje Dragpo Tsal.

You were known by the names of your three excellent manifestations: Padma Jungnae, Padmasambhava, and Tshokye Dorje. Your secret name was Dorje Dragpo Tsal.

ཐུགས་རྗེས་བདག་ལ་བྱིན་གྱིས་རློབས༔

THU JE DA LA JIN GYI LO

With your compassion please bless us!

བརྩེ་བས་བདག་སོགས་ལམ་སྣ་དྲོངས༔

TSE WAE DA SO LAM NA DRONG

Lead us to salvation with your loving care!

དགོངས་པས་བདག་ལ་དངོས་གྲུབ་སྩོལ༔

GONG PAE DA LA NGO DRUB TSOL

Grant us accomplishments with your presence!

ནུས་པས་བདག་སོགས་བར་ཆད་སོལ༔

NU PAE DA SO BAR CHE SOL

Remove our obstacles with your power!

ཕྱི་ཡི་བར་ཆད་ཕྱི་རུ་སོལ༔

CHI YI BAR CHE CHI RU SOL

Resolve outer obstacles where they are!

ནང་གི་བར་ཆད་ནང་དུ་སོལ༔

NANG GI BAR CHE NANG DU SOL

Resolve inner obstacles where they are!

གསང་བའི་བར་ཆད་དབྱིངས་སུ་སོལ༔

SANG WAI BAR CHE YING SU SOL

Resolve subtle obstacles in emptiness!

གུས་པས་ཕྱག་འཚལ་སྐྱབས་སུ་མཆི༔

GU PAE CHA TSHAL KYAB SU CHI

We prostrate with devotion and take refuge in you.

ༀ་ཨཱཿཧཱུྃ་བཛྲ་གུ་རུ་པདྨ་སིདྡྷི་ཧཱུྃ༔

OM   Aa   HUNG   BEN ZA   GU RU   PE MA   SID DHI   HUNG

Guru Padmasambhava with the indestructible body, speech and mind — please grant us the accomplishment of buddhahood.

With your compassion please bless us! Lead us to salvation with your loving care! Grant us accomplishments with your presence! Remove our obstacles with your power! Resolve outer obstacles where they are! Resolve inner obstacles where they are! Resolve subtle obstacles in emptiness! We prostrate with devotion and take refuge in you. Guru Padmasambhava with the indestructible body, speech and mind — please grant us the accomplishment of buddhahood.

བསམ་ཡས་མཆིམས་ཕུར་སྒྲུབ་པ་མཛད༔

SAM YAE CHIM PHUR   DRU PA   DZAE
at this cave near Samye Monastery   practice   did

You performed practice at Samye Chimphu, and

རྐྱེན་ངན་བཟློག་ཅིང་དངོས་གྲུབ་གནང༔

KYEN   NGAN   DOG CHING   NGO DRU   NANG
circumstances   bad   repelling   attainments   giving

Repelling all bad circumstances you bestowed accomplishments and

རྗེ་བློན་ཐར་པའི་ལམ་ལ་བཀོད༔

JE   LON   THAR PAI   LAM   LA   KOE
king   ministers   salvation   path   on   put

Placed the king and ministers on the path of liberation.

གདོན་གཟུགས་བོན་གྱི་བསྟན་པ་བསྣུབས༔

DON ZU   BON   GYI   TAN PA   NUB
evil system   Bon religion   of   doctrines   finished

You caused the demise of the doctrines of the demonic Bon and

ཆོས་སྐུ་དྲི་མེད་རིན་ཆེན་གཏེར༔

CHO KU   DRI ME   RIN CHEN   TER
dharmakaya, actuality   stainless   jewel, precious   treasure

With the precious treasure of the stainless dharmakaya

སྐལ་ལྡན་སངས་རྒྱས་ས་ལ་བཀོད༔

KAL DAN   SANG GYE   SA   LA   KO
fortunate ones   buddha's   stage   on   put, establish

You established the fortunate ones in the state of buddhahood.

You performed practice at Samye Chimphu and repelling all bad circumstances you bestowed accomplishments and placed the king and ministers on the path of liberation. You caused the demise of the doctrines of the demonic Bon and with the precious treasure of the stainless dharmakaya you established the fortunate ones in the state of buddhahood.

ཐུགས་རྗེས་བདག་ལ་བྱིན་གྱིས་རློབས༔

THU JE   DA   LA   JIN GYI LO

With your compassion please bless us!

བརྩེ་བས་བདག་སོགས་ལམ་སྣ་དྲོངས༔

TSE WAE   DA SO   LAM NA DRONG

Lead us to salvation with your loving care!

དགོངས་པས་བདག་ལ་དངོས་གྲུབ་སྩོལ༔

GONG PAE   DA LA   NGO DRUB   TSOL

Grant us accomplishments with your presence!

ནུས་པས་བདག་སོགས་བར་ཆད་སོལ༔

NU PAE   DA SO   BAR CHE   SOL

Remove our obstacles with your power!

ཕྱི་ཡི་བར་ཆད་ཕྱི་རུ་སོལ༔

CHI YI   BAR CHE   CHI RU   SOL

Resolve outer obstacles where they are!

ནང་གི་བར་ཆད་ནང་དུ་སོལ༔

NANG GI   BAR CHE   NANG DU   SOL

Resolve inner obstacles where they are!

གསང་བའི་བར་ཆད་དབྱིངས་སུ་སོལ༔

SANG WAI   BAR CHE   YING   SU   SOL

Resolve subtle obstacles in emptiness!

གུས་པས་ཕྱག་འཚལ་སྐྱབས་སུ་མཆི༔

GU PAE   CHA TSHAL   KYAB   SU   CHI

We prostrate with devotion and take refuge in you.

ཨོཾ་ཨཱ༔ཧཱུྃ་བཛྲ་གུ་རུ་པདྨ་སིདྡྷི་ཧཱུྃ༔

OM   Aa   HUNG   BEN ZA   GU RU   PE MA   SID DHI   HUNG

Guru Padmasambhava with the indestructible body, speech and mind
— please grant us the accomplishment of buddhahood.

*With your compassion please bless us! Lead us to salvation with your
loving care! Grant us accomplishments with your presence! Remove
our obstacles with your power! Resolve outer obstacles where they are!
Resolve inner obstacles where they are! Resolve subtle obstacles in
emptiness! We prostrate with devotion and take refuge in you. Guru
Padmasambhava with the indestructible body, speech and mind —
please grant us the accomplishment of buddhahood.*

དེ་ནས་ཨོ་རྒྱན་ཡུལ་དུ་བྱོན༔

DE NE	UR GYAN	YUL	DU	JON
then	*Oddiyana*	*country*	*to*	*went*

Then you went to the land of Urgyan where

ད་ལྟ་སྲིན་པོའི་ཁ་གནོན་མཛད༔

DAN TA	SIN POI		KHA NON	DZAE
now	*rakshasa, cannibal demons*		*subdue*	*to*

Now you tame the cannibal demons.

མི་རྣམས་ལྷག་གྱུར་ཡ་མཚན་ཆེ༔

MI NAM	LHA GYUR	YAM TSHAN	CHE
people	*supremely*	*wonderful*	*great*

Supremely wonderful for beings,

སྤྱོད་པ་རྨད་བྱུང་ངོ་མཚར་ཅན༔

CHO PA	MAE JUNG	NGO TSHAR CHAN
conduct	*amazing*	*tremendous one*

You are the marvellous one with the amazing deeds.

མཐུ་དང་རྫུ་འཕྲུལ་སྟོབས་པོ་ཆེ༔

THU	DANG	DZUN TRUL	TO PO	CHE
force	*and*	*miracles*	*strength*	*great*

Your power and miracles are very strong.

*Then you went to the land of Urgyan where now you tame the cannibal
demons. Supremely wonderful for beings, you are the marvellous one
with the amazing deeds. Your power and miracles are very strong.*

ཐུགས་རྗེས་བདག་ལ་བྱིན་གྱིས་རློབས༔

THU JE   DA   LA   JIN GYI LO

With your compassion please bless us!

བརྩེ་བས་བདག་སོགས་ལམ་སྣ་དྲོངས༔

TSE WAE   DA SO   LAM NA DRONG

Lead us to salvation with your loving care!

དགོངས་པས་བདག་ལ་དངོས་གྲུབ་སྩོལ༔

GONG PAE   DA LA   NGO DRUB   TSOL

Grant us accomplishments with your presence!

ནུས་པས་བདག་སོགས་བར་ཆད་སོལ༔

NU PAE   DA SO   BAR CHE   SOL

Remove our obstacles with your power!

ཕྱི་ཡི་བར་ཆད་ཕྱི་རུ་སོལ༔

CHI YI   BAR CHE   CHI RU   SOL

Resolve outer obstacles where they are!

ནང་གི་བར་ཆད་ནང་དུ་སོལ༔

NANG GI   BAR CHE   NANG DU   SOL

Resolve inner obstacles where they are!

གསང་བའི་བར་ཆད་དབྱིངས་སུ་སོལ༔

SANG WAI   BAR CHE   YING   SU   SOL

Resolve subtle obstacles in emptiness!

གུས་པས་ཕྱག་འཚལ་སྐྱབས་སུ་མཆི༔

GU PAE   CHA TSHAL   KYAB   SU   CHI

We prostrate with devotion and take refuge in you.

ཨོཾ་ཨཱཿཧཱུྃ་བཛྲ་གུ་རུ་པདྨ་སིདྡྷི་ཧཱུྃ༔

OM   Aa   HUNG   BEN ZA   GU RU   PE MA   SID DHI   HUNG

Guru Padmasambhava with the indestructible body, speech and mind
— please grant us the accomplishment of buddhahood.

With your compassion please bless us! Lead us to salvation with your loving care! Grant us accomplishments with your presence! Remove our obstacles with your power! Resolve outer obstacles where they are!

Removing Obstacles **163**

Resolve inner obstacles where they are! Resolve subtle obstacles in emptiness! We prostrate with devotion and take refuge in you. Guru Padmasambhava with the indestructible body, speech and mind — please grant us the accomplishment of buddhahood.

ཀྲུ་གསུང་ཐུགས་ལྡན་འགྲོ་བ་འདྲེན་པའི་དཔལ༔

KU	SUNG	THU	DAN	DRO WA	DREN PAI	PAL
body,	speech,	mind,	having	beings	guiding	glory,
nirmanakaya	sambhogakaya	dharmakaya				

Possessing the three kayas you are the supreme guide for beings.

སྒྲིབ་པ་ཀུན་སྤངས་ཁམས་གསུམ་ས་ལེར་མཁྱེན༔

DRI PA	KUN	JANG	KHAM	SUM	SA LER	KHYEN
obscurations	all	purified	worlds	three*	clearly	know

*the desire, form and formless worlds

Having purified all obscurations you know the three worlds clearly, just as they are.

དངོས་གྲུབ་མཆོག་བརྙེས་བདེ་ཆེན་མཆོག་གི་སྐུ༔

NGO DRU	CHO	NYE	DE CHEN	CHO	GI	KU
siddhi, attainment	supreme	got	joyful	supreme, excellent	of	body, form

Having gained the supreme accomplishments you have the body of supreme happiness.

Possessing the three kayas you are the supreme guide for beings. Having purified all obscurations you know the three worlds clearly, just as they are. Having gained the supreme accomplishment you have the body of supreme happiness.

ཐུགས་རྗེས་བདག་ལ་བྱིན་གྱིས་རློབས༔

THU JE   DA   LA   JIN GYI LO

With your compassion please bless us!

བརྩེ་བས་བདག་སོགས་ལམ་སྣ་དྲོངས༔

TSE WAE   DA SO   LAM NA DRONG

Lead us to salvation with your loving care!

དགོངས་པས་བདག་ལ་དངོས་གྲུབ་སྩོལ༔

GONG PAE   DA LA   NGO DRUB   TSOL

Grant us accomplishments with your presence!

ནུས་པས་བདག་སོགས་བར་ཆད་སོལ༔
NU PAE   DA SO   BAR CHE   SOL
Remove our obstacles with your power!

ཕྱི་ཡི་བར་ཆད་ཕྱི་རུ་སོལ༔
CHI YI   BAR CHE   CHI RU   SOL
Resolve outer obstacles where they are!

ནང་གི་བར་ཆད་ནང་དུ་སོལ༔
NANG GI   BAR CHE   NANG DU   SOL
Resolve inner obstacles where they are!

གསང་བའི་བར་ཆད་དབྱིངས་སུ་སོལ༔
SANG WAI   BAR CHE   YING   SU   SOL
Resolve subtle obstacles in emptiness!

གུས་པས་ཕྱག་འཚལ་སྐྱབས་སུ་མཆི༔
GU PAE   CHA TSHAL   KYAB   SU   CHI
We prostrate with devotion and take refuge in you.

ༀ་ཨཱཿཧཱུྃ་བཛྲ་གུ་རུ་པདྨ་སིདྡྷི་ཧཱུྃ༔
OM   Aa   HUNG   BEN ZA   GU RU   PE MA   SID DHI   HUNG
Guru Padmasambhava with the indestructible body, speech and mind
— please grant us the accomplishment of buddhahood.

With your compassion please bless us! Lead us to salvation with your loving care! Grant us accomplishments with your presence! Remove our obstacles with your power! Resolve outer obstacles where they are! Resolve inner obstacles where they are! Resolve subtle obstacles in emptiness! We prostrate with devotion and take refuge in you. Guru Padmasambhava with the indestructible body, speech and mind — please grant us the accomplishment of buddhahood.

རང་གི་སྣུབ་པ་རང་གིས་མཛད༔ རྗེས་འཇུག་རྡོ་རྗེ་མཆོ་རྒྱལ་གྱིས༔ ཕྱི་རབས་གང་
བག་བཀྱེད་འཛིན་གྱི༔བར་ཆད་སེལ་ཕྱིར་ཞུས་པ་ཡིན༔རྗེས་འཇུག་གང་བག་བཀྱེད་འཛིན་
རྣམས༔ ཉམས་སུ་ལོང་ལ་གསོལ་བ་ཐོབ༔ གསོལ་བ་ཆེར་གཅིག་བཏབ་པས་ཀྱང་༔ ཉིན་
ཞག་གཅིག་གི་བར་ཆད་སེལ༔ ཚེ་བསམས་འགྲུབ་པར་བྱེ་ཆོམ་མེད༔ བརྒྱད་འཛིན་དང་༔
ལྷུན་ཅིག་དང་འབྱུང་བར་ཤོག༔ སྤྲུལ་སྐུ་མཁའ་ལ་སྤྲུག་པོའི་གཏེར་མའོ༔
ས་མ་ཡ༔ རྒྱ་རྒྱ་རྒྱ༔

Padmasambhava wrote his practices by himself. I, his follower Jo-Mo Ye-Shes mTsho-rGyal requested this prayer in order to dispel the obstacles of the lineage-holders who will come later. The lineage-holding followers must practise and pray. To pray (with this prayer) just once will remove all obstacles for twenty-four hours. All that you wish for will undoubtedly be attained. May this text be found by a faithful lineage-holder.

This is the gTer-Ma treasure of Ba-mKhal sMug-Po (bZang-Po Grags-Pa).

Vows. Seal. Seal. Seal.

THE BARCHE LAMSEL, THE PRAYER WHICH REMOVES OBSTACLES FROM THE PATH

གསོལ་འདེབས་བསམ་པ་མྱུར་འགྲུབ་བཞུགས་སོ༎

The Prayer Which Quickly Fulfils Our Wishes

ཨེ་མ་ཧོཿ མཚོ་དབུས་གེ་སར་པདྨའི་སྡོང་པོ་ལ།

E MA HO	**TSHO WU**	**GE SAR**	**PE MAI**	**DONG PO**	**LA**
wonderful!	*lake centre**	*stamen*	*lotus*	*stem*	*on*

* Dhanakosa Lake, sunyata's symbol

Wonderful! In the centre of the lake, upon the stem and stamen of a lotus,

སྐུ་ལྔ་ཡེ་ཤེས་ལྷུན་གྱིས་གྲུབ་པའི་ལྷ།

KU	**NGA**	**YE SHE**	**LHUN GYI DRU PAI**	**LHA**
*kaya,mode**	*five*	*jnana, #*	*effortlessly arising*	*god (i.e. not a flesh body)*
		wisdom		

* The buddhas of the five families, and dharmakaya, sambhogakaya, nirmanakaya, svabha-vikakaya, and dharmadhatu jnanakaya, i.e. intrinsic mode, enjoyment mode, apparitional mode, integrative mode and hospitality of awareness mode

dharmadhatu jnana, adarsha jnana, samantajnana, pratika jnana, amoghasiddhi jnana, i.e. wisdom of infinite hospitality, mirror-like wisdom, wisdom of equality, wisdom of discernment, wisdom of accomplishment

Are you, the deity with the five modes and five wisdoms effortlessly arising,

རང་བྱུང་ཆེན་པོ་པདྨ་ཡབ་ཡུམ་ནི།

RANG JUNG	**CHEN PO**	**PE MA**	**YAB YUM**	**NI**
uncreated	*great*	*Padmasambhava*		*with his consort Yeshe Tsogyal*

Great spontaneous Padmasambhava and consort with

མཁའ་འགྲོ་སྤྲིན་ཕུང་འཕྲིགས་ལ་གསོལ་བ་འདེབས།

KHAN DRO	**TRIN**	**PHUNG**	**TRIG**	**LA**	**SOL WA DE**
dakinis	*cloud*	*many, a mass (i.e. a vast number)*	*gather*	*to*	*pray*

Vast clouds of dakinis gathered around you. We pray to you.

བསམ་པ་མྱུར་དུ་འགྲུབ་པར་བྱིན་གྱིས་རློབས།

SAM PA	**NYUR DU**	**DRU PAR**	**JIN GYI LO**
*wishes, thoughts**	*quickly*	*accomplish, fulfil*	*bless desires*

* which are in accordance with the Dharma

Bless us with the rapid fulfilment of our wishes.

Wonderful! In the centre of the lake, upon the stem and stamen of a lotus, are you, the deity with the five modes and five wisdoms effortlessly arising, great spontaneous Padmasambhava and consort with vast clouds of dakinis gathered around you. We pray to you. Bless us with the rapid fulfilment of our wishes.

ལས་ངན་སྨྱུད་པའི་སྟྲིན་མཐུས་བསྐྱེད་པའི།

LAE	NGAN	CHAE PAI	NAM MIN	THU	KYE PAI
actions, karmic activity	bad	done	maturing *	power	arising, developing, generating

* ripening to the point of giving a result

The power of the maturation of the bad karmic actions we have done, gives rise to

ནད་གདོན་བར་གཆོད་དམག་འཁྲུག་མུ་གེའི་ཚོགས།

NAE	DON	BAR CHOE	MAG	TRU	MU GEI	TSHO
illness	demons	obstacles, obstructions	war	fighting, like civil war	famine	(plural)

Illnesses, demons, obstacles, war, strife, and famine.

ཁྱོད་ཞལ་དྲན་པའི་མོད་ལ་ཟད་བྱེད་པའི།

KHYO	ZHAL	DREN PAI	MOE LA	ZAE	JE PAI
your	face	remember	immediately	finish (any troubles)	doing

You promised that when we bring your face to mind these troubles will end immediately.

ཞལ་བཞེས་སྙིང་ནས་གསོལ་ལོ་ཨོ་རྒྱན་རྗེ།

ZHAL ZHE	NYING	NAE	KUL LO	OR GYEN JE
promise *	heart	from	exhort, encourage	Padmasambhava

* Padmasambhava's promise to help those who have faith in him

Padmasambhava, from our hearts we call to you now, please help us.

བསམ་པ་མྱུར་དུ་འགྲུབ་པར་བྱིན་གྱིས་རློབས།

SAM PA	NYUR DU	DRU PAR	JIN GYI LO

Bless us with the rapid fulfilment of our wishes.

The power of maturation of the bad karmic actions we have done gives rise to illnesses, demons, obstacles, war, strife, and famine. You promised that when we bring your face to mind these troubles will end immediately. Padmasambhava, from our hearts we call to you now, please help us. Bless us with the rapid fulfilment of our wishes.

དད་དང་ཚུལ་ཁྲིམས་གཏོང་ལ་གོམས་པ་དང་།

DAE	DANG	TSHUL TRIM	TONG	LA	GOM PA	DANG
faith	and	morality	generosity	to, on	meditation, practice	and

Practicing faith, morality and generosity, and

ཐོས་པས་རྒྱུད་གྲོལ་ཁྲེལ་ཡོད་ངོ་ཚ་ཤེས།

THOE PAE	GYU	DROL	TREL YOE	NGO TSHA	SHE
by listening (to the dharma)	minds	free (from the afflictions)	fear of the bad opinion of others	shame (have a clear sense of good and bad)	know

Freeing our minds by listening to the Dharma, having modesty, shame, and

ཤེས་རབ་ཕུན་སུམ་ཚོགས་པའི་ནོར་བདུན་པོ།

SHE RAB	PHUN SUM TSHO PAI	NOR	DUN PO
prajna,	all good things, valuable things	wealth, riches	seven wisdom

Wisdom – these are the seven riches having true value.

སེམས་ཅན་ཀུན་གྱི་རྒྱུད་ལ་རབ་ཞུགས་ནས།

SEM CHEN	KUN	GYI	GYU	LA	RAB ZHU	NAE
sentient beings	all	of	mind	to	full entering	then

May they be fully absorbed by minds of all sentient beings, and

འཇིག་རྟེན་བདེ་སྐྱིད་ལྡན་པར་དབུགས་འབྱིན་མཛོད།

JIG TEN	DE KYI	DEN PAR	WUG JIN	DZOE
world	happiness, joy	having	giving confidence, lifting up and making and free	make

Bring them the confidence of enjoying happiness and joy in the world.

བསམ་པ་མྱུར་དུ་འགྲུབ་པར་བྱིན་གྱིས་རློབས།

SAM PA	NYUR DU	DRU PAR	JIN GYI LO

Bless us with the rapid fulfilment of our wishes.

Practicing faith, morality and generosity, and freeing our minds by listening to the Dharma, having modesty, shame, and wisdom – these are the seven riches having true value. May they be fully absorbed by the minds of all sentient beings, and bring them the confidence of enjoying happiness and joy in the world. Bless us with the rapid fulfilment of our wishes.

གང་ལ་ནད་དང་སྡུག་བསྔལ་མི་འདོད་རྐྱེན།

GANG	LA	NAE	DANG	DU NGAL	MI DOE	KYEN
someone,	to	sickness	and	sorrow,	undesirable	reasons,
whoever (for whoever					difficulty	situations
these difficulties come)						

For we who experience sickness, sorrow, undesirable situations,

འབྱུང་པོའི་གདོན་དང་རྒྱལ་པོའི་ཆད་པ་དང་།

JUNG POI	DON	DANG	GYAL POI	CHAE PA	DANG
elemental	demons	and	kings' government	troubles	and

Demonic forms of the elements, troubles from the state, and

མེ་ཆུ་གཅན་གཟན་ལམ་ཕྲང་འཇིགས་ལ་སོགས།

ME	CHU	CHEN ZAN	LAM TRANG	JI	LA SO
fire	water	dangerous	difficult paths	fears, frightening	and so on
		animas		things	

Fire, water, dangerous animals, difficult paths, fearful events and

ཚེ་ཡི་ཕ་མཐར་ཐུག་པའི་གནས་སྐབས་ཀུན།

TSHE YI	PHA THAR	THU PAI	NAE KAB	KUN
life	end, limit	at just that	occasions	all
		moment		

All occasions which can bring about the end of our life,

སྐྱབས་དང་རེ་ས་གཞན་ན་མ་མཆིས་པ།

KYAB	DANG	RE SA	ZHAN	NA	MA CHI PA
refuge	and	hope	other	if I look for	there is not

You are our only hope and refuge.

ཐུགས་རྗེས་གཟིགས་ཤིག་གུ་རུ་ཨོ་རྒྱན་རྗེ།

THU JE		ZI	SHI	GU RU	OR GYEN JE
with your compassion		look	please do!	guru	Padmasambhava

Please look on us with compassion, Guru Padmasambhava!

བསམ་པ་མྱུར་དུ་འགྲུབ་པར་བྱིན་གྱིས་རློབས།

SAM PA	NYUR DU	DRU PAR	JIN GYI LO

Bless us with the rapid fulfilment of our wishes.

For we who experience sickness, sorrow, undesirable situations, demonic forms of the elements, troubles from the state, and fire, water, dangerous animals, difficult paths, fearful events and all occasions which can bring about the end of our life, you are our only hope and refuge. Please look on us with compassion, Guru Padmasambhava! Bless us with the rapid fulfilment of our wishes.

མཁན་སློབ་ཆོས་གསུམ་རིང་ལུགས་ཆེ།

KHEN	LOB	CHO	SUM	RING LU	CHE
Shantarakshita	*Padmasambhava*	*King Trisong Deutsan*	*three*	*system*	*great*

With the great tradition of Shantarakshita, Padmasambhava and King Trisong Deutsan

འཛམ་གླིངས་གསུམ་ཁྱབ་པར་འཕེལ།

DZAM LING	SA SUM	KHYAE PAR	PHEL
world	*three places**	*pervasively*	*spread and increase*

*below the earth, on it and above it

Spreading throughout the three levels of the world, and

འགྲོ་རྒྱུད་མཆོག་གསུམ་སྣང་པ་དང་།

DRO	GYU	CHO SUM	NANG PA	DANG
beings	*minds*	*the three jewels*	*ideas and light*	*and*

The minds of all beings never separating from the illumination of the Three Jewels,

མི་འབྲལ་དུས་གསུམ་དགེ་ལེགས་ཤོག །

MI	DRAL	DU SUM	GE LE	SHO
not	*separated*	*three times*	*good luck, happiness*	*must be*

There must be good luck and happiness in the past, present and future!

With the great tradition of Shantarakshita, Padmasambhava and King Trisong Deutsan spreading throughout the three levels of the world, and the minds of all beings never separating from the illumination of the Three Jewels, there must be good luck and happiness in the past, present and future!

བདུད་འཇོམས་པས་སོ།། །།

By Dudjom Rinpoche

འདས་པའི་སངས་རྒྱས་ཀུན་གྱི་ཡུམ་ཆེན་མོ།

DAE PAI　**SANG GYE**　**KUN**　**GYI**　**YUM**　**CHEN MO**
past　*buddhas*　*all*　*of*　*mother*　*great*
　　　　　　　　　　　　　Prajnaparamita

Great Mother of all the buddhas of the past,

ད་ལྟར་སངས་རྒྱས་བསྐྱེད་ཅིང་རིག་པ་འཛིན།

DAN TAR　**SANG GYE**　**KYE CHING**　**RIG PA DZIN**
present　*buddhas*　*bringing forth*　*site of intrinsic awareness*
　　　　　　　　　　　　　Vidyadhari

Vidyadhari, giving rise to buddhas in the present,

མ་འོངས་སངས་རྒྱས་བསྐྱེད་མཛད་དབང་མོ་ཆེ།

MA ONG　**SANG GYE**　**KYE**　**DZAE**　**WONG MO**　**CHE**
future　*buddhas*　*develop,*　*doing*　*powerful lady*　*great*
　　　　　　　generate*　　　*Maha Karma*
　　　　　　　　　　　　　　Indrani

* causes them to attain enlightenment

Maha Karma Indrani, generating buddhas of the future –

དུས་གསུམ་རྒྱལ་བའི་ཡུམ་ལ་གསོལ་བ་འདེབས།

DU SUM　　　　**GYAL WAI**　　**YUM**　**LA**　**SOL WA DE**
three times (past　*jina's, buddha's*　*mother*　*la*　*pray*
present, future)

We pray to the mother of the buddha's of the three times.

Great Mother of all the buddhas of the past, Vidyadhari giving rise to buddhas of the present, Maha Karma Indrani, generating buddhas of the future – we pray to the mother of the bud-dhas of the three times.

ཞེས་རྡོ་རྗེ་རས།

By Vidyadhara

གསོལ་འདེབས་རྣམ་ཐར་དྲི་མེད་ནི།

The Prayer of the Stainless Biography

ཨེ་མ་ཧོ། རྣམ་ཐར་དྲི་མེད་ཡོན་ཏན་ཀུན་རྫོགས་ཤིང་།

E MA HO	NAM THAR	DRI ME	YON TAN	KUN DZO SHING
wonderful	*biography*	*stainless*	*good qualities*	*complete*

Wonderful! Your stainless life-story replete with all good qualities

ཡིད་བཞིན་ནོར་བུ་དབང་གི་རྒྱལ་པོ་ལྟར།

YI ZHIN NOR BU	WANG GI GYAL PO		TAR
wish-fulfilling gem	*(name of the highest one, royal power)*		*as*

Is like the Wangi Gyalpo wish-fulfilling gem.

བྱིན་རླབས་དངོས་གྲུབ་ཐམས་ཅད་འབྱུང་བའི་གནས།

JIN LAB	NGO DRU	THAM CHE	JUNG WAI NAE
blessing	*attainments*	*all*	*source*

The source of all blessings and accomplishments,

རྗེ་བཙུན་པདྨ་བདག་གིས་དུས་འདིར་དྲན།

JE TSUN	PAE MA	DA	GI	DU	DIR	DRAN
saintly, perfect	*Padmasambhava*	*me*	*by*	*time*	*at this*	*remember*

We think of you now, saintly Padmasambhava.

གསོལ་བ་འདེབས་སོ་ཨོ་རྒྱན་རིན་པོ་ཆེ།

SOL WA DE SO	OR GYAN	RIN PO CHE
pray	*Oddiyana*	*precious one*

Precious one from Orgyan, we pray to you.

བདག་སོགས་འགྲོ་ལ་དབང་བསྐུར་བྱིན་གྱིས་རློབས།

DA SO	DRO	LA	WANG KUR	JIN GYI LO
we	*beings*	*to*	*initiation*	*bless!*

Please grant initiation and blessing to all beings!

Wonderful! Your stainless life-story replete with all good qualities is like the Wangi Gyalpo wish-fulfilling gem. The source of all blessings and accomplishments, we think of you now, saintly Padmasambhava. Precious one from Orgyan, we pray to you. Please grant initiation and blessing to all beings!

ཐུབ་དབང་རྒྱལ་པོ་ཤཱཀྱའི་བསྟན་པ་ལ།

THUB WANG		GYAL PO	SHA KYAI	TAN PA	LA
munindra, powerful sage		*king, best*	*Shakyamuni*	*doctrines*	*to*

The doctrines of Buddha Shakyamuni, the greatest of all the powerful sages,

མཐའ་ཡས་སྤྲུལ་སྐུ་འགྲོ་བའི་དཔལ་དུ་ཤར།

THA YAE	TRUL KU	DRO WAI	PAL DU	SHAR
limitless	*emanations*	*beings*	*benefactor*	*arise, come*

Were spread by your countless emanations who act for the sake of beings.

རྨད་བྱུང་རྡོ་མཚར་མཚན་མཆོག་བརྒྱད་དང་ལྡན།

MAE JUNG	NGO TSHAR	TSHAN	CHO	GYAE	DANG DAN
amazing	*wonderful*	*identities, forms*	*excellent*	*eight*	*having*

You who show the marvellous and amazing eight excellent forms,

ཨོ་རྒྱན་པདྨ་བདག་གིས་དུས་འདིར་དྲན།

OR GYAN	PAE MA	DA GI	DU	DIR	DRAN
Oddiyana	*Padmasambhava*	*me by*	*time*	*at this*	*remember*

Padmasambhava of Orgyan, we think of you now.

གསོལ་བ་འདེབས་སོ་ཨོ་རྒྱན་རིན་པོ་ཆེ།

SOL WA DEB SO	OR GYAN	RIN PO CHE
pray	*Oddiyana*	*precious one*

Precious one from Orgyan, we pray to you.

བདག་སོགས་འགྲོ་ལ་དབང་བསྐུར་བྱིན་གྱིས་རློབས།

DA SO	DRO	LA	WANG KUR	JIN GYI LO
we	*beings*	*to*	*initiation*	*bless!*

Please grant initiation and blessing to all beings!

The doctrines of Buddha Shakyamuni, the greatest of all the powerful sages, were spread by your countless emanations who act for the sake of beings. You, who show the marvellous and amazing eight excellent forms, Padmasambhava of Orgyan, we think of you now. Precious one from Orgyan, we pray to you. Please grant initiation and blessing to all beings!

སྤྲུལ་སྐུའི་འབྱུང་གནས་རྒྱ་གར་ནུབ་ཕྱོགས་སུ།

TRUL KUI	JUNG NAE	GYA GAR	NUB	CHO	SU
nirmanakaya,	*source, i.e.*	*India*	*west*	*side*	*at*
i.e. Padmasambhava	*i.e. where arising*				

On the west side of India lies the place where your manifestation arose,

ཨོ་རྒྱན་དྲི་མེད་ཀོ་ཤའི་མཚོ་གླིང་དུ།

OR GYAN	DRI ME	KO SHAI	TSHO	LING DU
Oddiyana	*stainless*	*Dhanakosha*	*lake*	*in*

The stainless lake of Dhanakosha in the land of Orgyan.

མདངས་ལྡན་པདྨའི་སྙིང་པོར་རྫུས་ཏེ་འཁྲུངས།

DANG DAN	PAE MAI	NYING POR	DZU TE	TRUNG
shining	*lotus*	*in centre*	*miraculously*	*born*

There you were miraculously born in the centre of a shining lotus.

སྐྱེ་གནས་ཁྱད་འཕགས་ཨོ་རྒྱན་དུས་འདིར་དྲན།

KYE	NAE	KHYAE	PHA	OR GYAN	DU	DIR	DRAN
birth	*place*	*especially*	*noble,*	*Padmasambhava*	*time*	*at this*	*remember*
			elevated				

We remember now your most exalted birth place in Orgyan.

གསོལ་བ་འདེབས་སོ་ཨོ་རྒྱན་རིན་པོ་ཆེ།

SOL WA DEB SO	OR GYAN	RIN PO CHE
pray	*Oddiyana*	*precious one*

Precious one from Orgyan, we pray to you.

བདག་སོགས་འགྲོ་ལ་དབང་བསྐུར་བྱིན་གྱིས་རློབས།

DA SO	DRO	LA	WANG KUR	JIN GYI LO
we	*beings*	*to*	*initiation*	*bless!*

Please grant initiation and blessing to all beings!

On the west side of India lies the place where your manifestation arose, the stainless lake of Dhanakosha in the land of Orgyan. There you were miraculously born in the centre of a shining lotus. We remember now your most exalted birth place in Orgyan. Precious one from Orgyan, we pray to you. Please grant initiation and blessing to all beings!

ཞིང་ཁམས་ཁྱད་འཕགས་ཨོ་རྒྱན་ཕོ་བྲང་དུ།

ZHING KHAM	KHYAE	PHA	OR GYAN	PHO DRANG	DU
realm	*especially*	*noble, elevated*	*Oddiyana*	*palace*	*in*

In the palace of the most exalted realm of Orgyan

ཨྀནྡྲ་བོ་དྷི་སྲས་ཀྱི་སྐལ་བ་མཛད།

IN DRA BO DHI　　SAE　KYI　KAL WA　DZAE
(King of Oddiyana)　son　of　fortunate　did (according to the king's need)

You compassionately acted as King Indrabodhi's son and

མངའ་རིས་ཐམས་ཅད་བྱང་ཆུབ་ལམ་ལ་བཀོད།

NGA RI　THAM CHE　JANG CHU　　　LAM　LA　KOE
subjects　all　bodhi, enlightenment　path　on　put

Put all the subjects on the path to enlightenment.

ཆོས་ཀྱི་རྒྱལ་པོ་ཨོ་རྒྱན་རིན་པོ་ཆེ།

CHO KYI GYAL PO　　　　　OR GYAN　RIN PO CHE
Dharmaraja, king who fosters the dharma　Oddiyana　precious one

Precious one from Orgyan, you are the dharma king.

གསོལ་བ་འདེབས་སོ་ཨོ་རྒྱན་རིན་པོ་ཆེ།

SOL WA DEB SO　OR GYAN　RIN PO CHE
pray　Oddiyana　precious one

Precious one from Orgyan, we pray to you.

བདག་སོགས་འགྲོ་ལ་དབང་བསྐུར་བྱིན་གྱིས་རློབས།

DA SO　DRO　LA　WANG KUR　JIN GYI LO
we　beings　to　initiation　bless!

Please grant initiation and blessing to all beings!

In the palace of the most exalted realm of Orgyan you compassionately acted as King Indrabodhi's son and put all the subjects on the path to enlightenment. Precious one from Orgyan, you are the dharma king. Precious one from Orgyan, we pray to you. Please grant initiation and blessing to all beings!

རྒྱལ་སྲིད་སྤངས་ནས་དུར་ཁྲོད་གནས་སུ་གཤེགས།

GYAL SI　PANG　NE　DUR TRO　NAE　SU　SHE
kingdom　abandon　then　cemetery　place　to　went

You abandoned your kingdom and went to the cemeteries

ཞིང་སྐྱོང་མཁའ་འགྲོའི་ཚོགས་རྣམས་དབང་དུ་བསྡུས།

ZHING KYONG　KHAN DROI　TSHO NAM　WANG　DU　DU
land spirits　dakinis　hosts　power　under　drew, put

Where you put the hosts of local spirits and dakinis under your power, and

ཧྱ་ན་ཀུ་ཐེའི་སྦྱོར་སྒྲོལ་སྤྱོད་པ་མཛད།

TA NA   GA NAI   JOR   DROL   CHO PA   DZAE
union   liberation   union   liberation   practice, deeds   did

Performed the deeds of union and liberation.

བཏུལ་ཞུགས་རྨད་བྱུང་ཨོ་རྒྱན་རིན་པོ་ཆེ།

TUL ZHU   MAE JUNG   OR GYAN   RIN PO CHE
determined practice   wonderful   Oddiyana   precious one

Precious one from Orgyan, you are amazing in your arduous practice.

གསོལ་བ་འདེབས་སོ་ཨོ་རྒྱན་རིན་པོ་ཆེ།

SOL WA DEB SO   OR GYAN   RIN PO CHE
pray   Oddiyana   precious one

Precious one from Orgyan, we pray to you.

བདག་སོགས་འགྲོ་ལ་དབང་བསྐུར་བྱིན་གྱིས་རློབས།

DA SO   DRO   LA   WANG KUR   JIN GYI LO
we   beings   to   initiation   bless!

Please grant initiation and blessing to all beings!

You abandoned your kingdom and went to the cemeteries where you put the hosts of local spirits and dakinis under your power and performed the deeds of union and liberation. Precious one from Orgyan, you are amazing in your arduous practice. Precious one from Orgyan, we pray to you. Please grant initiation and blessing to all beings!

ཟ་ཧོར་ཡུལ་བྱོན་ཤཱཀྱའི་དགེ་སློང་མཛད།

ZA HOR   YUL   JON   SHA KYAI   GE LONG   DZAE
Zahor   country   went to   Shakyamuni's   bhikshu   did

As a bhikshu following Sahakyamuni you went to the land of Zahor.

ཚུལ་ཁྲིམས་རྣམ་དག་བསླབ་གསུམ་རྒྱན་གྱིས་མཛེས།

TSHUL TRIM   NAM DA   LAB   SUM   GYAN   GYI   DZE
morality   very pure   trainings   three   ornaments   with   beautiful
                          (morality, meditation, wisdom)

Keeping very pure morality you were made beautiful with the ornaments of the three trainings, you who

ཕ་རོལ་ཕྱིན་པ་བཅུ་ཡི་དོན་དང་ལྡན།

PHA ROL CHIN PA   CHU   YI   DON   DANG DAN
paramitas   ten   of   meaning and method   having

Possessed the realisation of the ten paramitas.

ཐར་པའི་ལམ་སྟོན་ཨོ་རྒྱན་རིན་པོ་ཆེ།

THAR PAI	LAM	TON	OR GYAN	RIN PO CHE
liberation	*path*	*showing*	*Oddiyana*	*precious one*

Precious one from Orgyan, you showed the path to liberation.

གསོལ་བ་འདེབས་སོ་ཨོ་རྒྱན་རིན་པོ་ཆེ།

SOL WA DEB SO	OR GYAN	RIN PO CHE
pray	*Oddiyana*	*precious one*

Precious one from Orgyan, we pray to you.

བདག་སོགས་འགྲོ་ལ་དབང་བསྐུར་བྱིན་གྱིས་རློབས།

DA SO	DRO	LA	WANG KUR	JIN GYI LO
we	*beings*	*to*	*initiation*	*bless!*

Please grant initiation and blessing to all beings!

As a bhikshu following Shakyamuni you went to the land of Zahor. Keeping very pure morality you were made beautiful with the ornaments of the three trainings, you who possessed the realisation of the ten paramitas. Precious one from Orgyan, you showed the path to liberation. Precious one from Orgyan, we pray to you. Please grant initiation and blessing to all beings!

འཇམ་དཔལ་བཤེས་གཉེན་ལ་སོགས་བླ་མ་ཡི།

JAM PAL SHE NYE	LA SO	LA MA	YI
Manjusritra	*and so on*	*guru*	*of*

You went to see Manjusrimitra and your other gurus and thus

སྤྱན་སྔར་བྱོན་ནས་སྒྲོ་འདོགས་མ་ལུས་བཅད།

CHEN NGAR	JON	NE	DRO DO	MA LU	CHAE
face to face	*went*	*then*	*doubts*	*all*	*destroyed*

Destroyed all your doubts.

ཐུགས་དམ་ཞལ་གཟིགས་མཁྱེན་གཉིས་མངོན་དུ་གྱུར།

THUG DAM	ZHAL ZI	KHYEN	NYI	NGON DU GYUR
transforming deity	*face saw*	*understandings**	*two*	*become manifest*

*mNgon-Gyur, evident and lKog-Gyur, hidden

Then you saw the face of your transforming deity and the two understandings arose clearly for you.

ཤེས་རབ་བློ་ལྡན་ཨོ་རྒྱན་རིན་པོ་ཆེ།

SHE RAB	LO DAN	OR GYAN	RIN PO CHE
supreme knowledge	*intelligent*	*Oddiyana*	*precious one*

Precious one from Orgyan, you possess great intelligence and supreme knowledge.

གསོལ་བ་འདེབས་སོ་ཨོ་རྒྱན་རིན་པོ་ཆེ།

SOL WA DEB SO   **OR GYAN**   **RIN PO CHE**
pray   *Oddiyana*   *precious one*

བདག་སོགས་འགྲོ་ལ་དབང་བསྐུར་བྱིན་གྱིས་རློབས།

DA SO   **DRO**   **LA**   **WANG KUR**   **JIN GYI LO**
we   *beings*   *to*   *initiation*   *bless!*

Please grant initiation and blessing to all beings!

You went to see Manjusrimitra and your other gurus and thus destroyed all your doubts. Then you saw the face of your transforming deity and the two understandings arose clearly for you. Precious one from Orgyan, you possess great intelligence and supreme knowledge. Precious one from Orgyan, we pray to you. Please grant initiation and blessing to all beings!

ཡེ་ཤེས་མཁའ་འགྲོ་དགེ་སློང་ཀུན་དགའ་མོས།

YE SHE   **KHAN DRO**   **GE LONG**   **KUN GA MOE**
pristine cognition   *dakini*   *Bhikshuni*   *Sarvananda*

The jnana dakini Bhikshuni Sarvananda

ཞལ་དུ་གསོལ་ནས་གསང་བའི་པདྨོར་བཏོན།

ZHAL   **DU**   **SOL**   **NE**   **SANG WAI**   **PAE MOR**   **TON**
mouth   *in*   *swallowed*   *than*   *secret*   *lotus*   *came out*

Swallowed you and emitted you from her secret lotus and

ཕྱི་ནང་གསང་བའི་དབང་རྣམས་རྫོགས་པར་བསྐུར།

CHI   **NANG**   **SANG WAI**   **WANG NAM**   **DZO PAR**   **KUR**
outer   *inner*   *secret*   *initiations*   *fully*   *given*

Thus you fully gained the outer, inner and secret initiations.

སྨིན་གྲོལ་མཐར་ཕྱིན་ཨོ་རྒྱན་རིན་པོ་ཆེ།

MIN   **DROL**   **THAR CHIN**   **OR GYAN**   **RIN PO CHE**
ripening   *liberating*   *fulfilled, completed*   *Oddiyana*   *precious one*
(initiation)   *(doctrines)*

Precious one from Orgyan, you have completed the stages of ripening and liberation.

གསོལ་བ་འདེབས་སོ་ཨོ་རྒྱན་རིན་པོ་ཆེ།

SOL WA DE SO   **OR GYAN**   **RIN PO CHE**
pray   *Oddiyana*   *precious one*

Precious one from Orgyan, we pray to you.

བདག་སོགས་འགྲོ་ལ་དབང་བསྐུར་བྱིན་གྱིས་རློབས།

DA SO   DRO   LA   WANG KUR   JIN GYI LO
we   beings   to   initiation   bless!

Please grant initiation and blessing to all beings!

The jnana dakini Bhikshuni Sarvananda swallowed you and emitted you from her secret lotus and thus you gained the outer, inner and secret initiations. Precious one from Orgyan, you have completed the stages of ripening and liberation. Precious one from Orgyan, we pray to you. Please grant initiations and blessing to all beings!

བླ་མས་ལུང་བསྟན་ཨོ་རྒྱན་ལ་སོགས་པའི།

LA MAE   LUNG TAN   OR GYAN   LA SO PAI
by guru   prediction   Oddiyana   and so on

In accordance with your guru's predictions

དུར་ཁྲོད་གནས་སུ་མཁའ་འགྲོ་བྱིན་བརླབས་ནས།

DUR TRO   NAE   SU   KHAN DROE   JIN LAB   NE
cemetery   place   in   by dakinis   blessed   then

You were blessed by dakinis in the cemeteries of Orgyan and so on, and

དངོས་གྲུབ་མཆོག་ཐོབ་དགོངས་པ་མངོན་དུ་གྱུར།

NGO DRU   CHO   THO   GONG PA   NGON DU GYUR
attainment   supreme   gained   wisdom   clearly manifest

Gaining the supreme accomplishment your wisdom was unobscured.

མཁའ་འགྲོའི་དབང་ཕྱུག་ཨོ་རྒྱན་རིན་པོ་ཆེ།

KHAN DROI   WANG CHU   OR GYAN   RIN PO CHE
dakinis   lord   Oddiyana   precious one

Precious one from Orgyan, you are the lord of the dakinis.

གསོལ་བ་འདེབས་སོ་ཨོ་རྒྱན་རིན་པོ་ཆེ།

SOL WA DEB SO   OR GYAN   RIN PO CHE
pray   Oddiyana   precious one

Precious one from Orgyan, we pray to you.

བདག་སོགས་འགྲོ་ལ་དབང་བསྐུར་བྱིན་གྱིས་རློབས།

DA SO   DRO   LA   WANG KUR   JIN GYI LO
we   beings   to   initiation   bless!

Please grant initiation and blessing to all beings!

In accordance with your guru's predictions you were blessed by dakinis in the cemeteries of Orgyan and so on, and gaining the supreme

accomplishment your wisdom was unobscured. Precious one from Orgyan, you are the lord of the dakinis. Precious one from Orgyan, we pray to you. Please grant initiation and blessing to all beings!

ཤར་ཕྱོགས་མ་ར་ཏི་ཀའི་གནས་མཆོག་ཏུ།

SHAR	CHO	MA RA TI KA'I	NAE	CHO	TU
east	*direction*	*(in Nepal)*	*place*	*excellent, sacred*	*in, at*

In the sacred place of Maratika that lies to the east

ལྷ་ལྕམ་མནྡྷ་ར་བ་ཡུམ་དང་བཅས།

LHA CHAM	MAN DHA RA WA	YUM	DANG CHE
princess	*Mandarava*	*consort*	*together*

You practised non-dual union with your consort

ཡབ་ཡུམ་གཉིས་མེད་ཚེ་ཡི་དངོས་གྲུབ་ཐོབ།

YAB YUM NYI ME	TSHE	YI	NGO DRU	THO
Padmasambhava and Mandarava	*long life*	*of*	*attainment*	*gained*

Princess Mandarava and gained the accomplishment of long life.

སྐྱེ་འཆི་གཉིས་སྤངས་ཨོ་རྒྱན་རིན་པོ་ཆེ།

KYE	CHI	NYI	PANG	OR GYAN	RIN PO CHE
birth	*death*	*both*	*discard, free of their compulsion*	*Oddiyana*	*precious one*

Precious one from Orgyan, you gained freedom from both birth and death.

གསོལ་བ་འདེབས་སོ་ཨོ་རྒྱན་རིན་པོ་ཆེ།

SOL WA DE SO	OR GYAN	RIN PO CHE
pray	*Oddiyana*	*precious one*

Precious one from Orgyan, we pray to you.

བདག་སོགས་འགྲོ་ལ་དབང་བསྐུར་བྱིན་གྱིས་རློབས།

DA SO	DRO	LA	WANG KUR	JIN GYI LO
we	*beings*	*to*	*initiation*	*bless!*

Please grant initiation and blessing to all beings!

In the sacred place of Maratika that lies to the east you practised non-dual union with your consort princess Mandarava and gained the accomplishment of long life. Precious one from Orgyan, you gained freedom from both birth and death. Precious one from Orgyan, we pray to you. Please grant initiation and blessing to all beings!

 གྱལ་པོའི་ཆད་པས་མེ་ལ་བསྲེགས་པའི་ཚེ།

GYAL POI   CHAE PAE   ME   LA   SE PAI   TSHE
king's   *punishment*   *fire*   *in*   *burnt*   *when*

When you suffered the king's punishment of being burnt in a fire

མཚོ་ཆེན་པདྨས་བརྒྱན་པའི་དབུས་ཉིད་དུ།

TSHO   CHEN   PAD MAE   GYAN PAI   WU NYI   DU
lake   *great*   *lotus*   *adorning*   *centre*   *in*

You transformed it into a great lake and sat like an ornament in the centre of a lotus

དངོས་སུ་བཞུགས་པས་ཐམས་ཅད་ངོ་མཚར་སྐྱེས།

NGO SU   ZHU PAE   THAM CHE   NGO TSHAR   KYE
really   *sitting*   *everyone*   *amazement*   *arose*

So that all were filled with amazement.

རླུང་སེམས་དབང་ཐོབ་ཨོ་རྒྱན་རིན་པོ་ཆེ།

LUNG   SEM   WANG   THOB   OR GYAN   RIN PO CHE
wind   *mind*   *power*   *got*   *Oddiyana*   *precious one*

Precious one from Orgyan, you gained the power of wind-mind.

གསོལ་བ་འདེབས་སོ་ཨོ་རྒྱན་རིན་པོ་ཆེ།

SOL WA DEB SO   OR GYAN   RIN PO CHE
pray   *Oddiyana*   *precious one*

Precious one from Orgyan, we pray to you.

བདག་སོགས་འགྲོ་ལ་དབང་བསྐུར་བྱིན་གྱིས་རློབས།

DA SO   DRO   LA   WANG KUR   JIN GYI LO
we   *beings*   *to*   *initiation*   *bless!*

Please grant initiation and blessing to all beings!

When you suffered the king's punishment of being burnt in a fire you transformed it into a great lake and sat like an ornament in the centre of a lotus so that all were filled with amazement. Precious one from Orgyan, you gained the power of wind-mind. Precious one from Orgyan, we pray to you. Please grant initiation and blessing to all beings!

ཨོ་རྒྱན་མཁའ་འགྲོའི་གླིང་དུ་སྤྱོད་པ་མཛད།

OR GYAN   KHAN DROI   LING   DU   CHOE PA   DZAE
Oddiyana   *dakini*   *place*   *at*   *practice*   *did*

You performed practice in the dakini land of Orgyan.

ཆུ་བོ་གྱེན་ལྡོག་ཉི་མ་སྟོད་ལ་མནན།

CHU WO	GYEN DOE	NYI MA	TOE	LA	NAN
river	*reverse*	*sun*	*high in the sky*	*at*	*fix*

Reversing the flow of a river, you fixed the sun high in the heavens and

རྫུ་འཕྲུལ་སྟག་ལ་བཅིབས་ནས་ནམ་མཁར་བཤེགས།

DZUN TRUL	TAG	LA	CHIB	NE	NAM KHAR	SHE
miraculous	*tiger*	*on*	*riding*	*then*	*in the sky*	*went*

Mounting on a miraculous tiger, you went riding in the sky.

གྲུབ་ཐོབ་རྒྱལ་པོ་ཨོ་རྒྱན་རིན་པོ་ཆེ།

DRU THOB	GYAL PO	OR GYAN	RIN PO CHE
siddhas, adepts	*king, best one*	*Oddiyana*	*precious one*

Precious one from Orgyan, you are the supreme adept.

གསོལ་བ་འདེབས་སོ་ཨོ་རྒྱན་རིན་པོ་ཆེ།

SOL WA DEB SO	OR GYAN	RIN PO CHE
pray	*Oddiyana*	*precious one*

Precious one from Orgyan, we pray to you.

བདག་སོགས་འགྲོ་ལ་དབང་བསྐུར་བྱིན་གྱིས་རློབས།

DA SO	DRO	LA	WANG KUR	JIN GYI LO
we	*beings*	*to*	*initiation*	*bless!*

Please grant initiation and blessing to all beings!

You performed practice in the dakini land of Orgyan. Reversing the flow of a river, you fixed the sun high in the heavens and, mounting on a miraculous tiger, you went riding in the sky. Precious one fron Orgyan, you are the supreme adept. Precious one from Orgyan, we pray to you. Please grant initiation and blessing to all beings!

བསིལ་བ་ཚལ་དུ་བཏུལ་ཞུས་མཛད་པའི་ཚེ།

SIL WA TSHAL	DU	TUL ZHU	DZAE PAI	TSHE
Sitavana cemetery	*in*	*determined practice*	*did*	*when*

When you performed determined practice at Silwa Tsal

ཕྱི་ནང་བཀའ་སྲུང་ཐམས་ཅད་དམ་ལ་བཏགས།

CHI	NANG	KA SUNG	THAM CHE	DAM	LA	TA
outer	*inner*	*doctrine guardians*	*all*	*vow*	*under*	*put*

You put all the outer and inner doctrine-guardians under vow and

འཇིག་རྟེན་དྲེགས་པ་ཀུན་གྱིས་སྲོག་སྙིང་ཕུལ།

JIG TEN	DREG PA	KUN	GYI	SO	NYING	PHUL
world	*proud spirits*	*all*	*by*	*life*	*essence*	*offer*

Forced all the arrogant worldly spirits to offer up their life-essence.

མ་རུངས་འདུལ་མཛད་ཨོ་རྒྱན་རིན་པོ་ཆེ།

MA RUNG		DUL	DZAE	OR GYAN	RIN PO CHE
rough, intractible beings		*tame*	*did*	*Oddiyana*	*precious one*

Precious one from Orgyan, you tamed the rough beings.

གསོལ་བ་འདེབས་སོ་ཨོ་རྒྱན་རིན་པོ་ཆེ།

SOL WA DEB SO	OR GYAN	RIN PO CHE
pray	*Oddiyana*	*precious one*

Precious one from Orgyan, we pray to you.

བདག་སོགས་འགྲོ་ལ་དབང་བསྐུར་བྱིན་གྱིས་རློབས།

DA SO	DRO	LA	WANG KUR	JIN GYI LO
we	*beings*	*to*	*initiation*	*bless!*

Please grant initiation and blessing to all beings!

When you performed determined practice at Silwa Tsal you put all the outer and inner doctrine-guardians under vow and forced all the arrogant worldly spirits to offer up their life essence. Precious one from Orgyan, you tamed the rough beings. Precious one from Orgyan, we pray to you. Please grant initiation and blessing to all beings!

ནཱ་ལནྡ་རུ་ཆོས་ཀྱི་འཁོར་ལོ་བསྐོར།

NA LAN DA		DU	CHO	KYI	KHOR LO	KOR
Nalanda University		*at*	*dharma*	*of*	*chakra*	*turn (i.e.teach)*

You taught the dharma at Nalanda and

བདུད་དང་མུ་སྟེགས་ཐམས་ཅད་ཚར་བཅད་ནས།

DU		DANG	MU TE	THAM CHE	TSHAR CHAE	NE
mara, demons		*and*	*anti-buddhists*	*all*	*destroy (i.e.make ineffective)*	*then*

Destroying all the demons and anti-buddhists

ཞི་བདེའི་ལམ་ལ་བཀོད་ནས་ཤཱཀྱ་ཡི།

ZHI	DEI	LAM	LA	KOE	NE	SHA KYA	YI
peace	*happiness*	*path*	*on*	*put*	*then*	*Buddha Shakyamuni*	*of*

You placed all beings on the path of peace and happiness.

བསྟན་པ་རྒྱས་མཛད་ཨོ་རྒྱན་རིན་པོ་ཆེ།

TAN PA GYE DZAE OR GYAN RIN PO CHE
doctrine spread do Oddiyana precious one

Precious one from Orgyan, you spread the doctrines of Shakyamuni.

གསོལ་བ་འདེབས་སོ་ཨོ་རྒྱན་རིན་པོ་ཆེ།

SOL WA DEB SO OR GYAN RIN PO CHE
pray Oddiyana precious one

Precious one from Orgyan, we pray to you.

བདག་སོགས་འགྲོ་ལ་དབང་བསྐུར་བྱིན་གྱིས་རློབས།

DA SO DRO LA WANG KUR JIN GYI LO
we beings to initiation bless!

Please grant initiation and blessing to all beings!

Please grant initiation and blessing to all beings! You taught the dharma at Nalanda and, destroying all the demons and anti-buddhists, you placed all beings on the path of happiness. Precious one from Orgyan, you spread the doctrines of Shakyamuni. Precious one from Orgyan, we pray to you Please grant initiation and blessing to all beings!

ཡང་ལེ་ཤོད་དུ་བདེ་གཤེགས་འདུས་པ་ཡི།

YANG LE SHO DU DE SHE DU PA YI
(in Nepal) at (bKa'-brGyad cycle) of

At Yanglesho when you set out the mandala of the

དཀྱིལ་འཁོར་བཞེངས་ནས་སྒྲུབ་པ་མཛད་པའི་ཚེ།

KYIL KHOR ZHENG NE DRU PA DZAE PAI TSHE
mandala set up then practise did when

Desheg Dupa and did that practice

རྒྱལ་བ་ཞི་ཁྲོའི་ལྷ་ཚོགས་ཞལ་གཟིགས་ནས།

GYAL WA ZHI KHROI LHA TSHO ZHAL ZI NE
jinas peaceful wrathful gods all face saw then

You saw the faces of all the divine peaceful and wrathful buddha forms.

དངོས་གྲུབ་མཆོག་ཐོབ་ཨོ་རྒྱན་རིན་པོ་ཆེ།

NGO DRUB CHO THO OR GYAN RIN PO CHE
attainment supreme gained Oddiyana precious one

Precious one from Orgyan, you gained the supreme accomplishment.

གསོལ་བ་འདེབས་སོ་ཨོ་རྒྱན་རིན་པོ་ཆེ།

SOL WA DEB SO   OR GYAN   RIN PO CHE
pray   Oddiyana   precious one

Precious one from Orgyan, we pray to you.

བདག་སོགས་འགྲོ་ལ་དབང་བསྐུར་བྱིན་གྱིས་རློབས།

DA SO   DRO   LA   WANG KUR   JIN GYI LO
we   beings   to   initiation   bless!

Please grant initiation and blessing to all beings!

At Yanglesho when you set out the mandala of the Desheg Dupa and did that practice you saw the faces of all the divine peaceful and wrathful buddha forms. Precious one from Orgyan, you gained the supreme accomplishment. Precious one from Orgyan, we pray to you. Please grant initiation and blessing to all beings!

མངའ་བདག་རྒྱལ་པོས་བོད་དུ་སྤྱན་དྲངས་ཚེ།

NGA DA GYAL POE   BOE   DU   CHAN DRAN   TSHE
powerful king, by (Trisong Deutsan) Tibet   to   invited   when

When you were invited to Tibet by this powerful king

འཇིག་རྟེན་དྲེགས་པ་བཏུལ་ནས་བསམ་ཡས་བཞེངས།

JIG TEN   DREG PA   DUL   NE   SAM YAE   ZHENG
world   proud spirits   tamed   then   Samyae monastery   raised
*   and demons*

You tamed the arrogant worldly spirits and raising the monastery of Samyae

རྒྱུ་འབྲས་ཐེག་ཆེན་ཆོས་ཀྱི་སྒྲོན་མེ་སྤར།

GYU   DRAE   THEG CHEN   CHO   KYI   DRON ME   PAR
sutra   tantra   mahayana   dharma   of   lamp   lit

You lit the lamp of the mahayana dharma of sutra and tantra.

བོད་ཁམས་མུན་སེལ་ཨོ་རྒྱན་རིན་པོ་ཆེ།

BOE   KHAM   MUN   SEL   OR GYAN   RIN PO CHE
Tibet   country   darkness   dispel   Oddiyana   precious one

Precious one of Orgyan, you dispelled all darkness in the land of Tibet.

གསོལ་བ་འདེབས་སོ་ཨོ་རྒྱན་རིན་པོ་ཆེ།

SOL WA DEB SO   OR GYAN   RIN PO CHE
pray   Oddiyana   precious one

Precious one from Orgyan, we pray to you.

བདག་སོགས་འགྲོ་ལ་དབང་བསྐུར་བྱིན་གྱིས་རློབས།

DA SO   DRO   LA   WANG KUR   JIN GYI LO
we   beings to   initiation bless!

Please grant initiation and blessing to all beings!

When you were invited to Tibet by the powerful king you tamed the arrogant worldly spirits and raising the monastery of Samyae you lit the lamp of the mahayana dharma of sutra and tantra. Precious one of Orgyan, you dispelled all darkness in the land of Tibet. Precious one from Orgyan, we pray to you. Please grant initiation and blessing to all beings!

ཏི་སྒྲོ་སྒྲགས་དང་མཆིམས་ཕུ་ལ་སོགས་པར།

TI DRO DRA   DANG   CHIM PHU   LA SO PAR
(place in Tibet) and   (place in Tibet) and at other places

At Tidrodrag, Chimpu and such places

མཚོ་རྒྱལ་ཡུམ་དང་གསང་སྤྱོད་མཛད་པའི་ཚེ།

TSHO GYAL   YUM   DANG   SANG CHO   DZAE PAI   CHE
Yeshe Tshogyal consort and   secret conduct, practising when
*   guhyacharya*

When you practised guhyacharya with your consort Yeshe Tshogyal

སྙན་བརྒྱུད་སྐུ་གསུང་ཐུགས་ཀྱི་གསང་སྒོ་ཕྱེ།

NYAN GYU   KU   SUNG   THU   KYI   SANG   GO   CHE
direct teaching   body speech mind of   secret door   opened
(she got from him)

You gave the teachings which reveal the secrets of body, speech and mind.

གདུལ་བྱ་སྨིན་གྲོལ་ཨོ་རྒྱན་རིན་པོ་ཆེ།

DUL JA   MIN   DROL   OR GYAN   RIN PO CHE
disciple ripening initiation liberating doctrines Oddiyana   precious one

Precious one from Orgyan, you ripen and liberate your disciples.

གསོལ་བ་འདེབས་སོ་ཨོ་རྒྱན་རིན་པོ་ཆེ།

SOL WA DEB SO   OR GYAN   RIN PO CHE
pray   Oddiyana   precious one

Precious one from Orgyan, we pray to you.

བདག་སོགས་འགྲོ་ལ་དབང་བསྐུར་བྱིན་གྱིས་རློབས།

DA SO   DRO   LA   WANG KUR   JIN GYI LO
we   beings to   initiation bless!

Please grant initiation and blessing to all beings!

At Tridro Drag, Chimpu and such places when you practised secret activity with your consort Yeshe Tshogyal you gave the teachings which reveal the secrets of body, speech and mind. Precious one from Orgyan, you ripen and liberate your disciples. Precious one from Orgyan, we pray to you. Please grant initiation and blessing to all beings!

བོད་ཡུལ་སྒྲུབ་གནས་གཚུག་ལག་ཁང་རྣམས་སུ།

BOE	YUL	DRUB	NAE	TSU LA KHANG	NAM	SU
Tibet	*country*	*practice*	*places*	*temples*	*many*	*in*

In the temples and practice places of Tibet

དགོངས་པ་མཛད་ནས་དམ་ཆོས་གཏེར་དུ་སྦས།

GONG PA	DZAE	NE	DAM	CHO	TER	DU	BAE
thought of what was suitable	*did*	*then*	*holy*	*dharma*	*treasure*	*as*	*hid*

You considered the future needs and then hid the holy dharma as treasure

སྙིགས་མ་ལྔ་བོད་གདུལ་བྱ་སྐྱོང་བར་མཛད།

NYIG MA	NGA	BOE	DUL JA	KYONG WAR	DZAE
degenerations	*five*	*Tibetan*	*disciples*	*protect*	*doing*

In order to protect your Tibetan disciples in the age of the five degenerations.

མ་འོངས་དོན་མཛད་ཨོ་རྒྱན་རིན་པོ་ཆེ།

MA ONG	DON	DZAE	OR GYAN	RIN PO CHE
future	*benefit*	*doing*	*Oddiyana*	*precious one*

Precious one from Orgyan, you acted for the benefit of future beings.

གསོལ་བ་འདེབས་སོ་ཨོ་རྒྱན་རིན་པོ་ཆེ།

SOL WA DEB SO	OR GYAN	RIN PO CHE
pray	*Oddiyana*	*precious one*

Precious one from Orgyan, we pray to you.

བདག་སོགས་འགྲོ་ལ་དབང་བསྐུར་བྱིན་གྱིས་རློབས།

DA SO	DRO	LA	WANG KUR	JIN GYI LO
we	*beings*	*to*	*initiation*	*bless!*

Please grant initiation and blessing to all beings!

In the temples and practice places of Tibet you considered the future needs and then hid the holy dharma as treasure in order to protect your Tibetan disciples in the age of the five degenerations. Precious one from Orgyan, you acted for the benefit of future beings. Precious one from Orgyan, we pray to you. Please grant initiation and blessing to all beings!

ལྨ་བརྒྱའི་དུས་སུ་ཁྱེད་ཀྱི་གཏེར་ཆོས་དང་།

NGAB GYAI	DU	SU	KHYE KYI	TER	CHO	DANG
five hundred	*period*	*in*	*your*	*treasure*	*dharma*	*and*

To those fortunate beings who would later meet

འཕྲད་པའི་སྐྱེས་བུ་གང་ཟག་ལས་ཅན་ལ།

TRAE PAI	KYE BU	GANG ZA	LAE CHAN	LA
meeting	*people*	*people*	*fortunate*	*to*

With your treasure dharma in the final five hundred year period

དབང་བསྐུར་ལུང་བསྟན་བྱིན་གྱིས་བརླབ་མཛད་པའི།

WANG KUR	LUNG TAN	JIN GYI LAB	DZAE PAI
initiations	*prediction*	*blessing*	*doing*

You gave initiations, predictions and blessings.

དངོས་གྲུབ་མཆོག་སྩོལ་ཨོ་རྒྱན་རིན་པོ་ཆེ།

NGO DRU	CHO	TSOL	OR GYAN	RIN PO CHE
attainment	*supreme*	*granting*	*Oddiyana*	*precious one*

Precious one from Orgyan, you grant the supreme accomplishment.

གསོལ་བ་འདེབས་སོ་ཨོ་རྒྱན་རིན་པོ་ཆེ།

SOL WA DEB SO	OR GYAN	RIN PO CHE
pray	*Oddiyana*	*precious one*

Precious one from Orgyan, we pray to you.

བདག་སོགས་འགྲོ་ལ་དབང་བསྐུར་བྱིན་གྱིས་རློབས།

DA SO	DRO	LA	WANG KUR	JIN GYI LO
we	*beings*	*to*	*initiation*	*bless!*

Please grant initiation and blessing to all beings!

To those fortunate beings who would later meet with your treasure dharma in the final five hundred year period you gave initiations, predictions and blessings. Precious one from Orgyan, you grant the supreme accomplishment. Precious one from Orgyan, we pray to you. Please grant initiation and blessing to all beings!

ཁ་བ་ཅན་དུ་བསྟན་པ་རྒྱས་པར་མཛད།

KHA WA CHAN	DU	TAN PA	GYAE PAR	DZAE
snowy land	*in*	*doctrine*	*spread*	*did*

You spread the doctrine in the Land of Snows and then went to

ལྷོ་ནུབ་ང་ཡབ་གླིང་ཕྲན་ཡུལ་དུ་བྱོན།

LHO NUB	NGA YAB	LING	TRAN	YUL	DU	JON
south-west	*Camara, whisk*	*island*	*small*	*country*	*to*	*went*

The small island shaped like a fly whisk lying to the south-west

ཞེ་སྡང་གདོང་དམར་སྲིན་པོའི་ཁ་གནོན་མཛད།

ZHE DANG	DONG	MAR	SIN POI		KHA NON	DZAE
anger	*face*	*red*	*rakasha, canibal demons*		*control, subdue*	*did*

Where you tamed the angry, red-faced cannibal demons.

འགྲོ་བའི་དཔལ་མགོན་ཨོ་རྒྱན་རིན་པོ་ཆེ།

DRO WAI	PAL	GON	OR GYAN	RIN PO CHE
beings	*glory*	*lord*	*Oddiyana*	*precious one*

Precious one from Orgyan, you are the lord and glory of all beings.

གསོལ་བ་འདེབས་སོ་ཨོ་རྒྱན་རིན་པོ་ཆེ།

SOL WA DEB SO	OR GYAN	RIN PO CHE
pray	*Oddiyana*	*precious one*

Precious one from Orgyan, we pray to you.

བདག་སོགས་འགྲོ་ལ་དབང་བསྐུར་བྱིན་གྱིས་རློབས།

DA SO	DRO	LA	WANG KUR	JIN GYI LO
we	*beings*	*to*	*initiation*	*bless!*

Please grant initiation and blessing to all beings!

You spread the doctrine in the Land of Snows and then went to the small island shaped like a fly whisk lying to the south-west where you tamed the angry, red-faced cannibal demons. Precious one from Orgyan, you are the lord and glory of all beings. Precious one from Orgyan, we pray to you. Please grant initiation and blessing to all beings!

གདུལ་བྱ་སྨིན་གྲོལ་མཛད་ནས་མཁའ་སྤྱོད་དུ།

DUL JA	MIN	DROL	DZAE	NE	KHA CHO	DU
disciples	*ripening*	*liberating*	*did*	*then*	*Khacera*	*to*
	(initiation)	*(doctrines)*			*(i.e. Zangdopalri or any higher realm he has visited)*	

You ripened and liberated your disciples and then went to Khacera

གནས་གསུམ་མཁའ་འགྲོའི་སྤྲིན་གྱི་ཚོགས་དབུས་སུ།

NAE	SUM	KHAN DROI	TRIN	GYI	TSHO	WU	SU
places	*three*	*dakinis*	*clouds*	*of*	*host*	*centre*	*in*
(body, speech and mind)			*(i.e. very many)*				

Where at the centre of a multitude of dakinis of the three places

གསང་སྔགས་དཀྱིལ་འཁོར་ཀུན་གྱི་གཙོ་བོར་བཞུགས།

SANG NGA **KYIL KHOR** **KUN** **GYI** **TSO WOR** **ZHU**
guhyamantra, tantric *mandala* *all* *of* *chief* *sit, stays*

You were the chief of all the tantric mandalas.

ཧེ་རུ་ཀ་དཔལ་ཨོ་རྒྱན་རིན་པོ་ཆེ།

HE RU KA **PAL** **OR GYAN** **RIN PO CHE**
Heruka *glorious* *Oddiyana* *precious one*

Precious one from Orgyan, you are the glorious Heruka.

གསོལ་བ་འདེབས་སོ་ཨོ་རྒྱན་རིན་པོ་ཆེ།

SOL WA DEB SO **OR GYAN** **RIN PO CHE**
pray *Oddiyana* *precious one*

Precious one from Orgyan, we pray to you.

བདག་སོགས་འགྲོ་ལ་དབང་བསྐུར་བྱིན་གྱིས་རློབས།

DA SO **DRO** **LA** **WANG KUR** **JIN GYI LO**
we *beings* *to* *initiation* *bless!*

Please grant initiation and blessing to all beings!

You ripened and liberated your disciples and then went to Khacera where at the centre of a multitude of dakinis of the three places you were the chief of all the tantric mandalas. Precious one from Orgyan, you are the glorious Heruka. Precious one from Orgyan, we pray to you. Please grant initiation and blessing to all beings!

དབང་ཆེན་སྤྲེའུ་ལོ་སྤྲེལ་ཟླའི་ཚེས་བཅུ་དང་།

WANG **CHEN** **TREU** **LO** **TREL** **DAI** **TSHE CHU** **DANG**
powerful *great* *monkey* *year* *monkey (sixth)* *month (lunar)* *tenth day* *and*

On the very powerful tenth day of the monkey month in the monkey year and

དུས་ཀྱི་རྒྱལ་པོ་ཚེས་བཅུ་ཐམས་ཅད་ལ།

DU **KYI** **GYAL PO** **TSHE CHU** **THAM CHE** **LA**
time *of* *king (most important)* *tenth day* *all* *on*

On all the lunar tenth days, these "kings of time",

སྐུ་གསུང་ཐུགས་ཀྱི་སྤྲུལ་པ་སྣ་ཚོགས་འགྱེད།

KU **SUNG** **THU** **KYI** **TRUL PA** **NA TSHO** **GYE**
body *speech* *mind* *of* *emanation* *many different* *send out*

You dispatch countless varied emanations of your body, speech and mind.

སྐལ་ལྡན་སྐྱོང་མཛད་ཨོ་རྒྱན་རིན་པོ་ཆེ།

KAL DAN	KYONG	DZAE	OR GYAN	RIN PO CHE
fortunate ones	*protecting*	*doing*	*Oddiyana*	*precious one*

Precious one from Orgyan, you protect the fortunate ones.

གསོལ་བ་འདེབས་སོ་ཨོ་རྒྱན་རིན་པོ་ཆེ།

SOL WA DEB SO	OR GYAN	RIN PO CHE
pray	*Oddiyana*	*precious one*

Precious one from Orgyan, we pray to you.

བདག་སོགས་འགྲོ་ལ་དབང་བསྐུར་བྱིན་གྱིས་རློབས།

DA SO	DRO	LA	WANG KUR	JIN GYI LO
we	*beings*	*to*	*initiation*	*bless!*

Please grant initiation and blessing to all beings!

On the very powerful tenth day of the monkey month in the monkey year and on all the lunar tenth days, these "kings of time", you dispatch countless varied emanations of your body, speech and mind. Precious one from Orgyan, you protect the fortunate ones. Precious one from Orgyan, we pray to you. Please grant initiations and blessing to all beings!

འགྲོ་མགོན་ཁྱེད་ཀྱི་མཚན་མཆོག་རིན་པོ་ཆེ།

DRO	GON		KYE KYI	TSHAN	CHO	RIN PO CHE
beings,	*lord, benefactor*	*your*		*name*	*excellent*	*precious*

Benefactor of beings, your excellent name is precious.

འགྲོ་བ་གང་གིས་མཐོང་ཐོས་དྲན་གྱུར་ཀྱང་།

DRO WA	GANG	GI	THONG	THO	DRAN	GYUR	KYANG
beings	*whoever*	*by*	*see*	*hear*	*remember*	*do*	*just*

Whoever sees, hears or remembers it will, just by that,

མི་མཐུན་རྐྱེན་དང་བར་ཆད་ཀུན་ཞི་ནས།

MI THUN	KYEN		DANG	BAR CHAE	KUN	ZHI	NE
difficult	*circumstances*	*and*		*obstacles*	*all*	*pacify*	*then, thus*

Have all their difficult circumstances and obstacles pacified.

དགོས་འདོད་རེ་སྐོང་ཨོ་རྒྱན་རིན་པོ་ཆེ།

GOE	DOE	RE	KONG	OR GYAN	RIN PO CHE
need	*wish*	*hope*	*fulfil*	*Oddiyana*	*precious one*

Precious one from Orgyan, you satisfy all needs, wishes and hopes.

 གསོལ་བ་འདེབས་སོ་ཨོ་རྒྱན་རིན་པོ་ཆེ།

SOL WA DEB SO   OR GYAN   RIN PO CHE
pray   Oddiyana   precious one

Precious one from Orgyan, we pray to you.

བདག་སོགས་འགྲོ་ལ་དབང་བསྐུར་བྱིན་གྱིས་རློབས།

DA SO   DRO   LA   WANG KUR   JIN GYI LO
we   beings   to   initiation   bless!

Please grant initiation and blessing to all beings!

Benefactor of beings, your excellent name is precious. Whoever sees, hears or remembers it will, just by that, have all their difficult circumstances and obstacles pacified. Precious one from Orgyan, you satisfy all needs, wishes and hopes. Precious one from Orgyan, we pray to you. Please grant initiation and blessing to all beings!

འཛམ་གླིང་བྱེ་བ་ཕྲག་བརྒྱའི་ཞིང་ཁམས་སུ།

DZAM LING   JE WA TRA GYAI   ZHING KHAM   SU
world   a thousand million   realms   in

In the thousand million realms

ཨོ་རྒྱན་པདྨ་བྱེ་བ་ཕྲག་བརྒྱའི་སྐུ།

OR GYAN   PE MA   JE WA TRA GYAI   KU
Padmasambhava   thousand million   bodies, forms

There are a thousand million forms of Orgyan Padma

གང་ལ་གང་འདུལ་དེ་ལ་དེར་སྟོན་པའི།

GANG   LA   GANG DUL   DE   LA   DER   TON PAI
whoever   to   whatever is necessary   that   to   with that   teach, show

Who teach whatever is necessary for taming each individual being.

འགྲོ་དོན་རྒྱས་མཛད་ཨོ་རྒྱན་རིན་པོ་ཆེ།

DRO   DON   GYE   DZAE   OR GYAN   RIN PO CHE
beings   benefit   vast   doing   Oddiyana   precious one

Precious one from Urgyan, your actions for the sake of beings are vast.

གསོལ་བ་འདེབས་སོ་ཨོ་རྒྱན་རིན་པོ་ཆེ།

SOL WA DEB SO   OR GYAN   RIN PO CHE
pray   Oddiyana   precious one

Precious one from Orgyan, we pray to you.

བདག་སོགས་འགྲོ་ལ་དབང་བསྐུར་བྱིན་གྱིས་རློབས།

DA SO	DRO	LA	WANG KUR	JIN GYI LO
we	*beings*	*to*	*initiation*	*bless!*

Please grant initiation and blessing to all beings!

In the thousand million world realms there are a thousand million forms of Orgyan Padma who teach whatever is necessary for taming each individual being. Precious one from Orgyan, your actions for the sake of beings are vast. Precious one from Orgyan, we pray to you. Please grant initiation and blessing to all beings!

ཨོ་རྒྱན་པདྨ་བླ་མའི་སྐུ་གཅིག་ལ།

OR GYAN PE MA	LA MAI	KU	CHI	LA
Padmasambhava	*guru's*	*form*	*one*	*in*

In just your single guru form of Orgyan Padma

དུས་གསུམ་སངས་རྒྱས་ཀུན་གྱི་བཀོད་པ་རྫོགས།

DU	SUM	SANG GYE	KUN	GYI	KOE PA	DZO
times	*three*	*buddhas*	*all*	*of*	*present, put*	*fully*

All the buddhas of the three times are present and complete

རྡོ་རྗེ་འཆང་ཆེན་ངོ་བོ་ཉིད་ཀྱི་སྐུ།

DOR JE CHANG CHEN	NGO WO NYI KYI KU
Mahavajradhara (highest level)	*Svabhavikakaya (integration of the three kayas)*

For you are the Mahavajradhara Svabhavikakaya.

རྒྱལ་སྲས་མཆོག་གཙོ་ཨོ་རྒྱན་རིན་པོ་ཆེ།

GYAL	SAE	CHO	TSO	OR GYAN	RIN PO CHE
jinas'	*son*	*excellent*	*chief*	*Oddiyana*	*precious one*

Precious one from Orgyan, you are the chief of all the excellent sons of the Victor.

གསོལ་བ་འདེབས་སོ་ཨོ་རྒྱན་རིན་པོ་ཆེ།

SOL WA DEB SO	OR GYAN	RIN PO CHE
pray	*Oddiyana*	*precious one*

Precious one from Orgyan, we pray to you.

བདག་སོགས་འགྲོ་ལ་དབང་བསྐུར་བྱིན་གྱིས་རློབས།

DA SO	DRO	LA	WANG KUR	JIN GYI LO
we	*beings*	*to*	*initiation*	*bless!*

Please grant initiation and blessing to all beings!

*In just your single guru form of Orgyan Padma all the buddhas of
the three times are present and complete, for you are Mahavajradhara
Svabhavikakaya. Precious one from Orgyan, you are the chief of all the
excellent sons of the Victor. Precious one from Orgyan, we pray to you.
Please grant initiation and blessing to all beings!*

མཐར་ཏུ་ཐུགས་རྒྱུད་བསྐུལ་བའི་ཕྱིར་བཛྲ་གུ་རུའི་བཟླས་པ་ཅི་ནུས་བྱས་མཐར།

After this, in order to move their minds, recite the Bendza Guru Mantra as
much as you can.

(According to the sMin-Grol Gling system)

ༀ་ཨཱཿཧཱུྃ་བཛྲ་གུ་རུ་པདྨ་སིདྡྷི་ཧཱུྃཿ

OM	Aa	HUNG	BEN ZA	GU RU	PE MA	SID DHI	HUNG
body	*speech*	*mind*	*vajra, indestructible*	*master*	*Padma-sambhava*	*attainments*	*give!*

Guru Padmasambhava with the indestructible body, speech and mind
— please grant us the accomplishment of buddhahood.

བླ་མའི་གནས་གསུམ་འབྲུ་གསུམ་ལས༔

LA MAI	NAE	SUM	DRU	SUM	LAE
guru's	*places*	*three*	*letters*	*three*	*from*
	(centres of his body, speech and mind with white Om at forehead, red Aa at throat and blue Hung at heart)				

From the three letters at the Guru's three centres

འོད་ཟེར་རིམ་དང་ཅིག་ཆར་འཕྲོས༔

WOE	ZER	RIM	DANG	CHI CHAR	TRO
light	*rays*	*in sequence (from Om first)*	*and*	*at once*	*radiate*

Rays of light radiate out in sequence and simultaneously.

བདག་གི་གནས་གསུམ་ཐིམ་པ་ཡི༔

DA GI	NAE	SUM	THIM PA	YI
my	*place*	*three*	*melt into*	*by*
	(forehead, throat, heart)			

They melt into my three centres and by this

དབང་བཞི་ཐོབ་ཅིང་སྒྲིབ་བཞི་དག༔

WANG	ZHI	THOB CHING	DRIB	ZHI	DA
initiations	*four#*	*gaining*	*obscurations**	*four*	*purify*

\# pot, secret, prajna-jnana and symbol
*due to karma, afflictions, dualistic cognitions and their traces

I gained the four initiations, my four obscurations are purified and

ལམ་བཞི་བསྒོམ་པའི་སྣོད་དུ་གྱུར༔

LAM	ZHI	GOM PAI		NOE	DU	GYUR
paths	four	meditating, practising		vessel	as	become

(bsKyed-Rim, rDzogs-Rim, Lhan-sKyes, rDzogs-Chhen)

I become qualified to practise the four paths.

མཐར་ནི་རང་ཐིམ་དབྱེར་མེད་ངང༔

THAR NI	RANG	THIM	YER ME		NGANG
finally, then	me	dissolves	inseperable, not different		nature

Then the Guru dissolves in me and I merge inseparably in his nature

བློ་འདས་ཆོས་སྐུའི་རང་ཞལ་བལྟ༔

LO	DAE	CHO KUI	RANG ZHAL	TA
intellectual conceptualisation	beyond	dharmakaya	own face, original nature	see

Where I see my true face, the dharmakaya beyond all conceptualisation.

From the three letters at the Guru's three centres rays of light radiate out in sequence and simultaneously. They melt into my three centres and by this I gain the four initiations, my four obscurations are purified and I become qualified to practise the four paths. Then the Guru dissolves in me and I merge inseparably in his nature where I see my true face, the dharmakaya beyond all conceptualisation.

Pure White Lotus
The Life of the Lotus Born From Oddiyana

From the Dakini Secret Treasure of the Truth of Phenomena
Revealed by Sera Khandro

CHAPTER 1.

How wonderful!

Emanated from the hearts of Limitless Light and
The Sage of the Shakyas,
You the Lotus Born[1], our second Buddha,
Manifested in the following way
In order to benefit those needing direction.

Due to ignorance[2]
Sentient beings wander on and on round the six realms[3] of existence.
In these degenerate times everything they do
Is suffused with the five poisons[4].
In order to educate these beings who resist all discipline[5]
You took birth on the top of a lotus in the lake
As a marvellous apparition[6] with all the marks and signs of perfection.

Dakinis[7] of the five classes along with heroes and heroines
Sang and danced and scattered auspicious flowers in welcome
As clouds of five-coloured rainbows filled the air.
Gods, nagas and all manner of beings rejoiced,
Bowing and praying as they sang your praises.

Hearing of all this, the King of Oddiyana
Went to welcome you, this young child.
He offered this praise to you, the apparition:

"Bodhisattva apparition of all of the Buddhas of the three times,
   Having come to Oddiyana you were born on the lake.
   Untouched by defilements you appeared on the heart of a lotus.
   Your radiant presence is fully endowed
   With the marks and signs of perfection.
   Meaningful to behold, we praise you, the Lotus King."

Following this praise the King led you into his palace and
Seated you on a jewelled throne[8] with fine silk cushions.
Offering you many gifts to please the senses,
He presented a vast banquet of many foods, both sweet and creamy.
The eight goddesses[9] proffered many gifts to you as,
Singing, dancing and performing,
They sang infinite praises to you, the apparition.

Marrying Enlightening Goddess[10], you ruled the Kingdom.
Again and again you saw the sufferings[11]
Of birth, old age, sickness and death.
Due to this you gradually renounced your throne.
Finally you left for India
Where you triumphed in your study of all branches of knowledge[12].

This completes Chapter One of PURE WHITE LOTUS: THE LIFE OF THE
LOTUS BORN FROM ODDIYANA telling how he came to this world and was
educated.

OM AA HUNG BENZA GURU PEMA SIDDHI HUNG

CHAPTER 2.

How wonderful!

You went to meet Ananda[13],
The principal attendant of Buddha Sakyamuni.
Receiving full monastic ordination from him
You donned the robes of a monk.

In the presence of the master Prabhahasti
You studied and practised the yogas of Maha, Anu and Ati[14].

From Garab Dorje, Buddhaguhya
Sri Singha, Manjushrimitra,
Humkara, Vimalamitra,
Dhanasanskrita and Nagarjuna[15]
You received the transmissions,
Practices, empowerments and instructions[16]
For the Heart Essence Great Completion[17],
The Secret Essence Tantra[18], the Great Supreme Heruka Tantra[19],
The Manjushri Body Tantra, the Lotus Speech Tantra,
The Most Pure Mind Tantra, the Amrita Quality Tantra,
The Nailing Activity Tantra, the Praise and Offering Tantra, and
The Subduing Wrathful Mantra Tantra.

From many other accomplished masters
You requested transmission of the three outer tantras[20],
The three inner tantras[21], as well as
All the instructions of the outer and inner tantras.
Fully ripening all the qualities of training
You became truly accomplished.

This completes Chapter Two of PURE WHITE LOTUS: THE LIFE OF THE
LOTUS BORN FROM ODDIYANA telling how he relied on Gurus, requested
teaching and ended doubts.

OM Aa HUNG BENZA GURU PEMA SIDDHI HUNG

CHAPTER 3.

How wonderful!

Then you went to the eight charnel grounds[22] in India.
Through your practice you beheld the deities and were
Granted their prophecies.
Fulfilling your practice,
You displayed various signs of accomplishment.
Eradicating all demons, you triumphed over the non-Buddhists.

You travelled to Zahor where you brought Princess Mandarava
Through the doorway of Dharma[23].
The King punished you with burning in a pyre.
The pyre transformed into a lake and you displayed many miracles.
Having attained the indestructible vajra body,
Nothing could harm you.
The King was amazed, and filled with faith and devotion,
In deep he regret confessed his mistake.
The whole Kingdom of Zahor was established in the Dharma.

Then at Maratika[24] you commenced the practice of immortality.
Completing the practice of longevity,
You met the Buddha Infinite Life.
Birth and death could not touch your ripened indestructible body.

You travelled to Dense Array[25] and the other pure lands
Of the buddhas of the five families
Where you conferred with the Happily Gone[26] who said:
"Other than your own mind there is no Buddha."

You practised Mahamudra at Yanglesho[27] and declared
"I have gained the supreme accomplishment of Mahamudra.[28]"

While you engaged in practice at Yarigong,
A dispute occurred with non-Buddhists
At the Vajra Seat at Bodhgaya.
The dakinis[29] advised the five hundred scholars there
To ask you to come with your entourage to the Vajra Seat.
Subduing all the non-Buddhists with your power to cause miracles
You established the true Dharma in India and
Preserved the doctrines of the secret mantra at the Vajra Seat.

This completes Chapter Three of PURE WHITE LOTUS: THE LIFE OF THE
LOTUS BORN FROM ODDIYANA telling of preserving the dharma doctrines
in India and establishing the land in the dharma.

OM AA HUNG BENZA GURU PEMA SIDDHI HUNG

CHAPTER 4.

How wonderful!

Due to the strength and intensity of his previous aspirations,
When the Dharma King Trisong Deutsen[30]
Was unable to tame the land on which to build his temple
The great scholar Bodhisattva Shantarakshita[31] predicted
The benefits of inviting you to come from India to Tibet.
Messengers were sent with gold and finely worded invitations.
When they arrived you discussed their request.
Seeing that the time was right you decided to go to Tibet and
Sent the three messengers on ahead of you.

When you reached Nepal local gods and demons
Created many disturbances, deceptive appearances and obstacles[32].
When you reached Mang-yul great problems occurred.
So for seven days you did the practice of Vitotama causing
All the obstacles to resolve naturally.
You bound all the local gods and cannibal spirits
Of Tibet to you under oath:
Some confessed and prayed, some offered you their life essence,
Some made promises, some paid respect,
Some took on the duty of protecting the doctrine,
Some revealed their body shape, and some kept their vows[33].

When you reached Tsang-rong you were greeted by gods and men.
In Tod-lung everyone welcomed you.
You displayed miracles and
The water used in practice became amrita[34].
Faith and devotion arose in all who met you.

You were met by the King at the Royal Tamarisk Grove.
Although the King was an emanation of Manjushri[35]
He made no obeisance due to his haughty arrogance.
You sang to him of your own power and greatness and
Performed wonders[36] so that faith arose in the King.

He prostrated before you, prayed to you, and
Invited you to sit on his golden throne.
He presented you with treasures and all that delights the senses.
All the gods and humans in Tibet made offerings to you.
Many troubling obstacles were created
By demon-supporting officials[37],
Whereas collaboration and harmonious conditions
Were offered by Dharma-supporting officials.

This completes Chapter Four of PURE WHITE LOTUS: THE LIFE OF THE
LOTUS BORN FROM ODDIYANA telling of the invitation from the King of
Tibet and the binding gods and demons under oath.

OM AA HUNG BENZA GURU PEMA SIDDHI HUNG

CHAPTER 5.

How wonderful!

Then you, the Master Lotus Born,
Manifested in the form of the very powerful wrathful Heruka[38].
Declaiming Hung! Hung!
You gathered in all the gods and demons.
Subduing them with orders, signs and actions,
You bound them by oath.
You blessed the site for the construction of Samye temple.
The four great Kings were placed in charge of the work.
Humans built by day, gods and demons built by night.
It was as if Samye was not constructed but simply grew.
Designed like Mount Meru
With the four great continents and the eight lesser ones,
Samye has inconceivable good qualities.

Images of peaceful and wrathful deities
Were displayed on the temple's three levels.
During the consecration auspicious flowers fell from the sky[39],
The images of the deities spoke and medicine fell like rain.
The stone stele blazed with fire and the copper dogs barked[40].

Wonderful auspicious signs appeared everywhere.
The King, his ministers, his subjects and entourage
Were all filled with joy.
Tibet became a land of good fortune, virtue and fulfilment.
The beneficial qualities of Samye are inconceivable.

This completes Chapter Five of PURE WHITE LOTUS: THE LIFE OF THE
LOTUS BORN FROM ODDIYANA telling of the construction of Samye
Temple and its consecration and flower scattering.

OM AA HUNG BENZA GURU PEMA SIDDHI HUNG

CHAPTER 6.

How wonderful!

In discussion with the scholar Shantarakshita you both agreed:

"Tibet is like a land of cannibal demons.
The people are like animals in not knowing
How to adopt virtue and reject vice.
The demon-supporting ministers
Are intensely jealous and make many obstacles,
So now it is time for us to prepare to return to our homelands."

When the King heard of this, he was heartbroken and wept.
He offered countless wonderful golden mandalas and
Prostrated so much that his crown fell off.
Wailing with the painful intensity of his devotion, he cried out:

"Alas! Alas! Kind apparition!
Scholar and Master, both so kind, please pay heed to me!
I Trisong Detsen have a vast virtuous intention[41], yet
This country of Tibet is like a land of barbarian cannibals.
Devoid of dharma and virtue we wander endlessly in samsara.
Scholar and Master, don't give up on us, please think of us with love.
You, the apparitions of the Buddhas, have come to a place of no virtue.
Please care for us with your compassionate enlightening minds."

The two Masters considered this request.
They indicated that the capable Tibetan children
Predicted by the Lotus Born
Should be sent to India to request instruction in the dharma[42].
Later they returned to Tibet
Bringing all the teachings of secret mantra tantra.
Then by listening, explaining, and meditating[43]
The doctrines were widely established.
Thus Trisong Deutsen's wishes were perfectly fulfilled.
He made offerings and grateful thanks
To the Masters, translators and scholars
To acknowledge their kindness and to extol the greatness of dharma.

The doctrines of the Buddha spread in the dark land of Tibet.
The translators and scholars returned to their homelands.
The doctrines of the dharma arose like the sun.

This completes Chapter Six of PURE WHITE LOTUS: THE LIFE OF THE
LOTUS BORN FROM ODDIYANA telling of the translators and scholars and
the translation of the sutras and tantras into Tibetan.

OM AA HUNG BENZA GURU PEMA SIDDHI HUNG

CHAPTER 7.

How wonderful!

Then you went to meditate in Chimpu[44].
The King and the other close disciples[45]
Offered you a mandala of gold and turquoise requesting
Instructions that were easy to do yet rich in blessing.
You revealed the meditation mandala
Of the Assembly of the Happily Gone.
During the empowerment each disciple threw a flower
To identify their specific practice[46].
Then they went off to meditate alone.
Each saw their deity, the sign of actual accomplishment.

Moreover, when you revealed the meditation mandalas of
The Assembly of Speech,
The Assembly of Visions of the Guru,
The Assembly of Visions of the Deity,
The Assembly of Visions of the Dakinis, and
The Assembly of Visions of the Protectors,
All these infinite mandalas were revealed
Through ripening empowerments and liberating instruction.
The King and the close disciples
Each went to their own place to practise.
In this way the instructions on meditation practice
Spread throughout Tibet.

This completes Chapter Seven of PURE WHITE LOTUS: THE LIFE OF
THE LOTUS BORN FROM ODDIYANA telling of how the King and the
disciples received empowerment and instruction and showed the signs of
accomplishment.

OM Aa HUNG BENZA GURU PEMA SIDDHI HUNG

CHAPTER 8.

How wonderful!

Then you, the Lotus Born, reflected:

"*Here in Tibet I have spread all the dharma of sutra and tantra,*
Including the outer and inner vajrayana.
Regarding the profound essential teachings
I have translated all the pith instructions
From Indian languages into Tibetan.
I have caused the teachings concerning study and meditation
To fully flourish.[47]

"*Now all of you, the King and my other close disciples,*
Must write down all I have taught you in magical terma letters[48] *and*
Hide them in many different secret places, both major and minor.

"I[49] have predicted which of you
  Will retrieve which treasures in future.
  I have written lists clearly describing the contents by their titles.
  I have sealed them with mantra."

Then each disciple made an aspiration
That they would fulfil the Guru's prediction in future.

  "In[50] the future degenerate times
  When life starts to fade by the age of twenty,
  When you find these treasures I will give you specific instruction.
  These secret teachings of mine are my legacy.
  On first approaching a treasure,
  Frightening visions and challenging events will occur.
  Do not react to them; simply rest in openness whatever comes[51].
  The dakinis and dharma protectors will help you and
  Bestow accomplishments.
  Do not talk about what has occurred.
  Keep it hidden within your heart.

  "Actively maintain morality
  Through the vows of renunciation, altruism and tantra.
  Suffering is inherent in all worldly activity.
  Do not waste this precious dharma life — practise virtue!
  Pray to your Guru and to the Buddha, Dharma and Sangha.
  Be careful to make no mistake
  In adopting virtue and abandoning non-virtue.

  "Recite the essential mantras OM MANI PEME HUNG and
  OM AA HUNG BENZA GURU PEMA SIDDHI HUNG
  Pray to me during the six periods of the day and night.
  Each morning and each evening I will come to you as I am[52].
  Let your mind relax and release. Free of artifice
  You will meet me in the open clear light of awareness.
  As a result you will awaken to the three modes of enlightenment present
  within you.

  "Whatever[53] prayerful request you make to me
  I will be like the true wishfulfilling gem.
  In this life, the intermediate state, and

The next, my protection is certain —
People of Tibet, do not doubt this or be unsure.
Maintain your faith and impartial pure vision.
Make supports[54] for Buddha's body, speech and mind.
Ransom those about to be killed.
On the tenth day during the waxing moon
On the twenty-fifth day during the waning moon
Make assembled offerings, burn butter lamps and give alms.
With the pure intention
That others are to be cherished more than yourself,
Take care of all sentient beings in the six realms
With your awakening mind.

"You,[55] the King, and my other close disciples present here now, will
By the purity of your heart intentions, manifest in future times
As the hundred treasure revealers in charge of the doctrines.
In each valley there will be a treasure revealer,
A meditation on me and a treasure site.
In each region each family will have
A worthy monk in residence and there will be
An accomplished meditator, a tantric master, a fully ordained monk,
A tantric subduer of demons, and an adept.
Each and everyone of these will be my emanation[56].
Those who follow me in future must develop pure vision![57]"

This completes Chapter Eight of PURE WHITE LOTUS: THE LIFE OF THE LOTUS BORN FROM ODDIYANA telling of concealing treasures, the offering of final advice, and prophecy concerning the treasure revealers.

OM AA HUNG BENZA GURU PEMA SIDDHI HUNG

CHAPTER 9.

How wonderful!

Then you, the Lotus Born Master, spoke again:[58]
 "Even though I have been very kind to Tibet
 This has not been appreciated.
 My work of guiding Tibet through my manifest body is finished.

Now I will leave and go to tame the cannibal demons.
If I do not subdue all those cannibals there is
No one else prophesied who has the means to tame them.
I will gather the cannibals to me and ensure their happiness.[59]*"*

Hearing this the King[60] was downcast.
With a troubled heart he wept and wailed[61]
In an effort to postpone your departure.
Yeshe Tshogyal tried to follow you, and beseeched:

"Alas! Alas! Precious Guru!
As a woman what Guru will accept me!
You are leaving all of us, the King and your disciples!
Who will we rely on? From whom can we request pith instructions?
Who will protect and shelter us? In whom can we place our hopes?
Who will dispel our negative karma and the resulting
Suffering of the people of Tibet?
Who can dissolve our doubts regarding view, meditation and conduct?
To whom can I bring my intimate questions
About meditation experiences?
Who will comprehend the degrees of heat[62]
Arising with experiences and awakening?
Alas! Oh Guru, hold us with your compassion!
Do not abandon your Tibetans! Protect us with your love!"

Lamenting strongly, she tearfully requested him to stay.
In response, the Master said:

"Worthy adept[63]*, you will never be separate from me.*
Always imagine me on the crown of your head or deep in your heart and
In future you will meet me in Lotus Light."
"For[64]*the sake of you, the King, and for my present close disciples, and*
For all sentient beings in the future,
I leave you prophecies as the representatives of my body along with
Hidden treasures as the representatives of my speech.
My mind will sustain my fortunate future followers.
If those sentient beings in the future who have not met me
Read and copy out my life story,
Memorise it correctly, and venerate it,
They will be born later in my pure land."

With these words, you eased the troubled minds
Of the King and your disciples.
Then King Mutig Tsenpo, Yeshe Tshogyal and
The disciples discussed amoungst themselves.
Offering a gold and turquoise mandala and a vast dharma feast[65]
Together they made their request with this prayer:

>   "We request a prayer of aspiration to remind us of your fine qualities
>   Using few words yet containing
>   The essence of profound instructions,
>   One which will pacify troubles in this life and
>   Lead us to your pure land in the next
>   Where we will live as teacher and disciples."

This pleased you and you gave this prayer of aspiration
Saying, "Remember me[66] as you pray like this!

>   How wonderful!

>   Supreme regent of all the Buddhas of the past,
>   Great source of all the Buddhas of the future,
>   Supreme manifestation of all the Buddhas of the present,
>   Lotus Born apparition, the Buddha of the Three Times:

>>   I pray to you, please bless me.
>>   Pacify all outer, inner and secret obstacles[67].
>>   With your compassion, keep me inseparably with you
>>   In this life, the intermediate and the next.
>>   OM Aa HUNG BENZA GURU PEMA SIDDHI HUNG
>   Your clear knowledge of everything is pervasive like the sky,
>   Your loving compassion protects all beings as if they were your children,
>   Your power and strength is limitless, precious Guru from Oddiyana.

>>   I pray to you, please bless me.
>>   Pacify all outer, inner and secret obstacles.
>>   With your compassion, keep me inseparably with you
>>   In this life, the intermediate and the next.
>>   OM Aa HUNG BENZA GURU PEMA SIDDHI HUNG

The Three Jewels: Buddha, Teachings and Community;
The Three Roots: Guru, Deity and Dakini;
The Supreme Presence: Essence, Immediacy and Potential[68]*;*
Supreme Refuge, perfect Buddha from Oddiyana

> *I pray to you, please bless me.*
> *Pacify all outer, inner and secret obstacles.*
> *With your compassion, keep me inseparably with you*
> *In this life, the intermediate and the next.*
> OM Aa HUNG BENZA GURU PEMA SIDDHI HUNG

Dispelling the darkness of ignorance,
You maintain the lifeblood of the doctrine.
Your brilliance disempowers the demonic hordes of
Experiences arising from the dualism of subject and object.
Establishing the foundation of secret mantra dharma
You are the protector of beings.
Oddiyana, you are kindness itself, the true Second Buddha.

> *I pray to you, please bless me.*
> *Pacify all outer, inner and secret obstacles.*
> *With your compassion, keep me inseparably with you*
> *In this life, the intermediate and the next.*
> OM Aa HUNG BENZA GURU PEMA SIDDHI HUNG

Epitome of the Buddhas' body, you are Jampal Heruka
Epitome of the Buddhas' speech, you are Padma Heruka
Epitome of the Buddhas' mind, you are Yangdag Heruka
Epitome of the Buddhas' qualities, you are Chemchog Heruka
Epitome of the Buddhas' activity, you are the body of Dorje Zhonu —
You are the very powerful Thod Treng Tsal,
The essence who encompasses them all.

> *I pray to you, please bless me.*
> *Pacify all outer, inner and secret obstacles.*
> *With your compassion, keep me inseparably with you*
> *In this life, the intermediate and the next.*
> OM Aa HUNG BENZA GURU PEMA SIDDHI HUNG

The representatives of your body,
Your many manifestations, will arise.
The representatives of your speech
Are the many treasures you have hidden.
You entrusted the visions of your mind[69] to your faithful children.
With great love you watch over all the people of Tibet.
With matchless kindness you are the Precious Guru.

   I pray to you, please bless me.
   Pacify all outer, inner and secret obstacles.
   With your compassion, keep me inseparably with you
   In this life, the intermediate and the next.
   Om Aa Hung Benza Guru Pema Siddhi Hung

We pray to you, our wish-fulfilling Guru!
For all of us, your future devoted disciples,
By the power of our one-pointed prayers to you
Please bestow on our body the blessing of your unchanging body.
Please bestow on our speech the blessing of your uninterrupted speech.
Please bestow on our mind the blessing of your undeluded mind.
May meditation experience and awakening become manifest!
May we all achieve enlightenment in this lifetime!
Om Aa Hung Benza Guru Pema Siddhi Hung"

"You must not forget to recite this prayer.
 Have no doubt that you will meet me in person."

This completes Chapter Nine of Pure White Lotus: the Life of the Lotus Born from Oddiyana telling of the intention to tame the cannibal demons, the request from Yeshe Tshogyal, and the gift of the supplicating aspiration.

Om Aa Hung Benza Guru Pema Siddhi Hung

CHAPTER 10.

How wonderful!

Then you went with your disciples to Mang-yul Gung-tang
Where you all gathered to enjoy the festivities of feast assembly.
Countless mandalas of gold and turquoise were offered to you.
Correcting any mistakes in each of your students' practice,
You removed all their doubts.
You gave advice, special wrapped instructions[70] and pith teachings.

Then you, the Master, told them,

> "Faithful people of Tibet
> In the future false teachings resembling discovered treasures will appear.
> People claiming to be my emanation will act without virtue.
> Deceiving themselves and deceiving others,
> Their behaviour will bring chaos.
> Destroying the difference between cause and effect,
> They will shamelessly say everything is empty.
> Yet those with discernment and good qualities will see the truth."

You gave many such prophecies concerning the future.

Dakinis of the four classes appeared in order to greet you.
You mounted the miraculous supreme horse.
You turned towards the southwest, fixed your gaze and departed.

Yeshe Tshogyal, the King and the disciples were sad as
They each returned to their own dwelling.

This completes Chapter Ten of PURE WHITE LOTUS: THE LIFE OF THE
LOTUS BORN FROM ODDIYANA telling of the prophecies and the departure
to tame cannibal demons.

OM AA HUNG BENZA GURU PEMA SIDDHI HUNG

COLOPHON

This account of the Master's life was written down later by Dorje Tsho and then hidden as treasure. In future may it be discovered by one with the good karma to do so. Having been found, may it bring immeasurable benefit to sentient beings. Hosts of haughty guardians of the doctrines protect this profound text. Do not let it fall into the hands of vow breakers.

Samaya! Gya Gya Gya! Guhya Dhatim

At the right time, the one with the terton name Sukha Vajra copied this down from The Dakinis' Secret Treasury, the Actuality of Phenomena when she was in her twenty-eighth year.

May this be virtuous! virtuous! virtuous!

Translated in 1974 by James Low with the help of Tsewang Dongyal (now Khenpo Rinpoche) at Chatral Rinpoche's Temple in Jorebungalow.

Notes

1. Following the final perfect enlightenment of Buddha Shakyamuni, the Sage of the Shakyas, suffering spread throughout the world of Jambudvipa. In Oddiyana there was famine and the King, Indrabhuti, had lost his faith in karma and dharma due to the death of his son and his becoming blind. Seeing this, Chenrezi asked Amitabha, Buddha of Limitless Light, to help. Buddha Amitabha miraculously caused a five-coloured (white, red, blue, yellow, green) udumbara lotus to appear on the Dhanakosha Lake. Then from his heart he sent a five-pointed vajra with his seed syllable, the letter HRI (ཧྲཱིཿ) into the centre of the lotus. From this, the Lotus Born instantly appeared in the form of an eight-year-old boy with pink complexion and charming personality.

2. Ignoring the intrinsic purity of the whole, of which they are an aspect, sentient beings arise from the reifying belief that they are

real autonomous beings. Being blind to the actual, they believe in the duality of the separate existence of all that they encounter, and acting with desire and aversion they generate habits and tendencies which are formative of their future experience.

3. These are the realms of the gods, of the jealous gods, of humans, of animals, of hungry ghosts, and of those experiencing the hells.

4. The root poison is a combination of mental dullness, assumption and lack of insight. This gives rise to desire, aversion, pride and jealousy.

5. Believing the unreal to be real, deluded beings experience hopes and fears and this agitation makes them both easily distracted and impulsive. They need to learn the basic discipline of focused attention and non-distraction if they are to become truly useful to themselves and to others.

6. The Lotus Born is a magical apparition arising from the Buddha's compassion. He is not a person with a flesh and blood body. He is a body of light that can be seen and yet is never damaged. Being free of the delusion that he is a fixed entity, he can manifest in many different forms, both peaceful and wrathful, according to the needs of beings. His body has the thirty-two major and eighty minor marks that are the sign of a perfect Buddha.

7. Dakinis are sky-dwelling goddesses who manifest as the energy of the mind of the Lotus Born. They arise with different colours according to which of the five Buddha families they belong: buddha, white; lotus, red; vajra, blue; jewel, yellow; karma, green. The heroes and heroines are powerful spirits acting for dharma.

8. With this King Indrabhuti signals that he will hand over control of the kingdom to the Lotus Born.

9. The goddesses of beauty, of garlands, of song, of dance, of flowers, of incense, of light and of perfume.

10. Light Bearing Goddess, 'Od-'Chang Lha-Mo, is the wife of the Lotus Born when he manifests as Lotus King, Padma rGyal-Po, when he is the ruler of Oddiyana.

11. These four sufferings arise with birth as a human. When one sees

that each suffering is an inevitable aspect of this form of life in samsara, one can come to appreciate why suffering is the first Noble Truth, the shocking fact that can turn us towards the dharma.

12. When Lotus Born reached the Indestructible Seat of Enlightenment at Bodhgaya people asked him who his Guru was. When he told them that he was the Self-Occurring Swayambhu Buddha and therefore without parents or master, they thought he must be a dangerous person. So in order to dispel the doubts of the people, and in order to show his own disciples the importance of the line of succession of the masters he decided he would search for Gurus.

13. At the Asura Cave in the hill above the shrine of Dakshinkali near Parping in Nepal.

14. He progressed from Mahayoga where the mandala develops in stages, to Anuyoga where it arises instantly, to Atiyoga where the intrinsic is everything.

15. These are the eight main Gurus of the Lotus Born.

16. For each practice he received the energy transmission (rLung), the text of the sadhana practice (sGrub), the empowerment (dBang), and the oral instruction (Man-Ngag). This gave him the full authority to awaken the potential of the practice.

17. This directly introduces the non-duality of mind and experience and illuminates the darkness of the delusion of the duality of subject and object.

18. The Guhyagarbha Tantra sets out the structure of Mahayoga practice.

19. The Great Supreme Heruka Tantra and the following seven tantras form the Eight Great Practices which ensure the complete dissolving of the basis of samsara and release enlightened energy to act for the benefit of beings.

20. Kriya, Charya and Upaya.

21. Maha, Anu and Ati.

22. These were wild and dangerous places where bodies were left to rot or to be eaten by wild animals. Many dakinis inhabited them

and they could appear in terrifying mode to the unworthy or as bestowers of blessing and accomplishment to devoted yogis.

23. Princess Mandarava was living as a nun in a closed Buddhist convent. The Lotus Born magically entered the convent and she became his tantric consort. When the King heard of this he thought that this stranger had forced his daughter to break her vows and so he ordered a huge pyre to be constructed and tied the Lotus Born on top. However, after seven days smoke was still rising and when the King went to investigate he found that a lake had formed and the Lotus Born was sitting smiling on a lotus in the middle of it. The lake can still be visited at Rewalsar in Himachal Pradesh, India.

24. Maratika is a deep cave in eastern Nepal.

25. This is a name for the Akanistha highest Buddha realm. Each Buddha has their own realm where their particular qualities for promoting enlightenment are manifest. Buddha Vairocana is in Akanistha Ghanavyuha, Amitabha is in Sukhavati, Ratnasambhava is in Shrimat, Akshobya is in Abhirati, Amoghasiddhi is in Prakuta.

26. Happily Gone, Sugata in Sanskrit, indicates Buddhas, those who have happily and easily gone to, or entered into, enlightenment. Due to this they are fully available to help all sentient beings.

27. Yanglesho cave near Parping in Nepal.

28. Mahamudra is to abide in non-duality free of conceptual elaboration.

29. The dakinis taught the scholars the following Seven Line Prayer. This powerful evocation of the Lotus Born ensured that he arrived at the indestructible seat and defeated the wrong views proposed by the non-Buddhists.

    In Orgyen Land where north and west meet,
    In lotus corolla and on stem,
    Wondrous supreme attainment gained:
    'Lotus Born' your name of fame.
    As your circle, dakini multitudes surround.
    Your followers, we practise!

Blessings, in order to bestow, please come here!
Guru Padma Siddhi Hung.

[translation following word order]

30. King Trisong Detsen wanted to securely establish the Buddha dharma. This wish arose in him due to the power of the prayer that he had made in a previous life at the great Swayambhu Stupa in Kathmandu. At that time he was a stable hand, the eldest son of Samvara. Now in Tibet he had to deal with those of his ministers who were attached to their Bon-po traditions. So he told them that they had a choice. They had to do one of these four options: 1) build a glass of stupa on top of a hill so that it could be seen from China ; 2) cover the River Tsangpo with copper; 3) cover a small province with gold dust, or 4) build a Buddhist temple. They chose the fourth option as it seemed to be the easiest.

31. Shantarakshita was already in Tibet and he had been directing the construction of the temple. But although the workers built up the walls during the day, at night the local gods belonging to the Bon pantheon pulled them down.

32. The Lotus born went Swayambhu Stupa to the west of Kathmandu. There he met Sakya Devi, the daughter of King Sukhadhara, the ruler of Nepal. She possessed the thirty-two major and the eighty minor signs of a perfect Buddha. They went to Yanglesho and meditated on the Shri Vishuddha mandala. The Lotus Born was imprisoned three times by local spirits so he sent his disciples Jila Jisa and Kunla Kunsa to India to meet Shri Prabhahasti and ask for help. He entrusted them with the Kilaya Vitotama Tantra and they delivered it to the Lotus Born. By means of this practice all the local gods and troublemaking spirits were subdued and bound by oath to protect the dharma.

33. Local gods and spirits are concerned with their own territory. Their view is small for they are preoccupied with controlling their possessions. Strongly biased, they attack those who do not support their narrow interests, and in this way they are like the individual ego. However Buddha Dharma is concerned with the benefit of all. Using the power of Vajrakilaya, the Lotus Born nailed their selfish tendencies and directed their energetic activity towards protecting the Dharma so that benefit for all could occur.

34. Amrita, bDud-rTsi, is the essence of demons. This essence is emptiness. The power of the demon arises from ignoring emptiness. When the emptiness, the illusoriness, of the demon is revealed their five poisons are transformed into the five wisdoms. The harmful has become helpful. In this miracle in Tod-Lung the Lotus Born caused water hidden in the rock to become amrita and flow from the rock.

35. Manjushri is famed for his sharp intelligence and wisdom. Being his emanation, the King should have been able to see the superior qualities of the Lotus Born. Yet his mind had been dulled by the adulation he had received through being the King.

36. The Lotus Born put his hands together in greeting and fire shot out from them, burning the clothes of the King.

37. Although the Lotus Born, the Precious Guru, had such power and blessing, those who actively turned away from him and were unavailable to work for the common good could still cause many difficulties. Although the Buddhas work tirelessly for the benefit of all, in order for that stream of blessings to be absorbed there has to be collaboration. No one can make someone else enlightened. There has to be intention and ripening and openness.

The government ministers opposing the Lotus Born were led by Ma-Zhang but he was tricked by Gogen ('Gos-rGan), the chief of the Dharma Ministers, who said that it was an astrologically dangerous year for the King and so the Chief Minister should spend three months in a pit underground in order to divert the danger. Ma-Zhang claimed this honour of being Chief Minister to the King but when he was in the pit the pro-Dharma ministers filled the pit with thorns and earth and rocks and thus defeated and scattered the opposition.

38. The many different manifestations of the Lotus Born arise from his open empty source, his clarity revealing the actual contours of each situation, and his kindness, his connective energy of illusion which takes on whatever forms are necessary to benefit beings. In this case he shows the form of a wrathful Buddha, a Heruka, an unimpedable force that dissolves the resistance of all negative forces.

39. Many dakinis gathered in the sky and scattered flowers.

40. There were stone stele pillars at each of the four corners. Each was surmounted by the copper statue of a female dog.

41. The intention to have all the Dharma scriptures translated.

42. Before they left for India the Lotus Born taught them Sanskrit. They returned to Tibet after twenty-five years of intense study.

43. The people listened, the translators explained, and then all accomplished the required meditation.

44. Chimpu is a complex of caves used for retreat located on the mountain above Samye. The Lotus Born dwelt there for a time in a cave known as Drakmar Keutsang.

45. The Lotus Born had twenty-five close disciples, including the king. They all heard most of the teachings. There was an inner group of five, including the King, and they heard all of the teachings and had many emanations as later treasure-revealers.

46. The five sections of the mandala are the sites of the transformation of the five poisons into the five wisdoms or aspects of original knowing. As each disciple, with blindfolded eyes, cast their flower, where it landed indicated the aspect of the practice particularly important for that disciple. Profound dharma is not a set of standard-issue practices to be followed but an invitation into a deeper relationship with the ground of one's own presence. There are many paths, all helpful, but we each must find our way.

47. In these four lines the Lotus Born is privately reflecting on what he has done. In the subsequent paragraphs he is addressing his followers.

48. Knowing how the transmission can subtly decline generation by generation as human thinking leaks into the pure revelation, the Lotus Born gave many teachings which were written down in special script and hidden as treasures to be discovered at different predicted times in the future. Statues, ritual implements, and other items blessed by the Lotus Born himself were also hidden. The discovery of these treasures brings fresh inspiration into the world and strengthens the clarity and commitment of those fortunate

enough to connect with these bearers of the Guru's smile. This brief biography is one such treasure.

49. These three lines are the Precious Guru's reflection on what he has done.

50. Now the Guru speaks directly to his disciples.

51. If a treasure revealer reacts with hope or fear, each of these emotions will cloud the clarity necessary for the transmission of the capacity to reveal. Just as with the instructions for the bardo intermediate periods after death, the key requirement is to recall the Dharma and to remain trusting in open emptiness and not be misled by the patterns of whatever is occurring. The visions that arise on approaching a treasure are produced by the Dharma Protectors who guard the treasure. They will ensure that only a worthy emanation of the close disciples will be able to find and reveal the treasure.

52. Although this is a biography, the Lotus Born manifests in many ways and on many levels. He is not other than your own mind yet he is veiled by your addiction to your own thoughts. Relax out of identification with whatever is occurring. In this openness there is the clear light, the unobstructed potential of awareness. This is intrinsic ungraspable freedom, the integrity of openness, immediacy and expression.

53. Having addressed the King and close disciples the Lotus Born now addresses all the people of Tibet (and of the world).

54. Statues and paintings to support the presence of the Buddha's body. Preparing and printing books to support the presence of the Buddha's speech. Making stupas to support the presence of the Buddha's mind.

55. This final section is once again directed to the King and the close disciples.

56. In truth, everything that appears is an emanation of the Lotus Born. The whole of samsara from top to bottom is not other than his mandala.

57. The current degenerate age is marked by evermore stimuli for

the senses. Agitation, distraction, and impulsivity increase the deluded sense of real existents. Therefore the pure vision of the non-duality of appearance and emptiness must be maintained if the hidden treasures are to be revealed.

58. After the death of King Trisong Detsen the Precious Guru ruled Tibet for thirteen years while the deceased King's youngest son, Prince Mutig Tsanpo, was still a child. He took the Prince, who thought that the Lotus Born was his father, to Hepori Hill near Samye Temple and spoke these lines.

59. The Lotus Born was indicating that when he left Tibet he would arrive instantly on the island known as Fly Whisk to the South East of the continent of Jambudvipa. There on the first night, without being seen, he would merge into the body of the king of the rakshasa cannibals and expel his mind stream to a pure rebirth. In the morning no one would notice the difference and life would go on as usual. Yet gradually the Lotus Born, in his new form as the king, would soften his behaviour and so gradually his subjects would follow suit. In this way all his subjects would gradually turn towards virtue.

60. King Mutig Tsenpo was still a young man. His elder brother Mune Tsenpo was killed by the son of a Bon minister when Trisong Detsen was still alive. The second son Murup Tsenpo only ruled for a few months.

61. The Lotus Born had been asked to come to Tibet to subdue the spirits so that Samye Temple could be built. More and more had been requested of him and he had fulfilled the wishes of the faithful. But now he had to leave since there were others who needed him more. The grief felt at his leaving was a painful reminder of the truth of impermanence.

62. As the mind frozen by ignorance, attachment and all the afflictions melts due to the rising sun of awareness, heat spreads through body and mind and they become pliable and creative.

63. Lotus Born says these three lines specifically to Yeshe Tshogyal. Lotus Light, Zangdopalri, is the pure land of the Lotus Born.

64. The following lines are his instructions to everyone.

65. A dharma feast or ganachakra is the ritual meeting where yogis practise together, make communal offerings and enjoy those blessed offerings together.

66. The Lotus Born refers to himself as *Nga-Nyid* — 'as I actually am'. He is encouraging us to see him as he is, an apparition of light and sound, and not as our dualistic delusions take him to be.

67. The outer obstacles are war, famine, theft, illness and so on. The inner obstacles are doubt, inflation, anxiety, distraction and so on. The secret obstacles are reification, objectification and dualising.

68. Essence or openness is the ungraspability of the mind itself. Immediacy is how its presence shows as the undivided non-dual field. Potential or expression is the non-dual energy of the mind free to reveal the intrinsic connection of all arisings with the ground.

69. These are the visions that will lead the treasure-revealers to where the treasures are hidden.

70. These are special instructions written on small pieces of paper and wrapped in cloth to keep them safe and secret.

༄༅། རྒྱལ་བ་ལྔ་པས་མཛད་པའི་པདྨའི་ཨོ་རྒྱན་ཆེན་པོའི་གསོལ་འདེབས་བྱིན་རླབས་སྤྲིན་ཕུང་མ་ནི།

The Great Cloud of Blessings
A Prayer to Padmasambhava
by the
Fifth Dalai Lama

ནུབ་ཕྱོགས་བདེ་བ་ཅན་ན་འོད་དཔག་མེད།

NUB	CHO	DE WA CHEN	NA	OE PA ME
west	*direction*	*sukhavati, the realm of great happiness*	*in*	*Amitabha (dharmakaya)*

Amitabha in Dewachen to the west,

གྲུ་འཛིན་པོ་ན་འཕགས་མཆོག་འཇིག་རྟེན་དབང་།

DRU DZIN PO	NA	PHA CHO	JI TEN WONG
potala palace	*in*	*arya, noble*	*excellent*	*Lokesvara, Chenrezi (sambhogakaya)*

The most excellent, noble Chenrezi in the Potala,

སིན་དྷུ་རྒྱ་མཚོར་མཚོ་སྐྱེས་རྡོ་རྗེའི་དཔལ།

SIN DHU	GYAM TSHO	TSHO	KYE	DOR JE	PAL
Sindhu	*ocean, in*	*lake*	*born (Padmasambhava)**	*vajra*	*sri, glory (nirmanakaya)*

* Padmasambhava is not different in nature from Amitabha and Chenrezi.

Glorious Tsokye Dorje in the Sindhu Ocean,

ཨུ་རྒྱན་ཡུལ་དུ་རྒྱལ་པོ་ཐོར་ཚོག་ཅན།

UR GYEN	YUL	DU	GYAL PO	THOR CHO CHEN
oddiyana	*country*	*of*	*king*	*Ushnadhara (Padmasambhava as a youth)*

King Thorchochan in the land of Urgyan –

གསོལ་བ་འདེབས་སོ་སྤྲུལ་སྐུ་པདྨ་འབྱུང་།

SOL WA DEB SO	TRUL KU	PAE MA JUNG
we pray	*nirmanakaya, apparition*	*Padmasambhava*

We pray to Padmasambhava, the apparition.

ཕྱིན་གྱིས་རློབས་ཤིག་འཆི་མེད་རིག་འཛིན་རྗེ།

JIN GYI LO   SHI   CHI ME RIG DZIN   JE
blessing   give   Amar Vidyadhara*   (honorific)
* undying holder of intrinsic awareness, a name of Padmasambhava

Grant us your blessings, Chime Rigdzin!

ཐུགས་རྗེས་གཟིགས་ཤིག་གངས་ཅན་ལྷ་ཅིག་པུ།

THU JE   ZI SHI   GANG CHEN   LHA   CHI PU
by compassion look   Tibet   god   only, sole

Look on us with compassion, you who are the sole deity of Tibet,

འདི་ཕྱིའི་བསམ་དོན་འགྲུབ་པར་བྱིན་གྱིས་རློབས།

DI   CHI   SAM DON   DRU PAR   JIN GYI LO
this next what we wish for   accomplish bless
(life) (life)

Bless us with the accomplishment of our aspirations in this and all our future lives.

Amitabha in Dewachen to the west, the most excellent noble Chenrezi in the Potala, glorious Tsokye Dorje in the Sindhu Ocean, King Thorchogchan in the land of Urgyan – we pray to the apparition Padmasambhava. Grant us your blessings, Chime Rigdzin! Look on us with compassion, you who are the sole deity of Tibet. Bless us with the accomplishment of our aspirations in this and all our future lives.

སྦྱོར་སྒྲོལ་སྤྱོད་པ་ཤནྟ་རཀྵི་ཏ།

JOR   DROL   CHO PA   SHAN TA RAK SHI TA
rejoining   destroying   practice,   (one form of Padmasambhava)
the separated apartness   conduct

Shantarakshita, practitioner of joining and elimination,

ལྷ་སྲིན་བྲན་འཁོལ་རྡོར་རྗེ་དྲག་པོ་རྩལ།

LHA   SIN   DRAN KHOL   DOR JE DRAG PO TSAL
local demons make servants of Vajrarudra, one form of Padmasambhava
gods

Dorje Dragpo Tsal who subjugates the local gods and demons,

ཞི་ཁྲོ་ཀུན་གཟིགས་ཤཀྱ་སེ་ངྷེའི་ཞབས།

ZHI   TRO   KUN   ZI   SHA KYA SENG GEI   ZHA
peaceful wrathful all   look   Shakhasimha   feet

Shakya Senge who sees all the peaceful and wrathful deities,

ཤེས་བྱ་ཀུན་མཁྱེན་བློ་ལྡན་མཆོག་སྲེད་དཔལ།

SHE JA	KUN	KHYEN	LO DEN CHO SE	PAL
things that can be known	*all*	*knows*	*Matiman Vararuci (a form of Padmasambhava)*	*sri, glory*

Glorious Loden Chogse who knows all that can be known –

གསོལ་བ་འདེབས་སོ་སྤྲུལ་སྐུ་པད་མ་འབྱུང༌།

SOL WA DE SO   TRUL KU   PAE MA JUNG

We pray to the apparition Padmasambhava.

བྱིན་གྱིས་རློབས་ཤིག་འཆི་མེད་རིག་འཛིན་རྗེ།

JIN GYI LOB   SHI   CHI ME RIG DZIN JE

Grant us your blessing, Chime Rigdzin!

ཐུགས་རྗེས་གཟིགས་ཤིག་གངས་ཅན་ལྷ་ཅིག་པུ།

THU JE   ZI SHI   GANG CHEN   LHA   CHI PU

Look on us with compassion, you who are the sole deity of Tibet.

འདི་ཕྱིའི་བསམ་དོན་འགྲུབ་པར་བྱིན་གྱིས་རློབས།

DI   CHI   SAM DON   DRU PAR   JIN GYI LO

Bless us with the accomplishment of our aspirations in this and all our future lives.

Shantarakshita, practitioner of joining and eliminating; Dorje Dragpo Tsal who subjugates the local gods and demons; Shakya Senge who sees all the peaceful and wrathful deities; glorious Loden Chogse who knows all that can be known – we pray to the apparition Padmasambhava. Grant us your blessings, Chime Rigdzin! Look on us with compassion, you who are the sole deity of Tibet. Bless us with the accomplishment of our aspirations in this and all our future lives.

འཆི་མེད་སྐུ་བརྙེས་ཚེ་དབང་རིག་འཛིན་རྗེ།

CHI ME	KU	NYE	TSHE WONG RIG DZIN	JE
undying	*body*	*got*	*Ayush Indra Vidyadhara (a title of Padmasambhava)*	*(honorific)*

Tshewang Rigdzin who gained the body of immortality,

ཟ་ཧོར་ཡུལ་དུ་པད་མ་སམྦྷ་ཝ།

ZA HOR	YUL	DU	PAD MA SAM BHA VA
Zahor	*country*	*in*	*Padmasambhava, Guru Rinpoche*

Padmasambhava in the country of Zahor,

ཨེ་དཔུང་མཚོ་རུ་བསྒྱུར་པའི་པདྨ་རྒྱལ།

ME PUNG TSHO RU GYUR PAI PE MA GYAL
fire heap lake to changed Padma Raja
(on which he was being burned) (a name of Padmasambhava)

Padma Gyalpo who turned a blazing pyre into a lake,

མུ་སྟེགས་འདུལ་མཛད་སེ་ངེའི་སྒྲ་སྒྲོགས་པ།

MU TE DUL DZAE SENG GEI DRA DRO PA
Tirthikas, discipline, Simharavana
those with control (a title of Padmasambhava)

Senge Dradog who disciplined those with wrong views –

གསོལ་བ་འདེབས་སོ་སྤྲུལ་སྐུ་པདྨ་འབྱུང་།

SOL WA DE SO TRUL KU PE MA JUNG

We pray to the apparition Padmasambhava.

བྱིན་གྱིས་རློབས་ཤིག་འཆི་མེད་རིག་འཛིན་རྗེ།

JIN GYI LOB SHI CHI ME RIG DZIN JE

Grant us your blessing, Chime Rigdzin!

ཐུགས་རྗེས་གཟིགས་ཤིག་གངས་ཅན་ལྷ་ཅིག་པུ།

THU JE ZI SHI GANG CHEN LHA CHI PU

Look on us with compassion, you who are the sole deity of Tibet.

འདི་ཕྱིའི་བསམ་དོན་འགྲུབ་པར་བྱིན་གྱིས་རློབས།

DI CHI SAM DON DRU PAR JIN GYI LO

Bless us with the accomplishment of our aspirations in this and all our future lives.

Tshewong Rigdzin who gained the body of immortality; Padmasambhava in the country of Zahor; Padma Gyalpo who turned a blazing pyre into a lake; Senge Dradog who disciplined those with wrong views – we pray to the apparition Padmasambhava. Grant us your blessings, Chime Rigdzin! Look on us with compassion, you who are the sole deity of Tibet. Bless us with the accomplishment of our aspirations in this and all our future lives.

དངོས་གྲུབ་མཆོག་བརྙེས་རྡོ་རྗེ་ཐོད་འཕྲེང་རྩལ།

NGO DRU CHO NYE DOR JE THO TRENG TSAL
siddhi, real supreme got Vajra Kapalamalin
attainment (enlightenment) (a name for Padmasambhava)

Dorje Tho Treng Tsal who gained the supreme accomplishment,

ཁྲི་སྲོང་བཞེད་པ་ཡོངས་སྐོངས་པད་འབྱུང་།

TRI SONG	ZHE PA	YONG KONG	PE MA JUNG
King Trisong Deutsan	*needs and desires*	*make full*	*Padmasambhava*

Padmasambhava who fulfilled the wishes and desires of King Trisong Deutsan

བདུད་དང་དམ་སྲི་འདུལ་མཛད་གྲོ་བོ་ལོད།

DUE	DANG	DAM SI	DUL DZAE	TRO WO LO
maras, demons	*and*	*vow-breakers**	*discipline,educate permanently control*	*Dorje Drolo, Vajrakrodha (form of Padmasambhava)*

*a class of demons who cause trouble for those who keep vows

Dorje Drolo who disciplined the demons and vow-breakers,

ཟངས་མདོག་དཔལ་རི་ཀརྨ་དྲག་པོ་རྩལ།

ZANG DO PAL RI   KAR MA DRAG PO TSAL
Zangdopalri*   *(a title of Padmasambhava in the form of the King of the Rakshasas)*
*the hill on the island of Ngayab to the southwest where Padmasambhava is at present, teaching dharma to the Rakshasa.

Karma Dragpo Tsal who resides at Zangdo Palri –

གསོལ་བ་འདེབས་སོ་སྤྲུལ་སྐུ་པད་འབྱུང་།

SOL WA DE SO   TRUL KU   PE MA JUNG
We pray to the apparition Padmasambhava.

བྱིན་གྱིས་རློབས་ཤིག་འཆི་མེད་རིག་འཛིན་རྗེ།

JIN GYI LOB   SHI   CHI ME RIG DZIN JE
Grant us your blessing, Chime Rigdzin!

ཐུགས་རྗེས་གཟིགས་ཤིག་གངས་ཅན་ལྷ་ཅིག་པུ།

THU JE   ZI SHI   GANG CHEN   LHA   CHI PU
Look on us with compassion, you who are the sole deity of Tibet.

འདི་ཕྱིའི་བསམ་དོན་འགྲུབ་པར་བྱིན་གྱིས་རློབས།

DI CHI   SAM DON   DRU PAR   JIN GYI LO
Bless us with the accomplishment of our aspirations in this and all our future lives.

Dorje Tho Treng Tsal who gained the supreme accomplishment; Padmasambhava who fulfilled the wishes and desires of King Trisong Deutsan; Dorje Drolo who disciplined the demons and vowbreakers; Karma Dragpo Tsal who resides at Zangdopalri – we pray to the apparition

Padmasambhava. Grant us your blessings, Chime Rigdzin! Look on us with compassion, you who are the sole deity of Tibet. Bless us with the accomplishment of our aspirations in this and all our future lives.

མགོན་ཁྱོད་འགྲོ་བ་ཀུན་གྱི་སྐྱབས་གྱུར་ཀྱང་།

GON	KHYO	DRO WA	KUN	GYI	KYAB	GYUR	KYANG
protector, benefactor	*you*	*beings, those moving in samsara*	*all*	*of*	*refuge*	*are*	*although*

Protector, although you are the refuge of all beings

བོད་ཡུལ་བསྟན་པ་ཉི་འོད་ལྟ་བུར་གསལ།

BOE YUL	TEN PA	NYI	OE	TA BUR	SAL
Tibet	*Buddha's doctrines*	*sun*	*light*	*like*	*shine, illuminate*

In the land of Tibet you caused the Buddha's doctrines to shine like the light of the sun.

རི་བྲག་མཚོ་སོགས་གནས་ཀུན་བྱིན་གྱིས་བརླབས།

RI	DRA	TSHO	SO	NAE	KUN	JIN GYI LA
hill	*rock*	*lake*	*and so on*	*places*	*all*	*you blessed*

You blessed the hills, rocks, lakes and each and every place,

ཟབ་གཏེར་གྲངས་མེད་རྒྱས་བཏབ་བཀའ་དྲིན་ཆན།

ZAB	TER	DRANG ME	GYE TAB	KA DRIN CHEN
profound	*terma, treasures**	*numberless*	*put away, away*	*very kind, most considerate to us*

*doctrines hidden for the benefit of future disciplines

You, the most kind one who hid numberless profound Treasures –

གསོལ་བ་འདེབས་སོ་སྤྲུལ་སྐུ་པདྨ་འབྱུང་།

SOL WA DE SO TRUL KU PE MA JUNG

We pray to the apparition Padmasambhava.

བྱིན་གྱིས་རློབས་ཤིག་འཆི་མེད་རིག་འཛིན་རྗེ།

JIN GYI LOB SHI CHI ME RIG DZIN JE

Grant us your blessing, Chime Rigdzin!

ཐུགས་རྗེས་གཟིགས་ཤིག་གངས་ཅན་ལྷ་ཅིག་པུ།

THU JE ZI SHI GANG CHEN LHA CHI PU

Look on us with compassion, you who are the sole deity of Tibet.

 འདི་ཕྱིའི་བསམ་དོན་འགྲུབ་པར་བྱིན་གྱིས་རློབས།

DI CHI   SAM DON   DRU PAR   JIN GYI LO

Bless us with the accomplishment of our aspirations in this and all our future lives.

Protector, although you are the refuge of all beings in the land of Tibet you caused the Buddha's doctrines to shine like the light of the sun. You blessed all the hills, rocks, lakes and each and every place, you, the most kind one who hid numberless profound Treasures – we pray to the apparition Padmasambhava. Grant us your blessings, Chime Rigdzin! Look on us with compassion, you who are the sole deity of Tibet. Bless us with the accomplishment of our aspirations in this and all our future lives.

འཕྲིན་ལས་གཞུང་བསྲངས་མཆོད་བསྟོད་གསོལ་འདེབས་ཤིང་།

TRIN LAE	**ZHUNG**	**SANG**	**CHOE**	**TOE**	**SON DEB SHING**
ritual meditation	*text*	*reading*	*offerings*	*praise, paean*	*praying*

By reciting ritual meditation texts, making offerings, and reciting praise and prayers

མི་ཕྱེད་གུས་པས་ཐུགས་དམ་རྒྱུད་བསྐུལ་ན།

MI	**CHE**	**GUE PAE**	**THUG DAM**	**GYU**	**KUL**	**NA**
not	*half, split*	*faith, with devotion*	*vows, integrity*	*mind*	*exhort, invoke*	*if, then*

(we remind him of his vows to help us)

With full devotion we exhort you by invoking your vows.

དུས་ཀྱི་རྒྱལ་པོ་ཚེས་བཅུ་རྣམས་ཤར་ལ།

DU	**KYI**	**GYAL PO**	**TSHE CHU**	**NAM**	**SHAR**	**LA**
time (i.e. very important)	*of*	*king*	*10th day of lunar month*	*when*	*coming*	*then*

Then when the tenth day, the king of time, arrives,

འབྱོན་པར་ཞལ་གྱི་བཞེས་པ་རྡོ་རྗེའི་གསུང་།

JON PAR	**ZHAL GYI ZHE PA**	**DOR JEI**	**SUNG**
coming	*you promised*	*vajra, indestructible (it is never retracted once spoken)*	*speech*

You will come as you have promised with your unchanging words.

By reciting ritual meditation texts, making offerings, and reciting praise and prayers with full devotion we exhort you by invoking your vows. Then when the tenth day, the king of time, arrives, you will come as you have promised with your unchanging words.

བསླུ་མེད་བདེ་པའི་འབྲས་བུ་ཡུལ་མེད་དུ།

LU ME	DEN PAI	DRAE BU	YOL ME DU
undeceiving, never cheating	*truth*	*result*	*not late, on time*

May the result of your unfailing truth be timely

ལེགས་པར་སྩོལ་ཞིག་ཨོ་རྒྱན་སྤྲུལ་པའི་སྐུ།

LEG PAR	TSOL ZHI	OR GYAN	TRUL PAI KU
well	*we request you (we hope you will do what we ask)*	*Oddiyana Padmasambhava*	*nirmanakaya*

In bringing benefit for us, you the apparition called Orgyan.

རེ་བ་སྐོངས་ཤིག་བསམ་འཕེལ་དབང་གི་རྒྱལ།

RE WA	KONG SHI	SAM PEL	WONG	GI	GYAL
hopes	*fulfil*	*wishes, satisfying (the king of wish-granting objects, the Cintamani)*	*power*	*of*	*king*

King of all wish-fulfilling powers, satisfy our hopes!

གསོལ་བཏབ་འབྲས་བུ་སྩོལ་ཞིག་པདྨ་འབྱུང་།

SOL TAB	DRAE BU	TSOL ZHI	PAE MA JUNG
prayer	*result*	*please give us*	*Padmasambhava*

Padmasambhava, please grant us the results we pray for.

You are the apparition called Orgyan. May the result of your unfailing truth be timely in bringing benefit for us. King of all wish-fulfilling powers, satisfy our hopes! Padmasambhava, please grant us the results we pray for.

སྙིང་ནས་གདུང་ཤུགས་དྲག་པོའི་དད་པ་དང་།

NYING	NAE	DUNG SHU	DRAG POI	DAE PA	DANG
heart	*from sincerely*	*devotion, craving for blessing (so that we are shaking and weeping)*	*fierce, strong*	*faith*	*and*

When with intense faith and devotion in our hearts

ངག་ནས་ལྷང་ལྷང་དབྱངས་ཀྱིས་གསོལ་འདེབས་ན།

NGA	NE	LHANG LHANG	YANG	KYI	SON DEB	NA
speech	*with*	*very loud*	*sound*	*by*	*prayer (using this prayer)*	*then, when*

Our voices are loud and fervent with this prayer,

ཟངས་མདོག་དཔལ་གྱི་རི་ནས་པདྨ་འབྱུང་།

ZANG	DO	PAL	GYI	RI	NAE	PAE MA JUNG
copper	*colour*	*glorious*	*of*	*mountain*	*from*	*Padmasambhava*
(The glorious copper coloured mountain where Padmasambhava is staying at present)						

From Zangdo Palri, you, Padmasambhava,

དཔའ་བོ་མཁའ་འགྲོའི་ཚོགས་བཅས་འདིར་གཤེགས་ལ།

PA WO	KHAN DRO	TSHO CHE	DIR	SHE	LA
viras	*dakinis*	*hosts*	*here*	*come*	*as, with (now he is here!)*

With your hosts of viras and dakinis will come here!

When, with intense faith and devotion in our hearts, our voices are loud and fervent with this prayer, you, Padmasambhava, with your hosts of viras and dakinis will come here from Zangdo Palri!

གསལ་གསལ་སྐུ་ཡི་སྣང་བ་མིག་ལ་སྟོན།

SAL SAL	KU YI	NANG WA	MIG	LA	TON
very clear	*body's*	*appearance*	*our eyes*	*to*	*show*

Show the appearance of your clear and shining body to our eyes!

སྙན་སྙན་གསུང་གི་ཆོས་སྒྲ་རྣ་བར་སྒྲོགས།

NYAN NYAN	SUNG	GI	CHO	DRA	NA WAR	DRO
very sweet	*speech*	*of*	*dharma*	*sound*	*our ears*	*sound*

Send the dharma sound of your sweet speech to our ears!

ལྷོད་ལྷོད་ཐུགས་ཀྱི་བྱིན་རླབས་སྙིང་ལ་སྟིམས།

LHO LHO	THU	KYI	JIN LAB	NYING	LA	TIM
soft, relaxed	*mind*	*of*	*blessing*	*our heart*	*to*	*melt, be absorbed in*

Let the blessing of your relaxed gentle mind melt into our hearts!

བྱིན་ཆེན་ཕོབ་ལ་དབང་བཞི་བསྐུར་དུ་གསོལ།

JIN	CHEN	PHOB	LA	WONG	ZHI	KUR DU	SOL
blessing	*great*	*strike us*	*with this*	*initiation, consecration*	*four**	*we request, exhort*	*pray*

*of his body, speech, mind, and all three together

Touch us with your great blessing! Please grant us the four initiations!

Show the appearance of your clear and shining body to our eyes! Send the dharma sound of your sweet speech to our ears. Let the blessing of your relaxed gentle mind melt into our hearts! Touch us with your great blessing! Please grant us the four initiations!

སྔོན་ལས་ལྷ་སྲིན་འཁྲུགས་པའི་འཕྲལ་རྐྱེན་གྱིས།

NGON	LAE	LHA	SIN	TRUG PAI	TRAL	KYEN	GYI
former lives	*actions, karmic deeds*	*local*	*demons*	*troubles, difficulties*	*emergency, coming quickly*	*reasons, causes, circumstances*	*by*

Due to our actions in former lives, local gods and demons cause sudden troubles and disasters such as

ཨི་ཕྱུགས་ནད་རིམས་སད་སེར་དབུལ་ཞིང་འཕོངས།

MI	CHU	NAE RIM	SAE	SER	UL ZHING PHONG
no	*wealth, cattle, possessions*	*disease, sickness*	*frost on crops*	*hail storms*	*very poor*

Lack of animals, disease, destruction of crops by frost and hail, and great poverty.

ཕྱོགས་བཞིའི་དམག་འཁྲུག་མཚོན་ཆའི་བསྐལ་པ་སོགས།

CHO	ZHI	MA TRU	TSHON CHAI	KAL PA SO
direction	*four*	*fighting, wars and strife*	*weapon's*	*time*

Now is the time of weapons, wars and strife in the four directions.

མ་ལུས་ཞི་ཞིང་བརླག་པར་བྱིན་གྱིས་རློབས།

MA LU	ZHI ZHING	DO PAR	JIN GYI LO
without exception	*pacifying, rendering ineffectual*	*send back*	*bless all beings*

Please bless us by repulsing these evils and pacifying them all without exception.

Due to our actions in former lives, local gods and demons cause sudden troubles and disasters such as lack of animals, disease, destruction of crops by frost and hail, and great poverty. Now is the time of weapons, with wars and strife in the four directions. Please bless us by repulsing these evils and pacifying them all without exception.

ཆར་ཆུདུས་བབས་ལོ་ཕྱུགས་རྟག་ཏུ་ལེགས།

CHAR CHU	DU BAB	LO	CHUG	TAG TU	LE
rainfall	*timely*	*harvest*	*cattle*	*always*	*good*

With timely rainfall may the harvests and herds always be plentiful, and

ཚེ་རིང་ནད་མེད་ལུས་ངག་ཡིད་གསུམ་བདེ།

TSHE	RING	NAE	ME	LU	NGA	YI	SUM	DE
life	*long*	*sickness*	*without*	*body*	*speech*	*mind*	*three*	*happy*

With long life free of sickness may there be happiness in body, speech and mind.

མཐའ་བཞིའི་འབྱོར་བའི་ལས་སྒོ་རྣམ་པར་ཕྱེ།

THA ZHI	JOR WAI	LAE	GO	NAM PAR	CHE
ends four*	*wealth (all good things)*	*from*	*door (i.e. we get everything)*	*fully*	*open*

* the ends of the four directions i.e. everywhere

Opening wide the door for wealth from the four ends of the universe,

ཛོགས་ལྡན་དགའ་སྟོན་རྒྱས་པར་བྱིན་གྱིས་རློབས། །

DZOE DEN	GA TON	GYE PAR	JIN GYI LO
golden period, yuga*	*happiness*	*spread*	*grant this bless*

* when all is good and there are no difficulties

Please bless us with the spreading of the happiness of the Golden Age.

With timely rainfall may the harvests and herds always be plentiful, and with long life free of sickness may there be happiness in body, speech and mind. Opening wide the door for wealth from the four ends of the universe, please bless us with the spreading of the happiness of the Golden Age.

ཁྱོད་འབངས་ནམ་ཡང་ཡལ་བར་མི་འདོར་ཞེས། །

KHYO	BANG	NAM YANG	YAL WAR	MI	DOR	ZHE
your	*subject*	*always*	*your remembrance*	*not*	*throw away, forget*	*you said*

You will never abandon or forget your people –

མངའ་བདག་ཡབ་སྲས་འབངས་ལ་ཞལ་འཆེས་པའི། །

NGA DA YAB	SE	BANG	LA	ZHAL CHE PAI
King Trisong Deutsan	*his son, Mutig Tsenpo*	*subjects*	*to*	*promised*
		(especially the inner disciples)		

You made this promise to King Trisong Deutsan, his son and their subjects

འགྱུར་མེད་རྡོ་རྗེའི་གསུང་གི་དོན་གྱི་འབྲས། །

GYUR ME	DOR JEI	SUNG	GI	DON	GYI	DRE
unchanging	*vajra, indestructible*	*speech*	*of*	*meaning*	*of*	*result*

With your changeless vajra speech. May it come to fruition

མངོན་སུམ་སྩོལ་བའི་དགའ་སྟོན་དུས་ལ་བབས། །

NGON SUM	TSOL WAI	GA TON	DU LA BAB
very clear, manifest	*give*	*happiness, festival*	*now, not delay*

With the immediate manifest granting of a great festival of happiness.

You will never abandon or forget your people – you made this promise with your changeless speech to King Trisong Deutsan, his son and their subjects. May it come to fruition with the immediate manifest granting of a great festival of happiness.

ཨ་དོར་ན་དེང་ནས་ལྷུན་གྲུབ་ཀུན་ཏུ་བཟང་།

DOR NA	DENG NAE	LHUN DRU	KUN TU ZANG
briefly	*from now*	*effortlessly arising, vibhusiddhi*	*Samantabhadra (enlightenment)*

In brief, from now on, for as long as effortlessly arising Samantabhadra

མ་ཐོབ་དེ་སྲིད་མགོན་པོ་ཁྱོད་ཉིད་ཀྱིས།

MA	THOB	DE SI	GON PO	KHYO NYI	KYI
not	*get*	*until*	*protector, benefactor*	*you*	*by*

Is not attained, Protector, you

རྗེས་སུ་བཟུང་ནས་མཆོག་དང་ཐུན་མོང་གི།

JE SU	ZUNG	NAE	CHO	DANG	THUN MONG	GI
after	*hold (hold and keep as disciples, look after our spiritual welfare)*		*supreme (enlightenment)*	*and*	*general, ordinary*	*of*

Must hold us as your disciples and satisfy us with

དངོས་གྲུབ་བདུད་རྩིའི་བཅུད་ཀྱིས་ཚིམས་པར་མཛོད།

NGO DRU	DU TSI	CHU	KYI	TSHIM PAR	DZO
siddhis, true accomplishment	*amrita, liberating elixir*	*essence*	*by*	*satisfy*	*we must get*

The essence of the elixir of supreme and general accomplishments.

In brief, from now on, for as long as effortlessly arising Samantabhadra is not attained, Protector, you must hold us as your disciples and satisfy us with the essence of the elixir of supreme and general accomplishments.

ཅེས་སློབ་དཔོན་ཆེན་པོ་པདྨ་འབྱུང་གནས་ལ་གསོལ་བ་འདེབས་པ་བྱིན་རླབས་སྤྲིན་ཕུང་མ་ཞེས་པ་འདི་ནི་འཕྲུལ་སྣང་ཆོས་བཅུ་པ་རྣམས་ཀྱི་ཉམས་ལེན་ལ་ཕན་པའི་ཆེད་དུ་བྱང་གླིང་བསམ་འགྲུབ་རྒྱལ་པོས་བསྐུལ་ངོར་ཟ་ཧོར་གྱི་བནྡེ་(རྒྱལ་བ་ལྔ་ཆེན་པོས་)སྦྱར་བའོ།། །།

This prayer to Maha Acharya Padmasambhava, which is a great cloud of blessing, was composed by Zahor Gyi Bande (The 5th Dalai Lama) at the request of Jang Ling Samdrub Gyalpo in order to help the sadhana practice on the 10th lunar day at the time of the 'Phrul sNang' (festival in Lhasa).

Translated by C.R. Lama and James Low, Bodha, Kathmandu,Nepal on the tshe chu, tenth day occurring in December 1977

བསྟོད་པ་ PRAISE

ཧཱུྃ༔ མ་བཅོས་སྤྲོས་བྲལ་བླ་མ་ཆོས་ཀྱི་སྐུ༔

HUNG   **MA CHOE**   **TOE DRAL**   **LA MA**   **CHOE KYI KU**
hung   *unartificial*   *without elaboration*   *guru*   *dharmakaya, intrinsic mode*

Hung. The guru free of artifice and elaboration is the intrinsic mode.

བདེ་ཆེན་ལོངས་སྤྱོད་བླ་མ་ཆོས་ཀྱི་རྗེ།

DE   **CHEN**   **LONG CHOE**   **LA MA**   **CHOE**   **KYI**   **JE**
bliss   *great*   *sambhogakaya, enjoyment*   *guru*   *dharma*   *of*   *lord*

The guru of great happiness, master of dharma, is the enjoyment mode.

པད་སྡོང་ལས་འཁྲུངས་བླ་མ་སྤྲུལ་པའི་སྐུ༔

PAE   **DONG**   **LAE**   **THRUNG**   **LA MA**   **TRUL PAI KU**
lotus   *stem*   *from*   *born*   *guru*   *nirmanakaya, apparitional mode*

The guru born from a lotus stem is the apparitional mode.

སྐུ་གསུམ་རྡོ་རྗེ་འཆང་ལ་ཕྱག་འཚལ་བསྟོད༔

KU   **SUM**   **DOR JE CHANG**   **LA**   **CHA TSAL**   **TOE**
body   *three*   *Vajradhara, the primordial buddha*   *to*   *prostrate*   *praise*

We salute and praise Vajradhara with these three modes.

Hung. The guru free of artifice and elaboration is the intrinsic mode. The guru of great happiness, master of dharma, is the enjoyment mode. The guru born from a lotus stem is the apparitional mode. We salute and praise Vajradhara with these three modes.

Imploring Padmasambhava

INVOCATION

བསླུ་མེད་གཏན་གྱི་སྐྱབས་གཅིག་འཁོར་ལོའི་མགོན།

LU ME	TEN GYI	KYAB CHI	KHOR LOI GON
unfailing, uncheating	permanent	protector	Chakranath, * lord of the wheel of the dharma

*Samantabhadra, dharmakaya, Vajradhara, Sunyata or dharmata

Unfailing, consistent protector, lord of the wheel of the dharma,

སངས་རྒྱས་ཀུན་དངོས་ཨོ་རྒྱན་རྡོ་རྗེ་འཆང་།

SANG GYE	KUN	NGO	OR GYEN DOR JE CHANG
buddhas	all	original, true nature	Padmasambhava (I pray to you)

The actuality of all the buddhas, Orgyen Dorje Chang –

ཉམ་ཐག་བདག་ལ་རེས་ཆྱེད་ལས་མེད།

NYAM THAB	DA	LA	RE SA	KHYE	LAE	ME
very difficult, very sad, many troubles	me (I and all sentient beings)	to	hope, something to rely on	you	other	without

With my many troubles, you are my only hope!

ཐུགས་རྗེ་གློག་ལྟར་མྱུར་བས་དུས་འདིར་དགོངས།

THU JE	LO	TAR	NYUR WAE	DU	DIR	GONG
compassion	lightning	like	quick	time (now)	here	think of me

With your compassion fast as lightning, please think of me now.

Unfailing consistent protector, the lord of the wheel of the dharma, the actuality of all the buddhas, Orgyen Dorje Chang – with my many troubles, you are my only hope! With your compassion fast as lightning, please think of me now.

RECALLING PADMASAMBHAVA'S KINDNESS

དེ་ནི་དུས་ངན་སྙིགས་མའི་མཐའ་ལ་ཐུག

DA NI	DU NGAN	NYIG MAI	THA	LA THU
now	bad time	degenerate period	end	reached

Now the evil time of the end of the degenerate period has come, and

བློན་ལོག་དམ་སྲི་སྤུན་དགུ་ཁ་དར་ནས།

MON	LO	DAM SI	PUN GU	KHA DAR	NAE
aspiration	*false,*	*demons who make trouble*	*nine*	*now spread and*	*then*
	wrong	*for vow keepers*	*brothers*	*grow strong*	

The misguided intentions of the vow destroying Nine Brothers spread
and grow strong and

མི་རྣམས་ཕལ་ཆེར་ཤེས་རྒྱུད་འགོང་པོས་བརྩམས།

MI NAM	PHAL CHER	SHE GYU	GONG POE	LAM
human beings	*ordinary*	*minds*	*demon*	*influence*

The minds of human beings are influenced by Gongpo demons.

ཁྱོད་འབངས་ཐུགས་རྗེ་ནམ་ཡང་མི་འདོར་བའི།

KHYO BANG	THU JE	NAM YANG MI	DOR WAI
your people, subjects	*compassion*	*never*	*forget, discard*
(all beings in samara)	*(Padmasambhava said he would help)*		

With a compassion that never forgets your people,

བརྩེ་བའི་སྐུ་རྟེན་ཅན་དེ་ཁྱེད་ལགས་ཀྱང་།

TSE WAI	KU	DRIN CHEN	DE	KHYE	LA	KYANG
compassion's	*body,*	*very kind*	*that*	*you*	*are*	*yet*
	one					

You are the most kind manifestation of loving concern.

*Now the evil time of the end of the degenerate period has come, the
misguided intentions of the vow destroying Nine Brothers spread and
grow strong and the minds of human beings are influenced by Gongpo
demons. With a compassion that never forgets your people you are the
most kind manifestation of loving concern.*

THE EVIL THAT BEINGS DO

ཁྲེལ་མེད་པོ་རྣམས་ལས་ངན་ཁ་མ་གང་།

TREL ME PO NAM	LAE NGAN	KHA MA GANG
shameless people	*bad actions*	*have not yet come full**

*i.e. don't have quite enough negativity for going to hell

Shameless people go on performing bad actions.

གུ་རུ་ཉིད་དང་ཁྱེད་ཀྱི་བསྟན་པ་དང་།

GU RU NYI	DANG	KHYE KYI	TEN PA	DANG
Padmasambhava	*and*	*your*	*doctrines*	*and*

You, Padmasambhava, and your doctrines and

ཁྱེད་ཀྱི་རྗེས་འཇུག་རྣམས་ལ་ཐན་དུ་བལྟ།

KHYE KYI	JE JU NAM	LA	THEN DU		TA
your	*followers*	*to*	*bad, inauspicious, troubling sign like a river flowing the wrong way*		*look*

Your followers are looked on as being bad and harmful.

བཀའ་དྲིན་ཁྱད་གསོད་ལོག་པའི་ལྟའི་འབར་ཤ་དིར།

KA DRIN	KHYE SOE	LOG TAI	BAR SHA DIR
kindness	*ignore, not feel any obligation to repay*	*wrong views*	*say and do many wrong things*

Kindness is repaid by harm, and with wrong views, people say and do many bad things.

མ་རུང་འགོང་པོར་རྒྱབ་བརྟེན་བློ་གཏད་འཆའ།

MA RUNG	GONG POR	GYAB TEN	LO TAE CHA
very bad	*obstructing demons**	*relying on them to back one up*	*believe what these demons say and do*

*they can show human form

Very bad Gongpo demons are relied on and believed in.

ཕྱི་ནང་དབྱེན་སློར་ཕྱུང་ཀྱུ་གས་ཟུར་སྟུ་འདྲེན།

CHI	NANG	WEN JOR	PHUNG TRU	JUR NA DREN
outer	*inner*	*cause trouble**	*telling tales about#*	*lead in a bad way+*

*with bad words   #people to cause trouble   +e.g the materialist doctrines

Outer and inner troubles are caused by bad words, discord is spread and people are led in false ways.

Shameless people go on performing bad actions. You, Padmasambhava, your doctrines and your followers are looked on as being bad and harmful. Kindness is repaid by harm, and with wrong views, people say and do many bad things. Very bad Gongpo demons are relied on and believed in. Outer and inner troubles are caused by bad words, discord is spread and people are led in false ways.

I ALSO HAVE GONE WRONG AND SO NOW GET TROUBLES

དམན་ས་བཟུང་ཡང་ཕྱོགས་ལྷུང་ཕྲག་དོག་ལྷང་།

MAN SA	ZUNG	YANG	CHO LHUNG	TRA DO	DANG
*low place**	*keep*	*yet, even if*	*partial, biased*	*jealous*	*grow up*

* without egoism, humble

I stay humbly in a low place, yet biased attitudes and jealousy develop towards me.

དྲང་པོར་གནས་ཀྱང་གཡོ་སྒྱུས་ནག་ཉེས་འགེལ།

DRANG POR	NAE	KYANG	YO GYUE	NA NYE GEL
straight	*stay*	*yet*	*cheating*	*get trouble*
(not doing bad things)				

I act straight-forwardly, yet I am disturbed by those who deceive and cheat.

མ་ཉེས་ཁ་ཡོག་རྐྱེན་ངན་རླུང་ལྟར་འཚུགས།

MA NYE	KHA YO	KYEN NGAN	LUNG	TAR	TSHU
I have not	*falsely*	*bad, difficult*	*storm*	*like*	*fiercely coming*
done wrong	*accused*	*situations*			

I don't act badly, yet I am falsely accused and difficult situations rage like a storm.

སྤྱོད་ངན་རང་གིས་སྤྱད་ནས་དུས་ངན་ཟེར།

CHOE NGAN	RANG	GI	CHAE	NAE	DU	NGAN	ZER
bad action	*I (sentient*	*by*	*done*	*then*	*times*	*bad*	*say*
	beings)				*(kali yuga)*		

I myself have done bad actions and yet I say that these times are evil.

I stay humbly in a low place, yet biased attitudes and jealousy develop towards me. I act straight forwardly, yet I am disturbed by those who deceive and cheat. I don't act badly, yet I am falsely accused and difficult situations rage like a storm. I myself have done bad actions and yet I say that these times are evil.

CALLING FOR HELP

ཅི་ལ་བསམ་ཡང་སྙིང་རླུང་སྟོད་དུ་འཚང་།

CHI LA SAM	YANG	NYING	LUNG	TOE DU TSANG
whatever I think	*also*	*heart*	*wind*	*go up*
about, all that I see		*(i.e. sighing because very sad)*		

Whatever I think about makes me very sad.

གཏིང་ནས་ཡིད་ཆད་སྐྱོ་བའི་གདུང་ཡུས་ཀྱིས།

TING	NAE	YI CHAE	KYO WAI	DUNG YU	KYI
deep	*from*	*heart broken,*	*very sad*	*crying and snivelling*	*with*
inside		*no hope*	*like a child*		

Completely heart broken, with a sad whimper,

སྨྲེ་སྔགས་འོ་དོད་འབོད་དགོས་དུས་བྱུང་ངོ་།

ME NGA	O DOE	BOE GO	DU JUNG NGO
sorrowing	*save me!*	*necessary*	*the time has come*
words	*cry for help*	*to say*	

I cry for help with the sorrowing words that must be said.

Whatever I think about makes me very sad. Completely heart broken,
with a sad whimper, I cry for help with the sorrowing words that must
be said.

REQUESTING HELP FROM PADMASAMBHAVA TO SEND TROUBLES AWAY

ཕ་གཅིག་ཁྱེད་ལ་མི་འབོད་སུ་ལ་འབོད།

PHA CHI	KHYE	LA	MI BOE	SU	LA	BOE
my sole father,	*you*	*to*	*not ask*	*who*	*to*	*ask (for help)*
Padmasambhava						

My only father, if I do not cry out to you then who else can I ask?

བརྩེ་ཆེན་ཁྱེད་ཀྱིས་མི་གཟིགས་སུ་ཡིས་གཟིགས།

TSE	CHEN	KHYE	KYI	MI ZI	SU	YI	ZI
compassion	*great*	*you*	*by*	*not see*	*who*	*by*	*look (on me and all*
							sentient beings)

If you who have great compassion do not look on me then who will?

ཐུགས་དམ་གནད་ནས་བསྐུལ་ལོ་ཐོད་ཕྲེང་རྩལ།

THU DAM	NAE NE	KUL LO	THOE TRENG TSAL
your mind's	*very strong,*	*invoke,*	*Padmasambhava vow*
	imperatively	*arouse*	

Thod Treng Tsal, I strongly invoke your bond with us.

དབྱིངས་ནས་དགོངས་པ་བསྐྱེད་ཅིག་གྲོ་བོ་ལོད།

YING	NAE	GONG PA	KYOE CHI	DRO WO LO
inside	*from*	*connection,*	*move (i.e. become*	*Dorje Trolo*
(dharmadhatu)		*intention*	*active)*	

Dorje Trolo, in unimpeded spaciousness manifest your instant connection.

མཐུ་སྟོབས་ནུས་པའི་རྩལ་ཤུགས་ཆུང་རེ་རན།

THU	TOB	NU PAI	TSAL SHU	CHUNG RE RAN
sharp effective	*power,*	*force*	*energy,*	*you must do as much as*
power	*strength*		*force*	*possible, utilise all your powers*

Using the energy of your sharp, effective power you must do everything possible.

མི་འདོད་རྐྱེན་ངན་འདི་ལས་མྱུར་དུ་སྒྲོལ།

MI DOE	KYE NGAN	DI LAE	NYUR DU	DROL
*without desire**	*bad circumstances*	*from this*	*quickly*	*save*

*without clinging to our present situation

Save me quickly from these bad circumstances towards which I have
no desire, and

བར་ཆད་བདུད་ཀྱི་དམག་དཔུང་ཕྱིར་ལ་བྱོལ།

BAR CHAE	DUE	KYI	MA PUNG	CHIR LA DO
obstructions	*maras**	*of*	*army, horde*	*send back, repulse*

* demons that keep the mind from enlightenment

Turn back the warring hosts of obstructing demons.

*My only father, if I do not cry out to you then who else can I ask?
If you who have great compassion do not look on me then who will?
Thod Treng Tsal, I strongly invoke your bond with us. Dorje Trolo, in
unimpeded spaciousness manifest your instant connection. Using the
energy of your sharp, effective power you must do everything possible.
Save me quickly from these bad circumstances towards which I have not
desire and turn back the warring hosts of obstructing demons.*

REQUESTING BENEFIT FROM PADMASAMBHAVA

གདུག་ཅན་རྩུང་སེམས་སྣང་བ་དབང་དུ་བསྡུས།

DU CHEN		LUNG	SEM	NANG WA	WONG DU DUE
very bad, dangerous		*volatile*	*mind*	*thinking,*	*put under your power*
people, trouble-makers				*ideas*	

Please put all dangerous beings, impulses and erroneous ideas under
your power.

སྐྱེ་འགྲོའི་བློ་ཡིད་ཕན་གྲོགས་དགེ་ལ་བསྒྱུར།

KYE DROI	LO YI	PHEN	DRO	GE	LA	GYUR
sentient	*mind,*	*help*	*friendship*	*virtue*	*to*	*become, go*
beings	*intellect*					

Turn the minds of sentient beings towards helpfulness, friendliness and
virtue.

མདོར་ན་བདག་སོགས་ཁྱེད་ཀྱི་གདུལ་བྱ་རྣམས།

DOR NA	DA SO		KHYE KYI	DUL JA NAM
briefly	*we (potentially all*		*your*	*followers, the ones open to your*
	beings in samsara)			*influence, those willing to be educated*

In brief, for myself and all your followers,

ལས་རྐྱེན་ངན་པའི་དབང་དུ་མ་བཏང་བར།

LAE	KYEN	NGAN PAI	WONG	DU	MA	TANG WAR
actions	*causes,*	*bad*	*power*	*under*	*not*	*send**
	reasons					

*i.e. allow us to go by our own wrong impulses

Do not send us under the power of bad actions and circumstances, but

ཕྱི་ནང་མི་འདོད་ཉེས་ཚོགས་དབྱིངས་སུ་སོལ།

CHI	NANG	MI DOE	NYE TSHO	YING SU SOL
outer	*inner*	*disagreeable*	*bad things*	*make empty in the sky, dissolve in the open expanse of emptiness*

Dissolve all outer and inner disagreeable problems and tendencies in the infinity of spaciousness.

Please put all dangerous beings, impulses and erroneous ideas under your power. Turn the minds of sentient beings towards helpfulness, friendliness and virtue. In brief, for myself and all your followers, do not send us under the power of bad actions and circumstances, but dissolve all outer and inner disagreeable problems and tendencies in the infinity of spaciousness.

PRAYING FOR BUDDHAHOOD AND THE SPREADING OF THE DHARMA

འདོད་དོན་བསམ་རྒུ་འབད་མེད་ཡིད་བཞིན་གྲུབས།

DOE DON	SAM GU	BAE ME	YI ZHIN	DRU
what we want	*what we think of, pleasure*	*without trying*	*as we desire*	*be accomplished*

Grant us what we want, what we think of, without effort, just as we desire.

གང་གི་རིང་ལུགས་འཛམ་གླིང་ཁྱབ་པར་སྤེལ།

GANG GI		RING LU	DZAM LING	KHYAE PAR PEL
Padmasambhava, the second Buddha		*dharma system*	*Jambudvipa**	*spread and fill*

*here this means the whole world

Padmasambhava's dharma system must spread and fill the whole world, and

དོན་གཉིས་ལྷུན་གྲུབ་ཕྱོགས་ལས་རྣམ་པར་རྒྱལ།

DON	NYI	LHUN DRU	CHO LAE	NAM PAR GYAL
benefit (i.e buddhahood	*two (self and others)*	*effortlessly*	*everywhere*	*completely victorious**

*the dharma's truth must overcome all wrong views

Effortlessly accomplishing the welfare of myself and others, must be completely victorious everywhere.

གུ་རུ་ཁྱེད་དང་མཉམ་པ་ཉིད་གྱུར་ནས།

GU RU	KHYE	DANG	NYAM PA NYI	GYUR	NAE
Padmasambhava	*you*	*and*	*equal*	*become**	*then*

* all beings in samsara must gain this stage

Padmasambhava, bless us that we may become equal to you, and thus

འཁོར་བ་དོང་སྤྲུགས་ནུས་པར་བྱིན་གྱིས་རློབས།

KHOR WA   DONG TRU   NU PAR   JIN GYI LO
samsara   upturn and empty   power   bless

Gain the power to upturn and empty samsara.

Grant us what we want, what we think of, without effort, just as we desire. Padmasambhava's dharma system must spread and fill the whole world, and , effortlessly accomplishing the welfare of myself and all others, must be completely victorious everywhere. Padmasambhava, bless us that we may become equal to you, and thus gain the power to upturn and empty samsara.

ཞེས་པ་འང་ཕྱི་ནང་གི་རྐྱེན་དུ་མས་ཡིད་སྐྱོངས་ཏེ་སེམས་སྐྱོ་བའི་གནས་སྐབས་ཤིག་ན་གདུང་
འབོད་ཀྱི་ངོ་དོད་བཙལ་ཐབས་སུ་ཐལ་ཏེ་འཇིགས་བྲལ་ཡེ་ཤེས་རྡོ་རྗེས་སོ།།   །།

Due to many inner and outer causes, some troubles arose in my mind one sad time. Then without trying, this fervent cry for help arose by itself in my mind. Jigtral Yeshe Dorje.

ༀ་རྒྱན་རིན་པོ་ཆེའི་རྗེན་བསྐྱེད་དང་རྡུགས་བསྟོད་བྱ་བ་ནི༔

The Precious Guru from Oddiyana

སྐྱབས་འགྲོ༔ REFUGE

ན་མོ༔ བླ་མ་བདེ་གཤེགས་འདུས་པའི་སྐུ༔

NA MO	**LA MA**	**DE SHE**	**DU PAI**	**KU**
salutation	*Guru as Padmasambhava*	*Buddhas, Happily Gone*	*encompass*	*body (Nirmanakaya)*

Salutation. Guru, you are the presence of the bodies of all the Buddhas and

དཀོན་མཆོག་གསུམ་གྱི་རང་བཞིན་ལ༔

KON CHO	**SUM**	**GYI**	**RANG ZHIN**	**LA**
*jewels	*three*	*of*	*nature*	*to*

* Buddha, Dharma, Sangha; Guru, Path Deity, Dakini; Dharmakaya, Sambhogakaya, Nirmanakaya

Are identical in nature to the Three Jewels.

བདག་ཉིད་བྱང་ཆུབ་མ་ཐོབ་བར༔

DA NYI	**JANG CHU**	**MA**	**THO**	**BAR**
I (and all beings)	*enlightenment*	*not*	*gain*	*until*

Until I gain enlightenment

སྒོ་གསུམ་གུས་པས་སྐྱབས་སུ་མཆི༔

GO	**SUM**	**GU PAE**	**KYAB**	**SU**	**CHI**
doors	*three*	*with reverence, devotion*	*refuge*	*for*	*go*

With the devotion of my body, speech and mind I go to you for refuge.

Salutation. Guru, you are the presence of the bodies of all the Buddhas and are identical in nature to the Three Jewels. With the devotion of my body, speech and mind I go to you for refuge until I gain enlightenment.

ན་མོ༔ བླ་མ་བདེ་གཤེགས་འདུས་པའི་གསུང་༔

NA MO	**LA MA**	**DE SHE**	**DU PAI**	**SUNG**
salutation	*Guru as Padmasambhava*	*Buddhas, Happily Gone*	*encompass*	*speech (Sambhogakaya)*

Salutation. Guru, you are the presence of the speech of all the Buddhas and

དཀོན་མཆོག་གསུམ་གྱི་རང་བཞིན་ལ༔

KON CHO	SUM	GYI	RANG ZHIN	LA
jewels	*three*	*of*	*nature*	*to*

Are identical in nature to the Three Jewels.

བདག་ཉིད་བྱང་ཆུབ་མ་ཐོབ་བར༔

DA NYI	JANG CHU	MA	THO	BAR
I (and all beings)	*enlightenment*	*not*	*gain*	*until*

Until I gain enlightenment

སྒོ་གསུམ་གུས་པས་སྐྱབས་སུ་མཆི༔

GO	SUM	GU PAE	KYAB	SU	CHI
doors	*three*	*with reverence, devotion*	*refuge*	*for*	*go*

With the devotion of my body, speech and mind I go to you for refuge.

Salutation. Guru, you are the presence of the speech of all the Buddhas and are identical in nature to the Three Jewels. With the devotion of my body, speech and mind I go to you for refuge until I gain enlightenment.

ན་མོ༔   བླ་མ་བདེ་གཤེགས་འདུས་པའི་ཐུགས༔

NA MO	LA MA	DE SHE	DU PAI	THU
salutation	*Guru as Padmasambhava*	*Buddhas, Happily Gone*	*encompass*	*mind (Dharmakaya)*

Salutation. Guru, you are the presence of the minds of all the Buddhas and

དཀོན་མཆོག་གསུམ་གྱི་རང་བཞིན་ལ༔

KON CHO	SUM	GYI	RANG ZHIN	LA
jewels	*three*	*of*	*nature*	*to*

Are identical in nature to the Three Jewels.

བདག་ཉིད་བྱང་ཆུབ་མ་ཐོབ་བར༔

DA NYI	JANG CHU	MA	THO	BAR
I (and all beings)	*enlightenment*	*not*	*gain*	*until*

Until I gain enlightenment

སྒོ་གསུམ་གུས་པས་སྐྱབས་སུ་མཆི༔

GO	SUM	GU PAE	KYAB	SU	CHI
doors	*three*	*with reverence, devotion*	*refuge*	*for*	*go*

With the devotion of my body, speech and mind I go to you for refuge.

Salutation. Guru, you are the presence of the minds of all the Buddhas and are identical in nature to the Three Jewels. With the devotion of my body, speech and mind I go to you for refuge until I gain enlightenment.

 སེམས་བསྐྱེད་ནི། DEVELOPING THE MIND OF ENLIGHTENMENT

སེམས་བསྐྱེད་འགྲོ་བ་ཀུན་དོན་དུ༔

SEM   **KYE**   **DRO WA**   **KUN**   **DON DU**
enlightening mind   *developing*   *beings*   *all*   *for the sake of*
Developing the mind of enlightenment for the sake of all beings

བླ་མ་སངས་རྒྱས་བསྒྲུབ་ནས་ནི༔

LA MA   **SANG GYE**   **DRUB**   **NAE**   **NI**
Guru as   *Buddha*   *practices till*   *then*
Padmasambhava   *enlightenment*
I will do the practice of my Guru Buddha.

གང་ལ་གང་འདུལ་འཕྲིན་ལས་ཀྱིས༔

GANG LA GANG   **DUL**   **TRIN LAE**   **KYI**
according to need   *disciplining*   *deeds*   *by*
Then, with the activity of educating according to need,

འགྲོ་བ་འདུལ་བར་སེམས་བསྐྱེད་དོ༔

DRO WA   **DUL WAR**   **SEM**   **KYE DO**
beings   *educate*   *mind*   *develop*
I will ripen beings. This is my altruistic aspiration.

Developing the mind of enlightenment for the sake of all beings I will do the practice of my Guru Buddha. Then, with the activity of educating beings according to their need, I will ripen them fully. This is my altruistic aspiration.

[Say this three times.]

According to the sMin-Grol-gLing system one should recite as follows:

ཚོགས་བསགས་ནི།   ACCUMULATING MERIT

བླ་མ་ཡི་དམ་མཁའ་འགྲོ་གཤེགས༔

LA MA	YI DAM	KHAN DRO	SHE
Guru	*path deity*	*dakini*	*please come*

Gurus, Path Deities and Dakinis, please come here and

ཉི་ཟླ་པདྨའི་གདན་ལ་བཞུགས༔

NYI	DA	PAE MAI	DEN	LA	ZHU
sun	*moon*	*lotus*	*cushion*	*on*	*sit*

Sit upon these cushions of lotus, sun and moon.

ལུས་ངག་ཡིད་གསུམ་གུས་ཕྱག་འཚལ༔

LU	NGA	YI	SUM	GUE	CHA TSHAL
body	*speech*	*mind*	*three*	*devotion*	*prostrate*

We bow to you with the devotion of our body, speech and mind, and

ཕྱི་ནང་གསང་བའི་མཆོད་པ་འབུལ༔

CHI	NANG	SANG WAI	CHO PA	BUL
outer	*inner*	*secret*	*offering*	*present*

Present the outer, inner and secret offerings.

Gurus, Path Deities and Dakinis, please come here and sit upon these cushions of lotus, sun and moon. We bow to you with the devotion of our body, speech and mind, and present the outer, inner and secret offerings.

ཉམས་ཆག་སྡིག་སྒྲིབ་མཐོལ་ཞིང་བཤགས༔

NYAM	CHA	DIG	DRIB	THOL ZHING	SHA
lapses	*breaches*	*sins*	*obscurations*	*with hands at heart*	*confess, ask forgiveness*

With our hands at our hearts we confess our lapses, breaches, sins and obscurations.

གསང་སྔགས་བསྒྲུབས་ལ་རྗེས་ཡི་རང་༔

SANG	NGA	DRU	LA	JE YI RANG
secret	*mantra (tantra)*	*practice*	*to*	*rejoice with*

We rejoice at the virtue of those who practise tantra.

སྨིན་གྲོལ་གསང་སྔགས་ཆོས་འཁོར་བསྐོར༔

MIN	DROL	SANG NGA	CHO	KHOR	KOR
ripening	*liberating*	*tantric*	*dharma*	*wheel*	*turn*
initiation	*doctrines*				

We request you to spread the tantric doctrines of ripening and liberation and

མྱ་ངན་མི་འདའ་བཞུགས་སུ་གསོལ༔

NYA NGAN	MI	DA	ZHU	SU SOL
sorrow	*not*	*pass*	*remain*	*please*
(do not die, do not enter nirvana)				

Ask you to remain with us and not pass away.

སྙིང་པོ་སེམས་ཅན་དོན་དུ་བསྔོ༔

NYING PO	SEM CHEN	DON	DU	NGO
*essence**	*sentient beings*	*benefit*	*for*	*dedicate, give*
* of our merit and wisdom and our pure nature				

We dedicate our essence for the benefit of sentient beings.

ཡང་དག་རྡོ་རྗེའི་དོན་རྟོགས་ཤོག༔

YANG	DA	DOR JEI	DON	TO	SHO
very	*pure*	*vajra, sunyata*	*nature*	*awaken to*	*we all must*

May we all awaken to our very pure indestructible nature.

With our hands at our hearts we confess our lapses, breaches, sins and obscurations. We rejoice at the virtue of those who practise tantra. We request you to spread the tantric doctrines of ripening and liberation and ask you to remain with us and not pass away. We dedicate our essence for the benefit of sentient beings. May we all awaken to our very pure indestructible nature.

བལྟས་པ་ཙམ་གྱིས་འགྲོ་རྣམས་དབང་དུ་སྡུད།

TAE PA	TSAM	GYI	DRO	NAM	WANG	DU	DUE
glance	*mere*	*by*	*beings*	*all*	*power*	*under*	*control, suppress*

By your mere glance all beings are gathered under your power.

སྤྱིགས་པ་ཙམ་གྱིས་སྡེ་བརྒྱད་བྲན་དུ་བཀོལ།

DIG PA	TSAM	GYI	DE	GYE	TRAN	DU	KOL
command, gesture	*mere*	*by*	*groups*	*eight*	*servant*	*as*	*make*

By your mere command the eight classes of spirits attend you as servants.

བསམ་པ་ཙམ་གྱིས་དགོས་འདོད་ཆར་ལྟར་འབེབས།

SAM PA	TSAM	GYI	GOE	DOE	CHAR	TAR	BE
thought, intention	*mere*	*by*	*need*	*wish for*	*rain*	*as*	*fall*

By your mere thought all we need and desire falls like rain.

ཨོ་རྒྱན་རིན་པོ་ཆེ་ལ་གསོལ་བ་འདེབས།

OR GYEN	RIN PO CHE	LA	SOL WA DE
Oddiyana	*precious one*	*to*	*pray*

Padmasambhava, we pray to you.

By your mere glance all beings are gathered under your power. By your mere command the eight classes of spirits attend you as servants. By your mere thought all we need and desire falls like rain. Padmasambhava, we pray to you.

ཧཱུྃ༔ ཨོ་རྒྱན་ཡུལ་གྱི་ནུབ་བྱང་མཚམས༔

HUNG	UR GYEN YUL	GYI	NUB JANG	TSHAM
vocative, seed letter of Padmasambhava	*Oddiyana, the dakinis' land*	*of*	*north-west*	*border, corner*

Hung. In the land of Urgyen's north-west corner,

པདྨ་གེ་སར་སྡོང་པོ་ལ༔

PAE MA	GE SAR	DONG PO	LA
lotus	*stamen*	*stem*	*on*

Upon a lotus stem and stamen,

ཡ་མཚན་མཆོག་གི་དངོས་གྲུབ་བརྙེས༔

YAM TSHEN	CHO GI	NGO DRU	NYE
marvellous, wonderful	*supreme (i.e. buddhahood)*	*siddhis, attainments*	*has got*

With marvellous and supreme accomplishments,

པདྨ་འབྱུང་གནས་ཞེས་སུ་གྲགས༔

PAE MA JUNG NAE		ZHE SU	DRA
Padmasambhava, Guru Rinpoche		*known as*	*famous (famed as)*

The Lotus Born is your famous name.

འཁོར་དུ་མཁའ་འགྲོ་མང་པོས་བསྐོར༔

KHOR	DU	KHAN DRO		MANG POE	KOR
retine	*as*	*dakinis, sky-goddesses (here it means all sky travelling deities)*		*many*	*by*	*surrounded*

As retinue many dakinis surround you.

ཁྱེད་ཀྱི་རྗེས་སུ་བདག་སྒྲུབ་ཀྱིས༔

KHYE   **KYI JE SU**   **DA**   **DRU**   **KYI**
you   *following after,*   *I*   *practice*   *by that*
      emulating

Following and relying on you, I do your practice, therefore,

བྱིན་གྱིས་བརླབ་ཕྱིར་གཤེགས་སུ་གསོལ༔

JIN GYI LAB   **CHIR**   **SHE SU SOL**
blessing   *in order to*   *please come*

In order to bless us, please come here!

གུ་རུ་པདྨ་སིདྡྷི་ཧཱུྃ༔

GU RU   **PAE MA**   **SID DHI**   **HUNG**
guru, master   *Padmasambhava*   *real attainment*   *give me!*

Guru Padmasambhava grant us the accomplishment of buddhahood!

Hung. In the land of Urgyen's north-west corner, upon a lotus stem and stamen, with marvellous and supreme accomplishments, the Lotus Born is your famous name. As retinue many dakinis surround you. Following and relying on you, I do your practice, therefore, in order to bless us, please come here!

ཞེས་ཅི་ནུས་དང་།

[Recite this as many times as you can with true devotion from your heart.]

རྟགས་བསྟོད་བྱ་བ་ནི༔

DESCRIPTION OF PADMASAMBHAVA PRAISING ALL THAT HE SIGNIFIES

ཧཱུྃ༔ སྐུ་གསུང་ཐུགས་རྟོགས་པདྨ་འབྱུང་གནས་ནི༔

HUNG   **KU**   **SUNG**   **THU**   **DZO**   **PAE MA**   **JUNG NAE**   **NI**
five   *body**   *speech#*   *mind+*   *complete*   *lotus*   *born*   *regarding*
wisdoms
*nirmanakaya   #sambhogakaya   +dharmakaya

Hung. Padmasambhava, your body, speech and mind are the presence of the three aspects of enlightenment.

རྒྱལ་བའི་གདུང་འཚོབ་འཁོར་བའི་གཡུལ་ངོ་བཟློག༔

GYAL WAI   **DUNG TSO**   **KHOR WAI**   **YUL NGO**   **DO**
jinas', victors'   *representative*   *samsara's,*   *troubles,*   *stop, repel*
Buddhas'   *world's*   *disturbance*

You are the representative of all the Buddhas, the one who repels the troubles of samsara.

ཐུགས་རྗེ་ཆེན་པོས་འགྲོ་བ་འདྲེན་མཛད་པའི༔

THU JE	CHEN POE	DRO WA	DREN	DZAE PAI
compassion, kindness	*great, non-dual with emptiness*	*wanderers, sentient beings*	*leading*	*doing*

With great compassion you lead all beings to liberation.

སྤྲུལ་སྐུ་འགྲོ་བ་འདྲེན་ལ་ཕྱག་འཚལ་བསྟོད༔

TRUL KU	DRO WA	DREN	LA	CHA TSAL	TOE
apparition, nirmanakaya	*sentient beings*	*guide*	*to*	*bow, prostrate*	*praise*

Salutation and praise to the apparition who guides all beings.

Hung. Padmasambhava, your body, speech and mind are the presence of the three aspects of enlightenment. You are the representative of all the Buddhas, the one who repels the troubles of samsara. With great compassion you lead all beings to liberation. Salutation and praise to the apparition who guides all beings.

རྣོད་ཀྱི་རྗེ་ལྡེམ་དྲུ་ལ་བཙུགས་པ་ནི༔

GOE	KYI	TSE DEM	U	LA	TSU PA	NI
vulture	*of*	*feather*	*head, hat*	*on*	*put*	*thus*

You have a vulture's feather on top of your hat,

སྒྲུབ་པ་མཐར་ཕྱིན་ཡེ་ཤེས་རྒྱས་པའི་རྟགས༔

DRU PA	THAR CHIN	YE SHE	GYE PAI	TA
practice	*completed*	*original knowing*	*spread*	*sign*

The sign of the vast spreading of original knowing arising from the completion of meditation practice.

དཔལ་ཆེན་ཞྭ་བའི་དབྱིབས་ཞུ་གསོལ་བ་ནི༔

PAL	CHEN	SHA WAI	YIB	ZHU SOL WA	NI
splendour	*great*	*hat*	*shape*	*wearing*	*thus*

You wear a very powerful and splendid hat,

ཐེག་ཆེན་ལྟ་བའི་དོན་དང་ལྡན་པའི་རྟགས༔

THEG CHEN	TA WAI	DON	DANG	DEN PAI	TA
mahayana	*view*	*meaning*	*and*	*have*	*sign*

The sign that you embody the meaning of the Mahayana view.

དབུ་སྐྲའི་ཐོར་ཚུགས་གྱེན་དུ་བཅིངས་པ་ནི༔

U	TRAI	TOR TSU	GYEN	DU	CHING PA	NI
head	*hair*	*piled high*	*up*	*as*	*tied*	*thus*

The hair on your head is bound up in a topknot,

དུས་གསུམ་སངས་རྒྱས་ཐམས་ཅད་འདུས་པའི་རྟགས༔

DU	SUM	SANG GYE	THAM CHE	DU PAI	TA
times	*three*	*Buddhas*	*all*	*encompass*	*sign*

The sign that your presence encompasses all the Buddhas of the three times.

You have a vulture's feather on top of your hat, the sign of the vast spreading of original knowing arising from the completion of meditation practice. You wear a very powerful and splendid hat, the sign that you embody the meaning of the Mahayana view. The hair on your head is bound up in a topknot, the sign that your presence encompasses all the Buddhas of the three times.

སྤྱན་གསུམ་དྲག་པོས་འགྲོ་ལ་གཟིགས་པ་ནི༔

CHEN	SUM	DRA POE	DRO	LA	ZI PA	NI
eyes	*three*	*fierce*	*sentient beings*	*to*	*look at*	*thus*

With your three fiercely alert eyes you see all who wander in samsara,

ཐུགས་རྗེ་ཆེན་པོས་འགྲོ་བ་འདྲེན་པའི་རྟགས༔

THU JE	CHEN PO	DRO WA	DREN PAI	TA
compassion (non-dual)	*great*	*sentient beings*	*guide*	*sign*

The sign that you guide all beings with great compassion.

འཛུམ་པའི་ཞལ་རས་མདངས་དང་ལྡན་པ་ནི༔

DZUM PAI	ZHAL RAE	DANG	DANG	DEN PA	NI
smiling	*expression, face*	*radiant*	*and*	*having*	*thus*

Your smiling face is bright and radiant,

བྱམས་དང་སྙིང་རྗེས་འགྲོ་བ་འདྲེན་པའི་རྟགས༔

JAM	DANG	NYING JE	DRO WA	DREN PAI	TA
love	*and*	*compassion*	*sentient beings*	*guide*	*sign*

The sign that you guide all sentient beings with love and compassion.

With your three fiercely alert eyes you see all who wander in samsara, the sign that you guide all beings with great compassion. Your smiling face is bright and radiant, the sign that you guide all sentient beings with love and compassion

ཟ་འོག་བེར་ཆེན་སྐུ་ལ་གསོལ་བ་ནི༔

ZA OG	BER	CHEN	KU	LA	SOL WA	NI
silk brocade	*gown (blue)*	*great*	*body*	*on*	*wear*	*thus*

On your body you wear a great gown of luxurious brocade,

སྒྲུབ་པ་བཀའ་བརྒྱད་སྐུ་ལ་རྫོགས་པའི་རྟགས༔

DRU PA	KAB GYAE	KU	LA	DZO PAI	TA
practice	*eight herukas*	*body*	*in*	*complete*	*sign*

The sign that all the deities of the Eight Practices are fully present in your body.

ལེ་བརྒན་དམར་པོའི་ཆོས་གོས་གསོལ་བ་ནི༔

LE GEN	MAR POI	CHO	GO	SOL WA	NI
poppy red	*red*	*dharma*	*robes*	*wear*	*thus*

You wear the very red dharma robes,

ཚུལ་ཁྲིམས་རྣམ་དག་སྡོམ་དང་ལྡན་པའི་རྟགས༔

TSUL TRIM	NAM	DA	DOM	DANG	DEN PAI	TA
morality	*very*	*pure*	*vows*	*and*	*have*	*sign*

The sign of your vows and pure morality.

བརྗིད་པའི་བེར་ཆེན་སྐུ་ལ་གསོལ་བ་ནི༔

JI PAI	BER	CHEN	KU	LA	SOL WA	NI
shining, impressive	*gown*	*great*	*body*	*on*	*wear*	*thus*

You wear a very splendid and imposing gown,

སྲིད་གསུམ་འགྲོ་བ་ཟིལ་གྱིས་གནོན་པའི་རྟགས༔

SI	SUM	DRO WA	ZIL	GYI	NON PAI	TA
worlds*	*three*	*sentient beings*	*splendour*	*by*	*suppress*	*sign*

*gods, nagas humans

The sign that you easily control all beings in the three worlds.

On your body you wear a great gown of luxurious brocade, the sign that all the deities of the Eight Practices are fully present in your body. You wear the very red dharma robes, the sign of your vows and pure morality. You wear a very splendid and imposing gown, the sign that you easily control all beings in the three worlds.

ཕྱག་གཡས་གསེར་གྱི་རྡོ་རྗེ་བསྣམས་པ་ནི༔

CHA	YAE	SER GYI	DOR JE	NAM PA	NI
hand	*right*	*golden*	*vajra*	*hold*	*thus*

In your right hand you hold a golden vajra,

ཡེ་ཤེས་ལྔ་ལྡན་ལོག་འདྲེན་འཇོམས་པའི་རྟགས༔

YE SHE	NGA	DEN	LOG	DREN	JOM PAI	TA
original knowing	*five*	*have*	*wrong way*	*leading*	*defeating*	*sign*

The sign that with your five original knowings you destroy those who lead others astray.

ཕྱག་གཡོན་བདུད་རྩིའི་ཐོད་པ་བསྣམས་པ་ནི༔

CHA   YON   DU TSI   THOE PA   NAM PA   NI
hand   left   amrita   skullcup   hold   thus*
*the pure essence of demons, released when they are freed of ignorance.

In your left hand you hold a skullcup full of amrita,

སྒྲུབ་པ་པོ་ལ་དངོས་གྲུབ་སྟེར་བའི་རྟགས༔

DRUB PA PO   LA   NGO DRUB   TER PAI   TA
meditators   to   accomplishment   giving   sign

The sign that you bestow true attainment upon practitioners.

ཁ་ཊྭཾ་རྩེ་གསུམ་སྐུ་ལ་བརྟེན་པ་ནི༔

KA TVAM   TSE   SUM   KU   LA   TEN PA   NI
trident   points   three   body   at   hold   thus

You hold a three-pointed khatvanga against your body,

ཐབས་དང་ཤེས་རབ་འདུ་འབྲལ་མེད་པའི་རྟགས༔

THAB   DANG   SHE RAB   DU   TRAL   ME PAI   TA
method,   and   discernment,   join   separate   without   sign
compassion   emptiness

The sign that method and discernment are always united within you.

In your right hand you hold a golden vajra, the sign that with your five original knowings you destroy those who lead others astray. In your left hand you hold a skullcup full of amrita, the sign that you bestow true attainments upon practitioners. You hold a three-pointed khatvanga against your body, the sign that method and discernment are always united within you.

མི་འགྱུར་ཞབས་གཉིས་སྐྱིལ་ཀྲུང་མཛད་པ་ནི༔

MI   GYUR   ZHAB   NYI   KYIL TRUNG   DZAE PA   NI
not   changing   feet   two   crossed over posture   do   thus

Your two feet are arranged in the unchanging posture,

ཆོས་ཀྱི་སྐུ་ལ་འདུ་འབྲལ་མེད་པའི་རྟགས༔

CHO KYI KU   LA   DU   TRAL   ME PAI   TA
dharmakaya   in   join   separate   without   sign

The sign that you are always united with the Dharmakaya.

ཉི་ཟླ་པདྨའི་གདན་ལ་བཞུགས་པ་ནི༔

NYI   DA   PAE MAI   DEN   LA   ZHU PA   NI
sun   moon   lotus   cushion   on   sit   thus

You sit on cushions of lotus, sun and moon,

འཁོར་བའི་ཉོན་མོངས་གཡུལ་ངོ་བཟློག་པའི་རྟགས༔

KHOR WAI	NYON MONG	YUL NGO	DOG PAI	TA
samsara's	*afflictions**	*troubled*	*repel*	*sign*

*mental dullness, desire, aversion, pride and jealousy

The sign that you put an end to the troubles the afflictions cause in samsara.

དྲག་པོའི་ཧཱུྃ་རིང་ཐུང་སྒྲོག་པ་ནི༔

DRA POI	HUNG	RING	HUNG	THUNG	DRO PA	NI
fierce	*sound of Hung*	*long*	*Hung*	*short*	*make, generate*	*thus*

You make the fierce sound of Hung, both long and abrupt,

མ་མོ་མཁའ་འགྲོ་དབང་དུ་སྡུད་པའི་རྟགས༔

MA MO	KHAN DRO	WANG	DU	DUE PAI	TA
mother goddess	*dakinis*	*power*	*under*	*control*	*sign*

The sign that you put the mamo and dakinis under your power.

Your two feet are arranged in the unchanging posture, the sign that you are always united with the Dharmakaya. You sit on cushions of lotus, sun and moon, the sign that you put an end to the troubles the afflictions cause in samsara. You make the fierce sound of Hung, both long and abrupt, the sign that you put the mamo and dakinis under your power.

འཇའ་ཡི་གུར་ཕུབ་འོད་ཟེར་འཕྲོ་བ་ནི༔

JA	YI	GUR PHU	OE ZER	TRO WA	NI
rainbow	*of*	*tent*	*light rays*	*radiate*	*thus*

A canopy of rainbows surrounds you radiating rays of light,

ཐུགས་རྗེ་ཐབས་ཀྱིས་འགྲོ་བ་འདྲེན་པའི་རྟགས༔

THU JE	THAB	KYI	DRO WA	DREN PAI	TA
compassion	*method*	*by*	*beings*	*guide*	*sign*

The sign that you guide sentient beings by means of compassion.

སངས་རྒྱས་འདུས་པའི་རྒྱལ་སྲས་པདྨ་འབྱུང༔

SANG GYE	DU PAI	GYAL	SAE	PAE MA JUNG
buddha	*encompassing*	*Buddha Amitabha*	*son*	*Lotus Born*

Padmasambhava, son of Amitabha, you encompass all the Buddhas and

སྣ་ཚོགས་ཐབས་ཀྱིས་འགྲོ་བ་འདྲེན་མཛད་པའི༔

NA TSO	THAB	KYI	DRO WA	DREN	DZAE PAI
diverse	*methods*	*by*	*beings*	*lead*	*do*

Guide all beings according to their diverse needs.

པད་འབྱུང་གནས་སྐུ་ལ་ཕྱག་འཚལ་བསྟོད༔

PAE MA	JUNG NE	KU	LA	CHA TSAL	TOE
lotus	*source*	*body*	*to*	*prostrate*	*praise*

Padmasambhava, we offer salutation and praise to your embodied presence.

A canopy of rainbows surrounds you radiating rays of light, the sign that you guide sentient beings by means of compassion. Padmasambhava, son of Amitabha, you encompass all the Buddhas and guide all beings according to their diverse needs. Padmasambhava, we offer salutation and praise to your embodied presence.

བསྟོད་པ་ PRAISE

ཧཱུྃ༔ མ་བཅོས་སྤྲོས་བྲལ་བླ་མ་ཆོས་ཀྱི་སྐུ༔

HUNG	MA CHOE	TOE DRAL		LA MA	CHOE KYI KU
Hung	*unartificial*	*without elaboration*		*guru*	*dharmakaya, intrinsic mode*

Hung. The guru without artifice or elaboration is the intrinsic mode.

བདེ་ཆེན་ལོངས་སྤྱོད་བླ་མ་ཆོས་ཀྱི་རྗེ༔

DE	CHEN	LONG CHO	LA MA	CHOE	KYI	JE
bliss	*great*	*sambhogakaya, enjoyment*	*guru*	*dharma*	*of*	*lord*

The guru of great happiness, master of dharma, is the enjoyment mode.

པད་སྡོང་ལས་འཁྲུངས་བླ་མ་སྤྲུལ་པའི་སྐུ༔

PAE	DONG	LAE	THRUNG	LA MA	TRUL PAI KU
lotus	*stem*	*from*	*born*	*guru*	*nirmanakaya, apparition mode*

The lotus born guru is the apparitional mode.

སྐུ་གསུམ་རྡོ་རྗེ་འཆང་ལ་ཕྱག་འཚལ་བསྟོད༔

KU	SUM	DOR JE CHANG	LA	CHA TSAL	TOE
body	*three*	*Vajradhara*	*to*	*prostrate*	*praise*

We salute and praise Vajradhara with these three modes.

Hung. The guru without artifice or elaboration is the intrinsic mode. The guru of great happiness, master of dharma, is the enjoyment mode. The lotus born guru is the apparitional mode. We salute and praise you, the Vajradhara having these three modes.

Translated by CR Lama and James Low

Lotus Source Practice

སྐྱབས་གསོལ། INITIAL REQUEST

སྐྱབས་གནས་བསྐུ་མེད་དཀོན་མཆོག་རིན་པོ་ཆེ།

KYAB	NAE	LU ME	KON CHO	RIN PO CHE
refuge,	*place,*	*unfailing,*	*jewel*	*precious*
protector		*never cheating*		

Precious jewel who is our unfailing refuge,

ཐུགས་རྗེ་མངའ་བའི་ཨུ་རྒྱན་པདྨ་ལ།

THU JE	NGA WAI	UR GYEN	PAE MA	LA
compassion	*possessor*	*Oddiyana*	*lotus*	*to*

Kind Pema from Oddiyana,

བདག་གི་ཇི་ལྟར་གསོལ་བ་བཏབས་པ་བཞིན།

DA GI	JI TAR	SOL WA	TA PA	ZHIN
my	*like what,*	*prayer,*	*made*	*like that,*
	how it is	*request*		*accordingly*

Precisely what we pray for

མྱུར་དུ་འགྲུབ་པར་བྱིན་གྱིས་བརླབས་དུ་གསོལ།

NYUR DU	DRU PAR	JIN GYI LAB	DU SOL
quickly	*accomplish*	*blessing*	*pray, request*

Please bless us with its rapid accomplishment.

Precious jewel our unfailing refuge, kind Pema from Oddiyana, please bless us with the rapid fulfilment of precisely what we pray for.

ཚིག་བདུན་གསོལ་འདེབས། SEVEN LINE PRAYER

ཧཱུྃཿ ཨུ་རྒྱན་ཡུལ་གྱི་ནུབ་བྱང་མཚམསཿ

HUNG	UR GYEN	YUL	GYI	NUB	JANG	TSHAM
seed syllable Lotus Source	Oddiyana	country	of	north	west	border, corner

Hung. Where north and west meet in the land of Oddiyana,

པདྨ་གེ་སར་སྡོང་པོ་ལཿ

PAE MA	GE SAR	DONG PO	LA
lotus	stamen	stem	on

Upon the stem and stamen of a lotus,

ཡ་མཚན་མཆོག་གི་དངོས་གྲུབ་བརྙེསཿ

YAM TSHEN	CHO	GI	NGO DRU	NYE
marvellous, wonderful	supreme	of	accomplishment, siddhi	got, has

Are you who have the marvellous and supreme accomplishment,

པདྨ་འབྱུང་གནས་ཞེས་སུ་གྲགསཿ

PAE MA	JUNG NAE	ZHE SU	DRA
lotus	source	famous	as

Lotus Source of great renown.

འཁོར་དུ་མཁའ་འགྲོ་མང་པོས་བསྐོརཿ

KHOR DU	KHAN DRO	MANG POE	KOR
retine as	dakinis*	many by	surrounded

*sky-goddesses, deities inseparable from space

With a retinue of many dakinis around you.

ཁྱེད་ཀྱི་རྗེས་སུ་བདག་སྒྲུབ་ཀྱིསཿ

KHYE KYI	JE SU	DA	DRU	KYI
you of	following after	I	practice	by that

Following and relying on you we do your practice, therefore,

བྱིན་གྱིས་བརླབ་ཕྱིར་གཤེགས་སུ་གསོལཿ

JIN GYI LAB	CHIR	SHE SU SOL
blessing	in order to	please come

In order to grant your blessings, please come here!

 གུ་རུ་པདྨ་སི་དྡྷི་ཧཱུྃ༔

GU RU   **PAE MA**   **SID DHI**   **HUNG**
guru, master *Padmasambhava* *real attainment* *give me!*

Guru Lotus Source grant us accomplishment!

Where north and west meet in the land of Oddiyana, upon the stem and stamen of a lotus, are you who have the marvellous supreme accomplishment, Lotus Source of great renown, with a retinue of many dakinis around you. Following and relying on you we do your practice, therefore, in order to grant your blessings, please come here! Guru Lotus Source grant us accomplishment!

ཞེས་ཅི་ནུས་དང་།
[Recite this three times]

 སྐྱབས་འགྲོ། TAKING REFUGE

ན་མོ་སྐྱབས་གནས་ཀུན་འདུས་བླ་མ་རྗེ༔

NA MO   **KYAB**   **NAE**   **KUN**   **DUE**   **LA MA**   **JE**
homage   *refuge*   *place*   *all*   *gathered together*   *guru*   *honorific*

Salutation! You are my noble guru encompassing all sites of refuge.

རིག་འཛིན་བླ་མའི་དཀྱིལ་འཁོར་དུ༔

RIG DZIN   **LA MAI**   **KYIL KHOR**   **DU**
vidyadhara, aware   *guru's*   *mandala*   *in, to*

Aware guru, in your mandala

བདག་སོགས་འགྲོ་དྲུག་སེམས་ཅན་རྣམས༔

DA SO   **DRO**   **DRU**   **SEM CHEN**   **NAM**
I and everyone   *going*   *six*   *sentient beings*   *(plural)*

I and all sentient beings wandering in the six realms of samsara

བྱང་ཆུབ་བར་དུ་སྐྱབས་སུ་མཆི༔

JANG CHU   **BAR DU**   **KYAB**   **SU**   **CHI**
bodhi, enlightenment   *until*   *refuge*   *for*   *go*

Take refuge from now until enlightenment is gained.

Salutation! You are my noble guru encompassing all the sites of refuge. From now on until enlightenment is gained, I and all sentient beings wandering in the six realms of samsara take refuge in the mandala of our aware guru.

ལན་གསུམ་རྗེས༔

[Recite this three times]

སེམས་བསྐྱེད། DEVELOPING INFINITE ALTRUISM

ཧོ༔ བདག་གིས་འགྲོ་བ་ཀུན་དོན་དུ༔

HO	DA	GI	DRO WA	KUN	DON	DU
Ho!	*me*	*by*	*sentient beings*	*all*	*benefit*	*for*

Ho! In order to benefit all sentient beings,

བླ་མ་རིག་འཛིན་ཁྱེད་བསྒྲུབ་ནས༔

LA MA	RIG DZIN	KYE	DRU	NAE
guru	*vidyadhara,*	*you*	*practice*	*and then*
	aware			

Aware guru, I will do your practice, and,

འགྲོ་དྲུག་སྡུག་བསྔལ་བསལ་བྱ་ཞིང༔

DRO	DRU	DU NGAL	SAL	JA ZHING
beings	*six*	*suffering*	*clear away*	*doing*

Removing the sufferings of all beings in the six realms

རིག་འཛིན་བླ་མའི་སར་འགོད་བྱུ༔

RIG DZIN	LA MAI	SAR	GOE JA
vidyadhara	*guru's*	*in place*	*establish*

Will establish them on the level of the aware guru.

Ho! In order to benefit all sentient beings, aware guru, I will do your practice, and, removing the sufferings of all beings in the six realms, I will establish them on the level of the aware guru.

ལན་གསུམ་རྗེས༔

[Recite this three times]

SEVEN BRANCH PRACTICE

ཕྱག་འཚལ་བ་དང་མཆོད་ཅིང་བཤགས་པ་དང་།

CHA TSAL WA	DANG	CHO CHING	SHA PA	DANG
salutation	*and*	*offerings*	*confession*	*and*

By salutations, offerings, and confession, and

རྗེས་སུ་ཡི་རང་བསྐུལ་ཞིང་གསོལ་བ་ཡི།

JE SU YI RANG	KUL ZHING	SOL WA	YI
rejoicing at the merit of others	*requesting dharma teaching*	*praying, requesting the buddhas to stay*	*of*

By rejoicing at the merit of others, beseeching dharma teaching, and requesting the buddhas not to leave –

དགེ་བ་ཆུང་ཟད་བདག་གིས་ཅི་བསགས་པ།

GE WA	CHUNG ZAE	DA	GI	CHI	SA PA
virtue	*small amount*	*me*	*by*	*whatever*	*collected*

Whatever small amount of virtue I have collected

ཐམས་ཅད་བདག་གིས་བྱང་ཆུབ་ཕྱིར་བསྔོ་འོ།།

THAM CHE	DA	GI	JANG CHU	CHIR	NGO O
all	*me*	*by*	*enlightenment, bodhi*	*for the sake of (for all beings)*	*dedicate*

I dedicate it all for the enlightenment of all beings.

By salutations, offerings and confession, and by rejoicing at the merit of others, beseeching dharma teaching and requesting the buddhas not to leave – whatever small amount of virtue I have collected by doing this, I dedicate it all for the enlightenment of all beings.

ༀ༔ བབ་དོན་རྡོ་རྗེ་སྙིང་པོ་ལས༔ ཡང་གསང་རིག་འཛིན་ཡོངས་རྫོགས་ཀྱི་བླ་མ་གུ་རུ་མཚན་བརྒྱད་བྲི་བག༔
ད་སྒྲུབ་པ་ཡེ་ཤེས་བདུད་རྩིའི་སྤྲིན་ཆར་བཞུགས༔

SWEET RAINFALL OF THE TRANSFORMATIVE ELIXIR OF WISDOM

which is the special practice of the eight forms of Lotus Source, in the Very Secret Awareness-abiding Complete Guru section of **The Profound Meaning of the Indestructible Heart**

ༀ༔   ཀ ཿ ཙ ༢ ༣ ༤

བླ་མ་མཁའ་འགྲོའི་ཚོགས་ལ་འདུད༔ བདག་འདི་ཨུ་རྒྱན་ཕོད་འཕྲེང་རས༔ རྒྱ་བལ་ཀུན་གྱི་ས་རྣམས་འགྲིམས༔ པཎ་གྲུབ་དུ་མ་བརྟེན་ནས་ནི༔ གསང་སྔགས་དཀྱིལ་འཁོར་དུ་མ་བསྐོར༔ དབང་དང་གདམས་པ་མ་ལུས་ཐོབས༔ ཕྱོགས་དུས་རྒྱལ་བ་རྒྱལ་སྲས་ཀྱི༔ སྐུ་གསུང་ཐུགས་ཡོན་རྩལ་རྫོགས་ནས༔ མ་ཆགས་སློན་གྱིས་མ་གོས་པ༔ མཚོ་ཆེན་པད་མའི་སྦུབས་སུ་འཁྲུངས༔ སྤྲུལ་ཀུང་འགྱུན་དུ་མི་བཏུབ་སྤྲུལ༔ དུར་འཁྲལ་བགོད་པ་དུ་མ་བསྟན༔ དུར་ཁྲོད་བརྒྱད་དུ་སྤྱོད་པ་མཛད༔ སྤྲུལ་པ་བརྒྱད་དུ་འགྱེད་པའི་ཚེ༔ གུ་རུ་མཚན་བརྒྱད་ཞེས་སུ་གྲགས༔ དེ་ལ་སློར་དངས་རྗེས་གསུམ་ལས༔ སློར་བ་དབེན་པར་ཡོ་བྱད༔ བསགས༔ སྐྱབས་འགྲོ་སེམས་བསྐྱེད་སྒྱུན་དུ་སོང༔ མདུན་མཁར་གུ་རུ་གསལ་བཏབས་ལ༔ གསོལ་བ་གདབ་པ་འདི་ལ་འབབ༔

Salutation to the Guru and the assembled dakinis!

I am the skull-garlanded one from the land of Oddiyana who has visited all the holy places of India and Nepal and, having engaged with many scholars and adepts, entered many tantric mandalas. I have received all the necessary empowerments and instructions. All aspects of all the buddhas and bodhisattvas of every time and place are complete in me and I am without desire and free of any fault. I was born on a lotus in the great ocean as the unequalled apparition. I have shown many magical forms and have been active in the eight great charnel grounds. When I emanated my eight manifestations I became known as the guru with eight names.

[There are three parts to this practice, the preparations, the main part and subsequent part. Firstly, as preparation, you should go to an isolated place and arrange all the items necessary for practice. Having completed taking refuge and developing an altruistic intention you should imagine Lotus Source in the sky just before and above you and earnestly recite the following prayer.]

བདུན་བསྐྱེད་ནི༔ VISUALISE DEITY

རང་མདུན་པད་ྨེ་ཉི་ཟླའི་སྟེང་༔

RANG	DUN	PAD MA	NYI	DAI	TENG
me	*in front of*	*lotus*	*sun*	*moon*	*upon*

Before me, on a lotus, sun and moon,

རིག་འཛིན་པད་འབྱུང་གསལ་བཏབས་ལ༔

RIG DZIN	PAE JUNG	SAL TAB LA
vidyadhara	*Padmasambhava*	*visualise*

I imagine Lotus Source the Aware.

Before me, on a lotus, sun and moon, I imagine Lotus Source the Aware.

གསོལ་འདེབས། PRAYER

ཀྱེཿ   རྗེ་བཙུན་གུ་རུ་རིན་པོ་ཆེཿ

KYE	JE TSUN	GU RU	RIN PO CHE
Ah!	*venerable*	*teacher,* *Lotus Source*	*precious*

Ah! Worthy teacher, so rare and precious,

རྒྱལ་བའི་སྐུ་གསུང་ཐུགས་ཡོན་རྫོགསཿ

GYAL WAI	KU	SUNG	THU	YON	DZO
Buddha's	*body*	*speech*	*mind*	*virtues*	*complete*

All the buddhas' body, speech, mind and qualities are fully present in you.

གསོལ་འདེབས་བུ་ལ་བྱིན་གྱིས་རློབསཿ

SON DE	BU		LA	JIN GYI LO
praying	*follower, child*		*to*	*bless*

Please bless your child who prays to you and

བསམ་པ་ལྷུན་གྱིས་འགྲུབ་པར་ཤོགཿ

SAM PA	LHUN GYI	DRU PAR	SHO
wishes	*immediately*	*fulfil*	*do*

Swiftly fulfil my wishes.

Ah! Worthy teacher, so rare and precious, all the buddhas' body, speech, mind, and qualities are fully present in you. Please bless your child who prays to you and fulfil grant my wishes.

[Recite this three times]

སྔགས། MANTRA

ཨོཾ་ཨཱཿཧཱུྃ་བཛྲ་གུ་རུ་པདྨ་སི་དྡྷི་ཧཱུྃཿ

OM Aa HUNG BENDZA GURU PAE MA SIDDHI HUNG

Indestructible three mode guru, Lotus Source grant us accomplishment!

བརྒྱ་སྟོང་ཁྲི་འབུམ་བཟླས་པར་བྱ༔

[This mantra should be recited 100, or 1000, or 10,000 or 100,000 times.]

[The Seven Line Prayer can also be recited many times here.]

 དེ་ནས་དབང་བཞི་བླང་བ་ནི༔ RECEIVING THE FOUR INITIATIONS

བླ་མའི་གནས་གསུམ་ལས་འོད་འཕྲོས༔

LA MAI	NAE SUM	LAE	OE	THROE
guru's	*three places**	*from*	*light*	*comes out*

* forehead, throat, heart

At the guru's forehead, throat and heart light manifests

ཨོཾ་ཨཱཿཧཱུྃ་ཡི་གེའི་རྣམ་པ༔

OM	Aa	HUNG	YI GE	NAM PA
Body's	*Speech's*	*Mind's*	*letter*	*form*
seed letter	*seed letter*	*seed letter*		
at forehead	*at throat*	*at heart*		
white	*red*	*blue*		

In the form of letters OM ཨོཾ, Aa ཨཱཿ, HUNG ཧཱུྃ and

རང་ཐིམ་དབང་བཞི་རྫོགས་སྒྲིབ་དག༔

RANG	THIM	WANG	ZHI	DZO	DRIB	DA
me	*absorbed into**	*initiations*	*four*	*complete, fully get*	*obscurations*	*purify*

*they melt sequentially into my forehead, throat and heart and then all together. This gives us the four initiations which unite us with our potential to awaken as buddhas.

Flows into me. I receive the four initiations, my obscurations are purified, and

སྐུ་དང་ཡེ་ཤེས་ལྔ་མངོན་གྱུར༔

KU	DANG	YE SHE	NGA	NGON GYUR
bodies, modes	*and*	*original knowing*	*five*	*manifest clearly*

The five kayas and the five original knowings manifest in me.

བླ་མ་རིན་པོ་ཆེ་མཁྱེན་ནོ༔

LA MA	RIN PO CHE	KHYEN NO
guru	*precious*	*hear me and give me these initiations!*

Precious guru, please hear me!

At the guru's forehead, throat and heart light manifests in the form of letters OM ཨོཾ, Aa ཨཱཿ, HUNG ཧཱུྃ and flows into me. I receive the four initiations, my obscurations are purified, and the five kayas and the five original knowings manifest in me. Precious guru, please hear me!

[A: If you have time, practise as follows, and then go to the first reciting line on the following page, *"In an instant of recollection I become..."*

Then imagine that Lotus Source is smiling radiantly at you. He comes to the top of your head and from the feet up and the head down he dissolves gradually (or instantaneously, whichever is easier for you) into a ball of light which is absorbed through the crown of your head and descends into your heart. Your body, which is now a body of light, merges into the ball of light so that your body, speech and mind become inseparably merged into the guru's Body, Speech and Mind, like water poured into water. Now the ball of light, your union, which is your sole focus of attention, becomes smaller and smaller until it vanishes. Now there is only simple infinite openness. Remain in that state without doing anything at all, at ease, calm and relaxed. Then allow appearance to gradually occur without adopting or rejecting and then, *"In an instant of recollection I become…"*

B. If you have less time do not follow the above paragraph but go straight to the following line below *"Lotus Source melts into my heart."*]

[གུ་རུ་རང་གི་སྙིང་དབུས་བསྟིམས༔

GU RU	RANG	GI	NYING	UE	TIM
guru	own	of	heart	centre	melt

Lotus Source melts into my heart.

རང་རིག་ཧྲཱི་ཡི་ཡོངས་གྱུར་ལས༔

RANG	RIG	HRI	YI	YONG	GYUR	LAE
my	mind	HRI	letter	totally	change	from

(Rays of light spread out from the HRI as offerings to all the buddhas and then gather back in it. Then I become Lotus Source)

My awareness becomes the letter HRI.

Lotus Source melts into my heart. My awareness becomes the letter HRI.]

དེ་ནས་དངོས་གཞི་བསྐྱེམ་པ་ལ༔ བདག་བསྐྱེད་ནི༔
THE MAIN PRACTICE: VISUALISING ONESELF

རང་ཉིད་སྐད་ཅིག་དྲན་རྫོགས་སུ༔

RANG NYI	KAE CHI	DRAN	DZO	SU
oneself	*instant*	*recollection*	*complete*	*in*

In an instant of recollection I become

པད་འབྱུང་དཀར་དམར་ཞི་མ་ཁྲོ༔

PAE	JUNG	KAR	MAR	ZHI MA	THRO
lotus	*born*	*white*	*red*	*peaceful*	*wrathful*

Lotus Source, pink in colour with an expression that is both peaceful and angry.

རྡོ་རྗེ་ཐོད་འཛིན་མཉེན་ཞུ་གསོལ༔

DOR JE	THOE	DZIN	NYEN ZHU	SOL
vajra	*skull*	*holding*	*lotus hat*	*wearing*

Holding a vajra and a skull cup, I wear a lotus hat.

ཕོད་ཁ་ཆོས་གོས་ཟ་བེར་མནབས༔

PHO KHA	CHOE	GOE	ZA BER	NAB
tunic	*dharma*	*robes*	*cloak*	*dressed*

Dressed in a tunic, red dharma robes and a cloak

མཚོ་སྐྱེས་པད་ཟླའི་གདན་ལ་བཞུགས༔

TSHO	KYE	PAE	DAI	DAN	LA	ZHU
lake	*born*	*lotus*	*moon, of*	*cushion*	*on*	*sitting*

I sit on a lotus with a moon cushion.

དམ་ཡེ་དབྱེར་མེད་ལྷུན་གྲུབ་རྫོགས༔

DAM	YE	YER ME	LHUN DRUB	DZO
visualised form	*wisdom form*	*inseparable*	*spontaneous*	*complete*

The form I imagine and the actual form are instantly inseparable.

ཨོཾ་ཨཿཧཱུྃ་བཛྲ་གུ་རུ་པདྨ་སིདྡྷི་ཧཱུྃ༔

OM Aa HUNG BENDZA GURU PAE MA SIDDHI HUNG

Indestructible three mode guru, Lotus Source grant us accomplishment!

In an instant of recollection I become Lotus Source, pink in colour with an expression that is both peaceful and angry. Holding a vajra and a skull cup, I wear a lotus hat. Dressed in a tunic, red dharma robes and a cloak, I sit on a lotus with a moon cushion. The form I imagine and the actual form are instantly inseparable.

OM Aa HUNG BENDZA GURU PAE MA SIDDHI HUNG

[Recite the mantra many times]

[The Seven Line Prayer can also be recited many times here.]

ཞེས་བརྗོད་བླ་མ་རིག་འཛིན་འགྲུབ༔ དཔེ་གས་མེད་ཁྱབ་བརྟལ་ངང་གིས་སྐྱོང༔

This concludes the mantra recitation of the awareness-abiding guru. The practice and you in your practice of it are protected within infinite presence beyond objectification.

བརྫས་ལ་ཡུ༔ རྒྱ་རྒྱ་རྒྱ༔ གཏེར་རྒྱ༔ སྦས་རྒྱ༔ ཟབ་རྒྱ༔ གསང་རྒྱ༔ མན྄༔ ༈ ཀྵ༔ །

Vajra vows. Triple seal. Treasure seal. Hidden seal. Profound seal. Secret seal. Mantra. It is like this.

མཆོད་པ། OFFERINGS

ༀ་བཛྲ་ཨརྒྷཾ་པ་དྱཾ་པུཥྤེ་དྷུ་པེ་ཨ་ལོ་ཀེ་གྷནྡྷེ་ནེ་ཝི་དྱེ་ཤབྡ་ཨ་ཧཱུྃ༔

OM BENDZA ARGHAM PADYAM PUSHPE DHUPE ALOKE GENDHE NEWIDYE
SHABDA A HUNG

We offer the forms of emptiness: drinking water, feet washing water,
flowers, incense, lamps, perfumed water, food, sound.

བསྟོད་པ། PRAISE

ཧཱུྃ༔ མ་བཅོས་སྤྲོས་བྲལ་བླ་མ་ཆོས་ཀྱི་སྐུ༔

HUNG	MA CHOE	TOE DRAL	LA MA	CHOE KYI KU
Hung	*uncontrived*	*unelaborated*	*guru*	*dharmakaya, intrinsic mode*

Hung. The guru without artifice or elaboration is the intrinsic mode.

བདེ་ཆེན་ལོངས་སྤྱོད་བླ་མ་ཆོས་ཀྱི་རྗེ༔

DE	CHEN	LONG CHO	LA MA	CHOE	KYI	JE
bliss	*great*	*sambhogakaya, enjoyment mode*	*guru*	*dharma*	*of*	*lord*

The guru of great happiness, master of dharma, is the enjoyment mode.

པད་སྡོང་ལས་འཁྲུངས་བླ་མ་སྤྲུལ་པའི་སྐུ༔

PAE	DONG	LAE	THRUNG	LA MA	TRUL PAI KU
lotus	*stem*	*from*	*born*	*guru*	*nirmanakaya, apparitional mode*

The lotus born guru is the apparitional mode.

སྐུ་གསུམ་རྡོ་རྗེ་འཆང་ལ་ཕྱག་འཚལ་བསྟོད༔

KU	SUM	DOR JE CHANG	LA	CHA TSAL	TOE
body	*three*	*Vajradhara*	*to*	*prostrate*	*praise*

We salute and praise Vajradhara with these three modes.

*Hung. The guru without artifice or elaboration is the intrinsic mode.
The guru of great happiness, master of dharma, is the enjoyment mode.
The lotus born guru is the apparitional mode. We salute and praise you,
the Vajradhara having these three modes.*

ཧཱུྃ། དེ་ལྟར་ཟབ་གསང་སྙིང་པོ་ཡི༔ ཡང་ཟབ་རིག་འཛིན་ཡོངས་རྫོགས་ཀྱི༔ སྒྲུབ་པའི་ཆ་ ཀྱེན་མང་དུ་བསྟན༔ འདི་ཉིད་གུ་རུ་མཚན་བརྒྱད་ཀྱི༔ སྤྱི་དང་བྱེ་བྲག་སྒྲུབ་པ་ལས༔ ལམ་ འདིར་མོས་པའི་དོན་དུ་བསྟན༔ སྦྱོར་དངོས་དེ་ལྟར་ཤེས་པར་བྱ༔

Many aspects within the domain of practice have been taught for the series of the Very Secret Awareness-abiding Complete Guru belonging to the Profound Secret Heart. Here, from the general and specific practices of the Guru's Eight Forms, I have shown this path in order to benefit the faithful. Learn the preparations and main part as I have shown.

གསུམ་པ་རྗེས་ཀྱི་རིམ་པ་ནི༔ རྗེས་ཤེས་སྣང་གྲགས་ཐམས་ཅད་ཀུན༔ བླ་མའི་སྐུ་གསུང་ ཐུགས་སུ་གོ༔ མོས་གུས་རྩེ་གཅིག་འབྲལ་མེད་བྱ༔ ཡོན་དན་བདེ་སྟོང་ལྷུན་གྱིས་གྲུབ༔ ཕྲིན་ལས་གང་བརྩམས་འགྲོ་བ་འདྲེན༔ ཡེ་ཤེས་མཐའ་རྒྱས་ཀློང་དུ་གྲོལ༔ ཨུ་རྒྱན་ཡུལ་དུ་ མཁའ་ལ་སྤྱོད༔ ཡར་གྱི་རེ་བ་གནས་དག༔ མར་གྱི་དགོ་དོགས་པ་བྲལ༔ འདི་བྲ་ འདི་བྱེད་ཆོས་ཀྱི་དབྱིངས༔ དབྱིངས་དང་ཡེ་ཤེས་ལྷུན་གྱིས་གྲུབ༔ བརྟས་མ་ཡུༀ རྒྱ་རྒྱ་རྒྱ༔ གཏེར་རྒྱ༔ ཟབ་རྒྱ༔ སྤས་རྒྱ༔ གསང་རྒྱ༔ ཏི་ཐིམ༔

The third part comprises the subsequent stages. Subsequent to the previous practice, one should experience all that is seen, heard and arises in the mind to be the body, speech and mind of the guru. With faith and devotion abide in this with unwavering one-pointed focus. The quality of emptiness and happiness will arise effortlessly. Whatever activity you commence will lead all manner of beings to liberation in the limitless infinity of original knowing. You will be at home in the sky over the land of Oddiyana. Your hopes of ascending will be fulfilled and your fears of descending to the states of woe will be ended. Each action and each intention is within the infinity of infinite hospitality as openness and original knowing are always inseparable. Indestructible vows. Seal Seal Seal. Transcendent seal. Profound seal. Hidden seal. Secret seal. All in infinity.

ཞེས་པ་འདི་ཡང་བདག་འདུ་འགྲོ་ཕན་གླིང་པ་གྲོ་ལོད་རྩལ་གྱིས་བདེ་མཆོག་རྡོ་རྗེ་ཤུགས་འཆང་ མགུལ་ནས་གདན་དྲངས་པའོ༔

I, Nuden Dorje Drophan Lingpa Drolo Tsal, found this treasure text in Tsoe village, Demchog Dorje Shug Chang mountain.

དེ་ལས་སླང་བར་བཙམས༔

[When you begin to arise from that state:]

འདི་ལྟར་མིག་གི་ཡུལ་དུ་སྣང་བ་ཡི༔

DI TAR	MI	GI	YUL	DU	NANG WA	YI
like this	eye,	of	objects,	as, of	appearances,	of
in this way	visual		field		visual experience	

As regards the objects of our vision, the appearances

ཕྱི་ནང་སྣོད་བཅུད་དངོས་པོ་ཐམས་ཅད་ཀུན༔

CHI	NANG	NOE	CHU	NGOE WO	THAM CHE	KUN
outer	inner	container	contents	entities, things	all	all
		i.e. universe	i.e. beings	held to as real		

Of absolutely all the outer and inner entities that constitute the universe and its inhabitants,

སྣང་ཡང་བདག་འཛིན་མེད་པའི་ངང་ལ་ཞོག༔

NANG	YANG	DAG DZIN	ME PAI	NGANG	LA	ZHO
appear, arise	yet, also	grasping and	without	state,	in	stay,
within the sphere		believing in		nature		maintain
of awareness		individual				
		reality or self-nature				

We maintain the state in which they appear yet without being grasped at as something inherently real,

གཟུང་འཛིན་དག་པ་གསལ་སྟོང་ལྷ་ཡི་སྐུ༔

ZUNG	DZIN	DA PA	SAL	TONG	LHA	YI	KU
graspable	grasping	purified	clarity,	emptiness,	god	of	body
object	mind	luminosity	depth		(divine form or		
					expression, nirmanakaya)		

For in fact they are the divine forms of clarity and emptiness, pure and inherently untainted by the false notions of graspable objects and grasping mind.

འདོད་ཆགས་རང་གྲོལ་གྱི་བླ་མ་ལ་གསོལ་བ་འདེབས༔

DOE CHAG	RANG DROL	GYI	LA MA	LA	SOL WA DE
desire	self-liberating,	of	guru	to	pray
	goes free by itself				

(The openness of this divine play of the non-duality of appearances and emptiness provides no ground for subject/object tension or the reification of the experiences of the six realms)

We pray to the guru who self-liberates desire.

ཨུ་རྒྱན་པདྨ་འབྱུང་གནས་ལ་གསོལ་བ་འདེབས༔

UR GYAN	PAE MA	JUNG NAE	LA	SOL WA DE
Oddiyana	lotus	source	to	pray
		(Padmasambhava)		

We pray to Lotus Source of Oddiyana.

As regards the objects of our vision, the appearances of absolutely all the outer and inner entities that constitute the universe and its inhabitants, we maintain the state in which they appear yet without being grasped at as something inherently real, for in fact they are the divine forms of clarity and emptiness, pure and inherently untainted by the false notions of graspable objects and grasping mind. We pray to the guru who self-liberates desire. We pray to Lotus Source of Oddiyana.

འདི་ལྟར་རྣ་བའི་ཡུལ་དུ་གྲགས་པ་ཡི༔

DI TAR	NA WAI	YUL	DU	DRA PA	YI
in this way	audition, the hearing power of the ear	objects	of, as	sound, that which is heard	of

As regards the objects of audition, the audible occurrences

སྙན་དང་མི་སྙན་འཛིན་པའི་སྒྲ་རྣམས་ཀུན༔

NYAN	DANG	MI NYAN	DZIN PAI	DRA	NAM	KUN
sweet, pleasant	and	bitter, unpleasant	grasped at	sound	(plural)	all

Comprising all the sounds that we grasp at as being pleasant and unpleasant,

གྲགས་སྟོང་བསམ་མནོ་བྲལ་བའི་ངང་ལ་ཞོག༔

DRA	TONG	SAM NO	DRAL WAI	NGANG	LA	ZHO
sound	emptiness	thought, ratiocination	without	state	in	stay, keep, maintain

(leaving the sound as immediate energy and not covering it in a layer of interpretation)

We remain in the state of sound and emptiness that is free of all conceptual interpretation,

གྲགས་སྟོང་སྐྱེ་འགགས་མེད་པ་རྒྱལ་བའི་གསུང༔

DRA	TONG	KYE	GA	ME PA	GYAL WAI	SUNG
sound	emptiness	beginning	interruption	without	Jina's, Buddha's	speech (Sambhogakaya)

For in fact they are sound and emptiness, the unborn and uninterrupted speech of the Buddha.

བྲགས་སྟོང་རྒྱལ་བའི་གསུང་ལ་གསོལ་བ་འདེབས༔

DRA   TONG   GYAL WAI   SUNG   LA   SOL WA DE
sound   emptiness   Jina's, Buddha's   speech   to   pray
(like mantra)

(This view should be applied to all the other senses, sense organs and their objects.)

We pray to the Buddha's speech of sound and emptiness.

ཨུ་རྒྱན་པདྨ་འབྱུང་གནས་ལ་གསོལ་བ་འདེབས༔

UR GYAN   PAE MA   JUNG NAE   LA   SOL WA DE

We pray to Lotus Source of Oddiyana.

As regards the objects of audition, the audible occurrences comprising all the sounds that we grasp at as being pleasant and unpleasant, we remain in the state of sound and emptiness that is free of all conceptual interpretation, for in fact they are sound and emptiness, the unborn and uninterrupted speech of the Buddha. We pray to the Buddha's speech of sound and emptiness. We pray to Lotus Source of Oddiyana.

འདི་ལྟར་ཡིད་ཀྱི་ཡུལ་དུ་འགྱུ་བ་ཡི༔

DI TAR   YI   KYI   YUL   DU   GYU WA YI
in this way   mental consciousness,   of   object   as   movement, restlessness,
mentation   quivering*

*i.e. thoughts and feeling coming and going causing agitation

As regards the objects of our mentation, these restless movements of

ཉོན་མོངས་དུག་ལྔའི་རྟོག་པ་ཅི་ཤར་ཡང་༔

NYON MONG   DU   NGAI   TO PA   CHI   SHAR   YANG
afflictions*   *poisons***   *five's*   *thoughts,*   *whatever*   *may arise*   *yet*
                                    feelings

* the source of all troubles   ** opacity, aversion, pride, desire, jealousy

Thoughts imbued with the five poisons, no matter what occurs

སྔོན་བསུས་རྗེས་དཔྱོད་བློ་ཡིས་བཅོས་མི་གཞུག༔

NGON SUE   JE CHOE   LO   YI   CHO   MI   ZHU
waiting expectantly   *analysing, following*   *intellect*   *by*   *artifice,*   *not*   *do,*
before thoughts come*   *after past thoughts***   *contrivance*   *enter*

* i.e. looking out for something** like a dog following footprints

We do not enter upon the intellect's contrivance of awaiting future thoughts and following after past thoughts.

འགྱུ་བ་རང་སར་བཞག་པས་ཆོས་སྐུར་གྲོལ༔

GYU WA	RANG SAR	ZHA PAE	CHO KUR	DROL
restlessness, infirmity	in its own place (leave it alone)	by keeping	dharmakaya intrinsic mode	liberated, free*

* Subject and object go free by themselves leaving awareness unobscured.

By leaving the restless movement in its own place we are liberated in the intrinsic mode.

རིག་པ་རང་གྲོལ་གྱི་བླ་མ་ལ་གསོལ་བ་འདེབས༔

RIG PA	RANG DROL	GYI	LA MA	LA	SOL WA DE
intrinsic awareness	self-liberating	of	guru	to	pray

We pray to the guru of self-liberating awareness.

ཨུ་རྒྱན་པདྨ་འབྱུང་གནས་ལ་གསོལ་བ་འདེབས༔

UR GYAN	PAE MA	JUNG NAE	LA	SOL WA DE

We pray to Lotus Source of Oddiyana.

As regards the objects of our mentation, these restless movements of thoughts imbued with the five poisons, no matter what occurs we do not enter upon the intellect's contrivance of awaiting future thoughts and following after past thoughts. By leaving the restless movement in its own place we are liberated in the intrinsic mode. We pray to the guru of self-liberating awareness. We pray to Lotus Source of Oddiyana.

ཕྱི་ལྟར་གཟུང་བའི་ཡུལ་སྣང་དག་པ་དང་༔

CHI	TAR	ZUNG WAI	YUL	NANG	DA PA	DANG
outer, outside	as	graspable	objects	images, appearances	purified	and

With the purification of all that appears as the outer objects of grasping, and

ནང་ལྟར་འཛིན་པའི་སེམས་ཉིད་གྲོལ་བ་དང་༔

NANG	TAR	DZIN PAI	SEM NYI	DROL WA	DANG
inner	as	grasping	mind	liberate	and

The liberating of the grasping mind within,

བར་དུ་འོད་གསལ་རང་ངོ་ཤེས་པ་རུ༔

BAR DU	OE SEL	RANG NGO	SHE PA	RU
at that time, when the sense of outer and inner dissolves	clarity, lucidity, luminosity	own face	awaken to	with, to

We awaken to our own intrinsic face of clear illumination.

དུས་གསུམ་བདེ་གཤེགས་རྣམས་ཀྱི་ཐུགས་རྗེ་ཡིས༔

DU	SUM	DE SHE NAM	KYI	THU JE	YI
times	three	sugatas, buddhas	of	compassion	by, with
(past, present, future)				(Their kindness shines through our obscurations revealing our actual presence.)	

By the kindness of the buddhas of the three times,

བདག་འདྲའི་རང་རྒྱུད་གྲོལ་བར་བྱིན་གྱིས་རློབས༔

DA	DRAI	RANG GYU	DROL WAR	JIN GYI LO
I	like *	our sense of personal continuity as someone	liberate	bless

*all beings who are like me in wandering in samsara yet having buddha nature

May I and all beings be blessed with liberation from our sense of self.

With the purification of all that appears as the outer objects of grasping, and the liberating of the grasping mind within, we awaken to our own intrinsic face of clear illumination. By the kindness of the buddhas of the three times, may I and all beings be blessed with liberation from our sense of self.

ཨི་རྟག་རྒྱུད་བསྐུལ་ནི།   WAKE UP TO IMPERMANENCE

ཨོཾ་ཨཱཿ་ཧཱུྂ་མ་ཧཱ་གུ་རུ་སརྦ་སིདྡྷི་ཧཱུྂ༔

OM	Aa	HUNG	MAHA	GURU	SARVA	SIDDHI	HUNG
Body	*Speech*	*Mind*	*great*	*teacher*	*all*	*true*	*actualise*

Body, Speech, Mind. Great Guru, actualise all accomplishments!

འཇིག་རྟེན་སྣང་བ་སྒྱུ་མར་གོ་ལགས་ཀྱང༔

JIG TEN	NANG WA	GYU MAR	GO LA	KYANG
worlds (all	*appearances,*	*illusory,*	*know, intellectual*	*yet*
(of samsara)	*ideas*	*magical*	*understanding*	

Although I know worldly appearances to be illusory

འཕྲུལ་སྣང་འདི་ལ་ད་དུང་བདག་འཛིན་སྐྱེས༔

THRUL	NANG	DI	LA	DA DUNG	DA	DZIN	KYE
bewildering,	*appearances*	*these*	*to*	*till now*	*self-*	*grasping*	*arises*
confusing ideas					*existent*		

I still grasp at these bewildering appearances as if they had real existence.

བདག་གི་ཉོན་མོངས་བག་ཆགས་མ་སྟོང་བར༔

DA GI	NYON MONG	BAG CHA	MA TONG WAR
my	*poisons, afflictions**	*traces***	*not finished, not experienced as empty clarity*

*opacity, anger, desire, pride, jealousy   ** the subtle traces of these afflictions

My afflictions and their subtle traces are not yet empty for me.

ཆགས་ཞེན་རྩད་ནས་ཆོད་པར་བྱིན་གྱིས་རློབས༔

CHA	ZHEN	TSAE	NAE	CHO PAR	JIN GYI LO
desire,	*hopes,*	*root*	*from*	*is cut*	*bless*
attachment	*expectations*	*(totally)*			

I awake to the self-eradication of hope and desire!

Body, Speech, Mind. Great Guru, actualise all accomplishments! Although I know worldly appearances to be illusory I still grasp at these bewildering appearances as if they had real existence. My afflictions and their subtle traces are not yet empty for me. I awake to the self-eradication of hope and desire!

ཨོཾ་ཨཱཿ་ཧཱུྂ་མ་ཧཱ་གུ་རུ་སརྦ་སིདྡྷི་ཧཱུྂ༔

OM Aa HUNG MAHA GURU SARVA SIDDHI HUNG

Body, Speech, Mind. Great Guru, actualise all accomplishments!

སྐྱིགས་མའི་ལས་ངན་མི་རྟག་རང་གཟུགས་ལ༔

NYIG MAI	LAE	NGEN	MI TA	RANG ZU	LA
Debased period of intense egotism	*actions*	*bad*	*impermanent*	*own form, this world I live in*	*to*

Towards the impermanent manifestations of the bad actions of this DEased period

ངེས་འབྱུང་སྐྱེས་ནས་ཆགས་ཞེན་ཡུལ་བོར་ཡང་༔

NGE JUNG	KYE	NAE	CHA	ZHEN	YUL	BOR	YANG
renunciation	*arises, is born*	*then*	*desire*	*hopes, attachments*	*objects*	*discard, throw out*	*yet*

Renunciation arises and I discard the objects of my hopes and desires.

ཕྱིས་ནས་རང་བདེའི་ཡུལ་འདོད་དུ་ཁས་མནར༔

CHI NAE	RANG	DEI	YUL	DOE	DU KHAE	NAR
later on	*my*	*happiness*	*objects*	*desire**	*suffering, by*	*pained, troubled*

*things I like and use like house, books, dharma statues, clothes, friends and so on

Yet later on I am troubled by the suffering arising from desire for the things that make me happy.

འདོད་སྲེད་རྩད་ནས་ཆོད་པར་བྱིན་གྱིས་རློབས༔

DOE	SE	TSAE NAE	CHO	PAR	JIN GYI LO
desire	*craving*	*root, totality*	*cut, destroy*	*as*	*bless*

I awake to the self-eradication of desire and craving!

Body, Speech, Mind. Great Guru, actualise all accomplishments! Towards the impermanent manifestations of the bad actions of this DEased period renunciation arises and I discard the objects of my hopes and desires. Yet later on I am troubled by the suffering arising from desire for the things that make me happy. I awake to the self-eradication of desire and craving!

ཨོཾ་ཨཱཿཧཱུྃ་མ་ཧཱ་གུ་རུ་སརྦ་སིདྡྷི་ཧཱུྃ༔

OM Aa HUNG MAHA GURU SARVA SIDDHI HUNG

Body, Speech, Mind. Great Guru, actualise all accomplishments!

དུག་གསུམ་ཉོན་མོངས་སེལ་བའི་ཐབས་ཆེན་པོ༔

DU	SUM	NYON MONG	SEL WAI	THAB	CHEN PO
poisons	*three**	*afflictions*	*clearing***	*method, means*	*great*

* opacity, anger, desire   **showing their emptiness

Great methods for making clear the nature of the afflicting three poisons

ཀྱུལ་བས་ལུང་བསྟན་མང་པོ་གསུང་ལགས་ཀྱང༔

GYAL   WAE   LUNG TEN   MANG PO   SUNG   LA   KYANG
*Jina *   by   teachings, books   many   spoke   did   yet*
*Buddha, one who is victorious over all limitations.

Have been taught by the buddhas in many instructions.

སྤོང་དཀའི་བག་ཆགས་དབང་དུ་ཉེས་ཆེར་ཤོར༔

PONG   KAI   BA CHA   WANG DU   SHAE CHER   SHOR
*abandon,   difficult   subtle traces   under the   very strongly   go down
discard   power of*

Yet I helplessly fall under the power of subtle karmic traces that are so
difficult to abandon.

ལས་ངན་རྩད་ནས་ཆོད་པར་བྱིན་གྱིས་རློབས༔

LAE   NGEN   TSAE   NAE   CHO PAR   JIN GYI LO
activity, deeds   bad   root   from   cut   as   bless*
*the bad deeds which keep us wandering and suffering in samsara
I awake to the self-eradication of bad actions!

*Body, Speech, Mind. Great Guru, actualise all accomplishments! Great
methods for making clear the nature of the afflicting three poisons have
been taught by the buddhas in many instructions yet I helplessly fall
under the power of subtle karmic traces that are so difficult to abandon.
I awake to the self-eradication of bad actions!*

ཨོཾ་ཨཿཧཱུྃ་མ་ཧཱ་གུ་རུ་སརྦ་སིདྡྷི་ཧཱུྃ༔

OM Aa HUNG   MAHA GURU SARVA SIDDHI HUNG
Body, Speech, Mind. Great Guru, actualise all accomplishments!

ཕྱི་རྐྱེན་ནང་རྐྱེན་དེས་ཐག་པའི་རྐྱེན༔

CHI   KYEN   NANG   KYEN   DE MA THA PAI   KYEN
outer   reason,   inner subject**   reason,   suddenly arising,#   reason,
(objects) situation   (consciousness) situation   immediately happening   situation*
*climbing a mountain   ** attention wandering
#due to the first two, falling off the mountain and being killed.

Outer situations, inner situations, and suddenly occurring situations,

ཐམས་ཅད་བསྐྱེད་པའི་རྩ་བ་གཉིས་འཛིན་དུ༔

THAM CHE   KYAE PAI   TSA WAI   NYI   DZIN   TU
all   arising, developing   root   duality   belief in   as

All arise from the root of belief in duality.

ད་གཟོད་གོ་ཡང་མདུད་པའི་རྩལ་མ་གྲོལ༔

DA ZOE	GO	YANG	DU PAI	TSAL	MA	DROL
now	*intellectual knowledge*	*yet*	*Mara's demon's**	*energy, wave*	*not*	*free from*

*the active forms of ignorance which are its bewildering energy

I know this now, yet I am not free from the power of Mara.

རང་སེམས་གཅེར་བུར་འཆར་བར་བྱིན་གྱིས་རློབས༔

RANG	SEM	CHER BUR	CHAR WAR	JIN GYI LO
my	*mind*	*naked, unobstructed*	*arise*	*bless*

I awake to the arising of my naked awareness!

Body, Speech, Mind. Great Guru, actualise all accomplishments! Outer situations, inner situations, and suddenly occurring situations, all arise from the root of belief in duality. I know this now, yet I am not free from the power of Mara. I awake to the arising of my naked awareness!

ༀ་ཨཱཿཧཱུྃ་མ་ཧཱ་གུ་རུ་སརྦ་སིདྡྷི་ཧཱུྃ༔

OM Aa HUNG   MAHA GURU SARVA SIDDHI HUNG

Body, Speech, Mind. Great Guru, actualise all accomplishments!

གཉིས་འཛིན་སྒྲོགས་ལས་གྲོལ་བར་བྱིན་གྱིས་རློབས༔

NYI	DZIN	DRO	LAE	DROL WAR	JIN GYI LO
duality	*believe*	*fetter*	*from*	*free*	*bless*

I awake to freedom from the fetter of belief in duality.

ཤེས་པ་གཟོ་མེད་རང་ལུགས་ལྷུག་པ་ལ༔

SHE PA	ZO ME	RANG LU	LHU PA	LA
mind itself, awareness	*unmade, uncontrived*	*own way* own mode*	*relaxed, easy, spontaneous*	*thus*

*unborn it arises of itself without stimulus

My mind as it is is unmade, at ease in every way.

མཁས་ཀྱང་ལེགས་པའི་རང་བཟོ་མ་བྱས་ཤིང་༔

KHAE	KYANG	LE PAI	RANG ZO	MA	JAE SHING
wise, Buddha	*also*	*good qualities (of nirvana)*	*own work, effort*	*not*	*making*

It is not made by the good deeds and qualities of the Buddha, and

བྱིང་འཐིབས་གཡེང་བའི་བཙོན་རར་མ་བཅིངས་པར༔

JING	THIB	YENG WAI	TSON RAR	MA	CHING PAR
sinking	*foggy*	*wavering, instability*	*prison (samsara)*	*not*	*bound*

It is not bound in the prison of sinking, fogginess and wavering.

བཀྲག་མདངས་རང་འོད་འཚེར་བའི་རིག་པ་འདི༔

TRAG	DANG	RANG	OE	TSER WAI	RIG PA	DI
brilliant	radiant	own, inherent	light, clarity	shining	presence, awareness	this

With my awareness shining with its brilliant, radiant, intrinsic light,

ཆོས་ཉིད་ཡངས་པའི་མ་དང་བུ་འཕྲད་ནས༔

CHOE NYI	YANG PAI	MA	DANG	BU	THRAE	NAE
dharmata, actuality	vast	mother*	and	child**	meet	therefore

*sunyata itself   ** experience of sunyata developed in practice

Actuality's vast mother and her child will meet.

ལེ་ལོ་རྐྱེན་གྱི་གྲོགས་ཕྱིར་མ་འཐོམས་པར༔

LE LO	KYEN	GYI	DRO	CHIR	MA	THOM PAR
lazy	reasons, situations	of	friends	due to	not	get stunned, not become stupid

So not being dulled by the false friends encouraging complacency,

ལེགས་པའི་ཁང་བུར་གཅེས་པའི་གཉེར་བྱས་ཏེ༔

LE PAI	KHANG BUR	CHE PAI	NYER	JAE	TE
good (sunyata)	house	loving, intimate	relation, friend	do	thus (must do practice)

I will lovingly befriend the good house of sunyata.

མྱུར་དུ་ཆོས་ཉིད་མ་དང་བུ་འཕྲད་ནས༔

NYUR DU	CHOE NYI	MA	DANG	BU	THRAE	NAE
quickly	dharmata	mother	and	son	meet*	then

*my mind will be permanently merged in sunyata's clear understanding

With this mother actuality and her child will quickly meet.

ཕྱིན་ཆད་འགྲོ་དོན་སྟོབས་ཆེན་བྱེད་པར་ཤོག༔

CHIN CHAE	DRO	DON	TOB	CHEN	JE PAR	SHO
from that time	beings in samsara	benefit	strength	great	do, act	emphatic

Then, from that time on I will act with all my power for the benefit of sentient beings!

བྱང་ཆུབ་སེམས་དཔའི་སྤྱོད་པ་བྱེད་པར་ཤོག༔

JANG CHU SEM PAI	CHO PA	JE PAR	SHO
bodhisattva's	conduct, deeds	do	emphatic

I will perform the deeds of a bodhisattva!

གཞན་དོན་དགེ་བ་རླབས་ཆེན་འགྲུབ་པར་ཤོག༔

ZHEN	DON	GE WA	LAB	CHEN	DRU PAR	SHO
other's	*benefit*	*virtue*	*wave*	*great*	*accomplish*	*emphatic*

I will create a great wave of virtue for the benefit of others!

འཁོར་བ་དོང་ནས་སྤུག་པའི་མཐུ་ཐོབ་ཤོག༔

KHOR WA	DONG	NAE	TRU PAI	THU	THO	SHO
samsara	*upturn*	*then*	*empty completely*	*effective power*	*get*	*emphatic*

I will gain the effective power to upturn and empty samsara!

Body, Speech, Mind. Great Guru, actualise all accomplishments! I awake to freedom from the fetter of belief in duality. My mind as it is is unmade, at ease in every way. It is not made by the good deeds and qualities of the Buddha, and it is not bound in the prison of sinking, fogginess and wavering. With my awareness shining with its brilliant, radiant, intrinsic light, actuality's vast mother and son will meet. So not being dulled by the false friends encouraging complacency I will lovingly befriend the good house of sunyata. With this mother actuality and her child will quickly meet. Then, from that time on I will act with all my power for the benefit of sentient beings! I will perform the deeds of a bodhisattva! I will create a great wave of virtue for the benefit of others! I will gain the effective power to upturn and empty samsara!

ཚོགས་བསྡུས་པ་ནི༔ SHARING THE OFFERING

རཾ་ཡཾ་ཁཾ་ཨོཾ་ཨཱཿཧཱུྂ༔

RAM	YAM	KHAM	OM	Aa	HUNG
fire burning	*air blowing*	*water washing*	*body**	*speech***	*mind#*
out impurities	*them away*	*away all traces*			

*nirmanakaya **sambhogakaya #dharmakaya
(The mantra purifies, consecrates and increases the offerings.)

ངོ་བོ་སྟོང་པའི་ཚོགས་གཞོང་དུ༔

NGO WO	TONG PAI	TSHO	ZHONG	DU
openness	*emptiness*	*offering*	*vessel*	*in*

The offering bowl of the emptiness of our open nature

རང་བཞིན་གསལ་བའི་ཚོགས་རྫས་བཤམས༔

RANG ZHIN	SAL WAI	TSHO DZAE	SHAM
presence	*clarity*	*offering articles*	*put*

Displays the offering of the clarity of our presence

ཐུགས་རྗེ་ཀུན་ཁྱབ་བྱིན་ཆེན་ཕོབ༔

THU JE	KUN KHYA	JIN CHEN	PHO
compassion	*all pervading*	*blessings*	*give*

Revealing our all-inclusive kindness.

མཆོག་གསུམ་རྩ་གསུམ་སྐུ་གསུམ་ལྷ༔

CHO	SUM	TSA	SUM	KU	SUM	LHA
jewels	*three*	*root*	*three*	*enlightened mode*	*three*	*god*

Three Jewels, three Roots, and three enlightened Modes,

ཀུན་འདུས་བླ་མ་འདིར་བྱོན་ལ༔

KUN DUE	LA MA	DIR	JON	LA
all together	*Guru*	*here*	*come*	*and*

Together with the Guru who encompasses you all – please come here and

བདེ་བ་ཆེན་པོའི་ཚོགས་མཆོད་བཞེས༔

DE WA	CHEN POI	TSHO	CHOE	ZHE
bliss	*great*	*assembled*	*offerings*	*accept*

Enjoy the great happiness of these assembled offerings.

ཉམས་ཆགས་ཉེས་ཚོགས་མཐོལ་ཞིང་བཤགས༔

NYAM	CHA	NYE	TSHO	THOL ZHING	SHA
lapses	breaches	faults	all	palms together	confess

With our palms held together at our hearts, we confess all our many breaches of vows, lapses and faults.

འཁྲུལ་སྣང་རྟོག་ཚོགས་དབྱིངས་སུ་བསྒྲལ༔

THRUL	NANG	TOG	TSHO	YING	SU	DRAL
deluded, bewildering	appearances	thoughts	all	infinite hospitality	in	liberate

All deluding appearances and thoughts are liberated within the infinitely hospitable ground, and

ཀ་དག་རིག་པའི་ཀློང་དུ་བསྟབས༔

KA DA	RIG PAI	LONG DU	TA
pure	awareness	inside	set forth

Displayed within the primordial purity of open awareness.

མགྲོན་བཞིའི་ཐུགས་དམ་བསྐང་གྱུར་ཅིག༔

DRON	ZHI	THU	DAM KANG	GYUR	CHI
guests	four	mind	satisfied	become	must

The four classes of guests must be completely satisfied.

ཚོགས་རྫོགས་དོན་གཉིས་ལྷུན་གྲུབ་ནས༔

TSHO	DZO	DON	NYI	LHUN DRU	NE
accumulation	complete	benefit	two	spontaneous	then

With all our accumulations of merit and wisdom complete may benefit for self and other arise effortlessly.

སྐུ་བཞིའི་རྒྱལ་སྲིད་མྱུར་ཐོབ་ཤོག༔

KU	ZHI	GYAL	SI	NYUR	THO	SHO
kayas	four	Jinas'	realm	quickly	attain	must

May all beings quickly awaken in the Buddhas' realm of the four enlightened modes.

The offering bowl of the emptiness of our open nature displays the offering of the clarity of our presence revealing our all-inclusive kindness. Three Jewels, three Roots, and three enlightened Modes, together with the Guru who encompasses you all – please come here and enjoy the great happiness of these assembled offerings. With our palms held together at our hearts, we confess all our many breaches of vows, lapses and faults. All deluding appearances and identifications are liberated within the infinitely hospitable ground, and displayed within the primordial purity

*of open awareness. The four classes of guests must be completely satisfied.
With all our accumulations of merit and wisdom complete may benefit
for self and other arise effortlessly. May all beings quickly awaken in the
Buddhas' realm of the four enlightened modes.*

འདོན་བདེའི་ཕྱིར་སྤྲར་ཟིལ་གནོན་གླིང་པས་བསྒྲིགས་པའོ༔

Arranged by Zilnon Lingpa (C.R. Lama), for easy reading.

ཧོ༔   ཞལ་ཟས་ཚོགས་མཆོད་དམ་པ་འདི༔

HO	ZHAL ZAE	TSHO	CHO	DAM PA	DI
Oh!	*food*	*assembled*	*offerings*	*excellent*	*this*

Oh! This excellent assembly of food offerings

འདོད་ཡོན་མ་སྤངས་ལོངས་སྤྱོད་རྒྱན༔

DON YON	MA PANG	LONG CHO	GYEN
all things pleasing to the senses	*not reject*	*enjoy, use*	*like an ornament*

Ornaments our enjoyment – so do not reject the pleasure!

དངོས་གྲུབ་སྣ་ཚོགས་འདི་ལས་འབྱུང༔

NGO DRU	NA TSHO	DI	LAE	JUNG
siddhi, true accomplishment	*many, different*	*this*	*from*	*arise, come*

From this enjoyment many different accomplishments arise.

རྣལ་འབྱོར་དགྱེས་པའི་ཚོགས་ལ་རོལ༔

NAL JOR	GYE PAI	TSHO	LA ROL
yogis, relaxed and open	*happily*	*assembled offerings*	*eat and enjoy*

Yogis, happily eat and enjoy these assembled offerings!

སིདྡྷི་ཕ་ལ་ཨ་ལ་ལ་ཧོ༔

SID DHI	PHA LA	A LA LA HO
true accomplishment	*result*	*wonderful!*

The result is true accomplishment – wonderful!

*Oh! This excellent assembly of food offerings ornaments our enjoyment
– so do not reject the pleasure! From this enjoyment many different
accomplishments arise. Yogis, happily eat and enjoy these assembled
offerings! The result is true accomplishment – wonderful!*

དགེ་བསྔོ། DEDICATION OF MERIT

དགེ་འདིས་བླ་མ་ཁྱེད་འགྲུབ་ནས།

GE	DI	LA MA	KHYE	DRU	NAE
virtue	*by this*	*Guru*	*your*	*practice*	*having*

By this virtue, by doing your practice

འགྲོ་ཀུན་ཉིད་དང་དབྱེར་མེད་ཤོག།

DRO	KUN	NYI	DANG	YER ME	SHO
living beings	*all*	*yourself*	*and*	*inseparable*	*must*

May all beings become inseparable from you, our guru.

འཇིག་རྟེན་བདེ་བའི་དཔལ་ལ་སྤྱོད།

JI TEN	DE WAI	PAL	LA	CHOE
worldly	*happiness*	*glory*	*with*	*enjoy*

May we all enjoy the rich happiness of this world and have

རིག་འཛིན་བླ་མའི་བཀྲ་ཤིས་ཤོག།

RIG DZIN	LA MAI	TRA SHI	SHO
Vidyadhara	*Guru, of*	*auspicious*	*must be*

The good fortune of our aware Guru.

By this virtue, by doing your practice may all beings become inseparable from you, our guru. May we all enjoy the rich happiness of this world and have the good fortune of our aware Guru.

ཕན་པར་བསམས་པ་ཙམ་གྱིས་ཀྱང་།

PHEN PAR   **SAM PA**   **TSAM**   **GYI**   **KYANG**
benefit   *think*   *only*   *by*   *even*

When merely the thought of helping others

སངས་རྒྱས་མཆོད་ལས་ཁྱད་འཕགས་ན།

SANG GYE   **CHO**   **LAE**   **KYE PHA**   **NA**
buddhas   *offering*   *than*   *excellent*   *thus*

Is more excellent than the worship of the Buddhas,

སེམས་ཅན་མ་ལུས་ཐམས་ཅད་ཀྱི།

SEM CHEN   **MA LUE**   **THAM CHE**   **KYI**
sentient beings   *without exception*   *all*   *of*

It is unnecessary even to mention the greatness of striving

བདེ་དོན་བརྩོན་པ་སྨོས་ཅི་དགོས།།

DE DON   **TSON PA**   **MOE**   **CHI**   **GOE**
benefit   *strive*   *say*   *what*   *need*

For the happiness and welfare of all beings without exception.

When merely the thought of helping others is more excellent than the worship of the Buddhas, it is unnecessary even to mention the greatness of striving for the happiness and welfare of all beings without exception.

སྤྱོད་འཇུག་ལས།

Verse from Entering the Way of the Bodhisattva by Shantideva.

བསྟན་པ་རྒྱས་པའི་སྨོན་ལམ། ASPIRATION FOR THE FLOURISHING OF DHARMA

ཉེར་འཚེ་མ་ལུས་ཞི་བ་དང་།

NYER TSE **MA LUE** **ZHI WA** **DANG**
difficulties, *without* *pacify* *and*
troubles *exception*

All difficulties without exception being pacified and

མཐུན་རྐྱེན་ནམ་མཁའི་མཛོད་བཞིན་དུ།

THUN **KYEN** **NAM KAI** **DZO** **ZHIN DU**
harmonious *situations* *sky's* *treasure* *like*

With harmonious conditions like the treasure of the sky,

རྒྱལ་དབང་པདྨ་འབྱུང་གནས་ཀྱི།

GYAL **WANG** **PAE MA JUNG NAE** **KYI**
Jina, Victor *lord* *Padmasambhava* *of*

The teachings of the powerful Victor Lotus Source

བསྟན་པ་ཡུན་རིང་འབར་གྱུར་ཅིག།

TAN PA **YUN RING** **BAR** **GYUR CHI**
doctrine *long life* *shining* *must*

Must live long and shine brightly!

ཨོཾ་ཨཱཿཧཱུྃ་བཛྲ་གུ་རུ་པདྨ་སིདྡྷི་ཧཱུྃཿ

OM **Aa** **HUNG** **BEN DZA** **GU RU** **PAE MA** **SID DHI** **HUNG**
Body *Speech* *Mind* *indestructible* *Guru* *Lotus* *accomplishment* *give*

Indestructible three mode guru, Lotus Source, grant us accomplishment!

All difficulties without exception being pacified, and with harmonious conditions like the treasure of the sky, the teachings of the powerful victor Lotus Source must live long and shine brightly! Indestructible three mode guru Lotus Source, grant us accomplishment!

ཟངས་མདོག་དཔལ་རི་སྨོན་ལམ།

Aspiration for Zangdopalri

གནས་མཆོག་དག་པ་སྤྲུལ་རྫ་ཡབ་ཟངས་མདོག་དཔལ་རི་པདྨ་འོད་ཀྱི་ཞིང་གི་སྨོན་ལམ་ལ་
བརྟེན་ནས་འཁོར་བ་ལས་བགྲོད་པའི་རྟ་ཕོ་མྱུར་མགྱོག་ཕྲགས་རྗེས་ལྱགས་ཀྱུ་བཞུགས་སོ༔

This aspiration is Padmasambhava's hook of kindness which quickly
carries us from samsara like a galloping stallion. Relying on this we
arrive at his Palace of Lotus Light on the glorious Copper-coloured
Mountain (Zangdopalri) in the pure and perfect place, the Land of
Tail Whisk lying to the south-west.

ༀ་ཨཱཿཧཱུྃ་བཛྲ་གུ་རུ་པདྨ་སི་དྡྷི་ཧཱུྃ༔

OM	Aa	HUNG	BEN DZA	GU RU	PAE MA		SID DHI	HUNG
Body	*Speech*	*Mind*	*indestructible*	*teacher*	*Padmasambhava*		*siddhis*	*grant*

Body speech mind indestructible teacher, bestow true attainments!

འཕགས་ཡུལ་ལྷོ་ནུབ་རྫ་ཡབ་གླིང་ཕྲན་ཡུལ༔

PHA	YUL	LHO	NUB	NGA	YAB	LING	TRAN	YUL
holy	*land*	*south*	*west*	*tail*	*end*	*island*	*small*	*land*

South-west of Bodhgaya and beyond the holy land of India is the small
island that resembles a tail whisk.

ཤིན་ཏུ་འཇིགས་རུང་ཟ་བྱེད་སྲིན་པོའི་གྲོང༔

SHIN TU	JIG RUNG	ZA JE	SIN POE	DRONG
very	*fearful*	*eater*	*cannibals*	*city*

There lies the city of the very frightening rakshasa cannibals with

རི་བྲག་དམར་ནག་མཚོན་ཆ་བཟེངས་འདྲའི་བསྐོར༔

RI	DRA	MAR	NAG	TSON CHA	ZENG	DRAI	KOR
mountain	*rock*	*red*	*black*	*weapons*	*raised*	*like*	*surrounded*

Red-black rocky mountains surrounding it like raised weapons.

སྲིན་གླིང་སོ་གཉིས་གྲོང་ཁྱེར་བརྗོད་ལས་འདས༔

SIN	LING	SO NYI	DRONG KYER	JOE LAE DAE
cannibal	*island*	*thirty-two*	*city*	*inexpressible, numberless*

There are thirty-two rakshasa cannibal islands with numberless cities.

*Body speech mind indestructible teacher, bestow true attainments!
South-west of Bodhgaya and beyond the holy land of India is the small
island that resembles a tail whisk. There lies the city of the very frightening rakshasa cannibals with red-black rocky mountains surrounding
it like raised weapons. There are thirty-two rakshasa cannibal islands
with numberless cities.*

དེ་དབུས་ས་གཞི་ཁོ་དུ་སྟོམས་ཡངས་ཞིང་ཟླུམ༔

DE WUE	SA ZHI	KHO NYOM	YANG SHING	DUM
in the centre of the main island	*land*	*flat very (as a table)*	*large*	*round*

In the centre there is a very large, round flat island

མེ་ཏོག་པདྨའི་ལྗོངས་དང་སྨན་སྣ་ཚོགས༔

ME TOG	PAE MAI	JONG	DANG	MAN	NA TSHO
flower	*lotus*	*garden*	*and*	*medicine*	*many different*

Which is a garden with lotuses and many flowers and medicinal plants.

དྲི་ངད་འཕུལ་ཞིང་དྲི་ཡིས་དབང་པོ་སངས༔

DRI	NGAE	THUL ZHING	DRI	YI	WANG PO	SANG
smell	*strong*	*volatile*	*smell*	*by*	*nose*	*refresh*

Their scent is intense and spreading easily it refreshes one's sense of
smell.

དཔག་བསམ་ཤིང་ཆེན་ཡལ་ག་ལོ་འབྲས་ལྡན༔

PA SAM SHING	CHEN	YAL GA	LO	DRAE	DAN
wish-fulfilling tree	*great*	*branch*	*leaves*	*fruit*	*having*

There is also a great wish-granting tree with many branches, leaves and
fruit.

*In the centre there is a very large, round and flat island which is a
garden with lotuses and many flowers and medicinal plants. Their scent
is intense and spreading easily it refreshes one's sense of smell. There is
also a great wish-granting tree with many branches, leaves and fruit.*

རིན་ཆེན་ས་གཞི་བདུད་རྩིའི་ཆུ་མིག་འབབས༔

RIN CHEN	SA ZHI	DUE TSI	CHU MI	BAB
precious jewel	*land*	*amrita*	*spring*	*come*

In this precious land liberating elixir bubbles up from springs.

བྱ་རིགས་སྣ་ཚོགས་ཆོས་ཀྱི་བརྡ་སྐད་ལེན༔

BYA	RIG	NA TSHO	CHOE	KYI	DA	LU LEN
bird	*kinds*	*diverse*	*dharma*	*of*	*symbol*	*singing*

Many kinds of birds sing the symbolic sounds of dharma.

 རི་དགས་དུད་འགྲོ་ཆུ་གནས་བུང་བ་སོགས༔

RI DA	DUN DRO	CHU	NAE	BUNG WA	SO
deer	*hooved animals*	*water*	*inhabitants*	*bees*	*and so on*

There are deer and other hooved animals, aquatic creatures, bees and other humming insects,

འཕུར་ལྡིང་རྩེ་འཛོ་དགའ་འགྲོ་སྤྱངས་སྤྱབས་བསྐོར༔

PHUR	DING	TSE JO	GA DRO	TANG TAB	KOR
flying	*jumping*	*playing*	*very happy*	*posture*	*inside*

Each expressing joy by flying, jumping and playing.

པདྨ་འོད་ཀྱི་ཞིང་དེར་སྐྱེ་བར་ཤོག༔

PAE MA	OE	KYI	ZHING	DER	KYE WAR	SHO
lotus	*light*	*of*	*land*	*there*	*born*	*must*

We must take birth in this land of Lotus Light.

In this precious land liberating elixir bubbles up from springs. Many kinds of birds sing the symbolic sounds of dharma. There are deer and other hooved animals, aquatic creatures, bees and other humming insects, each expressing joy by flying, jumping and playing. We must take birth in this land of Lotus Light.

དེ་དག་དབུས་སུ་ཡན་ལག་བརྒྱད་ལྡན་གྱི༔

DE DA	WUE	SU	YAN LA	GYE	DEN	GYI
these	*centre*	*in*	*good quality*	*eight*	*have*	*of*

In the centre, with water having the eight good qualities,

རྒྱ་མཚོ་ཆེན་པོ་ཟླུམ་འཁྱིལ་གཏིང་དཔལ་ལ༔

GYAM TSO	CHEN PO	DUM	KHYIL	TING	DRAL	LA
ocean	*great*	*round*	*swirl*	*deep*	*without*	*there*

Is a great swirling ocean of unfathomable depth.

ནང་ན་རིན་ཆེན་སྣ་ཚོགས་གཅལ་དུ་བཀྲམ༔

NANG NA	RIN CHEN	NA TSHO	CHAL	DU	TRAM
in there	*jewels*	*many*	*spread*	*out*	*strewn*

Many jewels are strewn over its floor.

ཀླུ་རིགས་དཔག་མེད་མཆོད་རྫས་ཐོག་ཏེ་མཆོད༔

LU	RIG	PA ME	CHOE	DZAE	THO TE	CHOE
naga	*class*	*numberless*	*offering*	*things*	*hold up*	*offer*

Countless naga snakes raise up and proffer diverse offerings.

པདྨ་འོད་ཀྱི་ཞིང་དེར་སྐྱེ་བར་ཤོག།

PAE MA   **OE**   **KYI**   **ZHING**   **DER**   **KYE WAR**   **SHO**
lotus   *light*   *of*   *land*   *there*   *born*   *must*

We must take birth in this land of Lotus Light.

In the centre, with water having the eight good qualities, is a great swirling ocean of unfathomable depth. Many jewels are strewn over its floor. Countless naga snakes raise up and proffer diverse offerings. We must take birth in this land of Lotus Light.

དེ་དབུས་གནས་མཆོག་ཟངས་མདོག་དཔལ་གྱི་རི།

DE   **WUE**   **NAE**   **CHO**   **ZANG**   **DO**   **PAL**   **GYI**   **RI**
that   *centre*   *place*   *excellent*   *copper*   *coloured*   *glorious*   *of*   *mountain*

In the centre of the ocean is the supreme place, the glorious copper coloured mountain.

ཙིཏྟའི་དབྱིབས་ཅན་རྩ་བ་མཆོར་ནུབ་ཅིང་།

TSIT   **TAE**   **YIB**   **CHEN**   **TSA WA**   **TSO**   **NUB CHING**
heart   *of*   *shape*   *with*   *root*   *ocean*   *sunk in*

Shaped like a heart, its root is in the ocean while

ལྷག་མ་ལྷུན་ཆགས་བརྗིད་ལྡན་གཟི་བརྗིད་འབར།

LHAG MA   **LHUN CHA**   **JI DEN**   **ZI JI**   **BAR**
the rest   *stable*   *splendid, impressive*   *shining*   *blazing*

The rest of it is unshakable, impressive and blazing with light.

མ་མོ་མཁའ་འགྲོ་ཐམས་ཅད་འདུ་བའི་གླིང་།

MA MO   **KHAN DRO**   **THAM CHE**   **DU WAI**   **LING**
mother goddesses   *dakinis*   *all*   *gather*   *place*

This is where all the mother goddesses and dakinis gather.

པདྨ་འོད་ཀྱི་ཞིང་དེར་སྐྱེ་བར་ཤོག།

PAE MA   **OE**   **KYI**   **ZHING**   **DER**   **KYE WAR**   **SHO**
lotus   *light*   *of*   *land*   *there*   *born*   *must*

We must take birth in this land of Lotus Light.

In the centre of the ocean is the supreme place, the glorious copper coloured mountain. Shaped like a heart, its root is in the ocean while the rest of it is unshakable, impressive and blazing with light. This is where all the mother goddesses and dakinis gather. We must take birth in this land of Lotus Light.

རི་རབ་དེ་ཡི་རྩེ་མོ་འོད་ལྔའི་ཀློང་ༀ

RI RAB	**DE**	**YI**	**TSE MO**	**OE**	**NGAI**	**LONG**
mountain	*that*	*of*	*top*	*colour**	*five**	*in the*

*white, red, blue, yellow, green

The sky around the top of that excellent mountain shines in the five colours.

ཤེལ་དང་བཻ་ཌཱུརྻ་དང་ར་ག་དང་ༀ

SHEL	**DANG**	**BE DUR YA**	**DANG**	**RA GA**	**DANG**
crystal	*and*	*lapis lazuli*	*and*	*coral*	*and*
(east side)		*(south side)*		*(west side)*	

White crystal, blue lapis lazuli, red coral, and

ཨིནྡྲ་ནི་ལ་ལ་སོགས་རིན་ཆེན་གྱི༔

IN DRA NI LA		**LA SO**	**RIN CHEN**	**GYI**
indranila, like a green emerald		*and so on*	*precious*	*of*
(north side)				

Green indranila and so on are the precious materials

རྩིག་པ་ལྔ་ལྡན་གྲུ་བཞི་སྒོ་བཞི་པ༔

TSIG PA	**NGA**	**DEN**	**DRU**	**ZHI**	**GO**	**ZHI PA**
walls	*five*	*have*	*corners*	*four*	*doors*	*four*

Which form the walls of the palace five layers thick. There are four corners, four doors and

ཚད་དང་མཚན་ཉིད་ཡོངས་རྫོགས་གཞལ་མེད་ཁང་༔

TSAE	**DANG**	**TSHEN NYI**	**YONG DZO**	**ZHAL**	**ME**	**KHANG**
measure	*and*	*symbols*	*complete*	*measure*	*without*	*palace*
				(	*mandala*	)

The measurements, symbols and attributes are perfect in this infinite palace.

པདྨ་འོད་ཀྱི་ཞིང་དེར་སྐྱེ་བར་ཤོག༔

PAE MA	**OE**	**KYI**	**ZHING**	**DER**	**KYE WAR**	**SHO**
lotus	*light*	*of*	*land*	*there*	*born*	*must*

We must take birth in this land of Lotus Light.

The sky around the top of that excellent mountain shines in the five colours. White crystal, blue lapis lazuli, red coral and green indranila are the precious materials which form the walls of the palace five layers thick. There are four corners, four doors and the measurements, symbols and attributes are perfect in this infinite palace. We must take birth in this land of Lotus Light.

ཁང་བརྩེགས་ལྔ་པ་སྒོ་ཁང་རྟ་བབ་ལྡན༔

KHANG	TSE	NGA PA	GO KHANG	TA BAB	DEN
building	levels	five	porch	archway	have

The palace has five stories with porches and archways.

རཏྣ་རིགས་ཀྱི་ཕ་གུ་དྲ་བ་དང་༔

RATNA	RIG	KYI	PHA GU	DRA WA	DANG
jewels	different	of	cornice	decorative chains	and

Different jewels decorate each cornice. There are decorative chains and

ཟ་ཕྱེད་མདའ་ཡབ་པུ་ཤུད་ནོར་བུའི་ཏོག༔

TRA CHE	DA	YAB	PU SHU	NOR BUI	TO
half chains	covered	veranda	rain spouts	jewelled	pinnacle

Half chains, roofed verandas, rain spouts and a jewelled pinnacle.

འཕན་གདུགས་རྒྱལ་མཚན་དར་དཔྱང་དྲིལ་གཡེར་སྒྲས༔

PHEN DU	GYAL TSEN	DAR CHANG	DRIL	YER	TRAE
canopies	victory banners	silk tassels	bells	small	adorned

There are ribbon banners on the pillars, ceiling canopies, victory banners and silk tassels with bells and small bells attached.

པདྨ་འོད་ཀྱི་ཞིང་དེར་སྐྱེ་བར་ཤོག༔

PAE MA	OE	KYI	ZHING	DER	KYE WAR	SHO
lotus	light	of	land	there	born	must

We must take birth in this land of Lotus Light.

The palace has five stories with porches and archways. Different jewels decorate each cornice. There are decorative chains and half chains, roofed verandas, rain spouts and a jewelled pinnacle. There are ribbon banners on the pillars, ceiling canopies, victory banners and silk tassels with bells and small bells attached. We must take birth in this land of Lotus Light.

འདོད་སྣམ་རྣམས་ལ་མཆོད་པའི་ལྷ་མོ་ཡིས༔

DOE NAM		NAM	LA	CHOE PAI	LHA MO	YI
balcony, veranda		(pl.)	on	offering	goddesses	by

On the balconies and verandas are offering goddesses

མཆོད་རྫས་དུ་མ་ཐོགས་ཏེ་མཆོད་པར་བྱེད༔

CHO	DZAE	DU MA	THOG TE	CHO PAR	JE
offering	articles	various	hold up	offer to	do

Who bear aloft diverse gifts.

ཕྱི་ནང་སྒྲིབ་མེད་ཡེ་ཤེས་ཟང་ཐལ་ཀློང་༔

CHI	NANG	DRIB	ME	YE SHE	ZANG THAL	LONG
outer	inner	obscuring	not	wisdom	direct	depth

The walls are translucent. With original knowing one can see everything directly and

མཐའ་དབུས་མ་འདྲེས་ཕོ་བྲང་ཟང་ཐལ་འཆར་༔

THA	WUE	MA	DRE	PHO DRANG	ZANG THAL	CHAR
edge	centre	not	mixed	palace	direct	arise

Without merging centre and periphery since the entire palace is immediately present.

པདྨ་འོད་ཀྱི་ཞིང་དེར་སྐྱེ་བར་ཤོག༔

PAE MA	OE	KYI	ZHING	DER	KYE WAR	SHO
lotus	light	of	land	there	born	must

We must take birth in this land of Lotus Light.

On the balconies and verandas are offering goddesses who bear aloft diverse gifts. The walls are translucent. With original knowing one can see everything directly and without merging centre and periphery since the entire palace is immediately present. We must take birth in this land of Lotus Light.

ཡེ་ཤེས་རང་འོད་ཕོ་བྲང་དེ་ཡི་མཐར༔

YE SHE	RANG	OE	PHO DRANG	DE	YI	THAR
original knowing	self-arising	light	palace	that	of	end, edge

At the perimeter of this palace manifesting from the intrinsic light of original knowing

རིན་ཆེན་དུ་མ་ལས་གྲུབ་ལྕགས་རིས་བསྐོར༔

RIN CHEN	DU MA	LAE DRU	CHA	RI	KOR
jewel	many	built up	iron	mountain	circle

Is an encircling wall of jewels resembling the iron mountains surrounding our world.

སྟེང་ན་སྐུ་གདུང་འོད་འབར་འཕན་གདུགས་དང་༔

TENG NA	KU DUNG	OE BAR	PHAN DU	DANG
on top of	stupa	shining	banners and canopies	and

The top of the wall is ornamented with shining reliquaries, banners, canopies and

 དར་ཆེན་སྟག་གི་རྒྱལ་མཚན་དྲ་བས་སྤྲས༔

DAR	CHEN	TA	GI	GYAL TSEN	DRA WAE	TRAE
banner	*great*	*tiger*	*of*	*victory banner*	*garlands*	*ornamented*

Great banners, tiger victory banners and garlands.

དྲིལ་གཡེར་རླུང་བསྐྱོད་ཆོས་སྒྲས་སྟོང་གསུམ་ཁྱབ༔

DRIL	YER	LUNG	KHYO	CHOE	DRAE	TONG SUM	KHYA
bells	*small bells*	*wind*	*moved*	*dharma*	*sound*	*everywhere*	*spreads*

The large and small bells are shaken by the wind and their dharma sound is heard in every world.

པདྨ་འོད་ཀྱི་ཞིང་དེར་སྐྱེ་བར་ཤོག༔

PAE MA	OE	KYI	ZHING	DER	KYE WAR	SHO
lotus	*light*	*of*	*land*	*there*	*born*	*must*

We must take birth in this land of Lotus Light.

At the perimeter of this palace manifesting from the intrinsic light of original knowing is an encircling wall of jewels resembling the iron mountains surrounding our world. The top of the wall is ornamented with shining reliquaries, banners, canopies and great banners, tiger victory banners and garlands. The large and small bells are shaken by the wind and their dharma sound is heard in every world. We must take birth in this land of Lotus Light.

གསང་མཆོག་བླ་མེད་ཕོ་བྲང་དེའི་དབུས་སུ༔

SANG	CHO	LA ME	PHO DRANG	DEI	WUE	SU
secret	*excellent*	*unsurpassed*	*palace*	*that*	*centre*	*of*

In the centre of this secret, excellent, unsurpassed palace

རིན་ཆེན་ཟུར་བརྒྱད་ཉི་ཟླ་པདྨའི་སྟེང༔

RIN CHEN	ZUR	GYAE	NYI	DA	PAE MAI	TENG
jewels	*face, side*	*eight*	*sun*	*moon*	*lotus*	*on*

Is an eight-sided jewelled throne. There, sitting on top of sun, moon and lotus,

བདེ་གཤེགས་ཀུན་འདུས་རྗེ་བཙུན་སྤྲུལ་པའི་སྐུ༔

DE SHE	KUN DUE	JE TSUN	TRUL PAI KU
tathagatas buddhas	*including, encompassing*	*venerable*	*nirmanakaya, apparition*

Is the venerable nirmanakaya who encompasses all the Happily Gone,

མཚོ་སྐྱེས་རྡོ་རྗེ་རྣམ་འགྱུར་མ་ངེས་བཞུགས༔

TSO	KYE	DOR JE	NAM	GYUR	MA NGE	ZHU
lake	born	vajra	form		changing	sits, stays

Tsokye Dorje, whose form is not fixed.

པདྨ་འོད་ཀྱི་ཞིང་དེར་སྐྱེ་བར་ཤོག༔

PAE MA	OE	KYI	ZHING	DER	KYE WAR	SHO
lotus	light	of	land	there	born	must

We must take birth in this land of Lotus Light.

In the centre of this secret, excellent, unsurpassed palace is an eight-sided jewelled throne. There, sitting on top of sun, moon and lotus, is the venerable nirmanakaya who encompasses all the Happily Gone, Tsokye Dorje, whose form is not fixed. We must take birth in this land of Lotus Light.

གཡས་གཡོན་ཡེ་ཤེས་མཁའ་འགྲོ་རྣམས་གཉིས་དང་༔

YAE	YON	YE SHE	KHAN DRO	NAM	NYI	DANG
right	left	wisdom	dakini	(pl.)	two	and
			(Mandarava and Yeshe Tsogyal)			

On his right and left are the two wisdom dakinis along with

རྒྱ་བོད་རིག་འཛིན་དཔག་ཏུ་མེད་པ་ཡིས༔

GYA	BOE	RIG DZIN	PA TU		ME PA	YI
India	Tibet	vidyadharas	measure, number		without	by

Numberless sages from India and Tibet.

བླ་མེད་རྡོ་རྗེ་སྙིང་པོའི་ཆོས་འཁོར་བསྐོར༔

LA	ME	DOR JE	NYING POE	CHOE	KHOR	KOR
highest	without	vajra	essence	dharma	wheel	turning

Their dharma practice is the unsurpassed indestructible essence.

རྔ་ཆེན་གླིང་བུ་ལ་སོགས་རོལ་མོ་དཀྲོལ༔

NGA	CHEN	LING BU	LA SO	ROL MO	DROL
drum	big	flute	and so on	cymbals	play

They play big drums, flutes, cymbals, and other musical instruments.

པདྨ་འོད་ཀྱི་ཞིང་དེར་སྐྱེ་བར་ཤོག༔

PAE MA	OE	KYI	ZHING	DER	KYE WAR	SHO
lotus	light	of	land	there	born	must

We must take birth in this land of Lotus Light.

On his right and left are the two wisdom dakinis along with numberless

*sages from India and Tibet. Their dharma practice is the unsurpassed
indestructible essence. They play big drums, flutes, cymbals, and other
musical instruments. We must take birth in this land of Lotus Light.*

གསང་མཆོག་བླ་མེད་ཕོ་བྲང་བར་ཁང་དུ༔

SANG	CHO	LA ME	PHO DRANG	BAR	KHANG	DU
secret	*excellent*	*unsurpassed*	*palace*	*middle*	*room, floor*	*in*

On the middle floor of this unsurpassed secret excellent palace

བཅོམ་ལྡན་དཔལ་ཆེན་ཆེ་མཆོག་ཉི་རུ་ཀ༔

CHOM DEN	PAL CHEN	CHEM CHO	HE RU KA
bhagawan	*glorious*	*Chemchog*	*Heruka*

Is the perfect one, glorious Chemchog Heruka surrounded by the

སྒྲུབ་པ་སྡེ་དགུ་ཕག་ཁྲོས་སེང་གེའི་གདོང་༔

DRU PA	DE	GU	PHA	THROE	SENG GEI	DONG
sadhana	*group*	*nine, many*	*sow**	*wrathful***	*lion's#*	*face*

*Dorje Phagma   **Troma Nagmo   #Senge Dongma

Deities of the eight sadhanas along with Dorje Phagmo, Troma Nagmo,
Senge Dongma,

རྡོ་རྗེ་རྣལ་འབྱོར་གསང་བ་ཡེ་ཤེས་དབྱིངས༔

DOR JE NAL JOR	SANG WA	YE SHE	YING
vajra yogini	*secret*	*wisdom*	*space*

Vajra Yogini and Sangwa Yeshe Ying.

ཕ་མ་གཉིས་མེད་རྒྱུད་སྡེའི་འཁོར་གྱིས་བསྐོར༔

PHA	MA	NYI ME	GYU	DEI	KHOR GYI KOR
father	*mother*	*non-dual, neutral*	*tantras*	*of*	*surrounded*

They are surrounded by the deities of the father, mother and non-dual
tantras.

པད་འོད་ཀྱི་ཞིང་དེར་སྐྱེ་བར་ཤོག༔

PAE MA	OE	KYI	ZHING	DER	KYE WAR	SHO
lotus	*light*	*of*	*land*	*there*	*born*	*must*

We must take birth in this land of Lotus Light.

*On the first floor of this unsurpassed secret excellent palace is the
perfect one, glorious Chemchog Heruka surrounded by the deities of
the eight sadhanas along with Dorje Phagmo, Troma Nagmo, Senge
Dongma, Vajra Yogini and Sangwa Yeshe Ying. They are surrounded
by the deities of the father, mother and non-dual tantras. We must take
birth in this land of Lotus Light.*

གསང་མཆོག་བླ་མེད་སྟེང་ཁང་དང་པོའི་ནང་༔

SANG	CHO	LA ME	TENG	KHANG	DANG POI	NANG
secret	*excellent*	*unsurpassed*	*above*	*room*	*first*	*in*

On the second floor of this unsurpassed secret excellent palace is

བདེ་གཤེགས་དྲུག་པ་རྡོ་རྗེ་འཆང་ཆེན་ལ༔

DE SHE	DRU PA	DOR JE CHANG	CHEN	LA
buddha	*sixth*	*Vajradhara*	*great*	*with*

The sixth Buddha, the great Vajradhara

གཞི་བཅུ་རྩ་གཉིས་ཞི་བའི་ལྷ་ཚོགས་དང་༔

ZHIB CHU TSA NYI	ZHI WAI	LHA	TSHO	DANG
forty-two	*peaceful*	*deities*	*host*	*and*

Surrounded by the forty-two peaceful deities and by

ས་བཅུ་བྱང་ཆུབ་སེམས་དཔའི་ཚོགས་ཀྱིས་བསྐོར༔

SA	CHU	JANG CHU SEM	PAI	TSHO	KYI	KOR
ten	*stage*	*bodhisattvas*	*of*	*host*	*by*	*surrounded*

The Bodhisattvas of the tenth stage.

པདྨ་འོད་ཀྱི་ཞིང་དེར་སྐྱེ་བར་ཤོག༔

PAE MA	OE	KYI	ZHING	DER	KYE WAR	SHO
lotus	*light*	*of*	*land*	*there*	*born*	*must*

We must take birth in this land of Lotus Light.

On the second floor of this unsurpassed secret excellent palace is the sixth Buddha, the great Vajradhara surrounded by the forty-two peaceful deities and by the Bodhisattvas of the tenth stage. We must take birth in this land of Lotus Light.

གསང་མཆོག་བླ་མེད་སྟེང་ཁང་བར་མའི་ནང་༔

SANG	CHO	LA ME	TENG	KHANG	BAR MAI	NANG
secret	*excellent*	*unsurpassed*	*above*	*room*	*middle*	*in*

On the third floor of this unsurpassed secret excellent palace is

ལོངས་སྐུའི་འཕགས་པ་སྤྱན་རས་གཟིགས་དབང་ཕྱུག༔

LONG KUI	PHA PA	CHEN RE ZI	WANG CHU
sambhogakaya	*noble*	*Avalokitesvara*	*powerful*

The sambhogakaya, noble powerful Chenrezi.

 འགྲོ་དྲུག་འདུལ་མཛད་ཐུབ་པ་དྲུག་རྣམས་ལ༔

DRO DRU	DUL DZE	THU PA	DRU	NAM	LA
beings six	*educate*	*muni, buddha*	*six*	*all*	*with*

The protectors of beings in the six realms, the six munis, and

ལོངས་སྤྱོད་རྫོགས་པའི་སྐུ་ཡི་འཁོར་གྱིས་བསྐོར༔

LONG CHO DZO PAE KU		YI	KHOR	GYI	KOR
sambhogakaya		*of*	*retinue*	*by*	*surround*

All the sambhogakaya forms surround him.

པདྨ་འོད་ཀྱི་ཞིང་དེར་སྐྱེ་བར་ཤོག༔

PAE MA	OE	KYI	ZHING	DER	KYE WAR	SHO
lotus	*light*	*of*	*land*	*there*	*born*	*must*

We must take birth in this land of Lotus Light.

On the third floor of this unsurpassed secret excellent palace is the sambhogakaya, noble, powerful Chenrezi. The protectors of beings in the six realms, the six munis, and all the sambhogakaya forms surround him. We must take birth in this land of Lotus Light.

གསང་མཆོག་བླ་མེད་ཕོ་བྲང་ཡང་ཐོག་ཏུ༔

SANG	CHO	LA ME	PHO DRANG	YANG	THO TU
secret	*excellent*	*unsurpassed*	*palace*	*further*	*above*

On the fourth floor of this unsurpassed secret excellent palace is

ཆོས་སྐུའི་རྒྱལ་བ་མགོན་པོ་འོད་དཔག་མེད༔

CHO KUI	GYAL WA	GON PO	OE PA ME
dharmakaya	*buddha*	*lord*	*Amitabha*

The dharmakaya buddha, our Protector Amitabha

ས་བཅུ་བྱང་ཆུབ་སེམས་དཔའི་ལྷ་ཚོགས་རྣམས༔

SA	CHU	JANG CHU SEM PAI	LHA	TSHO	NAM
ten	*stage*	*bodhisattvas*	*of*	*gods*	*host*	*all*

Surrounded by bodhisattvas of the tenth stage and hosts of deities.

ཐུགས་རྗེའི་སྤྱན་གྱིས་བདག་སོགས་འགྲོ་ལ་གཟིགས༔

THU JEI	CHEN	GYI	DA SO	DRO	LA	ZI
compassion's	*eye*	*by*	*we*	*beings*	*on*	*look*

They all look at us with their eyes of compassion.

པད་འོད་ཀྱི་ཞིང་དེར་སྐྱེ་བར་ཤོག༔

PAE MA	OE	KYI	ZHING	DER	KYE WAR	SHO
lotus	*light*	*of*	*land*	*there*	*born*	*must*

We must take birth in this land of Lotus Light.

On the fourth floor of this unsurpassed secret excellent palace is the dharmakaya buddha, our Protector Amitabha surrounded by bodhisattvas of the tenth stage and hosts of deities. They all look at us with their eyes of compassion. We must take birth in this land of Lotus Light.

གཙང་ཁང་རྣམས་ལ་རིག་འཛིན་ལྷ་ཡི་ཚོགས༔

TSANG	KHANG	NAM	LA	RIG DZIN	LHA	YI	TSHO
pure	*room*	*many*	*in*	*vidyadharas*	*gods*	*of*	*hosts*

In the many shrine rooms of the palace are hosts of sages,

སོ་སོར་མ་འདྲེས་འགྲོ་བའི་མོས་ངོ་རུ༔

SO SOR	MA	DRE	DRO WAI	MOE	NGO	RU
each other	*not*	*mixed*	*beings*	*wish*	*appear*	*according to*

Each manifesting distinctly according to the wishes of sentient beings.

སྣང་བརྙན་ཅིར་ཡང་འཆར་བ་སྤྲུལ་པའི་སྐུ༔

NANG	NYEN	CHIR YANG	CHAR WA	TRUL PAI KU
appearance	*form*	*whatever*	*arise*	*nirmanakaya*

These apparitions can manifest in any possible form

གང་ལ་གང་འདུལ་གདུལ་བྱའི་རེ་བ་སྐོང་༔

GANG LA GANG	DUL	DUL JEI	RE WA	KONG
to each as required	*discipline*	*disciples'*	*hopes*	*fulfil*

In order to provide what is necessary to fulfil the hopes of the faithful.

པད་འོད་ཀྱི་ཞིང་དེར་སྐྱེ་བར་ཤོག༔

PAE MA	OE	KYI	ZHING	DER	KYE WAR	SHO
lotus	*light*	*of*	*land*	*there*	*born*	*must*

We must take birth in this land of Lotus Light.

In the many rooms of the palace are hosts of sages, each manifesting distinctly according to the wishes of sentient beings. These apparitions can manifest in any possible form in order to provide what is necessary to fulfil the hopes of the faithful. We must take birth in this land of Lotus Light.

ཕྱོགས་བཅུའི་སངས་རྒྱས་བྱང་སེམས་ཉན་རང་དང༔

CHO	CHUI	SANG GYE	JANG SEM	NYEN	RANG	DANG
directions	ten	buddhas	bodhisattvas	sravakas	pratyeka buddhas	and

There are buddhas of the ten directions, bodhisattvas, sravakas and pratyekabuddhas,

དགུ་ལྡན་བླ་མ་ཡི་དམ་རྒྱུད་བཞི་དྲུག༔

GU	DEN	LA MA	YI DAM	GYU	ZHI	DRU
nine	having	guru	path deity	tantra	four	six

Gurus who hold the nine transmissions, path deities of the four and six classes of tantra,

དཔའ་བོ་མཁའ་འགྲོ་ཆོས་སྐྱོང་གཏེར་གྱི་བདག༔

PA WO	KHAN DRO	CHOE YING	TER	GYI	DA
heroes	dakinis	dharma protectors	treasure	of	masters

Heroes, dakinis, dharma protectors, treasure keepers,

དཔའ་རྟུལ་དུང་སྨན་ལ་སོགས་སྤྲིན་ལྟར་གཏིབས༔

PA	TUL	DUNG MEN	LA SO	TRIN	TAR	TIB
heroes	wild	goddesses	and so on	clouds	like	surround

Intrepid heroes, goddesses and many more, gathering like clouds.

པད་འོད་ཀྱི་ཞིང་དེར་སྐྱེ་བར་ཤོག༔

PAE MA	OE	KYI	ZHING	DER	KYE WAR	SHO
lotus	light	of	land	there	born	must

We must take birth in this land of Lotus Light.

There are buddhas of the ten directions, bodhisattvas, sravakas and pratyekabuddhas, gurus who hold the nine transmissions, the path deities of the four and six classes of tantra, heroes, dakinis, dharma protectors, treasure keepers, intrepid heroes, goddesses and many more, gathering like clouds. We must take birth in this land of Lotus Light.

གནས་དེའི་ཕྱོགས་མཚམས་རིག་འཛིན་རྒྱ་མཚོ་དང༔

NAE	DEI	CHO	TSHAM	RIG DZIN	GYAM TSO	DANG
place	that	directions	borders	vidyadharas	ocean	and

Extending into the eight directions are an ocean of sages and their

དཔའ་བོ་དཔའ་མོ་གྲངས་མེད་འཁོར་བཅས་ཀྱི༔

PA WO	PA MO	DRANG	ME	KHOR	CHAE	KYI
heroes	heroines	number	without	circles	with	of

Retinues of numberless heroes and heroines.

ཟབ་བཏུང་དཔག་མེད་ཟག་མེད་བདུད་རྩིར་བསྒྱུར༔

ZA	TUNG	PA	ME	ZA	ME	DU TSIR	GYU
food	*drink*	*measure*	*without*	*sin*	*without*	*amrita*	*make*

They offer food and drink beyond measure, offerings free of defilement which have become lib-erating elixir.

ཚོགས་ཀྱི་འཁོར་ལོའི་བར་མེད་མཆོད་པ་འབུལ༔

TSHO KYI	KHOR LOI	BAR	ME	CHO PA BUL
offering	*circle*	*gap*	*without*	*offering*

All this is offered as an unending ganachakra offering feast.

པདྨ་འོད་ཀྱི་ཞིང་དེར་སྐྱེ་བར་ཤོག༔

PAE MA	OE	KYI	ZHING	DER	KYE WAR	SHO
lotus	*light*	*of*	*land*	*there*	*born*	*must*

We must take birth in this land of Lotus Light.

Extending into the eight directions are an ocean of sages and their retinues of numberless heroes and heroines. They offer food and drink beyond measure, offerings free of defilement which have become liberating elixir. All this is offered as an unending ganachakra offering feast. We must take birth in this land of Lotus Light.

ཡེ་ཤེས་ཊ་ཀི་དཀར་སེར་དམར་ལྗང་མཐིང༔

YE SHE	DAK KI	KAR	SER	MAR	JANG	THING
wisdom	*dakini*	*white*	*yellow*	*red*	*green*	*blue*

Many wisdom dakinis, white, yellow, red, green, and blue in colour,

རབ་མཛེས་ཡིད་འོང་མང་པོས་བྲོ་གར་བླུ༔

RAB DZE	YI ONG	MANG POE	TRO GAR	LU
very beautiful	*lovely*	*many*	*dancing*	*singing*

Beautiful and lovely, sing and dance with

འཕན་གདུགས་རྒྱལ་མཆན་རོལ་མོ་སྣ་ཚོགས་སོགས༔

PHAN	DU	GYAL TSEN	ROL MO	NA TSHO	SO
pendants	*umbrellas*	*victory banners*	*musical instruments*	*various*	*and so on*

Pendants, umbrellas, victory banners, and various musical instruments.

འཇིག་རྟེན་འདིར་སྣང་མཆོད་རྫས་ཕོགས་ཏེ་མཆོད༔

JIG TEN	DIR	NANG	CHOE	DZAE	TO TE	CHOE
world	*here*	*appear*	*offering*	*articles*	*to hold up*	*offer*

As offerings they bear aloft all that is available in this world

པདྨ་འོད་ཀྱི་ཞིང་དེར་སྐྱེ་བར་ཤོག༔

PAE MA	OE	KYI	ZHING	DER	KYE WAR	SHO
lotus	*light*	*of*	*land*	*there*	*born*	*must*

We must take birth in this land of Lotus Light.

Many wisdom dakinis, white, yellow, red, green, and blue in colour, beautiful and lovely, sing and dance with pendants, umbrellas, victory banners and various musical instruments As offerings they bear aloft all that is available in this world. We must take birth in this land of Lotus Light.

ཞིང་དེའི་མདུན་ངོས་བྲག་རི་བུམ་པའི་དབྱིབས༔

ZHING	DEI	DUN NGOE	DRAG RI	BUM PAE	YIB
realm	*that*	*in front of*	*rocky mountain*	*vase*	*shape*

In front of this holy realm is a rocky mountain in the shape of a vase.

མགུལ་ལ་པདྨའི་ཕྱག་རྗེས་ཕྱག་མཐིལ་ནས༔

GUL	LA	PAE MAI	CHA JE	CHA	THIL	NAE
neck	*at*	*Padmasambhava's*	*hand noble*	*hands*	*palm*	*from*

At its neck are two handprints of Padmasambhava and from their palms

ཡེ་ཤེས་བདུད་རྩིའི་ཆུ་རྒྱུན་སྐྱེད་ཚལ་འབབས༔

YE SHE	DU TSI	CHU	GYUN	KYE TSAL	BAB
wisdom	*amrita*	*water*	*flows*	*garden*	*falls*

Holy amrita flows into the garden below.

མཐའ་བསྐོར་ལྕགས་རིས་ཡོངས་བསྐོར་མཚོ་དེའི་དཀྱིལ༔

THA KOR	CHA RI	YONG	KOR	TSO	DEI	KYIL
surrounding	*outer wall*	*fully*	*surround*	*lake*	*of*	*centre*

This garden is fully surrounded by an outer wall and at its centre is a lake of liberating elixir.

པདྨའི་སྦུགས་ནས་ལས་ལྡན་དཔག་མེད་འཁྲུངས༔

PAE MAI	BUE	NAE	LAE DEN	PA ME	TRUNG
lotus	*hollow*	*from*	*fortunate ones*	*numberless*	*born*

From the hollows within the many lotus flowers growing there numberless fortunate beings are born.

པདྨ་འོད་ཀྱི་ཞིང་དེར་སྐྱེ་བར་ཤོག༔

PAE MA OE	KYI	ZHING	DER	KYE WAR	SHO
Padmasambhava	*of*	*land*	*there*	*born*	*must*

We must take birth in this land of Lotus Light.

*In front of this holy realm is a rocky mountain in the shape of a vase.
At its neck are two handprints of Padmasambhava and from their
palms holy amrita flows into the garden below. This garden is fully
surrounded by an outer wall and at its centre is a lake of liberating
elixir. From the hollows within the many lotus flowers growing there
numberless fortunate beings are born. We must take birth in this land
of Lotus Light.*

གནས་ཀྱི་ཕྱོགས་མཚམས་སྲིན་ཡུལ་གླིང་རྣམས་སུ༔

NAE	KYI	CHO	TSAM	SIN	YUL	LING	NAM	SU
place	*of*	*directions*	*boundary*	*cannibal*	*country*	*islands*	*every*	*in*

Around the holy mountain in every direction, on every island in this
country of cannibals,

པད་འབྱུང་སྤྲུལ་པ་གྲངས་མེད་ཆོས་འཁོར་བསྐོར༔

PAE JUNG		TRUL PA	DRANG ME	CHOE	KHOR	KOR
Padmasambhava		*emanation*	*numberless*	*dharma*	*wheel*	*turn*

Are numberless emanations of Padmasambhava teaching the dharma.

གང་ལ་གང་འདུལ་ཐབས་ཀྱིས་འགྲོ་དོན་མཛད༔

GANG LA	GANG	DUL	THAB	KYI	DRO	DON	DZAE
whoever	*whatever*	*educate*	*methods,*	*by*	*beings'*	*benefit*	*do*
(doing what is necessary)			*skilful means*				

They use whatever methods of education are necessary for each
individual in order to benefit beings.

སྤྱོད་པ་རྨད་བྱུང་རིག་འཛིན་རྒྱལ་བའི་ཞིང༔

CHO PA	MAE JUNG	RIG DZIN	GYAL WAI	ZHING
deeds	*wonderful*	*vidyadharas*	*victors'*	*realm*

Many wonderful deeds are done by the sages of this buddha realm.

པད་འོད་ཀྱི་ཞིང་དེར་སྐྱེ་བར་ཤོག༔

PAE MA	OE	KYI	ZHING	DER	KYE WAR	SHO
lotus	*light*	*of*	*land*	*there*	*born*	*must*

We must take birth in this land of Lotus Light.

*Around the holy mountain in every direction, on every island in this
country of cannibals, are numberless emanations of Padmasambhava
teaching the dharma. They use whatever methods of education are
necessary for each individual in order to benefit beings. Many wonderful
deeds are done by the sages of this buddha realm. We must take birth in
this land of Lotus Light.*

ཞིང་མཆོག་རྣམ་དག་དེ་ཡི་ཕྱོགས་མཚམས་སུ༔

ZHING	CHO	NAM DA	DE	YI	CHO	TSHAM	SU
realm	*excellent*	*very pure*	*that*	*of*	*directions*	*boundary*	*in*

In every direction around this excellent pure place,

ནམ་མཁའ་ས་གཞི་བར་སྣང་ཡོངས་གང་བའི༔

NAM KHA	SA ZHI	BAR NANG	YONG	GANG WAI
sky	*land*	*atmosphere*	*fully*	*fill*

In the sky, in the air, and on the land, are many, many

ཡེ་ཤེས་ལྔ་ལྡན་འཇའ་འོད་ཐིག་ལེའི་ཀློང༔

YE SHE	NGA	DEN	JA OE	THIG LE	LONG
wisdom	*five*	*having*	*rainbow*	*light ball*	*inside*

Rainbows and spheres of light with the colours of the five wisdoms.

པད་འབྱུང་གྲངས་མེད་ཉི་དུལ་ཇི་བཞིན་འཁྲིགས༔

PAE JUNG		DRANG ME	NYI	DUL	JI ZHIN	TRI
Padmasambhava		*numberless*	*sun*	*dust*	*similar*	*gather*

Within them are emanations of Padmasambhava as numerous as dust specks in the rays of the sun.

པདྨ་འོད་ཀྱི་ཞིང་དེར་སྐྱེ་བར་ཤོག༔

PAE MA	OE	KYI	ZHING	DER	KYE WAR	SHO
Padmasambhava	*of*	*land*	*there*	*born*		*must*

We must take birth in this land of Lotus Light.

In every direction around this excellent pure place, in the sky, in the air, and on the land, are many, many rainbows and spheres of light with the colours of the five wisdoms. Within them are emanations of Pad-masambhava as numerous as dust specks in the rays of the sun. We must take birth in this land of Lotus Light.

ཞིང་དེའི་ཡོན་ཏན་བསམ་འདས་བརྗོད་མི་ལང༔

ZHING	DEI	YON TEN	SAM DAE	JOE MI LANG
realm	*of*	*quality*	*incomprehensible*	*unspeakable, inexpressible*

To see this realm of inconceivable inexpressible qualities

མཐོང་བས་ཡིད་འཕྲོག་དྲན་པས་སྡུག་བསྔལ་སེལ༔

THONG WAE	YI	THRO	DRAN PAE	DU NGAL	SEL
by seeing	*mind*	*captivated*	*remember*	*misery*	*save from*

Is to wish to go there, and even to think of it is to be freed from suffering.

ཐོས་པས་སེམས་སྐྱོ་བདེ་ཆེན་རྒྱལ་བའི་ཞིང༔

THOE PAE SEM LONG DE CHEN GYAL WAE ZHING
by hearing mind arouse happy great Buddha realm

To hear of it awakens great happiness in the mind.

མི་བཟོད་གདུངས་ཤུགས་དྲག་པོས་གསོལ་བ་འདེབས༔

MI ZOE DUNG SHU DRA POE SOL WA DE
unbearable faith, longing force fierce pray

To this realm of the Buddha we pray with fierce and unbearable longing.

པདྨ་འོད་ཀྱི་ཞིང་དེར་སྐྱེ་བར་ཤོག༔

PAE MA OE KYI ZHING DER KYE WAR SHO
lotus light of land there born must

We must take birth in this land of Lotus Light.

To see this realm of inconceivable inexpressible qualities is to wish to go there, and even to think of it is to be freed from suffering. To hear of it awakens great happiness in the mind. We pray to this realm of the Buddha with fierce and unbearable longing. We must take birth in this land of Lotus Light.

ཕྱི་ལྟར་བརྡ་དོན་རྟགས་རྫོགས་ང་ཡབ་གླིང༔

CHI TAR DA DON TA DZO NGA YAB LING
outer as symbol meaning signs perfect Zangdopalri

Outwardly, there is Zangdopalri, perfect in symbols, meaning and signs.

ནང་ལྟར་རང་ལུས་རྩ་ཁམས་མཁའ་འགྲོའི་གླིང༔

NANG TAR RANG LUE TSA KHAM KHAN DROI LING
inner as own body channels constituents dakinis' land

Inwardly, there is the dakinis' land within the channels and constituents of our own body.

གསང་བ་ཡེ་ཤེས་རང་སྣང་དཔལ་གྱི་ཞིང༔

SANG WA YE SHE RANG NANG PAL GYI ZHING
secret, deep wisdom unmade vision shining of realm

Secretly, there is the glorious realm of the uncontrived display of original knowing.

དད་དམ་མོས་གུས་དྲག་པོས་གསོལ་བ་འདེབས༔

DAE DAM MOE GUE DRA POE SOL WA DE
faith pure longing devotion strongly pray

With pure faith, longing and devotion we pray fiercely to experience this.

པདྨ་འོད་ཀྱི་ཞིང་དེར་སྐྱེ་བར་ཤོག

PAE MA	OE	KYI	ZHING	DER	KYE WAR	SHO
lotus	*light*	*of*	*land*	*there*	*born*	*must*

We must take birth in this land of Lotus Light.

Outwardly, there is Zangdopalri, perfect in symbols, meaning and signs. Inwardly, there is the dakinis' land within the channels and constituents of our own body. Secretly, there is the glorious realm of the uncontrived display of original knowing. With pure faith, longing and devotion we pray fiercely to experience this.We must take birth in this land of Lotus Light.

བདག་སོགས་ཚེ་འདིའི་སྣང་བ་འགགས་མ་ཐག

DA	SO	TSE	DI	NANG WA	GA	MA THA
self	*others*	*life*	*this*	*appearances, experiences*	*end, stop*	*immediately*

Immediately at the ending of the experiences of this life

འཆི་བ་འོད་གསལ་རང་ངོ་འཕྲོད་པ་དང་

CHI WA	OE	SAL	RANG	NGO	TROE PA	DANG
death	*light*	*clear*	*self*	*face*	*meet*	*and*

May we recognise our own original face as the clear light at death.

བར་དོར་འཇིགས་སྐྲག་སྡུག་བསྔལ་མི་འབྱུང་ཞིང་

BAR DO	JIG TRA	DU NGAL	MI	JUNG ZHING
bardo	*fear, terror, alarm*	*sufering*	*not*	*arising*

With no fear or suffering arising in the intermediate bardo

རིག་འཛིན་དཔའ་བོ་མཁའ་འགྲོའི་བསུ་མར་བཅས

RIG DZIN	PA WO	KHAN DROI	SU MAR	CHE
vidyadharas	*dakas, heroes*	*dakinis*	*reception, welcome party*	*together, with*

May we be welcomed by the sages, heroes and dakinis.

པདྨ་འོད་ཀྱི་ཞིང་དེར་སྐྱེ་བར་ཤོག

PAE MA	OE	KYI	ZHING	DER	KYE WAR	SHO
lotus	*light*	*of*	*land*	*there*	*born*	*must*

We must take birth in this land of Lotus Light.

Immediately at the ending of the experiences of this life may we recognise our own original face as the clear light at death. With no fear or suffering arising in the intermediate bardo may we be welcomed by the sages, heroes and dakinis. We must take birth in this land of Lotus Light.

ཏདྱ་ཐ་ཀྲི་ཡ་ཨ་ཨ་འབྷོ་དྷ་ནི་སྭ་ཧཱ༔

TA DYA THA   **PAN TSA**   **KRI YA**   **A VA**   **BHO DHA NI**   **SWA HA**
like this   *five*   *deeds*   *get*   *buddhahood*   *reach*

It is like this. We must accomplish the five transformations and reach Buddhahood!

བདག་འདྲ་པདྨ་ནུས་ལྡན་རྡོ་རྗེ་འགྲོ་ཕན་གླིང་པ་གྲོ་ལོད་རྩལ་གྱི་སྐུ་ལས་དག་སྣང་དུ་ཟངས་
མདོག་དཔལ་རིར་ཕྱིན་སྐབས་རྒྱ་བོད་རིག་འཛིན་རྣམས་དང་ལྷན་དུ་འཚོངས་ནས་ཐམས་ཅད་
ཀྱིས་མགྲིན་གཅིག་ཏུ་བཏོན་པ་མཁའ་འགྲོས་ལུང་གི་མ་བརྗེད་ཡིད་ལ་ཟུང་ཅེས་གསུང་བཀའ་
བཞིན་འཁོར་ལོའི་གདོང་ནས་སྤེལ།

I, Padma Nudan Dorje Drophan Lingpa Drolo Tsal went to Zang-dopalri by means of pure vision and dream. At that moment the vidyadharas of India and Tibet gathered together and all with one voice, told me to hold on to and not to forget the instructions given to me by the dakinis. In accordance with their order, I wrote this down in Khordong Monastery.

ཟངས་མདོག་དཔལ་རིའི་བཀོད་པ༔

A Description of Zangdopalri

ཧཱུྃ༔ ཆོས་དབྱིངས་སྤྲོས་དང་བྲལ་བའི་ཞིང་ཁམས་སུ༔

HUNG	CHO	YING	TOE DANG DRAL WAI	ZHING KHAM	SU
potential	*dharmadhatu,*		*free of conceptual elaboration*	*sphere, realm*	*in*
	infinite hospitality				

Hung. In the sphere of infinite hospitality free of all conceptual elaboration

བདེ་གཤེགས་ཡུམ་ལྔའི་མཁའ་དབྱིངས་འབྱུང་ལྔའི་སྟེང༔

DE SHE	YUM	NGAI	KHA YING	JUNG	NGAI	TENG
Buddhas	*wives*	*five*	*creative space*	*elements*	*five*	*upon*

(Buddhas and wives and elements: Vairocana and Dharmadhatisvari, space; Akshobya and Buddhalocana and water; Amitabha and Pundarika, fire; Ratnasambhava and Mamaki, earth; Amoghasiddhi and Samayastava, wind)

Within the wombs of the wives of the five Buddhas the five elements arise and upon them

འདི་ནས་ཉི་མ་ལྷོ་ནུབ་མཚམས་ཤེད་ན༔

DI	NAE	NYI MA	LHO NUB	TSHAM SHE	NA
here	*from*	*sun (set)*	*south-west*	*side, area*	*at, in*

In the area south-west of here, towards the setting sun,

གནས་ཆེན་རྡོ་རྗེ་གདན་གྱི་ནུབ་ཕྱོགས་ན༔

NAE	CHEN	DOR JE	DEN	GYI	NUB	CHO	NA
place	*great (i.e.holy)*	*indestructible**	*seat*	*of*	*west*	*direction*	*at*

* At Bodh Gaya beneath the bodhi tree where Prince Siddhartha became Buddha Sakyamuni.

To the west of the holy place of Dorje Den,

རྔ་ཡབ་གླིང་ཕྲན་ཟ་བྱེད་སྲིན་པོའི་ཡུལ༔

NGA YAB	LING	TRAN	ZA JE	SIN POI	YUL
tail whisk	*island*	*small*	*cannibal*	*rakshasas, fierce*	*country*
(Camaradvipa, where				*demonic barbarians*	
Zangdaplri is situated)					

Lies the country of the cannibal rakshasas, the small island named Tail Whisk,

དུས་གསུམ་སངས་རྒྱས་རྣམས་ཀྱིས་བྱིན་བརླབས་པའི༔

DU	SUM	SANG GYE	NAM	KYI	JIN LAB PAI
times	*three*	*Buddhas*	*all*	*by*	*blessed, purified*

Which has been blessed by the Buddhas of the three times.

ཀུན་ཁྱབ་རང་བྱུང་གླིང་མཆོག་ཁྱད་པར་ཅན༔

KUN	KHYA	RANG	JUNG	LING	CHO	KHYAE PAR CHAN
all	pervading	self	arising	island	excellent	special

Self-arising and all-pervading, this excellent island is truly special.

To the south-west of here and west of the holy site of the Indestructible Seat, in the direction of the setting sun, lies the small island of Tail Whisk, the country of the cannibal rakshasas which has been blessed by the Buddhas of the three times. It rests on the five elements which arise from the wombs of the five Buddhas within the sphere of infinite hospitality free of all conceptual elaboration. Self-arising and all-pervading, this excellent island is truly special.

སྔོན་གྱི་བསྐལ་པ་དང་པོ་འདས་པའི་དུས༔

NGON GYI	KAL PA	DANG PO	DAE PAI	DUE
former	kalpa, aeon	first	ending	time
(very, very long ago)				

At the end of the first of the previous aeons

མ་ཏྲཾ་རུ་ཏྲ་བསྒྲལ་བའི་ཟས་བརྒྱད་ལ༔

MA TRAM RU TRA	DRAL WAI	DZE	GYAE	LA
name of the great demon who was destroyed by Heruka	killing	articles, parts*	eight	at

*two arms, two legs, head, upper torso, lower torso, and genitals

The eight parts from the killing of Matram Rudra

གསང་སྔགས་འབྱོན་པའི་གནས་བརྒྱད་བྱིན་གྱིས་བརླབས༔

SANG NGA	JON PAI	NAE	GYAE	JIN GYI LA
tantric, guhyamantra	coming	place*	eight**	blessing

* The holy places where the tantras were taught and practised.

**The eight places where the parts of the demon's body landed after they were thrown by Heruka.

Gave rise to the eight blessed places special to tantra.

ཙི་ཏ་ཨུ་རྒྱན་གནས་སུ་བབས་པ་ལས༔

TSI TA	UR GYAN	NAE	SU	BA PA	LE
citta, heart	Oddiyana	country	in	fell	from
(but Nyingmapa believe that)	(here this means wherever Padmasambhava)				
(this refers to the genitals)	(is staying i.e now it is Zangdopalri)				

The citta fell in the land of Urgyan and due to this

རྟེན་འབྲེལ་ཁྱད་པར་ཅན་གྱིས་གནས་མཆོག་ན༔

TEN DREL	KHYAE PAR	CHAN	GYI	NAE	CHO	NA
connection (i.e. this land is not an ordinary place)	special	very important	of	place	excellent	there

Very special connection it is an excellent place.

At the end of the first of the previous aeons the eight articles from the killing of Matram Rudra gave rise to the eight blessed places special to tantra. The citta fell in the land of Urgyan and due to this very special connection it is an excellent place.

ཪྡོ་རྗེ་ཕག་མོས་བྱིན་གྱིས་བརླབས་པའི་གནས༔

DOR JE PHA MOE	JIN GYI LAB PAI	NAE
by Vajravarahi	*blessed*	*place*

Blessed by Dorje Phamo,

མ་མོ་མཁའ་འགྲོ་ཐམས་ཅད་འདུ་བའི་གླིང༔

MA MO	KHAN DRO	THAM CHE	DU WAI	LING
mother goddesses	*dakinis*	*all*	*gathering*	*island, place*

This is the island where all the mamo and dakinis gather, and where

གསང་སྔགས་བརྡ་ཡི་རང་སྒྲ་དི་རི་རི༔

SANG NGA	DA	YI	RANG	DRA	DI RI RI
guhyamantra,	*symbols, signs,*	*of*	*own*	*sound*	*vibrating, resonant sound*
tantric	*vajras and so on*		*(like the murmuring of many muttered mantras)*		

Sounds emanate from tantric symbols, resonating di-ri-ri.

གནས་དེར་ཕྱིན་པ་ཙམ་གྱིས་བྱང་ཆུབ་ཐོབ༔

NAE	DER	CHIN PA	TSAM	GYI	JANG CHU	THO
place	*here*	*reach, arrive*	*only, merely*	*by*	*bodhi, enlightenment*	*get*

By merely reaching it enlightenment is gained.

བྱིན་ཆེན་གནས་མཆོག་ཁྱད་པར་ཅན་དེ་རུ༔

JIN	CHEN	NAE	CHO	KHYAE PAR CHAN	DE	RU
blessing	*great*	*place*	*excellent, holy*	*special*	*there*	*in*

This is the special holy place with great blessing.

Blessed by Dorje Phamo, this is the island where all the mamo and dakinis gather, and where sounds emanate from tantric symbols, resonating di-ri-ri. By merely reaching it, enlightenment is gained. This is the special holy place with great blessing.

རང་སྣང་ཟངས་མདོག་དཔལ་རི་ཙིཏྟའི་དབྱིབས༔

RANG	NANG	ZANG DO PAL RI	TSIT TAI	YIB
spontaneous	*appearance*	*sri tamaraparvat,*	*heart*	*shaped*
(arising from awareness)		*tamaravarni sri parvat**		

*the place where Padmasambhava is staying)

This spontaneous appearance, the Glorious Copper-Coloured Mountain, is shaped like a heart.

ཙ་བ་ཀླུ་ཡི་རྒྱལ་པོའི་གནས་སུ་ཟུག༔

TSA WA	LU	YI	GYAL POI	NAE	SU	ZU
root, base	*naga, snake gods*	*of*	*raja, king*	*place (i.e the ocean)*	*in*	*built, erected*

Its base is in the domain of the king of the nagas.

ཀེད་པ་ལྷུན་ཆགས་མཁའ་འགྲོའི་གླིང་ན་བརྗིད༔

KE PA	LHUN CHA	KHAN DROI	LING	NA	JI
middle part	*very attractive*	*dakinis'*	*island, place*	*in*	*splendid, impressive*

Its middle is the very splendid, most attractive island of the dakinis, while

ཙེ་མོ་ཚངས་པོའི་འཇིག་རྟེན་སྙེག་པ་འདྲ༔

TSE MO	TSHANG PAI	JIG TEN	NYE PA	DRA
peak	*Brahma's*	*world*	*reach*	*similar*
(the formless spheres above those of form and desire, i.e it is very high)				

Its peak is as high as the worlds of Brahma.

རི་བོ་གཞན་ལས་རི་རྒྱལ་ཁྱད་པར་ཅན༔

RI WO	ZHEN	LAE	RI	GYAL	KHYAE PAR CHAN
mountain	*others*	*compared with*	*mountain*	*king*	*special*

Compared with others this special mountain is the king.

This spontaneous appearance, the Glorious Copper-Coloured Mountain, is shaped like a heart. Its base is in the domain of the king of the nagas. Its middle is the very splendid most attractive island of the dakinis, while its peak is as high as the worlds of Brahma. Compared with others this special mountain is the king.

དཔལ་གྱི་རི་བོ་འབར་བའི་རྩེ་མོ་ན༔

PAL GYI RI WO	BAR WAI	TSE MO	NA
sriparvat, glorious mountain	*shining, very bright*	*peak, top*	*at, on*

On the shining peak of this glorious mountain

མ་བཙལ་ལྷུན་གྲུབ་ཡེ་ཤེས་གཞལ་ཡས་ཁང༔

MA	TSAL	LHUN DRU	YE SHE	ZHAL YAE KHANG
without	*careful endeavour*	*effortlessly arising knowing*	*original*	*divine mansion, mandala*

Is the divine mansion of original knowing which arose effortlessly without careful endeavour.

ཤར་ཕྱོགས་ཤེལ་ལ་ལྷོ་ཕྱོགས་བཻ་ཌཱུ་རྱ༔

SHAR	CHO	SHEL	LA	LHO	CHO	BE DUR YA
east	*side*	*crystal (white)*	*with*	*south*	*side*	*lapis lazuli or cornelian (blue)*

With its east side of crystal and bedurya on the south,

ནུབ་ཕྱོགས་རཱ་ག་བྱང་ཕྱོགས་ཨིནྡྲ་ནཱི་མ་དོག༔

NUB	CHO	RA GA	JANG	CHO	IN DRAI	DO
west	*side*	*dark red stone, like ruby*	*north*	*side*	*indranil (green)*	*colour*

Its western side of raga and north side the colour of indranil,

ཕྱི་ནང་མེད་པར་གསལ་བའི་གཞལ་ཡས་ཁང༔

CHI	NANG	ME PAR	SAL WAI	ZHAL YAE KHANG
outside	*inside*	*without*	*clear, transparent*	*palace, infinitude, mandala*

It is the divine transparent mansion with no distinction of inside and outside.

པདྨ་འོད་ཀྱི་ཕོ་བྲང་ཁྱད་པར་ཅན༔

PAE MA	OE	KYI	PHO DRANG	KHYAE PAR CHAN
lotus	*light*	*of*	*palace*	*special, superior*

This is the very special palace of Lotus Light.

On the shining peak of this glorious mountain is the divine mansion of original knowing which arose effortlessly without careful endeavour. With its east side of crystal and bedurya on the south, its western side of raga and north side the colour of indranil, it is the divine transparent mansion with no distinction of inside and outside. This is the very special palace of Lotus Light.

གཞལ་ཡས་ཆེན་པོའི་ཕྱོགས་བཞི་མཚམས་བརྒྱད་དང༔

ZHAL YAE	CHEN POI	CHO	ZHI	TSHAM	GYAE	DANG
divine mansion, infinitude	*great*	*directions*	*four*	*intermediate points (four)*	*eight (all together)*	*and*

The entirety of this great divine mansion, all that lies in the four cardinal and the four intermediate directions, and

སྟེང་འོག་ཐམས་ཅད་རིན་པོ་ཆེ་ལས་གྲུབ༔

TENG	OG	THAM CHE	RIN PO CHE	LE	DRU
above	*below*	*everywhere*	*jewels*	*from*	*made*

Above and below, is made from jewels.

ཁྱམས་དང་གྲུ་ཆད་ལྐོ་འབུར་རིས་བཞི་ཡང་༔

KHYAM	DANG	DRU CHAE	LO BUR	RI	ZHI	YANG
courtyard	*and*	*inner corner*	*projections*	*sides*	*four*	*also*

On each of the four sides, the courtyards, the inner corner areas and projections

འཕྲིན་ལས་བཞི་ཡི་ཁ་དོག་སོ་སོར་གསལ༔

TRIN LE	ZHI	YI	KHA DO	SO SOR	SAL
*activity**	*four*	*of*	*colours**	*each, separately*	*clear, shining*

*east-white-pacifying, south-yellow-increasing, west-red-dominating, north-green-destroying

Shine with the colour of the appropriate activity.

རང་བྱུང་ལྷུན་གྲུབ་གཞལ་ཡས་ཁང་ཆེན་པོ༔

RANG JUNG	LHUN DRU	ZHAL YAE KHANG	CHEN PO
spontaneous	*effortlessly arising*	*divine mansion*	*great*

This naturally arising great divine mansion is instantly present.

The entirety of this great divine mansion, all that lies in the four cardinal and the four intermediate directions and above and below, is made from jewels. On each of the four sides, the courtyards, the inner corner areas and projections shine with the colour of the appropriate activity. This naturally arising great divine mansion is instantly present.

རྩིག་པ་འདོད་སྙམས་ཕ་གུ་དྲ་བ་དང་༔

TSIG PA	DOE NYAM		PHA GU	DRA WA	DANG
walls	*ledges (adorned with articles that please the senses)*		*pillar, top*	*draped garland*	*and*

The walls, adorned ledges, pillar tops, draped garlands,

དྲ་ཕྱེད་མདའ་ཡབ་རིན་ཆེན་སྣ་ལྔ་གསལ༔

DRA CHE	DA YAB	RIN CHEN	NA	NGA	SAL
chain, loop, quarter circle	*eaves*	*precious substances*	*kinds*	*five**	*shining*

* gold, silver, copper, iron and lead

Half chains, and eaves are all shining with the five kinds of precious substances.

སྒོ་བཞི་ྟ་བབས་ཆོས་འཁོར་རྒྱན་རྣམས་ཀུན༔

GO	ZHI	TA	BAB	CHO KHOR	GYAN NAM	KUN
doors	*four*	*horse**	*descend*	*dharmachakra, wheel*	*ornaments, features*	*all*

*the entrance archway where horses are dismounted

The four doors, the entrance arches, the dharma wheels above the doors, and all the other features

སྣ་ཚོགས་རིན་པོ་ཆེ་ཡིས་མཛེས་པར་བརྒྱན༔

NA TSHO	RIN PO CHE	YI	DZE PAR	GYAN
many different	*jewels*	*with*	*beautifully*	*ornamented*

Are beautifully adorned with many different jewels.

ཀུན་ལས་ཁྱད་འཕགས་རིན་ཆེན་གཞལ་ཡས་ཁང༔

KUN	LAE	KHYAE	PHA	RIN CHEN	ZHAL YAE KHANG
all	*compared with*	*special*	*excellent*	*precious*	*mandala mansion*

This precious divine mansion is the most excellent of all.

The walls, adorned ledges, pillar tops, draped garlands, half chains, and eaves are all shining with the five kinds of precious substances, The four doors, the entrance arches, the dharma wheels above the doors, and all the other features are beautifully adorned with many different jewels. This precious divine mansion is the most excellent of all.

དཔག་བསམ་ཤིང་དང་བདུད་རྩིའི་ཆུ་མིག་དང༔

PAG SAM SHING	DANG	DU TSI	CHU MI	DANG
wish-fulfilling tree	*and*	*amrita's, liberating elixir's*	*spring*	*and*

Wish-fulfilling trees, springs of liberating elixir, and

འཇའ་ཚོན་སྣ་ལྔས་ཕྱི་ནང་སྤྲིན་ལྟར་གཏིབས༔

JA TSHON	NA	NGAE	CHI	NANG	TRIN	TAR	TIB
rainbow	*kinds**	*five*	*outer*	*inner*	*clouds***	*as*	*gather, assemble*

*white, red, blue, yellow, green   * *i.e. very many

Rainbows of the five colours appear within and without like masses of gathering clouds, and

མེ་ཏོག་པདྨའི་འོད་ཀྱིས་བར་སྣང་ཁེངས༔

ME TO	PAE MAI	OE	KYI	BAR NANG	KHENG
flowers	*lotus*	*light*	*by*	*sky up to the sun*	*fill, pervade*

The sky is filled with light from lotus flowers.

གནས་དེ་དྲན་པ་ཙམ་གྱིས་བདེ་ཆེན་ཐོབ༔

NAE	DE	DRAN PA	TSAM	GYI	DE	CHEN	THO
place	*that*	*remember, think of*	*only*	*by*	*happiness*	*great*	*get*

The mere remembrance of this place brings great happiness.

པདྨ་འོད་ཀྱི་གཞལ་ཡས་ཁྱད་པར་འཕགས༔

PAE MA OE	KYI	ZHAL YAE	KHYAE PAR	PHA
(name) (where the light arises from lotuses)	*of*	*mansion*	*especially*	*excellent*

The divine mansion of Lotus Light is the most excellent.

Wish-fulfilling trees, springs of liberating elixir, and rainbows of the five colours appear within and without like masses of gathering clouds, and the sky is filled with light from lotus flowers. The mere remembrance of this place brings great happiness. The divine mansion of Lotus Light is the most excellent.

གཞལ་ཡས་ཆེན་པོ་དེ་ཡི་ནང་ཤེད་ན༔

ZHAL YAE	CHEN PO	DE	YI	NANG SHE NA
divine mansion	great	that	of	inside

Within this great divine mansion

རིན་ཆེན་ཟུར་བརྒྱད་ཉིས་ཟླ་བའི་གདན༔

RIN CHEN	ZUR	GYAE	NYI MA	DA WAI	DEN
jewel	corner	eight	sun	moon	cushion
(like an eight petalled lotus)					

There is an eight-cornered jewel structure with sun and moon cushions.

མ་ཆགས་པད་འབར་བའི་སྡོང་པོ་ལ༔

MA CHA	PAE MA	BAR WAI	DONG PO	LA
without desire	lotus	shining	stem, stalk	on
(symbol of that)				

On top of this is the shining stalk of the lotus of freedom from desire

པད་འབྱུང་གནས་བདེ་གཤེགས་འདུས་པའི་སྐུ༔

PAE MA JUNG NAE	DE SHE	DU PAI	KU
Padmasambhava	Sugatas, Buddhas	encompassing	body
	(i.e. their natures are all contained within him)		

Upon which you sit, you, Padmasambhava, whose body is the presence of all the Buddhas.

སྣང་མཐའི་ཐུགས་ལས་རང་བྱུང་སྤྲུལ་པའི་སྐུ༔

NANG THAI	THU	LAE	RANG JUNG	TRUL PAI KU
Amitabha's	heart, mind	from	spontaneous	Nirmanakaya, apparition

You are the Nirmanakaya emanation spontaneously arising from the heart of Amitabha.

Within this great divine mansion there is an eight-cornered jewel structure with sun and moon cushions. On top of this is the shining stalk of the lotus of freedom from desire upon which you sit, you, Padmasambhava, whose body is the presence of all the Buddhas. You are the Nirmanakaya emanation arising spontaneously from the heart of Amitabha.

ཞི་རྒྱས་དབང་དྲག་དོན་ལ་དགོངས་པའི་ཕྱིར༔

ZHI	GYE	WANG	DRA	DON	LA	GONG PAI	CHIR
pacifying	*expanding*	*over-powering*	*destructive*	*beneficial*	*as*	*consider*	*in order to*

(i.e. in order to perform the various activities according to need)

In order to benefit beings by the four activities of pacifying, increasing, overpowering and destroying,

སྐུ་མདོག་ཕྱག་མཚན་རྒྱན་རྣམས་མ་ངེས་ཀྱང་༔

KU	DO	CHA TSHAN	GYEN NAM	MA NGE	KYANG
body	*colour (form, shape)*	*hand implements, symbols*	*ornaments*	*not fixed*	*yet*

Your body colour, hand implements, and ornaments change according to need, yet

ཉི་མ་སྟོང་གི་འོད་ལས་གཟི་མདངས་ཆེ༔

NYI MA	TONG	GI	OE	LAE	ZI DANG	CHE
sun	*a thousand*	*of*	*light*	*(comparative)*	*splendour, radiant majesty*	*greater*

Your splendour is always greater than the light of a thousand suns and

རི་རྒྱལ་ལྷུན་པོ་བས་ཀྱང་བརྗིད་རེ་ཆེ༔

RI GYAL LHUN PO	BAE	KYANG	JI	RE CHE
Mt Meru, the king of mountains	*(comparative)*	*also*	*impressive*	*greater*

Your grand majesty surpasses that of Mount Meru.

མཚོ་སྐྱེས་རྡོ་རྗེ་ཡ་མཚན་སྤྲུལ་པའི་སྐུ༔

TSHO	KYE	DOR JE	YAM TSHAM	TRUL PAI KU
lake	*born (lotus)*	*vajra*	*amazing, wonderful*	*emanation, apparition*

You are the wonderful apparition, Tsokye Dorje, the Lotus Born Vajra.

In order to benefit beings by the four activities of pacifying, increasing, overpowering and destroying, your body colour, hand implements and ornaments change according to need, yet your splendour is always greater than the light of a thousand suns, and your grand majesty surpasses that of Mount Meru. You are the wonderful apparition, Tsokye Dorje, the Lotus Born Vajra.

ཐུགས་ཀྱི་སྤྲུལ་པ་འཇིག་རྟེན་ཁྱབ་པར་འགྱེད༔

THU	KYI	TRUL PA	JIG TEN	KHYAE PAR	GYE
mind	*of*	*emanations**	*world*	*filling*	*send out, disperse*

*forms which perform his compassionate deeds

The emanations of your mind spread out to fill all the worlds and

སྤྱན་ཙ་ཉི་ཟླ་ལྟ་བུར་དཀྱིལ་ཞིང་གཟིགས༔

CHAN TSA	NYI	DA	TA BUR	KYIL ZHING	ZI
eyes	sun	moon	similar	large, round and powerful	looking

You look at us with your large round eyes shining like the sun and moon.

ནམ་མཁའི་གློག་ལས་ཕྱགས་རྗེ་འཕྲིན་ལས་མྱུར༔

NAM KHAI	LO	LAE	THU JEI	TRIN LAE	NYUR
sky's	lightning	(comparative)	compassionate	deeds	quicker

Your compassionate deeds are more rapid than lightening, while

དགོངས་པ་ཟབ་མོ་ནམ་མཁའི་ཀློང་དང་མཉམ༔

GONG PA	ZAB MO	NAM KHAI	LONG	DANG	NYAM
awareness	deep	sky's	depth, expanse	and	equal

Your profound awareness equals the vastness of space.

འགྲོ་ལ་བརྩེ་མཛད་ཐུགས་རྗེ་ཁྱད་པར་ཅན༔

DRO	LA	TSE	DZE	THU JE	KHYAE PAR CHAN
beings	to	kindly	act	compassion	special

With your very special compassion you act with kindness towards all.

The emanations of your mind spread out to fill all worlds and you look at us with your large round eyes shining like the sun and moon. Your compassionate deeds are more rapid than lightning, while your profound awareness equals the vastness of space. With your very special compassion you act with kindness towards all.

འགྲོ་ལ་བརྩེ་བའི་ཐབས་ཀྱིས་འགྲོ་དོན་མཛད༔

DRO	LA	TSE WAI	THAB	KYI	DRO	DON	DZAE
beings	to	compassionate	method	by	beings	benefit	doing

With compassionate methods you act for the benefit of beings.

ཞལ་འཛུམ་མཛེས་པའི་མདངས་ལྡན་ཡ་ལ་ལ༔

ZHAL	DZUM	DZE PAI	DANG DEN	YA LA LA
face	smiling	beautiful	visage, complexion	very attractive

Your smiling face has a most beautiful and attractive complexion.

འབྲུག་སྟོང་ལྡིར་པས་གསུང་གི་གདངས་སྒྲ་ཆེ༔

DRUG	TONG	DIR PAE	SUNG	GI	DANG	DRA	CHE
dragon	thousand (i.e. peals of thunder)	booming, rolling	speech	of	expression	sound	greater

Your expressive speech louder than a thousand dragons' roar

གསང་སྔགས་ཟབ་མོའི་ཆོས་སྒྲ་དི་རི་རི༔

SANG NGA		ZAB MOI	CHO	DRA	DI RI RI
tantric, secret mantra		*deep*	*dharma*	*sound*	*resonant, vibrant*

Is vibrant with the sound of the profound tantric dharma.

མཁའ་མཉམ་ཀུན་ཁྱབ་ཚངས་པའི་གསུང་དབྱངས་སྒྲོག༔

KHA	NYAM	KUN	KHYA	TSHANG WAI	SUNG	YANG	DRO
sky	*equalling*	*all*	*pervading*	*Brahma's*	*speech**	*melody*	*give voice to*

* the sixty perfect tones

With all the tones of Brahma your melodious speech resounds everywhere and fills the sky.

*With compassionate methods you act for the benefit of beings. Your
smiling face has a most beautiful and attractive complexion. Your
expressive speech louder than a thousand dragons' roar is vibrant with
the sound of the profound tantric dharma. With all the tones of Brahma
your melodious speech resounds everywhere and fills the sky.*

སྤྲུལ་སྐུ་ཆེན་པོའི་ཕྱོགས་བཞི་མཚམས་བརྒྱད་ན༔

TUL KU	CHEN POI	CHO	ZHI	TSHAM	GYAE	NA
nirmanakaya, emanation (Padmasambhava)	*great's*	*cardinal directions*	*four*	*intermediate directions (four)*	*eight (four + four)*	*in*
		(i.e. one of the Kabgyae groups in each direction)				

Around you, the great incarnation, in the four cardinal directions and
four intermediate directions,

ལོག་པའི་དགྲ་བགེགས་བརྫིས་པའི་གདན་སྟེང་དུ༔

LOG PAI	DRA	GEG	DZI PAI	DEN	TENG DU
wrong, false	*enemies*	*obstructors*	*trampled down*	*cushions*	*on top of*

Upon cushions of the trampled-down misleading enemies and obstructors,

སྐུ་གསུང་ཐུགས་དང་ཡོན་ཏན་འཕྲིན་ལས་ཀྱི༔

KU	SUNG	THU	DANG	YON TAN	TRIN LE	KYI
body	*speech*	*mind*	*and*	*good qualities*	*deeds*	*of*

Are the hosts of mara-subduing fierce forms of

རིགས་ལྔ་བདེ་གཤེགས་བདུད་འདུལ་ཁྲོ་བོའི་ཚོགས༔

RIG	NGA	DE SHE	DU	DUL	TRO WOI	TSHO
families	*five**	*Sugatas, Buddhas*	*maras, demons*	*subduing*	*fierce forms*	*hosts, groups*

*vajra, ratna, padma, karma and buddha

The body, speech, mind, good qualities and deeds of the Sugatas of the
five families.

སྒྲུབ་ཆེན་བཀའ་བརྒྱད་ཀྱི་ལྷ་ཚོགས་རྣམས་ཀྱིས་བསྐོར༔

DRU	CHEN	KAB GYAE	KYI	LHA	TSHO	NAM	KYI	KOR
practice	*great*	*eight herukas*	*of*	*gods*	*hosts*	*all*	*by*	*surrounded*

All the gods of the Drubchen Kabgyae surround you.

Around you, the great incarnation, in the four cardinal directions and four intermediate directions, are the hosts of mara-subduing fierce forms of the body, speech, mind, good qualities and deeds of the Sugatas of the five families, each upon cushions of the trampled down misleading enemies and obstructors. Around you are all the gods of the Drubchen Kabgyae.

ཕྱོགས་བཞི་པདྨ་འདབ་བཞི་གདན་སྟེང་དུ༔

CHO	ZHI	PAE MA	DAB	ZHI	DEN	TENG DU
direction	*four*	*lotus*	*petal*	*four*	*cushions*	*on top of*

In the four directions upon cushions of four-petalled lotuses

རིགས་བཞི་གིང་དང་མཁའ་འགྲོ་སྡེ་བཞི་ཚོགས༔

RIG	ZHI	GING	DANG	KHAN DRO	DE	ZHI	TSHO
families	*four*	*agents*	*and*	*dakinis*	*class*	*four*	*hosts*

Are the hosts of agents of the four families and the dakinis of the four classes.

ཐམས་ཅད་མ་ལུས་དུར་ཁྲོད་རྒྱན་དང་ལྡན༔

THAM CHAE	MA LU	DUR TRO	GYAN	DANG DEN
all	*without exception*	*cemetery*	*dress and ornaments*	*having*

They are all adorned with the cemetery attire and

མཛེས་པའི་རྒྱན་དང་རོལ་པའི་སྟབས་སུ་བཞུགས༔

DZE PAI	GYAN	DANG	ROL PAI	TAB	SU	ZHU
beautiful	*ornaments*	*and*	*dancing*	*mode, style*	*in, as*	*staying, being*

Beautiful ornaments, and they appear in the dancing posture.

ཡེ་ཤེས་མཁའ་འགྲོ་ཡབ་ཡུམ་རྣམས་ཀྱིས་བསྐོར༔

YE SHE	KHAN DRO	YAB YUM	NAM	KYI	KOR
original knowing	*dakinis*	*with consort*	*all*	*by*	*surrounded*

All the dakinis of original knowing with their consorts surround you.

In the four directions upon cushions of four-petalled lotuses are the hosts of agents of the four families and the dakinis of the four classes. They are all adorned with the cemetery attire and beautiful ornaments, and they appear in the dancing posture. Around you are all the dakinis of original knowing with their consorts.

གཞལ་ཡས་ཆེན་པོའི་ཕྱོགས་བཞིའི་བར་ཁྱམས་དང་༔

ZHAL YAE	CHEN POI	CHO	ZHI	BAR KHYAM	DANG
divine mansion	*great*	*direction*	*four*	*courtyards,*	*and*
				outer empty areas	

In the four directions within the divine mansion, the courtyards,

གྲུ་ཆད་སྒྲོ་འབུར་རིག་འཛིན་མཁའ་འགྲོས་ཁེངས༔

DRU CHAE	LO BUR	RIG DZIN	KHAN DRO	KHENG
corner area	*inner projections*	*vidyadharas*	*dakinis*	*filled with*

Corner areas, and inner projecting quadrangles are filled with vidyadharas and dakinis.

ལྷ་དང་ལྷ་མོ་མང་པོ་སྤྲིན་ལྟར་གཏིབས༔

LHA	DANG	LHA MO	MANG PO	TRIN	TAR	TIB
gods	*and*	*goddesses*	*many*	*clouds*	*as*	*gather, assemble*

Many gods and goddesses gather like clouds and

ཕྱི་ནང་གསང་བའི་མཆོད་པ་སྣ་ཚོགས་འབུལ༔

CHI	NANG	SANG WAI	CHO PA	NA TSHO	BUL
outer	*inner*	*secret*	*offerings*	*many different*	*offer*

Present various outer, inner and secret offerings.

མ་མོ་མཁའ་འགྲོའི་ལྷ་ཚོགས་རྣམས་ཀྱིས་བསྐོར༔

MA MO	KHAN DROI	LHA	TSHO	NAM	KYI	KOR
mother goddesses	*dakinis*	*gods*	*hosts*	*all*	*by*	*surrounded*

All the mamo and dakinis surround you.

The courtyards, corner areas, and the inner projections lying in the four directions within the divine mansion are filled with vidyadharas and dakinis. Many gods and goddesses gather like clouds and present various outer, inner, and secret offerings. Around you are all the mamo and dakinis.

རིན་ཆེན་གཞལ་ཡས་ཁང་གི་འདོད་སྣམ་ལ༔

RIN CHEN	ZHAL YAE KHANG	GI	DOE NYAM	LA
jewel	*divine mansion*	*of, for*	*ledges filled*	*to, with*
			with offerings	

On the ledges of the jewelled palace

མཆོད་པའི་ལྷ་མོ་ཆར་སྤྲིན་ལྟ་བུར་གཏིབས༔

CHOE PAI	LHA MO	CHAR TRIN	TA BUR	TIB
offering	*goddesses*	*raincloud*	*as*	*gather*

Offering goddesses gather like rainclouds.

འདོད་ཡོན་དྲུག་གི་མཆོད་པས་འཇིག་རྟེན་ཁེངས༔

DOE YON	DRU	GI	CHOE PAE	JIG TEN	KHENG
desirable qualities	*six*	*of*	*with offerings*	*world*	*fill*
(i.e whatever is pleasing to the six senses)					

The whole world is filled with offerings having the six desirable qualities, and

ཀུན་ཏུ་བཟང་པོའི་མཆོད་པས་བདེ་གཤེགས་མཆོད༔

KUN TU ZANG POI		CHOE PAI	DE SHE	CHOE
Bodhisattva Samantabhadra's		*by offering*	*Happily Gone,*	*offer*
(as described in the bZang-sPyod sMon-Lam)			*Buddhas*	

They are presented to the Happily Gone One according to Kuntuzangpo's infinite offering system.

ཡོན་ཏན་ཀུན་འབྱུང་གི་ལྷ་ཚོགས་དུ་མས་བསྐོར༔

YON TAN	KUN JUNG	GI	LHA	TSHO	DU MAE	KOR
good qualities	*source*	*of*	*gods*	*hosts*	*by many*	*surrounded*
(allthat pleases)						

You are surrounded by many gods who are the source of all good qualities.

On the ledges of the jewelled palace offering goddesses gather like rainclouds and the whole world is filled with offerings having the six desirable qualities. They are presented to you, the Happily Gone One, according to Kuntuzangpo's infinite offering system. Around you are many gods, the source of all good qualities.

གཞལ་ཡས་ཆེན་པོའི་ཕྱོགས་བཞི་སྒོ་བཞི་ན༔

ZHAL YAE	CHEN POI	CHO	ZHI	GO	ZHI	NA
divine mansion	*great's*	*directions*	*four*	*door*	*four*	*in*

At the four doors in the four directions of this great divine mansion

རྒྱལ་ཆེན་སྡེ་བཞི་བསྐོ་བའི་བཀའ་ཉན་མཛད༔

GYAL	CHEN	DE	ZHI	GO WAI	KA	NYAN	DZAE
king	*great*	*groups*	*four**	*orders, instructions*	*order*	*hear*	*do*
				from Padmasambhava	*(i.e.obey)*		

* Dhritarashtra, Berudhaka, Berupaksha and Vaisramana

Are the four great kings who listen to the orders they are given and

ལྷ་སྲིན་སྡེ་བརྒྱད་བྲན་དང་ཕོ་ཉར་འགྱེད༔

LHA SIN	DE	GYAE	DRAN	DANG	PHO NYAR	GYE
local gods and demons	*groups*	*eight*	*servant*	*and*	*messengers*	*scatter, disperse*

Send out the eight groups of gods and demons as their servants and messengers

བདུད་དང་མུ་སྟེགས་དྲལ་ཕྲན་བཞིན་དུ་འདུལ༔

DU	DANG	MU TE		DUL TRAN	ZHIN DU	DUL
maras, demons	*and*	*enemies of dharma*		*fine dust*	*like that*	*control, destroy*

To grind the maras and dharma enemies down to dust.

ཆོས་སྐྱོང་སྲུང་མའི་ལྷ་ཚོགས་འཁོར་གྱིས་བསྐོར༔

CHO KYONG	SUNG MAI	LHA	TSHO	KHOR	GYI	KOR
dharma protectors	*guardians*	*gods*	*hosts*	*retinue*	*by*	*surrounded*

You are surrounded by your hosts of dharma-protectors and guardians.

At the four doors in the four directions of this great divine mansion are the four great kings who listen to the orders they are given and send out the eight groups of gods and demons as their servants and messengers to grind the maras and dharma enemies down to dust. Around you are your hosts of dharma-protectors and guardians.

དབྱིངས་དང་གནས་ཡུལ་འབུམ་ཕྲག་མཁའ་འགྲོའི་ཚོགས༔

YING	DANG	NAE	YUL	BUM TRA	KHAN DROI	TSHO
dharmadhatu	*and*	*32 places*	*24 sites*	*100,000*	*dakinis*	*hosts*

The countless hosts of dakinis residing in the space of all phenomena and at the thirty-two places and the twenty-four sites,

དཔའ་བོ་མཁའ་འགྲོ་ཆོས་སྐྱོང་བསྲུང་མར་བཅས༔

PA WO	KHAN DRO	CHO KYONG	SUNG MAR	CHAE
viras, heroes	*dakinis*	*dharma protectors*	*guardian*	*together*

Together with the heroes, dakinis, dharma-protectors and guardians

དཔག་མེད་སྤྲིན་ཕུང་འཁྲིགས་བཞིན་གསལ་བ་ཡི༔

PA ME	TRIN	PHUNG	TRIG	ZHIN	SAL WA	YI
numberless	*clouds*	*masses*	*gathering*	*like, as*	*clear vision*	*of*

All gather together clearly like countless massing of clouds.

རང་བྱུང་རང་ཤར་གསལ་ལ་འཛིན་མེད་བསྒོམ༔

RANG JUNG	RANG	SHAR	SAL	LA DZIN	ME	GOM
spontaneous	*self-arising*	*visualise*	*to*	*grasping*	*without*	*meditate*

Meditate without grasping at this spontaneous self-arising clarity.

The countless hosts of dakinis residing in the space of all phenomena and at the thirty-two places and the twenty-four sites, together with the heroes, dakinis, dharma-protectors and guardians all gather together clearly like countless massing of clouds. Meditate without grasping at this spontaneous self-arising clarity.

ཧཱུྂ༔ ཨོ་རྒྱན་ཡུལ་གྱི་ནུབ་བྱང་མཚམས༔

HUNG	UR GYEN YUL	GYI	NUB JANG	TSHAM
vocative, seed letter of Padmasambhava	*Oddiyana, the dakinis' land*	*of*	*north-west*	*border, corner*

Hung. In the land of Urgyen's north-west corner,

པདྨ་གེ་སར་སྡོང་པོ་ལ༔

PAE MA	GE SAR	DONG PO	LA
lotus	*stamen*	*stem*	*on*

Upon a lotus stem and stamen,

ཡ་མཚན་མཆོག་གི་དངོས་གྲུབ་བརྙེས༔

YAM TSHEN	CHO GI	NGO DRU		NYE
marvellous, wonderful	*supreme (i.e. buddhahood)*	*siddhis, attainments*		*has got*

With marvellous and supreme accomplishments,

པདྨ་འབྱུང་གནས་ཞེས་སུ་གྲགས༔

PAE MA JUNG NAE		ZHE SU	DRA
Padmasambhava, Guru Rinpoche		*known as*	*famous (famed as)*

The Lotus Born is your famous name.

འཁོར་དུ་མཁའ་འགྲོ་མང་པོས་བསྐོར༔

KHOR DU	KHAN DRO		MANG POE	KOR
retinue as	*dakinis, sky-goddesses (here it means all sky travelling deities)*		*many by*	*surrounded*

As retinue many dakinis surround you.

ཁྱེད་ཀྱི་རྗེས་སུ་བདག་སྒྲུབ་ཀྱིས༔

KHYE	KYI JE SU	DA	DRU	KYI
you	*following after, emulating*	*I*	*practice*	*by that*

Following and relying on you, I do your practice, therefore,

བྱིན་གྱིས་བརླབ་ཕྱིར་གཤེགས་སུ་གསོལ༔

JIN GYI LAB	CHIR	SHE SU SOL
blessing	*in order to*	*please come*

In order to bless us, please come here!

གུ་རུ་པདྨ་སིདྡྷི་ཧཱུྃ༔

GU RU	PAE MA	SID DHI	HUNG
guru, master	*Padmasambhava*	*real attainment*	*give me!*

Guru Padmasambhava grant us the accomplishment of buddhahood!

Hung. In the land of Urgyen's north-west corner, upon a lotus stem and stamen, with marvellous and supreme accomplishments, the Lotus Born is your famous name. As retinue many dakinis surround you. Following and relying on you, I do your practice, therefore, in order to bless us, please come here!

ཞེས་ཅི་ནུས་དང་།

[Recite this as many times as you can with true devotion from your heart.]

ཧཱུྃ༔ བཞེངས་ཤིག་པདྨ་འབྱུང་གནས་མཁའ་འགྲོའི་ཚོགས༔

HUNG	ZHENG SHI	PAE MA JUNG NAE	KHAN DROI	TSHO
five jnana and vocative	*arise!*	*Padmasambhava*	*dakinis*	*host*
	(Come from the dharmadhatu, the space of all phenomena.)			

Hung. Padmasambhava and your hosts of dakinis, arise!

དགོངས་ཤིག་ཕྱོགས་བཅུ་དུས་གསུམ་བདེ་གཤེགས་རྣམས༔

GONG SHI	CHO CHU	DU SUM	DE SHE NAM
pay attention to our request	*ten directions (everywhere)*	*three times (past, present, future)*	*Sugatas, Buddhas, Happily Gone*

Happily Gone of the three times and ten directions, pay heed!

རྗེ་བཙུན་ཆེན་པོ་པདྨ་ཐོད་ཕྲེང་རྩལ༔

JE TSUN	CHEN PO	PAE MA	THO THRENG TSAL
noble, worthy of respect	*great*	*(a form of Padmasambhava)*	

Most reverend Padma Tho Treng Tsal,

རིག་འཛིན་མཁའ་འགྲོའི་གནས་ནས་གཤེགས་སུ་གསོལ༔

RIG DZIN	KHAN DROI	NAE	NE	SHE SU SOL
vidyadharas	*dakini's*	*land*	*from*	*please come*

(i.e. We invite Padmasambhava to come from Zangdopalri where he resides at present surrounded by hosts of vidyadharas and dakinis. When he comes, his entire retinue follows automatically, just as with a great king.)

Please come from the land of the vidyadharas and dakinis!

Hung. Padmasambhava and your hosts of dakinis, arise! Happily Gone of the three times and ten directions, pay heed! Most reverend Padma Tho Treng Tsal, please come from the land of the vidyadharas and dakinis!

དབུ་སྐྲ་མཛེས་པའི་ཐོར་ཚོག་ཤིགས་སེ་ཤིག༔

WU TRA	DZE PAI	THOR CHO	SHI SE SHI
hair on head	*beautiful*	*long hair loose and tied up*	*loosely swishing*

Your beautiful long hair swishes, shi-se-shi.

རིན་ཆེན་རྒྱན་ཆ་མང་པོ་སི་ལི་ལི༔

RIN CHEN	GYAN CHA	MANG PO	SI LI LI
jewel	*ornaments*	*many*	*jangling with a sound like incessant rain*

Many jewel ornaments are tinkling, si-li-li.

དུར་ཁྲོད་རུས་ཆེན་རྒྱན་ཆ་ཁྲོ་ལོ་ལོ༔

DUR TRO	RU	CHEN	GYAN CHA	TRO LO LO
cemetery	*bones*	*great*	*ornaments*	*rattle together*

The great cemetery bone ornaments rattle, tro-lo-lo.

སྒྲ་དང་རོལ་མོ་མང་པོ་ཨུ་རུ་རུ༔

DRA	DANG	ROL MO	MANG PO	U RU RU
sounds	*and*	*music, cymbals*	*much*	*whirring*

Sounds and music vibrate, u-ru-ru.

Your beautiful long hair swishes, shi-se-shi. Many jewel ornaments are tinkling, si-li-li. The great cemetery bone ornaments rattle, tro-lo-lo. Sounds and music vibrate, u-ru-ru.

ཡི་དམ་ལྷ་ཚོགས་ཧཱུྃ་སྒྲ་དི་རི་རི༔

YI DAM	LHA	TSHO	HUNG	DRA	DI RI RI
path	*gods*	*hosts*	*Hung*	*sound*	*strong, flowing sound*

Hosts of path deities cry resonant Hungs, di-ri-ri.

མཁའ་འགྲོ་སྡེ་ལྔའི་གར་བྱེད་ཤིགས་སེ་ཤིག༔

KHAN DRO	DE		NGA	GAR JE	SHI SE SHI
dakinis	*kulas, families*		*five*	*dancing*	*swinging from side to side*

Dakinis of the five families dance gracefully, shi-se-shi.

གིང་ཆེན་དཔའ་བོའི་བྲོ་བརྡུངས་ཁྲབས་སེ་ཁྲབ༔

GING	CHEN	PA WOI	TRO DUNG	TRAB SE TRAB
agents	*great*	*viras, heroes*	*strong dancing*	*stomping step*

The great agents and pawo dance strongly, stomping trab-se-trab.

མ་མོ་མཁའ་འགྲོ་སྤྲིན་ལྟར་ཐིབས་སེ་ཐིབ༔

MA MO		KHAN DRO	TRIN	TAR	THIB SE THIB
Mothers, goddesses		*dakinis*	*clouds*	*like*	*gather swiftly and easily*

Mamo and dakinis gather like clouds, thib-se-thib.

Hosts of path deities cry resonant Hungs, di-ri-ri. Dakinis of the five families dance gracefully, shi-se-shi. The great agents and pawo dance strongly, stomping trab-se-trab. Mamo and dakinis gather like clouds, thib-se-thib.

ཆོས་སྐྱོང་སྡེ་བརྒྱད་ལས་བྱེད་ཁྱུགས་སེ་ཁྱུག༔

CHO	KYONG	DE	GYAE	LAE JE	KHYU SE KHYU
direction	protectors	class	eight	workers, active ones	very swiftly

The eight classes of dharma protectors and the workers rush on, khyug-se-khyug.

ཞུབ་ཆེན་སྟོང་གི་སྒྲ་སྐད་སི་ལི་ལི༔

ZHUB	CHEN	TONG GI	DRA KAE	SI LI LI
armour	great	a thousand-strong military division	sound	vibrating iron sound

A thousand armoured solders clatter, si-li-li.

གཡས་ན་ཕོ་རྒྱུད་ཐམས་ཅད་ཤ་ར་ར༔

YAE	NA	PHO GYU	THAM CHE	SHA RA RA
right	on	male gods, devas	all	come quickly

On the right all the male gods come quickly, sha-ra-ra.

གཡོན་ན་མོ་རྒྱུད་ཐམས་ཅད་ཤ་ར་ར༔

YON	NA	MO GYU	THAM CHE	SHA RA RA
left	on	female gods, devis	all	come quickly

On the left all the goddesses come quickly, sha-ra-ra.

The eight classes of dharma protectors and the workers rush on, khyug-se-khyug. A thousand armoured soldiers clatter, si-li-li. On the right all the male gods come quickly, sha-ra-ra. On the left all the goddesses come quickly, sha-ra-ra.

བར་སྣང་ཐམས་ཅད་དར་དུ་གདུགས་ལྷབས་སེ་ལྷབ༔

BAR NANG	THAM CHE	DAR	DU	LHAB SE LHAB
sky	all	flags	umbrellas	flutter to and fro, shimmer

The entire sky has flags and parasols fluttering, lhab-se-lhab.

དྲི་ཞིམ་སྤོས་ཀྱི་དྲད་པ་ཐུ་ལུ་ལུ༔

DRI	ZHIM	POE	KYI	NGAE PA	THU LU LU
smell	pleasing	incense	of	good strong smell	spreading everywhere

The good scent of pleasant smelling incense pervades, thu-lu-lu.

མཁའ་འགྲོ་གསང་བའི་བརྡ་སྐད་དི་རི་རི༔

KHAN DRO   **SANG WAI**   **DA KAE**   **DI RI RI**
dakinis   *secret*   *symbol language*   *strong flowing sound*

The dakinis' secret symbol language reverberates, di-ri-ri.

གིང་ཆེན་དཔའ་བོའི་བཤུགས་སྒྲ་ཀྱུ་རུ་རུ༔

GING CHEN   **PA WOI**   **SHU LU**   **KYU RU RU**
great agents   *viras*   *whistling*   *whistling sound*

The great agents' and pawos' whistling echoes, kyu-ru-ru.

The entire sky has flags and parasols fluttering, lhab-se-lhab. The good scent of pleasant-smelling incense pervades, thu-lu-lu. The dakinis' secret symbol language reverberates, di-ri-ri. The great agents' and pawos' whistling echoes, kyu-ru-ru.

ཧཱུྃ་གི་སྒྲང་སྒྲ་མང་པོ་དི་རི་རི༔

HUNG   **GI**   **NANG LU**   **MANG PO**   **DI RI RI**
hung   *of*   *wild, careless singing*   *many*   *strong flowing sound*

The wild sound of hung flows freely, di-ri-ri.

ཕཊ་ཀྱི་བརྡ་སྐད་དྲག་པོ་སངས་སེ་སང༔

PHAT   **KYI**   **DA KAE**   **DRA PO**   **SANG SE SANG**
Phat!   *of*   *symbol sound*   *strong*   *clear and sharp sound*

The fierce symbol sound Phat! blasts clear and sharp, sang-se-sang.

བདག་དང་འགྲོ་དྲུག་སེམས་ཅན་ཐམས་ཅད་ལ༔

DA   **DANG**   **DRO DRU**   **SEM CHEN**   **THAM CHE**   **LA**
I   *and*   *moving in the six realms of samsara*   *sentient being*   *all*   *to*

Please look on me and all beings moving in the six realms

ཐུགས་རྗེས་གཟིགས་ལ་གནས་འདིར་གཤེགས་སུ་གསོལ༔

THU JE   **ZI**   **LA**   **NAE**   **DIR**   **SHE SU SOL**
with compassion   *look*   *then*   *place*   *here*   *please come*

With compassion, and then come here.

The wild sound of hung flows freely, di-ri-ri. The fierce symbol sound Phat! blasts clear and sharp, sang-se-sang. Please look with compassion on me and all beings moving in the six realms and then come here.

གནས་འདིར་ཐུགས་རྗེས་དགོངས་ཏེ་གཤེགས་ནས་ཀྱང་༔

NAE	DIR	THU JE		GONG	TE	SHE	NE	KYANG
place	*here*	*with compassion*		*think*	*then*	*come*	*then*	*also*

Please think of this place with compassion and come here.

བདག་གིས་བྱང་ཆུབ་སྙིང་པོ་མ་ཐོབ་བར༔

DA		GI	JANG CHU NYING PO	MA	THO	BAR
me (I and all beings)		*by*	*the heart of enlightenment*	*not*	*get*	*until*

Until we gain the heart of enlightenment,

བགེགས་དང་ལོག་འདྲེན་བར་ཆད་འདུལ་བ་དང༔

GEG	DANG	LOG DREN	BAR CHAE		DUL WA	DANG
obstructors	*and*	*misleaders*	*interruptors, obstacles*		*subdue*	*and*

Please subdue the obstructors, misleaders and interruptors and

མཆོག་དང་ཐུན་མོང་དངོས་གྲུབ་རྩལ་དུ་གསོལ༔

CHO	DANG	THUN MONG	NGO DRU	TSAL DU	SOL
supreme	*and*	*general*	*siddhis*	*grant*	*please*

Bestow supreme and general accomplishments.

འཁོར་བ་སྡུག་བསྔལ་གྱི་རྒྱ་མཚོ་ལས་བསྒྲལ་དུ་གསོལ༔

KHOR WA	DU NGAL	GYI	GYAM TSHO	LAE	DRAL	DU	SOL
samsara	*suffering*	*of*	*ocean*	*from*	*free, take*	*out*	*please*

Please free us from samsara's ocean of suffering

Please think of this place with compassion and come here. Then, until we gain the heart of enlightenment, please subdue the obstructors, misleaders and interruptors and bestow supreme and general accomplishments. Please free us from samsara's ocean of suffering.

གསོལ་འདེབས་ལེའུ་བདུན་མའི་ནང་ཚན་མཁའ་འགྲོ་ཡེ་ཤེས་མཚོ་རྒྱལ་ལ་གསུངས་པ་ཁ་
བསྐྱར་བྱས་པ།།

Adapted by C.R. Lama from the prayer taught by Padmasambhava to Yeshe Tshogyal contained in *The Seven Chapters of Prayer*.

འཆི་བ་ལམ་འཁྱེར་གདམས་ངག་ཟབ་མོ་སྤྱར་བཅར་མ་བཞུགས་སོ།

In One's Own Hand
The Profound Instructions for Using Death as the Path

ༀ། འཆི་བ་ལམ་འཁྱེར་གདམས་ངག་ཟབ་མོ་སྤྱར་བཅར་མ་བཞུགས་སོ།
གུ་རུ་སྤྲུ་སྡི་ཏྲི་ཧཱུྃ། རྣལ་འབྱོར་པ་འཆི་ཁའི་ཚེ་ཉམས་སུ་བླང་བ་ནི། བདག་ལ་འཆི་ཁ་
བར་དོ་འཁར་དུས་འདིར། ཀུན་ལ་ཆགས་སྣང་འཛིན་ཞེན་སྤྱངས་བྱས་ནས། གདམས་
ངག་གསལ་བའི་དང་ལ་མ་ཡེངས་འཇུག །རང་རིག་སྐྱེ་མེད་ནམ་མཁའི་དབྱིངས་སུ་འཕོ།
ཞེས་གསུངས་པ་ལྟར་ཚེ་འདིའི་ཞེན་ཆགས་ཐམས་ཅད་སྤངས། གདམས་ངག་ནི་ད་ལྟ་སྐྱེ་
གནས་བར་དོར་ཐོས་བསམ་བསྒོམ་གསུམ་མ་ཐར་ཕྱིན་པ་ཡོད་ཚེ། དེའི་འཕུས་བུ་བར་
དོར་འབྱིན་དགོས་པས། ལྷ་བ་ཀ་དག་ཕྱོགས་ནས་གདང་ཞིབ་ལ་ཡོད་ན་དགུགས་ཆད་
འཕུལ་རྐྱེན་སེམས་དབུ་མར་ཆུད་སྐབས་རང་རྒྱུད་ཀྱི་རིག་པ་དོ་ཤེས་ཏེ་འོད་གསལ་མ་བུ་རོ་
འཕྲོད། འཆི་བ་འོད་གསལ་ཆོས་སྐུར་སངས་རྒྱ་ཐུགས་དང་ལ་བཞུགས་སྐབས་འདི་ཡིན།
ལུས་གྲུབ་སྣང་བ་བཞིའི་ལམ་ལ་རྣམས་འཁྱུར་ཡོད་ཚོགག་དག་གི་རང་མདངས་འགགས་མེད་དུ་
ཤར་བའི་སྐུ་འོད་ཟེར་གསུམ་ཞི་ཁྲོའི་ལྷ་རྣམས་རིག་རྩལ་ལྷུན་གྲུབ་ཏུ་རོ་འཕོད་དེ། བར་དོར་
ཕོངས་སྐུར་གྲོལ་བ་འམ་རང་བཞིན་སྤྲུལ་སྐུར་སངས་རྒྱ། བསྐྱེད་རིམ་གསལ་བ་ཆོམ་དང་
སྐུགས་ལམ་དུ་ལྔགས་པ་རྣམས་སྐྱི་དཔ་བར་དོར་ལྷོག་གི་གདམས་པས་ཕྱིན་མཆོངས་སྐྱོར་
བ་སོགས་ཡིན། རྗེ་མི་ལས་ཀྱི་འཆི་བ་འོད་གསལ་ཆོས་སྐུར་གྲོལ་བ་ཕྱག་ཆེན་དང་འོད་
གསལ་འོངས་སྐུར་གྲོལ་བ་བསྐྱེད་རིམ་སྐུ་ལུས་སྤྲི་ལས་སྤྲུལ་སྐུར་གྲོལ་བ་ལ་གཏུམ་མོ་དང་
ཐབས་ལས་དགོས་པར་གསུངས། ས་སྐུ་པ་རྣམས་བར་དོ་དོན་པ་རྣམ་གསུམ་ཞེས། ཧྲྭ་མ་
དན་པ། ཡི་དམ་ཀྱི་ལྷ་དན་པ། གསང་མཆེན་དན་པ་གསུམ་ཀྱིས་གྲོལ་བར་བཤད། མདོར་
ནས་བཀའ་རྙིང་གསུམ་ཀྱི་ཐབ་གནད་དེ་ལྟར་ཡིན་ཀྱང་། དེ་ལས་ཟབ་པ་དབུགས་ཆད་པ་དང་
མཚམ་དུ་མ་ཁན་སྦྱད་དུ་བསྒྲད་པའི་ཐབས་ཞིང་ཁམས་སྦྱང་བ་འདི་རང་ཟབ་པས་འཕོ་བ་ཡང་
འདིར་འདུས། དེ་ལ་ཁྱེད་ལྦགས་བདེ་ཆན་དང་མཚོན་དགའ་གོགས་རང་གང་འབྲད་རིག་
པ་གཏོད་པ་ཡིན་ཀྱང་། དེད་རང་རྣམས་ཟངས་མདོག་དཔལ་རི་རང་སྐྱབས་སུ་བབས་པས།
བདེ་བ་ཅན་ཡང་དེ་ཁ་ཡིན་པས། ད་ལྟ་རིག་པ་གསལ་དུས་དམིགས་པ་འདི་བཞིན་མཛོད།

Guru Padma Siddhi Hung   Regarding the practice that yogis must employ at the time when they come to die, the Bar-Do Thos-Grol says:

"Now as the bardo of death is arising for me I abandon all desire, anger, grasping and hope. Unwavering, I will maintain the state of clear understanding of the teachings and send my mind into the unborn sky-like dharmadhatu."

Accordingly, you must abandon all hopes and desires for this life. Now, during the period from birth until death (sKyes-gNas Bar-Do), you must perfect the three stages of hearing, reflecting and meditating so that the result will be gained in the bardo period after death. (Moreover if your mind is ready there is no reason why you cannot go fully to Zangdopalri before the time when you would die.)

If you have full confidence in the view of the primordial purity of your mind (Ka-Dag), then with your final exhalation (when you go unconscious at the time of death) put the wind/mind (rLung Sems) into the avadhuti central channel. Then self-occurring awareness will shine forth and mother and child clear light will manifest. You who are dying must practise staying merged in the Buddhahood of clear light Dharmakaya. (At death you should try to maintain this for seven to twenty-one days).

When you have full practice power of the path of the effortlessly arising four visionary appearances then the intrinsic radiance of primordial purity (Ka-Dag) will arise ceaselessly as sound, light and rays. (The four visionary appearances are 1. direct appearance of the actuality of phenomena; 2. increased in experiences in meditation; 3. the limit of awareness; 4. ceasing to cling to the actuality of phenomena.) Then you must recognise the peaceful and wrathful Gods as the effortlessly arising energy of awareness. With this, in the bardo you will be liberated in the Sambhogakaya. Or else you will easily gain Buddhahood as Nirmanakaya (as these forms develop later in Bar-Dos.)

Those who only have clear practice of the developing system (bsKyed-Rim) and have just entered upon the tantric path must try in the bardo of birth (Srid-Pa'i Bar-Do) to avoid being born in a lower existence. (By the power of their practice they must strive to be born in a human womb in a family where Dharma is practised.)

Milarepa said, *"At death liberation in the clear light Dharmakaya arises through mahamudra (Phyag-Chen). Liberation in the clear light Sambhogakaya arises through the developing system (bsKyed-Rim), illusory body (sGyu-Lus) and dream practice (rMi-Lam). While for liberation in the Nirmanakaya gTum-Mo and Thabs-Lam practice is necessary."*

The Sa-sKya-Pa have the teaching of the three remembrances for the Bar-Do at death. These are the remembrance of the Guru, remembrance of the Path Deity, and remembrance of the name received at the time of initiation. They explain that liberation will be gained by means of them.

In brief these are the profound essential points of the Sa-sKya, bKa'-brGyud and rNying-Ma teachings. But deeper than these is to be able at the time of the final exhalation at death to go immediately to the mKha-sPyod pure land. This method of going to the Buddha realm (Zhing-Khams) is very deep and important and so the transference ('Pho-Ba) technique is given here briefly. The way to practise this is to take as your mind's object bDe-Ba-Can or mNgon-dGa' or whatever Buddha realm you like. But especially for we rNying-Ma-Pa our 'chance' or 'portion' (Rang-sKabs-Su Babs-Pa) is Zangdopalri (Zangs-mDog dPal-Ri) though we can also focus on Dewachen (bDe-Ba-Can).

Now, keeping your mind clear, you must think as follows:

སྐྱབས་འགྲོ་དང་སེམས་བསྐྱེད། REFUGE AND BODHICITTA

སངས་རྒྱས་ཆོས་དང་ཚོགས་ཀྱི་མཆོག་རྣམས་ལ།

SANG GYE CHO DANG TSO KYI CHO NAM LA
buddha dharma and sangha of supreme (plural) to
(the assembly of committed practitioners)

To the Buddha, Dharma and Assembly of the Excellent Ones

བྱང་ཆུབ་བར་དུ་བདག་ནི་སྐྱབས་སུ་མཆི།

JANG CHU BAR DU DA NI KYAB SU CHI
enlightenment until I refuge for go

I go for refuge until enlightenment is gained.

བདག་གིས་སྦྱིན་སོགས་བགྱིས་པའི་བསོད་ནམས་ཀྱིས།

DA GI JIN SO GYI PAI SO NAM KYI
I by generosity other perfections* doing, practising virtue through
*discipline, patience, diligence, meditation, wisdom

Through the virtue of practising generosity and the other perfections

འགྲོ་ལ་ཕན་ཕྱིར་སངས་རྒྱས་འགྲུབ་པར་ཤོག།

DRO LA PHEN CHIR SANG GYE DRU PAR SHO
all beings to benefit in order to buddha accomplish may it happen

May I attain buddhahood for the benefit of all beings

I go for refuge to the Buddha, Dharma and Assembly of the Excellent Ones until enlightenment is gained. Through the virtue of practising generosity and the other perfections may I attain buddhahood for the benefit of all beings.

ལན་གསུམ་རྗེས༔

[Recite this three times.]

སངས་རྒྱས་དང་བྱང་ཆུབ་སེམས་དཔའ་རྣམས་ལ་ར་མ་དར་སྤྲུན་པའི་སྨོན་ལམ་བཞུགས་སོཿ

THE PRAYER OF ASPIRATION REQUESTING HELP FROM THE BUDDHAS
AND BODHISATTVAS

དཀོན་མཆོག་གསུམ་ལ་དངོས་སུ་འབྱོར་པ་དང་ཡིད་ཀྱི་སྤྲུལ་པའི་མཆོད་པ་འབུལཿ ལག་དུ་
སྤོས་དེ་ཞིམ་པོ་ཐོགས་ཏེཿ གདུང་བ་དྲག་པོས་འདི་སྐད་དོཿ

Make offerings to the Three Jewels with the gifts that you actually have, water,
rice and so on, and also with those that you imagine in your mind (as in the
system of Bodhisattva Samantabhadra). Hold some fragrant incense in your
hands, which are held together in prayer, and recite the following with deep
faith.

[This should be practised for oneself before the time of death and before
'Pho-Ba practice. Only meditators with true power can actually benefit
others by practising this for them. C. R. Lama.]

ཕྱོགས་བཅུ་ན་བཞུགས་པའི་སངས་རྒྱས་དང་

CHO	CHU	NA	ZHU PAI	SANG GYE	DANG
directions	*ten*	*in*	*staying*	*buddhas*	*and*

You, the compassionate Buddhas and

བྱང་ཆུབ་སེམས་དཔའ་ཐུགས་རྗེ་དང་ལྡན་པཿ

JANG CHU SEM PA	THU JE	DANG DEN PA
bodhisattvas	*compassion*	*possessing*

Bodhisattvas who reside in the ten directions,

མཁྱེན་པ་དང་ལྡན་པཿ སྤྱན་དང་ལྡན་པཿ

KHYEN PA	DANG DEN PA	CHAN	DANG DEN PA
deep knowledge, understanding	*possessing*	*eye (of wisdom)*	*possessing*

You who have true understanding, who have the eye of wisdom,

བརྩེ་བ་དང་ལྡན་པཿ འགྲོ་བའི་སྐྱབས་སུ་གྱུར་པ་རྣམསཿ

TSE WA	DANG DEN PA	DRO WAI	KYAB	SU	GYUR PA	NAM
kindness (they have the power to help)	*possessing*	*sentient beings*	*protect*	*as*	*are*	*(plural)*

You who are kind — protector of beings,

ཐུགས་རྗེའི་དབང་གིས་གནས་འདིར་བྱོན་ཅིག༔

THU JEI   WANG   GI   NAE   DIR   JON CHI
compassion's   power   by   place   here   come!

By the power of your compassion, you must come here!

དངོས་སུ་འབྱོར་བ་དང་ཡིད་ཀྱི་སྤྲུལ་པའི་མཆོད་པ་བཞེས་ཤིག༔

NGO SU   JOR WA   DANG   YI   KYI   TRUL PAI   CHO PA   ZHE   SHI
actually   gathered   and   mind   of   emanated,   offerings   accept   must
                                         imagined   (as payment for your help)

These offerings that I have actually assembled and all those that I create in my mind – you must accept them all!

ཐུགས་རྗེ་ཅན་ཁྱེད་རྣམས་ལ་མཁྱེན་པའི་ཡེ་ཤེས༔

THU JE CHEN   KHYE   NAM   LA   KHYEN PAI   YE SHE
compassionate ones   you   all   with   true understanding   original knowing

You are the compassionate ones with the true understanding of original knowing.

བརྩེ་བའི་ཐུགས་རྗེ༔   མཛད་པའི་འཕྲིན་ལས༔

TSE WAI   THU JE   **DZAE PAI   TRIN LAE**
kind   compassion   *doing,   activity, deeds*
                            performing   for others

You have kind compassion. You perform helpful activity.

སྐྱོབ་པའི་ནུས་མཐུ་བསམ་གྱིས་མི་ཁྱབ་པ་མངའ་བ་ལགས་པས༔

KYOB PAI   NU   THU   SAM GYI MI KHYA PA   NGA WA LA   PAE
protective   strength   power   inconceivable   possessing   by

You possess inconceivable protective strength and power.

You, the compassionate Buddhas and Bodhisattvas who reside in the ten directions, you who have true understanding, who have the eye of wisdom, you who are kind – protectors of beings, by the power of your compassion you must come here! These offerings that I have actually assembled and all those that I create in my mind – you must accept them all! You are the compassionate ones with the true understanding of original knowing. You have kind compassion. You perform helpful activity. You possess inconceivable protective strength and power.

ཕྱག་རྗེ་ཅན་ཁྱེད་རྣམས་ཀྱིས་བདག་ནི་   [ཆེ་གེ་མོ་ཞེས་བྱ་བ་འདི་ནི]༔

THU JE CHEN KHYE NAM	KYI	DA NI	CHE GE MO ZHE JA WA	DI NI
compassionate ones you all	*by*	*I/me*	*this person called*	*is this*
(buddhas and bodhisattvas)				

Compassionate ones, I call on you! I am [*or* this person called .... is]

འཇིག་རྟེན་འདི་ནས་ཕ་རོལ་ཏུ་ནི་འགྲོ༔

JIG TEN	DI	NAE	PHA ROL TU	NI	DRO
*world**	*this*	*from*	*away from, beyond*		*going*

*their present situation

Crossing over from my familiar world.

འཇིག་རྟེན་འདི་ནས་ནི་བོར༔   སྐྱེས་ཆེན་པོ་ནི་འདེབས༔

JIG TEN	DI	NAE NI BOR	KYAE CHEN PO NI	DE
world	*this*	*discard, thrown off*	*death, the great movement that carries one helplessly*	*struck, hit by*

My world is now abandoned. I am struck by the great irresistible change.

གྲོགས་ནི་མེད༔   སྡུག་བསྔལ་ནི་ཆེ༔   སྐྱབས་ནི་མེད༔

DRO NI	ME	DU NGAL NI	CHE	KYAB NI	ME
*friend**	*without*	*suffering*	*great*	*protection*	*without*

* All those one has known in this life must be left behind.

I am friendless, in great suffering and without protection.

མགོན་ནི་མེད༔   དཔུང་གཉེན་ནི་མེད༔

GON NI	ME	PUNG NYEN NI	ME
lord,	*without*	*assistant, helper*	*without*

I have no benefactor. I have no aid.

ཚེ་འདིའི་སྣང་བ་ནི་ནུབ༔

TSHE	DI	NANG WA	NI NUB
life	*this*	*ideas, appearances*	*declining, passing away*

The ideas of this life are passing away.

འགྲོ་བ་གཞན་དུ་ནི་འགྲོ༔   མུན་ནག་འཐུག་པོར་ནི་འཇུག༔

DRO WA	ZHAN	DU NI	DRO	MUN NA	THU POR NI	JU
beings	*other*	*to**	*going*	*dark*	*very gloomy*	*enter, start on*

* going to be reborn in another place among other beings

I am going off to be among strangers. I am entering upon great darkness.

གཡང་ཆེན་པོར་ནི་ལྷུང༔

YANG CHEN POR NI   **LHUNG**
great danger (like going over a precipice)   *fall*

I am falling into great danger.

རྣམ་རྟོག་གི་ནགས་ཁྲོད་འཐུག་པོར་ནི་འཇུག༔

NAM TO   **GI**   **NAG TRO**   **THU POR NI**   **JU**
thoughts   *of*   *forest*   *great, thick*   *enter*

I am entering the thick forest of discursive thoughts.

ལས་ཀྱི་དབང་གིས་ནི་དེད༔   དགོན་པ་ཆེན་པོར་ནི་འགྲོ༔

LAE   **KYI**   **WANG**   **GI NI**   **DE**   **GON PA**   **CHEN POR NI**   **DRO**
karma   *of*   *power*   *by*   *carried*   *isolated place*   *big*   *going*

I am carried off by the power of karma. I am advancing into great isolation.

རྒྱ་མཚོ་ཆེན་པོར་ནི་ཁྱེར༔   ལས་ཀྱི་རླུང་གིས་ནི་བཏེས༔

GYAM TSHO   **CHEN POR**   **NI KHYER**   **LAE KYI**   **LUNG**   **GI NI**   **DAE**
ocean (of the   *great*   *swept,*   *karma's*   *wind*   *by*   *pushed*
afflictions)   *(can't escape)*   *carried*

I am swept along by the great ocean. I am pushed by the wind of karma.

ས་ཚུགས་མེད་པའི་ཕྱོགས་སུ་ནི་འགྲོ༔

SA TSHU   **ME PAI**   **CHO SU NI**   **DRO**
resting place, halt   *without*   *onward*   *going*
(not recognise anything)

Without any resting place I must keep travelling on.

གཡུལ་ངོ་ཆེན་པོར་ནི་འཇུག༔

YUL NGO   **CHEN POR**   **NI JU**
frightful ideas, hostile appearances   *great, many*   *entering, coming*
(like a great battlefield)

I am encountering frightening appearances.

གདོན་ཆེན་པོས་ནི་ཟིན༔

DON   **CHEN POE**   **NI ZIN**
trouble, harm   *great*   *caught*
                (many demonic forms)

I am caught up in great harm.

གཤིན་རྗེའི་ཕོ་ཉས་ནི་འཇིགས་ཤིང་སྐྲག༔

SHIN JEI   **PHOE NYAE NI**   **JIG SHING**   **TRA**
yama's, the lord of death's   *messengers, agents*   *frightened*   *terrified*

I am frightened and terrorised by the agents of Yama.

ལས་ཀྱི་སྲིད་གནས་པ་ལ་ནི་འཇུག་ཡང་ཆིང༔   དབང་ནི་མེད༔

LAE	KYI	SI		NAE PA	LA NI	JU	YANG CHING	WANG	NI ME
karma	of	possible	places		into	enter	also	power	without

(*i.e. not get free from the realms of karmic compulsion*)

I may enter any of the places made possible by my actions. I am powerless.

*Compassionate ones I call on you! I am [or this person called .... is]
crossing over from my familiar world. My world is now abandoned.
I am struck by the great irresistible change. I am friendless, in great
suffering and without protection. I have no benefactor. I have no aid.
The ideas of this life are passing away. I am going off to be among
strangers. I am entering upon great darkness. I am falling into great
danger. I am entering the thick forest of discursive thoughts. I am
carried off by the power of karma. I am advancing into great isolation. I
am swept along by the great ocean. I am pushed by the wind of karma.
Without any resting place I must keep traveling on. I am encountering
frightening appearances. I am caught up in great harm. I am frightened
and terrorised by the agents of Yama. I may enter any of the places
made possible by my actions. I am powerless.*

གཅིག་པོར་འགྲོགས་མེད་པར་འགྲོ་དགོས་པའི་དུས་ལ་བབས་ན་

CHI POR	DRO ME PAR	DRO	GOE PAI	DU	LA BAB	NA
alone	friendless	go	necessary	time	comes	when (now)

Now that the time has come when I must go alone and friendless,

ཐུགས་རྗེ་ཅན་རྣམས་ཆེ་གེ་མོ་སྐྱབས་མེད་པ་

THU JE CHEN NAM	CHE GE MO	KYAB ME PA
compassionate ones (the buddhas and so on)	the one who has died	protector-less

You, the compassionate ones, must give refuge

བདག [འདི་] ལ་སྐྱབས་མཛོད་ཅིག༔

DA	[DI]	LA	KYAB	DZO	CHI
I	[this]	to	protect, give refuge	do	must

To me [or this person ....] for I am without refuge!

མགོན་མེད་པ་ལ་མགོན་མཛོད་ཅིག༔

GON	ME PA	LA	GON	DZO	CHI
protector	without	to	benefit	do	must

Protect me for I am without protection!

དཔུང་གཉེན་མེད་པ་ལ་དཔུང་གཉེན་མཛོད་ཅིག༔

PUNG NYEN   ME PA   LA   PUNG NYEN   DZO   CHI
helper, assistant   without   to   assistance   do   must

Assist me for I am without assistance!

བར་དོའི་མུན་ནག་ཆེན་པོ་ལས་སྐྱོབས་ཤིག༔

BAR DOI   MU NA   CHEN PO   LAE   KYOB   SHI
intermediate state   dark, gloomy   great   from   protect   must

You must protect me from the great darkness of the bardo.

ལས་ཀྱི་རླུང་དམར་ཆེན་པོ་ལས་བཟློག་ཅིག༔

LAE   KYI   LUNG   MAR   CHEN PO   LAE   DO   CHI
karma   of   wind   red   great   from   repel   must
  (pushing me from behind)

You must repel the storm wind of karma.

གཤིན་རྗེའི་འཇིགས་སྐྲག་ཆེན་པོ་ལས་སྐྱོབས་ཤིག༔

SHIN JEI   JI   DRA   CHEN PO   LAE   KYOB   SHI
Yama   terror   fear   great   from   protect   must

Protect me from the great terror of the Lord of Death.

བར་དོའི་འཕྲང་རིང་ཆེན་པོ་ལས་སྒྲོལ་ཅིག༔

BAR DOI   TRANG   RING   CHEN PO   LAE   DROL   CHI
bardo's   narrow   long   difficult way   from   save   must

You must save me from the long and narrow passage of the bardo.

ཐུགས་རྗེ་ཅན་ཁྱེད་རྣམས་ཀྱི་ཐུགས་རྗེ་མ་ཆུང་ཅིག༔

THU JE CHEN   KHYE   NAM   KYI   THU JE   MA CHUNG   CHI
compassionate ones   you   all   of   compassion   not grow less   must

Compassionate ones, your compassion must not weaken!

རམ་དའ་མཛོད་ཅིག༔   ངན་སོང་གསུམ་དུ་མ་བཏང་ཅིག༔

RAM DA DZO   CHI   **NGEN SONG   SUM DU   MA   TANG   CHI**
help,   do   must   *states of woe   three*   not   send   must*
assistance   *(do not let his bad karma*
                                                  send him there)

*hells, insatiable ghosts, animals

You must render assistance. Do not send me into the three lower realms.

སྔོན་གྱིས་དམ་བཅའ་མ་གཡེལ་བར༔

NGON   GYI   DAM CHA   MA   YEL WAR
former   of   vows   not   stray from
(their vows to help all beings)

Keep firmly to the vows you made in former times.

ཕྱགས་རྗེའི་ཕྱགས་སྟོབར་དུ་ཕྱུང་ཞིག༔

THU JEI   SHU   NYUR DU   CHUNG   ZHI
compassion's   power   quickly   make full   must
(in order to help me)

Your compassionate power must quickly reach full strength.

སངས་རྒྱས་དང་བྱང་ཆུབ་སེམས་དཔའ་རྣམས་ཀྱིས༔

SANG GYE   DANG   JANG CHU SEM PA   NAM   KYI
buddhas   and   bodhisattvas   all   by

Buddhas and bodhisattvas,

ཆེ་གེ་མོ་བདག[འདི]་ལ་

CHE GE MO   DA   [DI]   LA
person   I   [this]   to

For me [or this person ....]

ཕྱགས་རྗེས་ཐབས་དང་ནུས་པ་མ་ཆུང་ཞིག༔

THU JE   THAB   DANG   NU PA   MA   CHUNG   ZHI
compassion   method   and   power   not   lessen   must

Your compassionate methods and power must not be allowed to decrease!

ཕྱགས་རྗེས་བཟུང་ཞིག༔

THU JE   ZUNG   ZHI
compassion   hold   must

You must hold me with compassion.

སེམས་ཅན་ལས་ངན་པའི་དབང་དུ་མ་གཏོང་ཞིག༔

SEM CHEN   LAE   NGEN PAI   WANG   DU   MA   TONG   ZHI
sentient beings   karma   bad   of   power   under   not   put, go   must

Prevent beings from falling under the power of our own bad karma.

དཀོན་མཆོག་གསུམ་གྱིས་བདག་ཅག་

KON CHO SUM   GYI   DA CHA
The Three Jewels   by   us

Buddha, Dharma, and Sangha

བར་དོར་སྡུག་བསྔལ་ལས་སྐྱོབས་ཏུ་གསོལ༔

BAR DOR   DU NGAL LAE KYOB TU SOL
bardo   in   suffering from protect please

Please protect us from the sufferings of the bardo.

Now that the time has come when I must go alone and friendless, you, the compassionate ones, must give refuge to me [or this person ....] for I am without refuge! Protect me for I am without protection! Assist me for I am without assistance. You must protect me from the great darkness of the bardo. You must repel the storm wind of karma. Protect me from the great terror of the Lord of Death. You must save me from the long and narrow passage of the bardo. Compassionate ones, your compassion must not weaken! You must render assistance. Do not send me into the three lower realms. Keep firmly to the vows you made in former times. Your compassionate power must quickly reach full strength. Buddhas and bodhisattvas, for this person me [or 'person's name'], your compassionate methods and power must not be allowed to decrease. You must hold me with compassion. Prevent beings from falling under the power of our own bad karma. Buddha, Dharma and Sangha please protect us from the sufferings of the bardo.

ཆེས་མོས་གུས་དྲག་པོའི་སྒོ་ནས༔ བདག་གཞན་ཐམས་ཅད་ཀྱིས་ལན་གསུམ་བྱའོ༔ དེ་ནས་བར་དོ་ཐོས་གྲོལ་དང་འཕྲང་སྒྲོལ་འཇིགས་སྐྱོབ་མའི་སྨོན་ལམ་བཏབ་པར་བྱའོ༔ སངས་རྒྱས་དང་བྱང་ཆུབ་སེམས་དཔའ་རྣམས་ལ་རམ་འདར་སྐྱན་པའི་སྨོན་ལམ་རྫོགས་སོ༔ ས་མ་ཡ༔ རྒྱ་རྒྱ་རྒྱ༔

With the most intense devotion we and all other beings must pray like this three times. Then read the prayers of aspiration for protection from fear given in the Bar-Do Thos-Grol and the Bar-Do 'Phrang-Grol. This concludes The Prayer of Aspiration Requesting Help from the Buddhas and Bodhisattvas. Vows. Seal. Seal. Seal.

ཀརྨ་གླིང་པའི་ཞི་ཁྲོ་ལས་སོ།
[From the Karling Zhitro.]

ཕྱོགས་བཅུའི་དུས་གསུམ་བདེ་གཤེགས་རྣམས༔

CHO	CHUI	DU	SUM	DE SHE NAM
directions	*ten*	*times*	*three*	*Sugatas, Buddhas, also Bodhisattvas*
(i.e. everywhere)		*(past, present, future)*		

Buddhas of the ten directions and the three times

མདུན་གྱི་ནམ་མཁར་སྤྱན་དྲངས་ལ༔

DUN GYI	NAM KHAR	CHEN DRANG	LA
in front of me	*sky*	*to invite*	*then*

I invite you to appear in the sky before me.

རྩེ་གཅིག་གུས་པས་ཕྱག་འཚལ་ལོ༔

TSE CHI	**GU PAE**	**CHA TSHAL LO**
one pointed, unwavering	*devotion, by*	*offer obeisance, salutation*

With one-pointed devotion I offer you salutation.

ཨོཾ་བཛྲ་ས་མ་ཡ་ཛ་ཛ༔

OM	**BEN DZA**	**SA MA YA**	**DZA DZA**
vocative	*vajra, indestructible*	*vows, bonds*	*come! come!*

Om. Keep your vajra vows. Come! Come!

Buddhas of the ten directions and the three times, I invite you to appear in the sky before me. With one-pointed devotion I offer you salutation. Om. Keep your vajra vows. Come! Come!

བཅོམ་ལྡན་འདས་དེ་བཞིན་གཤེགས་པ་དགྲ་བཅོམ་པ་

CHOM DEN DAE	**DE ZHIN SHE PA**	**DRA CHOM PA**
Bhagawan, Victorious	*Tathagata, Buddha*	*Arhat, Triumphant*

Victorious, Thus Gone, Triumphant,

ཡང་དག་པར་རྫོགས་པའི་སངས་རྒྱས།

YANG DA PAR	**DZO PAI**	**SANG GYE**
perfect	*complete*	*Buddha*

(Samyak Sambuddha)

Complete and Perfect Buddha,

མགོན་པོ་འོད་དཔག་ཏུ་མེད་པ་ལ་

GON PO	**OE PA TU ME PA**	**LA**
benefactor	*Amitabha*	*to*

Benefactor Amitabha – to you

ཕྱག་འཚལ་ལོ། མཆོད་དོ། སྐྱབས་སུ་མཆིའོ།

CHA TSHAL LO	**CHO DO**	**KYAB SU CHI O**
salutation, obeisance	*offering*	*go for refuge*

(We salute him because he vowed never to forget those who call on him and to bring them to Dewachen.)

We make salutation, present offerings, and go for refuge.

Victorious, Thus Gone, Triumphant, Complete and Perfect Buddha, Benefactor Amitabha – to you we make salutation, present offerings, and go for refuge.

[Say this three times or more.]

བཅོམ་ལྡན་འདས་དེ་བཞིན་གཤེགས་པ་དགྲ་བཅོམ་པ་

CHOM DEN DAE **DE ZHIN SHE PA** **DRA CHOM PA**
Bhagawan, Victorious *Tathagata, Buddha* *Arhat, Triumphant*

Victorious, Thus Gone, Triumphant,

ཡང་དག་པར་རྫོགས་པའི་སངས་རྒྱས།

YANG DA PAR **DZO PAI** **SANG GYE**
perfect *complete* *Buddha*
   (*Samyak Sambuddha*)

Complete and Perfect Buddha,

མཚན་ལེགས་པར་ཡོངས་བསྒྲགས་དཔལ་གྱི་རྒྱལ་པོ་ལ་

TSHAN **LEG PAR** **YONG** **DRA** **PAL GYI** **GYAL PO** **LA**
name *well* *full* *reading or calling* *glorious* *king* *to*
(The name of the Buddha who promised to save all those who say his name.)

Tshan Legpar Yong Drag Palgyi Gyalpo – to you

ཕྱག་འཚལ་ལོ།   མཆོད་དོ།   སྐྱབས་སུ་མཆིའོ།

CHA TSHAL LO **CHO DO** **KYAB SU CHI O**
salutation, obeisance *offering* *go for refuge*

We make salutation, present offerings, and go for refuge.

Victorious, Thus Gone, Triumphant, Complete and Perfect Buddha,
Tshan Legpar Yong Drag Palgyi Gyalpo – to you we make salutation,
present offerings, and go for refuge.

[At this point you can also read the names of the 1,000 Buddhas.]

བཅོམ་ལྡན་འདས་དེ་བཞིན་གཤེགས་པ་དགྲ་བཅོམ་པ་

CHOM DEN DAE **DE ZHIN SHE PA** **DRA CHOM PA**
Bhagawan, Victorious *Tathagata, Buddha* *Arhat, Triumphant*

Victorious, Thus Gone, Triumphant,

ཡང་དག་པར་རྫོགས་པའི་སངས་རྒྱས།

YANG DA PAR **DZO PAI** **SANG GYE**
perfect *complete* *Buddha*
   (*Samyak Sambuddha*)

Complete and Perfect Buddha,

(འདས་པའི་)སངས་རྒྱས་མར་མེ་མཛད་ལ་

DAE PAI **SANG GYE** **MAR ME DZE** **LA**
passed *Buddha* *Dipamkara* *to*

Earlier Buddha Dipamkara – to you,

ཕྱག་འཚལ་ལོ།   མཆོད་དོ།   སྐྱབས་སུ་མཆིའོ།

CHA TSHAL LO   **CHO DO**   **KYAB SU CHIO**
salute   *offer*   *go for refuge*

We make salutation, present offerings, and go for refuge.

Victorious, Thus Gone, Triumphant, Complete and Perfect Buddha,
Earlier Buddha Dipamkara – to you we make salutation, present
offerings, and go for refuge.

བཅོམ་ལྡན་འདས་དེ་བཞིན་གཤེགས་པ་དགྲ་བཅོམ་པ་

CHOM DEN DAE   **DE ZHIN SHE PA**   **DRA CHOM PA**
Bhagawan, Victorious   *Tathagata, Buddha*   *Arhat, Triumphant*

Victorious, Thus Gone, Triumphant,

ཡང་དག་པར་རྫོགས་པའི་སངས་རྒྱས།

YANG DA PAR   **DZO PAI**   **SANG GYE**
perfect   *complete*   *Buddha*
   (*Samyak Sambuddha*)

Complete and Perfect Buddha,

(མ་འོངས་པའི་)སངས་རྒྱས་བྱམས་པ་མགོན་པོ་ལ་

MA ONG PAI SANG GYE   **JAM PA GON PO**   **LA**
future buddha   *Maitreyanath*   *to*

Future Buddha, Buddha Maitreyanath – to you

ཕྱག་འཚལ་ལོ།   མཆོད་དོ།   སྐྱབས་སུ་མཆིའོ།

CHA TSHAL LO   **CHO DO**   **KYAB SU CHIO**
salute   *offer*   *go for refuge*

We make salutation, present offerings, and go for refuge.

Victorious, Thus Gone, Triumphant, Complete and Perfect Buddha,
the future Buddha, Buddha Maitreyanath – to you we make salutation,
present offerings, and go for refuge.

བཅོམ་ལྡན་འདས་དེ་བཞིན་གཤེགས་པ་དགྲ་བཅོམ་པ་

CHOM DEN DAE   **DE ZHIN SHE PA**   **DRA CHOM PA**
Bhagawan, Victorious   *Tathagata, Buddha*   *Arhat, Triumphant*

Victorious, Thus Gone, Triumphant,

ཡང་དག་པར་རྫོགས་པའི་སངས་རྒྱས།

YANG DA PAR   **DZO PAI**   **SANG GYE**
perfect   *complete*   *Buddha*
   (*Samyak Sambuddha*)

Complete and Perfect Buddha,

དཔལ་རྒྱལ་བ་ཤཱཀྱ་ཐུབ་པ་ལ་

PAL   **GYAL WA**   **SHA KYA THUB PA**   **LA**
glorious   *victor*   *Shakyamuni*   *to*

The glorious Victor, Shakyamuni – to you

ཕྱག་འཚལ་ལོ།   མཆོད་དོ།   སྐྱབས་སུ་མཆིའོ།

CHA TSHAL LO   **CHO DO**   **KYAB SU CHIO**
salutation   *offer*   *go for refuge*

We make salutation, present offerings, and go for refuge.

Our teacher, Victorious, Thus Gone, Triumphant, Complete and Perfect Buddha, the glorious Victor, Shakyamuni – to you we make salutation, present offerings, and go for refuge.

བྱང་ཆུབ་སེམས་དཔའ་སེམས་དཔའ་ཆེན་པོ་

JANG CHU SEM PA   **SEM PA CHEN PO**
Bodhisattva   *Mahasattva*

Bodhisattva, Great Being,

འཕགས་པ་སྤྱན་རས་གཟིགས་འཇིག་རྟེན་དབང་ཕྱུག་ལ་

PHA PA   **CHEN RAE ZI**   **JIG TEN**   **WANG CHU**   **LA**
Arya   *Avalokitesvara*   *world*   *powerful*   *to*

Pure Avalokitesvara[1] powerful in the world – to you

ཕྱག་འཚལ་ལོ།   མཆོད་དོ།   སྐྱབས་སུ་མཆིའོ།

CHA TSHAL LO   **CHO DO**   **KYAB SU CHIO**
salutation   *offer*   *go for refuge*

We make salutation, present offerings, and go for refuge.

Bodhisattva, Great Being, Pure Avalokitesvara powerful in the world – to you we make salutation, present offerings, and go for refuge.

བྱང་ཆུབ་སེམས་དཔའ་སེམས་དཔའ་ཆེན་པོ་

JANG CHU SEM PA   **SEM PA CHEN PO**
Bodhisattva   *Mahasattva*

Bodhisattva, Great Being,

འཕགས་པ་མཐུ་ཆེན་ཐོབ་པ་ལ་

PHA PA   **THU CHEN THO PA**   **LA**
Arya   *Vajrapani, having great power*   *to*

Pure Vajrapani – to you

ཕྱག་འཚལ་ལོ།   མཆོད་དོ།   སྐྱབས་སུ་མཆིའོ།

CHA TSHAL LO   **CHO DO**   **KYAB SU CHIO**
salutation   *offer*   *go for refuge*

We make salutation, present offerings, and go for refuge.

Bodhisattva, Great Being, Pure Vajrapani – to you we make salutation, present offerings, and go for refuge.

བྱང་ཆུབ་སེམས་དཔའ་སེམས་དཔའ་ཆེན་པོ་

JANG CHU SEM PA   **SEM PA CHEN PO**
Bodhisattva   *Mahasattva*

Bodhisattvas, Great Beings,

འཕགས་པ་ཉེ་བའི་སྲས་ཆེན་པོ་བརྒྱད་ལ་

PHA PA   **NYE WAI**   **SAE**   **CHEN PO**   **GYAE**   **LA**
Arya   *close*   *disciples²*   *great*   *eight*   *to*

Arya, eight great close disciples – to you

ཕྱག་འཚལ་ལོ།   མཆོད་དོ།   སྐྱབས་སུ་མཆིའོ།

CHA TSHAL LO   **CHO DO**   **KYAB SU CHIO**
salutation   *offer*   *go for refuge*

We make salutation, present offerings, and go for refuge.

Bodhisattvas, Great Beings, Pure eight great close disciples – to you we offer salutation, present offerings, and go for refuge.

རྗེ་བཙུན་པདྨའི་བྱིན་བརླབ་ཉེར་ཐོབ་ཅིང་།

JE TSUN PAE MAI   **JIN LAB**   **NYER**   **THO CHING**
Padmasambhava's   *blessing*   *fully*   *gained*

You fully gained the blessing of Padmasambhava and

སྦས་ཡུལ་གནས་སྒོ་འབྱེད་ཅིང་ཟབ་གཏེར་བཏོན།

BAE YUL   **NAE**   **GO**   **JE CHING**   **ZAB**   **TER**   **TON**
secret land   *place*   *door*   *opening*   *profound*   *treasures**   *took out, showed*
*the Khordong Terchen Tersar (He got the key directly from Padma Trinlae.)

Opening the door of a secret land you revealed the profound treasure.

གྲུབ་པའི་དབང་ཕྱུག་ནུས་ལྡན་རྡོ་རྗེ་ལ།

DRU PAI   **WONG CHU**   **NU DEN DOR JE**   **LA**
siddhas,   *Lord, powerful*   *(name of Khordong terchen*   *to*
saints   *one*   *Dropan Lingpa Nuden Dorje)*

Nuden Dorje, lord of siddhas, –

 གསོལ་བ་བདེབས་སོ་འཕོ་བའི་ལམ་བསྒྲོད་ཤོག།

SOL WA DE SO	PHO WAI	LAM	DROE	SHO
pray	*transference*	*path*	*go well*	*must*

We pray to you that our practice of transference will go well.

You fully gained the blessing of Padmasambhava, and opening the door of a secret land you revealed the profound treasure. Nuden Dorje, lord of siddhas, we pray to you that our practice of transference will go well.

ཡེ་ནས་རང་རིག་གདོད་མའི་ཆོས་དབྱིངས་སུ།

YE NE	RANG	RIG	DOE MAI	CHO YING	SU
from the beginning	*intrinsic*	*awareness*	*primordial, original*	*dharmadhatu, infinite hospitality*	*in*

From the very beginning in the primordial infinite hospitality intrinsic awareness

ཆོས་ཀུན་རྣམ་པར་གྲོལ་བའི་སྒྱུ་འཕྲུལ་གྱིས།

CHO	KUN	NAM PAR DROL WAI		GYU TRUL	GYI
phenomena	*all*	*fully freed*		*illusions*	*by*

Completely liberates all phenomena as illusion.

མཐའ་ཡས་རྒྱལ་བའི་འཁོར་ལོའི་མགོན་གཅིག་པུ།

THA YAE	GYAL WAI	KHOR LOI	GON	CHI PU
limitless	*Jina, Victor (Gonpo Wangyal)*	*doctrines*	*lord*	*one, sole (i.e. great one)*

You are the sole master of the limitless doctrines of the buddha,

དབང་བསྒྱུར་གྲུབ་པའི་བླ་མ་གང་དེ་ལ།

WANG GYUR	DRU PAI	LA MA	GANG DE	LA
powerful	*gained*	*Guru*	*him*	*to*

Powerful siddha guru –

 གསོལ་བ་འདེབས་སོ་འཕོ་བའི་ལམ་བསྒྲོད་ཤོག།

SOL WA DE SO	PHO WAI	LAM	DROE	SHO
pray	*transference*	*path*	*go well*	*must*

We pray to you that our practice of transference will go well.

From the very beginning in the primordial infinite hospitality intrinsic awareness completely liberates all phenomena as illusion. You are the sole master of the limitless doctrines of the buddha, powerful siddha guru – we pray to you that our practice of transference will go well.

ཀལ་ལྡན་སྨིན་གྲོལ་ཨུ་རྒྱན་གླིང་མཆོག་ཏུ།

KAL DEN	MIN	DROL	UR GYEN	LING	CHO	TU
fortunate	*ripening*	*liberating*	*Padma**	*island*	*excellent*	*in*
	(initiation)	*(doctrines)*				

* He went to Zangdopalri and got blessings, initiations and doctrines from Padmasambhava.

You, the fortunate one ripening and liberating in the excellent realm of Padmasambhava

བདེ་སྟོང་ཟུང་འཇུག་འོད་གསལ་ཆེན་པོའི་དོན།

DE	TONG	ZUNG JU	OE SAL	CHEN POI	DON
happiness	*sunyata*	*fully merged*	*clear light*	*great*	*direct meaning*

Awakened to the great clear light, the union of bliss and emptiness.

མངོན་སུམ་སྟོན་མཛད་རོལ་པའི་རྡོ་རྗེ་ལ།

NGON SUM	TON	DZAE	ROL PAI DOR JE	LA
manifesting	*show*	*did*	*Dechen Rolpai Dorje**	*to*
(He was able to teach these				
methods to others)				

* He was the second incarnation of Nuden Dorje

Dechen Rolpai Dorje, you clearly taught this to others.

གསོལ་བ་འདེབས་སོ་འཕོ་བའི་ལམ་བསྒྲོད་ཤོག

SOL WA DE SO	PHO WAI	LAM	DROE	SHO
pray	*transference*	*path*	*go well*	*must*

We pray to you that our practice of transference will go well.

You, the fortunate one ripening and liberating in the excellent realm of Padmasambhava awakened to the great clear light, the union of bliss and emptiness. Dechen Rolpai Dorje, you clearly taught this to others. We pray to you that our practice of transference will go well.

དམ་པ་དེ་དག་ཀུན་གྱིས་རྗེས་བཟུང་ཞིང་།

DAM PA	DE DA	KUN	GYI	JE ZUNG ZHING
holy one	*these*	*all*	*by*	*held as disciple*
(all the lineage gurus)				

You are held as a disciple by all the holy ones,

ངུར་སྨྲིག་འཛིན་པ་བཏུལ་ཞུགས་དམ་པ་ཡི།

NGUR MIG	DZIN PA	TUL ZHU	DAM PA	YI
red robes	*wearing*	*determined*	*holy, excellent*	*of*
(he was a monk)		*practitioner*		

Most excellent determined practitioner dressed in red,

ক্রুন্'ন্মুব'উন্'র্ম্বিক'ন্রীনিম্বিপ্রান্মেন্মত্তব্ব|

GYAL	TEN	NYING MOR	JE PAI	LHA	SAM	CHEN
Jina,	*doctrine*	*daytime*	*as*	*doing*	*good,*	*thought*	*possessor*
Buddha					*superior*		

You whose superior intentions bring about the daytime of the doctrines of the Buddha,

ক্রুন্'ট্রিমম'নর্ত্ত'র্মবি'ত্রন্ম'ন'নার্ম্ন'ন'ন্বেন্ন্ম|

TSHUL TRIM ZANG POI	ZHAB	LA	SOL WA DE
(He was an incarnation of	*feet*	*to*	*pray*
Vimalamitra and the guru of C R Lama)			

Tshultrim Zangpo, at your feet we pray.

ন্বেন্'নবি'মন্ব'র্ষ্ন্'নেন্রুন্'নহ'ট্রিব'ট্রীম'র্ষ্লুনম|

PHO WAI	KHA CHO	DRU PAR	JIN GYI LO
transference	*Khacho*	*accomplish*	*bless*
	pure realm		

Please bless us that we may succeed in our transference to the pure realm of Khacho.

You who are held as a disciple by all the holy ones, most excellent determined practitioner dressed in red, you whose superior intentions bring about the daytime of the doctrines of the Buddha – please bless us that we may succeed in our transference to the pure realm of Khacho.

নন্'স্লুব'ৰিন্'ন্'স্লুন'মবন'ন্বিন'ম্বি'নেগ্রুন|

DE DEN ZHING	DU	NANG THA	OE MI GYUR
Sukhavati Kshetra,	*in*	*Amitabha*	*Unchanging Light*
Dewachen realm			*(Dharmakaya form)*

Amitabha Unchanging Light, in the realm of Dewachen,

ৰিম্ব'ন্'মন্'নেমনাম'মৰ্ক্তনা'ষ্ণিন্'ৰ্ত্তবি'নানিন|

RI	PO TA LAR	PHA	CHO	NYING JEI	TER
Mt.	*Potala*	*in*	*arya, pure,*	*excellent*	*compassion's*	*treasure*
			noble		*(Chenrezi, Sambhogakaya form)*

Chenrezi, the noble treasure of compassion at Mt. Potala,

ৰ'অন'ষ্লিন্'ন্'ন্মু'র্মন'ম্বিন'ৰ্ক্তন|

NGA YAB LING	DU	PAE MA THO TRENG TSAL
Fly-Whisk Island, site	*in*	*a wrathful form of Padmasambhava*
of Zangdo Palri, the Pure		*(Nirmanakaya form)*
Land of Padmasambhava		

Padma Thod Treng Tsal at Zangdo Palri —

དབྱེར་མེད་སྐྱབས་ཀུན་འདུས་ཞལ་བླ་མ་རྗེ།

YER ME	KYAB	KUN	DU	ZHAL	LA MA	JE
not different, inseparable	*refuge*	*all*	*assemble*	*face*	*Guru*	*special*

These, our inseparable protectors, are gathered within our Guru.

Amitabha Unchanging Light, in the realm of Dewachen, Chenrezi, the noble treasure of compassion at Mt. Potala, Padma Thod Treng Tsal at Zangdo Palri — these, our inseparable protectors, are gathered within our Guru.

ཚིག་བདུན་གསོལ་འདེབས།   SEVEN LINE PRAYER

ཧཱུྃ༔ ཨོ་རྒྱན་ཡུལ་གྱི་ནུབ་བྱང་མཚམས༔

HUNG	UR GYEN YUL	GYI	NUB JANG	TSHAM
vocative, seed letter of Padmasambhava	*Oddiyana, the dakinis' land*	*of*	*north-west*	*border, corner*

Hung. In the land of Urgyen's north-west corner,

པདྨ་གེ་སར་སྡོང་པོ་ལ༔

PAE MA	GE SAR	DONG PO	LA
lotus	*stamen*	*stem*	*on*

Upon a lotus stem and stamen,

ཡ་མཚན་མཆོག་གི་དངོས་གྲུབ་བརྙེས༔

YAM TSHEN	CHO GI	NGO DRU	NYE
marvellous, wonderful	*supreme*	*siddhis, attainments (i.e. buddhahood)*	*has got*

With marvellous and supreme accomplishments,

པདྨ་འབྱུང་གནས་ཞེས་སུ་གྲགས༔

PAE MA JUNG NAE		ZHE SU	DRA
Padmasambhava, Guru Rinpoche		*known as*	*famous*

The Lotus Born is your famous name.

འཁོར་དུ་མཁའ་འགྲོ་མང་པོས་བསྐོར༔

KHOR	DU	KHAN DRO	MANG POE	KOR
retinue	*as*	*dakinis, sky-goddesses (here it means all sky travelling deities)*	*many* *by*	*surrounded*

As retinue many dakinis surround you.

ཁྱེད་ཀྱི་རྗེས་སུ་བདག་སྒྲུབ་ཀྱིས༔

KHYE   KYI JE SU   DA   DRU   KYI
you   following after,   I   practice   by that
emulating

Following and relying on you, I do your practice, therefore,

བྱིན་གྱིས་བརླབ་ཕྱིར་གཤེགས་སུ་གསོལ༔

JIN GYI LAB   CHIR   SHE SU SOL
blessing   in order to   please come

In order to bless us, please come here!

གུ་རུ་པདྨ་སིདྡྷི་ཧཱུྃ༔

GU RU   PAE MA   SID DHI   HUNG
guru, master   Padmasambhava   real attainment   give me!

Guru Padmasambhava grant us the accomplishment of buddhahood!

*Hung. In the land of Urgyen's north-west corner, upon a lotus stem
and stamen, with marvellous and supreme accomplishments, the Lotus
Born is your famous name. As retinue many dakinis surround you.
Following and relying on you, I do your practice, therefore, in order to
bless us, please come here!*

ཞེས་ཅི་ནུས་དང་།

[Recite this as many times as you can with true devotion from your heart.]

བསྟོད་པ་ PRAISE

ཧཱུྃ༔   མ་བཅོས་སྤྲོས་བྲལ་བླ་མ་ཆོས་ཀྱི་སྐུ༔

HUNG   MA CHOE   TOE DRAL   LA MA   CHOE KYI KU
Hung   unartificial   without elaboration   guru   dharmakaya, intrinsic mode

Hung. The guru without artifice or elaboration is the intrinsic mode.

བདེ་ཆེན་ལོངས་སྤྱོད་བླ་མ་ཆོས་ཀྱི་རྗེ༔

DE   CHEN   LONG CHO   LA MA   CHOE   KYI   JE
bliss   great   sambhogakaya,   guru   dharma   of   lord
enjoyment

The guru of great happiness, master of dharma, is the enjoyment mode.

པད་སྡོང་ལས་འཁྲུངས་བླ་མ་སྤྲུལ་པའི་སྐུ༔

PAE   DONG   LAE   THRUNG   LA MA   TRUL PAI KU
lotus   stem   from   born   guru   nirmanakaya, apparition mode

The lotus born guru is the apparitional mode.

ཀུ་གསུམ་རྡོ་རྗེ་འཆང་ལ་ཕྱག་འཆལ་བསྟོད༔

KU	SUM	DOR JE CHANG	LA	CHA TSAL	TO
body	*three*	*Vajradhara*	*to*	*prostrate*	*praise*

We salute and praise Vajradhara with these three modes.

Hung. The guru without artifice or elaboration is the intrinsic mode. The guru of great happiness, master of dharma, is the enjoyment mode. The lotus born guru is the apparitional mode. We salute and praise you, the Vajradhara having these three modes.

སྙིང་ནས་མོས་གདུང་དྲག་པོས་གསོལ་འདེབས་ན།

NYING	NE	MOE	DUNG	DRAG POE	SOL DE	NA
heart, i.e. sincerely	*from*	*faith*	*devotion*	*very strong, with*	*pray*	*due to this therefore*

We pray to you from our hearts with fierce faith and devotion, so

རྟག་ཏུ་བརྩེ་བས་རྗེས་བཟུང་བྱིན་རླབས་སྩོལ།

TAG TU	TSE WAE	JE ZUNG	JIN LAB	TSOL
always	*compassion*	*hold all sentient beings*	*blessing*	*bestow*

Please always hold us always with your compassion and bestow your blessing.

གནས་སྐབས་ཕྱི་ནང་འགལ་རྐྱེན་བར་ཆད་ཞི།

NAE KAB	CHI	NANG	GAL KYEN	BAR CHAE	ZHI
in this life, on occasion	*outer*	*inner*	*difficult situations*	*obstacles*	*pacify*

Pacify outer and inner difficulties and obstacles as they occur, and

ཚེ་རིང་བདེ་འབྱོར་བསམ་དོན་ལྷུན་གྱིས་འགྲུབ།

TSHE	RING	DE	JOR	SAM DON	LHUN GYI DRU
life	*long*	*happiness*	*riches*	*whatever I desire*	*get easily*

Grant us long life, happiness, riches and the effortless accomplishment of our wishes.

We pray to you from our hearts with fierce faith and devotion, so please always hold us with your compassion and bestow your blessing. Pacify outer and inner difficulties and obstacles as they occur and grant us long life, happiness, riches and the effortless accomplishment of our wishes.

ཆོས་མིན་ལྟ་ངན་རྒྱུད་ལ་མི་སྐྱེ་བར།

CHO	MIN	TA	NGAN	GYU	LA	MI	KYE WAR
dharma	not	views	bad	mind	in	not	arising

With wrong views and non-dharma not arising in our minds

ཆོས་མཐུན་དཀར་པོའི་བསམ་སྦྱོར་གོང་དུ་འཕེལ།

CHO THUN	KAR POI	SAM	JOR	GONG DU PHEL
dharmic	pure, virtuous	thoughts	actions	increasing more to more

May our dharmic virtuous intentions and actions increase evermore.

ནམ་ཞིག་འཆི་ཁ་གནད་གཅོད་མི་སྨྱོང་ཞིང་།

NAM ZHI	CHI KHA	NAE	CHO	MI	NYONG ZHING
when	moment of death	sickness	trouble	not	experiencing

Not experiencing sickness and trouble at the moment of death,

འཕོས་མ་ཐག་ཏུ་མཁའ་འགྲོས་མདུན་བསུས་ནས།

PHO	MA THAG TU	KHAN DRO	DUN	SU	NE
go out from the top of the head	immediately	dakinis	before me	wait for	then

May we immediately leave our bodies and meet the dakinis waiting to guide us.

With wrong views and non-dharma not arising in our minds, may our dharmic virtuous intentions and actions increase evermore. Not experiencing sickness and trouble at the moment of death, may we immediately leave our bodies and meet the dakinis waiting to guide us.

པདྨ་འོད་ཀྱི་ཞིང་དུ་སྐྱེས་ནས་ཀྱང་།

PAE MA	OE	KYI	ZHING	DU	KYE	NE	KYANG
lotus	light	of	realm	in	born	then	also

Taking birth in the realm of Lotus Light, may we

གུ་རུའི་ཞལ་མཐོང་གསུང་གི་ལུང་ནོད་དེ།

GU RUI	ZHAL	THONG	SUNG	GI	LUNG	NOE	DE
Padmasambhava's	face	see	speech	of	instructions	hear	then

See the face of Padmasambhava and hear teaching from him.

ས་ལམ་ཡོན་ཏན་མིག་འཕྲུལ་ལྟ་བུར་འགྲོད།

SA	LAM	YON TEN	MIG TRUL	TA BUR	TRO
bhumi 10 stages	marga 5 paths	good qualities	miracle	like	go up, gain

May we miraculously ascend the Stages and Paths and gain all good qualities.

 རང་གཞན་དོན་གཉིས་མཐར་རུ་ཕྱིན་པར་ཤོག།

RANG	ZHEN	DON	NYI	THA RU CHIN PAR	SHO
myself	*others*	*benefit*	*both*	*fully accomplished*	*may*
(i.e. Buddhahood)					

May we fulfil profound benefit for ourselves and all others.

Taking birth in the realm of Lotus Light, may we see the face of Padmasambhava and hear him teach. May we miraculously ascend the Stages and Paths and gain all good qualities. May we achieve profound benefit for ourselves and all others.

འདོད་དོན་གསོལ་བ་ནི༔ PRAYING FOR WHAT WE WANT

ཕྱི་ལྟར་བརྡ་དོན་རྟགས་རྫོགས་རྔ་ཡབ་གླིང༔

CHI	TAR	DA DON	TA	DZO	NGA YAB LING
outer	*as*	*symbolic*	*signs[3]*	*perfected*	*Fly-Whisk Island*
generally		*meaning*			*(where Padmasambhava is now)*

Generally, on Fly-Whisk Island where the perfect signs indicate profound meaning,

ནང་ལྟར་རང་ལུས་ཕུང་ཁམས་མཁའ་འགྲོའི་གྲོང༔

NANG	TAR	RANG	LUE	PHUNG	KHAM	KHA DROI	DRONG
inner	*as*	*own*	*body*	*five[4]*	*eighteen[5]*	*dakinis'*	*place, city[6]*
				skandhas	*dhatus*		

In particular, in the dakinis' city of the constituents and generative factors of our own body,

གསང་བ་བདེ་སྟོང་དབྱེར་མེད་ཐིག་ལེའི་ཀློང༔

SANG WA	DE TONG	YER ME	THIG LEI	LONG
secret[7],	*emptiness and*	*not different,*	*ball's,[8]*	*centre*
deeply	*great bliss*	*inseparable*	*sphere's*	

Secretly, in the vastness of the sphere of the inseparability of bliss and emptiness,

ཡང་གསང་བྱ་རྩོལ་བྲལ་བ་གཉུག་མའི་གཤིས༔

YANG	SANG	JA	TSOL	DRAL WA	NYUG MAI	SHI
very	*secret[9]*	*deed*	*effort[10]*	*without[11]*	*original, unchanging*	*nature*

And most secretly, in and as our original unchanging nature free of deeds and effort,

རང་བྱུང་རང་ཤར་རང་གྲོལ་བདེ་བ་ཆེ༔

RANG JUNG	RANG SHAR	RANG DROL	DE WA	CHE
spontaneous	*self-arising*	*self-liberating, self-vanishing*	*happiness*	*great, empty*

There is the spontaneous self-arising self-liberating great happiness

གཉིས་མེད་རྒྱལ་པོ་དོན་གྱི་ཧེ་རུ་ཀ༔

NYI ME		GYAL PO	DON GYI	HE RU KA
non-dual, free of both samsara or nirvana[13]		*king of*	*genuine, original*	*Heruka*[12]

The king of nonduality, the genuine original Heruka,

གནས་གསུམ་མཁའ་འགྲོའི་གཙོ་བོ་པདྨ་འབྱུང༔

NAE	SUM	KHA DROI	TSO WO	PAE MA JUNG
places	*three**	*dakinis"*	*chief*	*Padmasambhava***

* Three places of body, speech and mind, where they stay and function.
** In his various aspects Padmasambhava resides in all those places.

Padmasambhava the chief of the dakinis of the three places.

སྐུ་གསུམ་དབྱེར་མེད་ཞབས་ལ་གསོལ་བ་འདེབས༔

KU	SUM	YER ME	ZHAB	LA	SOL WA DE
bodies, modes	*three**	*not different, not separate*	*feet*	*to*	*I pray*

* Dharmakaya, Sambhogakaya, Nirmanakaya

We pray to you in whom the three modes are inseparable.

Generally, on Fly-Whisk Island where the perfect signs indicate profound meaning; in particular in the dakinis' city of the constituents and generative factors of our own body; secretly in the vastness of the sphere of the inseparability of bliss and emptiness; and most secretly, in and as our original, unchanging nature free of deeds and effort, there is the spontaneous self-arising self-liberating great happiness, the king of nonduality, the genuine original Heruka, Padmasambhava, the chief of the dakinis of the three places. We pray to you in whom the three modes are inseparable.

ཞེས་གྲང་མང་བཟླས་རེས༔

[Pray like this three or more times.]

 དེ་ལྟར་གསོལ་བ་བཏབ་པའི་བྱིན་རླབས་ཀྱིས༔

DE TAR   SOL WA TA PAI   JIN LAB   KYI
like that   praying's   blessing   by

By the blessing of having prayed in this way

ཚེ་འདིར་མངོན་སུམ་ཁྱོད་ཞལ་མྱུར་མཇལ་ནས༔

TSE   DIR   NGON SUM   KHYO   ZHAL   NYUR   JAL   NAE
life   this   clearly,   your   face   quickly   meet, see   then
          manifestly   by the blessing of that

(See that we are not other than Padmasambhava)

In this life may we quickly see your face directly.

ཉོན་མོངས་ཤེས་བྱའི་སྒྲིབ་པ་ཀུན་དག་ཅིང༔

NYON MONG   SHE JAI   DRIB PA   KUN   DA   CHING
afflictions   subtle traces**   obscurations#   all   purify   then*
*stupidity, anger, desire, pride, jealousy ** habits from the long practice of stupidity and sin
whatever hides the truth, the afflictions and their traces

Then with all obscurations arising from the afflictions and subtle traces
being purified,

གཞོན་ནུ་བུམ་སྐུའི་རང་ཞལ་མཇལ་བར་ཤོག༔

ZHON NU   BUM   KUI   RANG   ZHAL   JAL WAR   SHO
youthful   pot   body   own   face   meet, see   may I, we*
                           (my own original presence)
* Our original nature of emptiness is always young and fresh, yet it is hidden in the pot of
our afflictions.

May we see our own true face, the ever-young original presence !

*By the blessing of having prayed in this way in this life may we quickly
see your face directly. Then with all obscurations arising from the afflictions and subtle traces being purified may we see our own true face, the
ever-young original presence!*

འདི་སྣང་ནུབ་ཚེ་དཔའ་བོ་མཁའ་འགྲོའི་ཚོགས༔

DI   NANG   NUB   TSE   PA WO   KHA DROI   TSO
this   life[14]   ending   time   viras, heroes   dakinis   host

When this life is ending, may hosts of viras and dakinis

རོལ་མོ་སྒྲ་སྙན་གླུ་དབྱངས་དམ་ཆོས་སྒྲས༔

ROL MO   DRA   NYEN   LU   YANG   DAM   CHOE   DRAE
music   sound   sweet   songs   melodies   holy   dharma   sound

Make sweet-sounding music and melodious songs, all with the sound
of the holy Dharma.

ཌཱ་མ་རུ་དང་མཆོད་རྫས་ཐོགས་བྱས་ནས༔

DA MA RU	DANG	CHO DZAE	THO JAE	NAE
damaru, double-headed hand drum	and	offering things	hold aloft, i.e. using	then

Holding damarus and offerings,

ས་སྤྱོད་ཌཱ་ཡབ་དཔལ་རིར་འཁྲིད་པར་ཤོག༔

SA CHO	NGA YAB	PAL RIR		TRI PAR	SHO
those who move on the land	Fly Whisk	Glorious Mountain (Padmasambhava's palace at Zangdopalri)		lead, guide	may they

May they guide us to the glorious mountain on Fly Whisk Island.

When this life is ending may hosts of viras and dakinis make sweet-sounding music and melodious songs, all with the sound of the holy Dharma. Holding damarus and offerings may they guide us to the glorious mountain on Fly Whisk Island[15].

དེ་མ་ཐག་པར་གུ་རུ་ཡབ་ཡུམ་གྱི༔

DE MA THAG PAR	GU RU	YAB YUM	GYI
immediately, at that time	Padmasambhava	with his consort	of

Immediately on arriving there may we see the face of Padmasambhava with his consort

ཞལ་མཇལ་གསུང་ཐོས་གདམས་ངག་ཀུན་ཐོབ་ནས༔

ZHAL	JAL	SUNG	THOE	DAM NGA	KUN	THO	NAE
face	meet	speech	hear	instruction	all	get	then

Hear his speech and receive all instructions from him.

ས་ལམ་མཐར་ཕྱིན་རིག་འཛིན་རྣམ་པ་བཞིའི༔

SA	LAM	THAR CHIN	RIG DZIN	NAM PA	ZHI
ten stages, or bhumis	five paths[16], or margas	fulfil, finish, complete	vidydhara, holder of natural awareness.	kinds, degrees	four

Then, completing the Stages[17] and Paths[18], may we quickly ascend the four[19] ranks of sages.

གོ་འཕང་མྱུར་ཐོབ་ཨོ་རྒྱན་པདྨ་དང༔

GO PHANG	NYUR	THO	UR GYEN PAE MA	DANG
stages, rank	quickly*	get	Padmasambhava	and

* All this can be during just one deep meditation.

Then becoming identical with Padmasambhava

དབྱེར་མེད་འགྲོ་བའི་དཔལ་དུ་བདག་གྱུར་ནས༔

YER ME	DRO WAI	PAL	DU	DA	GYUR	NAE
not different from	*beings in samsara*	*benefit*	*for*	*I*	*become*	*then*

May we be of great benefit for those who move in samsara, and

མཁའ་མཉམ་འགྲོ་བ་མ་ལུས་འདྲེན་པར་ཤོག༔

KHA	NYAM	DRO WA	MA LUE	DREN PAR	SHO
sky	*equalling*	*beings in samsara*	*without exception*	*guide, leader*	*may I be*

May we be guides for all beings without exception, as many as would equal the sky.

Immediately on arriving there may we see the face of Padmasambhava with his consort, hear his speech and receive all instructions from him. Then, completing the Stages and Paths, may we quickly ascend the four ranks of sages. Then becoming identical with Padmasambhava may we be of great benefit for those who move in samsara, and may we be guides for all beings without exception, as many as would equal the sky.

Gentle Transference

རང་གི་སྙིང་ཁ་ནས་རྟ་ཡབ་དཔལ་རིའི་བར་དུ་

RANG GI	NYING KHA		NAE	NGA YAB	PAL RI	BAR DU
my	*mind, heart centre*		*from*	*Fly Whisk*,*	*Zangdopalri*	*up to, until*

*the rakashasa island where Padmasambhava stays

From my heart centre to the glorious mountain of Zangdopalri

འོད་ལྔའི་ལམ་གསལ་ཞིང་འཚེར་བ་ཐལ་ལེ་འཇུག་པའི་

OE	NGAI*	LAM	SAL ZHING	TSHER WA	THAL LE	JU PAI
light	*five*	*path*	*clear*	*shining*	*direct*	*emerge, joining*

*white, red, blue, yellow, green

A path of five-coloured light emerges, clear, shining and direct.

སྟེང་དུ་རང་སེམས་རང་གཟུགས་ཀྱི་རྣམ་པ་ཅན་གྱི་

TENG DU	RANG	SEM	RANG	ZU	KYI	NAM PA	CHEN	GYI
on top of	*own*	*mind*	*own*	*form*	*of*	*form (one's present body of this life)*	*having*	*of*

My mind travels along it with the form of my present body.

གཡས་གཡོན་མདུན་རྒྱབ་ཐམས་ཅད་དཔའ་བོ་རིག་འཛིན་མཁའ་འགྲོའི་

YAE	YON	DUN	GYAB	THAM CHE	PA WO	RIG DZIN	KHAN DROI
right side	*left side*	*in front*	*at the back*	*everywhere*	*viras*	*vidyadhara*	*dakinis*

On my right and on my left, in front and behind, are all the heroes, vidyadharas and dakinis.

ཚོགས་ཀྱི་གྲོགས་དང་བཅས་ཏེ་

TSHO	KYI	DRO		DANG CHE	TE
hosts	*of*	*friends,helpers*		*together*	*then*

Together with these hosts of helpers,

འོད་ཀྱི་ལམ་གྱི་སྟེང་ན་ཕར་

OE	KYI	LAM	GYI TENG NA	PHAR
light	*of*	*path*	*on top of*	*beyond*

To the far end of this path of light

ཉམས་དགའ་ཡལ་ཡལ་བྱིན་འཐིབ་འཐིབ་

NYAM	GA	YAL YAL	JIN	THIB THIB
feeling	*happy*	*light and happy*	*blessing*	*enveloping haze*

(we get happier and happier the nearer we come to Zangdopalri)

I travel instantly, effortlessly, happily,

སྣང་བ་བདེ་ཆམ་ཆམ་ཕྱིན་ཏེ་

NANG WA   **DE**   **CHAM CHAM**   **CHIN**   **TE**
idea, feeling   *happy*   *spontaneous*   *go there*   *then*
(we get happier and happier the nearer we come to Zangdopalri)

Joyfully, enveloped in blessing.

འཇིག་རྟེན་མི་ཡུལ་གྱི་སྣང་བ་

JIG TEN   **MI**   **YUL GYI**   **NANG WA**
world*   *human*   *country's*   *ideas*
*and all of samsara

The appearances and recollections of human life in this world

ཐིབ་ཐིབ་ནུབ་ཏེ་ཕྱིར་ཕྱིར་ལུས་

THIB THIB   **NUB**   **TE**   **CHIR CHIR**   **LU**
fade away   *decline and vanish*   *then*   *successively*   *left behind*

Fade and vanish one after another until all are left far behind.

མཁའ་སྤྱོད་ཟངས་མདོག་དཔལ་རི་བཀྲ་ལམ་ལམ་ཤར།

KHA CHO ZANG DO PAL RI   **TRA**   **LAM LAM**   **SHAR**
Zangdopalri, as approached   *bright*   *vivid*   *arises*
through the sky

Then Khacho Zangdopalri appears clear and vivid in front of me.

ཨོ་རྒྱན་པདྨ་རིག་འཛིན་ཡི་དམ་མཁའ་འགྲོའི་དབུས་ན་

OR GYEN PAE MA   **RIG DZIN**   **YI DAM**   **KHAN DROI**   **WU**   **NA**
Padmasambhava   *vidyadharas*   *path deity*   *dakinis*   *centre*   *in*

In the centre of many vidyadharas, path deities, and dakinis Padmasambhava is

བཞུགས་པ་དང་ཇེ་ཉེར་སོང་ཏེ་མཐར་རང་གཟུགས་

ZHU PA   **DANG**   **JE NYER SONG**   **TE**   **THAR**   **RANG**   **ZU**
Sitting   *and*   *we approach nearer and nearer*   *then*   *finally*   *own*   *body*

Sitting and I approach closer and closer until finally my body

གུ་རུའི་ཐུགས་ཀར་སིབ་ཀྱིས་ཐིམ་པར་བསམ།

GU RUI   **THU KAR**   **SIB**   **KYI**   **THIM PAR**   **SAM**
Guru Rinpoche's   *his heart, in*   *melt*   *by*   *absorbed, as*   *believe*
(like two drops of water merging inseparably)

Is absorbed into his heart and dissolves in it.

From my heart centre to the glorious mountain of Zangdopalri a path of five-coloured light emerges, clear, shining and direct. My mind travels along it with the form of my present body. On my right and on my

left, in front and behind, are all the heroes, vidyadharas and dakinis. Together with these hosts of helpers, to the far end of this path of light I travel instantly, effortlessly, happily, joyfully, enveloped in blessing. The appearances and recollections of human life in this world fade and vanish one after another until all are left far behind. Then Khacho Zangdopalri appears clear and vivid in front of me. In the centre of many vidyadharas, path deities, and dakinis Padmasambhava is sitting and I approach closer and closer until finally my body is absorbed into his heart and dissolves in it.

ལ་བདེ་འབོལ་ལེ་བཞག།

[Then remain there relaxed and happy.]

ཚིག་བདུན་གསོལ་འདེབས། SEVEN LINE PRAYER

ཧཱུྂ༔ ཨོ་རྒྱན་ཡུལ་གྱི་ནུབ་བྱང་མཚམས༔

HUNG   **UR GYEN YUL**   **GYI**   **NUB JANG**   **TSHAM**
vocative, seed letter   *Oddiyana, the*   *of*   *north-west*   *border,*
of Padmasambhava   *dakinis' land*   *corner*

Hung. In the land of Urgyen's north-west corner,

པདྨ་གེ་སར་སྡོང་པོ་ལ༔

PAE MA   **GE SAR**   **DONG PO**   **LA**
lotus   *stamen*   *stem*   *on*

Upon a lotus stem and stamen,

ཡ་མཚན་མཆོག་གི་དངོས་གྲུབ་བརྙེས༔

YAM TSHEN   **CHO GI**   **NGO DRU**   **NYE**
marvellous,   *supreme*   *siddhis, attainments*   *has got*
wonderful   *(i.e. buddhahood)*

With marvellous and supreme accomplishments,

པདྨ་འབྱུང་གནས་ཞེས་སུ་གྲགས༔

PAE MA JUNG NAE   **ZHE SU**   **DRA**
Padmasambhava, Guru Rinpoche   *known as*   *famous*
                                (famed as)

The Lotus Born is your famous name.

འཁོར་དུ་མཁའ་འགྲོ་མང་པོས་བསྐོར༔

KHOR   **DU**   **KHAN DRO**   **MANG POE**   **KOR**
retinue   *as*   *dakinis, sky-goddesses*   *many*   *by*   *surrounded*
              (here it means all sky travelling deities)

As retinue many dakinis surround you.

ཁྱེད་ཀྱི་རྗེས་སུ་བདག་སྒྲུབ་ཀྱིས༔

KHYE	KYI JE SU	DA	DRU	KYI
you	following after, emulating	I	practice	by that

Following and relying on you, I do your practice, therefore,

བྱིན་གྱིས་བརླབ་ཕྱིར་གཤེགས་སུ་གསོལ༔

JIN GYI LAB	CHIR	SHE SU SOL
blessing	in order to	please come

In order to bless us, please come here!

གུ་རུ་པད་མ་སིདྡྷི་ཧཱུྃ༔

GU RU	PAE MA	SID DHI	HUNG
guru, master	Padmasambhava	real attainment	give me!

Guru Padmasambhava grant us the accomplishment of buddhahood!

Hung. In the land of Urgyen's north-west corner, upon a lotus stem and stamen, with marvellous and supreme accomplishments, the Lotus Born is your famous name. As retinue many dakinis surround you. Following and relying on you, I do your practice, therefore, in order to bless us, please come here!

ཞེས་ཅི་ནུས་དང་།

[Recite this as many times as you can with true devotion from your heart.]

PRAY

ཧཱུྃ༔ མ་བཅོས་སྤྲོས་བྲལ་བླ་མ་ཆོས་ཀྱི་སྐུ༔

HUNG	MA CHOE	TOE DRAL	LA MA	CHOE KYI KU
hung	unartificial	without elaboration	guru	dharmakaya, intrinsic mode

Hung. The guru free of artifice and elaboration is the intrinsic mode.

བདེ་ཆེན་ལོངས་སྤྱོད་བླ་མ་ཆོས་ཀྱི་རྗེ།

DE	CHEN	LONG CHOE	LA MA	CHOE	KYI	JE
bliss	great	sambhogakaya, enjoyment	guru	dharma	of	lord

The guru of great happiness, master of dharma, is the enjoyment mode.

པད་སྡོང་ལས་འཁྲུངས་བླ་མ་སྤྲུལ་པའི་སྐུ༔

PAE	DONG	LAE	THRUNG	LA MA	TRUL PAI KU
lotus	stem	from	born	guru	nirmanakaya, apparitional mode

The guru born from a lotus stem is the apparitional mode.

སྐུ་གསུམ་རྡོ་རྗེ་འཆང་ལ་གསོལ་བ་འདེབས༔

KU	SUM	DOR JE CHANG	LA	SOL WA DE
body	three	Vajradhara, the primordial buddha	to	pray

We pray to Vajradhara with these three modes.

Hung. The guru free of artifice and elaboration is the intrinsic mode.
The guru of great happiness, master of dharma, is the enjoyment mode.
The guru born from a lotus stem is the apparitional mode. We pray to
the Vajradhara with these three modes.

འཕོ་བ་   TRANSFERENCE

ཧྲཱིཿ   སྙིང་ཀའི་པདྨ་འདབ་བརྒྱད་གྱེས་པའི་དབུས༔

HRI	NYING KAI	PAE MA	DAB	GYAE	GYE PAI	WU
bija*	heart centre	lotus	petal	eight	open	in the centre of

*of whichever deity is meditated on

HRI. In the centre of an open eight-petalled lotus in my heart,

རྣམ་པར་ཤེས་པ་མ་གསར་སྒོ་ང་ཙམ༔

NAM PAR SHE PA	MA SAR	GO NGA	TSAM
consciousness	about to hatch	egg	as

Like an egg from which the chick is about to hatch,

ལང་ལིང་འཕར་བའི་ཟེར་མ་དང་ས་ཡར་འཕོས་པས༔

LANG LING	PHAR WAI	ZER	DANG	YAR	TROE PAE
shaking	shimmering	rays	bright	up*	radiate, by

*You must fully believe that your mind is completely leaving your body and travelling on shining light rays into the deity's heart.

My consciousness is jumping, ready to go — then it shoots upwards on bright shimmering rays of light and

པདྨ་འབྱུང་གནས་ཐུགས་ཀར་ཐིམ་པར་གྱུར༔

PAE MA JUNG NAE	THU KAR	THIM PAR	GYUR
Padmasambhava[20] (in Zangdopalri)	heart, into mind	absorb, melt	becomes

Merges into the mind of Padmasambhava.

ཧྲིཀ༔   ཧྲིཀ༔   ཧྲིཀ༔   ཕཊ༔   ཕཊ༔   ཕཊ༔

HIK	HIK	HIK	PHAT	PHAT	PHAT
Go!	Go!	Go!	Cut!	Cut!	Cut!

Hik! Hik! Hik! Phat! Phat! Phat!

*In the centre of an open eight-petalled lotus in my heart, like an egg
from which the chick is about to hatch, my consciousness is jumping
ready to go — then it shoots upwards on bright shimmering rays of
light and merges into the mind of Padmasambhava. Hik! Hik! Hik!
Phat! Phat! Phat!*

དམིགས་པ་འདི་ཡང་ཡང་བསྒྱུར། རྣམ་རྟོག་འཕོ་ན་འཆི་བ་མ་ཡིན། ཟང་མདོག་དཔལ་རིར་
ཨོ་རྒྱན་གྱི་ཞབས་དྲུང་དུ་འགྲོ་བ་ཡིན། དལན་དངོས་སུ་མཇལ་བ་ཡིན། དལས་དགའ་བ་
སུ་ཡོད་སྙམ་བྱེད། ཡང་བག་ཆགས་ཀྱི་དབང་གིས་འཇིགས་སྣང་དང་ཟ་ཟིའི་འཁྲུལ་པ་ཅི་
བྱུང་ཡང་རྨི་ལམ་དང་སྒྱུ་མ་ལྟ་བུ་ཡིན། བདེ་པར་གྲུབ་པ་རྡུལ་ཙམ་ཡང་མེད་པར་བདེན་
ཀྱིས་གཏན། བདེན་མེད་དང་སྒྱུ་མ་ལྟ་བུར་དྲན་པ་འདི་བར་དོ་སྒོང་བའི་ཐབས་ཟབ་ཕོས་ཡིན།
འདིའི་རང་ལ་དབུགས་སོང་ན་མི་ཡུལ་དུ་ཤི་བ་དང་། མཁའ་སྤྱོད་དུ་སྐྱེ་བ་དུས་མཉམ་ཡིན།

You must repeat this practice again and again. If discursive thoughts
(of fear, regret and so on) arise do not think that you are dying but
believe that you are now going immediately to be with Padmasambhava in Zangdo Palri. *"Now I will really see him. Who could feel more
happy than me!"* You must develop this feeling.

Moreover due to the power of subtle karmic habits, frightening
ideas and cloudy, confused meditation may arise. But no matter
what occurs you must see it to be like a dream or a magic form. You
must be clear that they have not even an atom's worth of substantial
reality. Remembering them to be devoid of inherent existence and to
be like magical forms is the most profound and important method
of practice in the Bar-Do. If one breathes one's last breath in that
state then one will die in the realm of humans and will be born at
the same moment in mKha'-sPyod, the dakinis' realm of Zangdo
Palri.

*[C.R. Lama said that this should only be practised with the intention to
leave the body immediately when 1) one is dying, 2) one is being tortured
or has a slow painful death, or 3) is forced to stop Dharma practice.]*

ཁམས་ཀྱིས་ལྷོག་ན།
[Then, if possible, you should recite this:]

ནམ་ཞིག་ཚེ་ཟད་འཆི་བའི་དུས་བྱུང་ཚེ༔

NAM ZHI		TSHE	ZAE	CHI WAI	DU	JUNG	TSHE
when, sometime		*life-span*	*finished*	*death's*	*time*	*arising*	*time, when*

When the time of death comes with the exhaustion of our life-span,

གནད་གཅོད་སྡུག་བསྔལ་དྲག་པོས་ཉེན་པ་ན༔

NAE	CHO	DU NGAL	DRA POE	NYEN PA	NA
illness	*fatal*	*suffering*	*intense, by terrible*	*disturbed, endangered*	*if, when*

If we are troubled by the fierce suffering of a fatal illness

ཡིད་གཉིས་ཐེ་ཚོམ་མེད་པར་གསོལ་བ་ཐོབ༔

YI NYI	THE TSHOM	ME PAR	SOL WA THO
two minds	*doubt*	*without*	*must pray*

We must pray without doubt and uncertainty

ཨོ་རྒྱན་སྣང་བ་མཐའ་ཡས་སྤྲུལ་པ་སྟེ༔

OR GYAN NANG WA THAE YAE				TRUL PA	TE
this is the name of Padmasambhava in the form of Amitabha				*apparition*	*then*

To the apparition of Orgyen Amitabha

བདེ་བ་ཅན་གྱི་ཞིང་དུ་ངེས་པར་སྐྱེ༔

DE WA CHEN	GYI	ZHING	DU	NGE PAR	KYE
Dewachen, Sukhavati	*of*	*realm*	*in*	*truly, certainly*	*born*

That we may surely be born in Dewachen.

ཨོ་རྒྱན་པདྨ་འབྱུང་གནས་ལ་གསོལ་བ་འདེབས༔

OR GYAN	PAE MA JUNG NAE		LA	SOL WA DE
the land where he was born	*Padmasambhava*		*to*	*pray*

We pray to Padmasambhava of Orgyen.

When the time of death comes with the exhaustion of our life-span, if we are troubled by the fierce suffering of a fatal illness we must pray without doubt and uncertainty to the apparition of Orgyen Amitabha that we may surely be born in Dewachen. We pray to Padmasambhava of Orgyen.

ཞེས་དང་

[Say this many times and also,]

འགྲོ་བའི་མགོན་པོ་ཨོ་རྒྱན་རིན་པོ་ཆེ༔

DRO WAI	GON PO	OR GYEN RIN PO CHE
sentient beings	*benefactor*	*Padmasambhava*

Benefactor of beings, Orgyen Rinpoche,

ཞིང་ཁམས་གནས་མཆོག་གང་ན་བཞུགས་གྱུར་ཀྱང་༔

ZHING KHAM	NAE	CHO	GANG	NA	ZHU GYUR	KYANG
pure realm	*place*	*supreme*	*wherever, whichever*	*in*	*stay*	*yet*

Wherever you might be staying, in whatever excellent pure place,

ཐུགས་རྗེས་མྱུར་མགྱོགས་ལྦུན་པའི་ལྕགས་ཀྱུ་ཡིས༔

THU JE	NYUR	GYO	DEN PAI	CHA KYU	YI
by compassion	*quickly*	*rushing*	*having*	*iron hook*	*by*

With the lightning iron hook of your compassion

བདག་སོགས་ཁྱེད་ཀྱི་གདུལ་བྱར་གྱུར་པ་རྣམས༔

DA SO	KHYE KYI	DUL JAR	GYUR PA	NAM
we	*your*	*disciples, subjects*	*are*	*(plural)*

You must free us, your disciples,

འཁོར་བའི་ཆུ་བོ་ཆེ་ལས་བསྒྲལ་ནས་ཀྱང་༔

KHOR WAI	CHU WO	CHE	LAE	DRAL	NAE	KYANG
samsara's	*river*	*great*	*from*	*free*	*then*	*also*

From the great river of samsara and then

ཨོ་རྒྱན་མཁའ་སྤྱོད་གནས་སུ་དྲང་དུ་གསོལ༔

OR GYEN KHA CHOE	NAE	SU	DRANG DU	SOL
Zangdopalri	*place*	*to*	*lead us*	*please, we pray*

Lead us to your pure land of Orgyen Khacho.

Benefactor of beings, Orgyen Rinpoche, in whatever excellent pure place you might be staying, with the lightning iron hook of your compassion you must free us, your disciples, from the great river of samsara and then lead us to your pure land of Orgyen Khacho.

ཞེས་སོགས་ཀྱིས་གསོལ་བ་དྲག་དུ་བཏབ། མ་ཐྤོག་ན་ཐུགས་ཡིད་གཅིག་ཏུ་བསྲེས། རབ་ཏུ་དདག་གི་དང་ནས་ཐ་མ་རང་སེམས་དབྱེར་མེད་དུ་སྤྲོ་བསྒོམ། འདི་ལྟར་སྒྲུབ་ན་ཤི་བས་འཆོངས་པ་ཡི་ནོ།

You must pray with very strong devotion using these and other similar prayers. If you are not able to pray then you must try to merge your mind completely with the Guru's mind. If in that state of fusion you can remain relaxed and clear in the inseparability of the Guru's mind and your own that is the best. If you practise like this then death will lead to happiness.

ཞེས་པ་འདི་ཡང་མགྲོན་གཉེར་ཀུན་དགའ་ཤེས་རབ་འབམས་ཀྱིས་གྲོ་འཚལ་ཏེ་ལྭ་པའི་ལམ་དུ་ཉེ་
བར་གྱུར་པ་ན་རིག་འཛིན་ཆེན་པོ་ཀུན་བཟང་པདྨ་འཕྲིན་ལས་ཀྱིས་བརྩེ་བ་ཆེན་པོས་གདམས་
པ་སྨྲ་བཅངས་སུ་རྩལ་བ་ཡིན་པ་ལས་ཕྱིས་སྨྲ་དང་ལྡད་འཁྲུག་མང་པོར་མ་དག་རྒྱན་
འཐུམས་ཀྱི་དཔེ་སྣ་རེ་འདུག་ཀྱང་། འདི་ནི་མ་ཕྱི་ཕྱར་མ་ལས་བཤུས་པའོ།། །།

Regarding this text, when his personal assistant Kun-dGa' Shes-Rab developed rheumatism and was dying, Rig-'Dzin Chen-Po Kun-bZang Padma 'Phrin-Las felt great compassion for him and so gave him these practice instructions that he had prepared definitively. Later on, after Padma 'Phrin-Las himself died, others wrote many extra incorrect things and put them in the text so that many wrong versions appeared. But the text given here is free of all later additions [C.R. Lama].

Transference Relying on Chenrezi

རང་ཉིད་དམ། ཚེ་འདས་མིང་འདི་ཞེས་བྱ་བ་

RANG NYI   DAM   TSHE   DAE   MING   DI   ZHE JA WA
I   or   life   gone   name   this   called
(This practice can be used both for one's own transference or for helping someone who
has died)

For oneself or the one called [   ] who has died,

ཁྱོད་ཀྱི་ལུས་འདི་འཕགས་པ་སྤྱན་རས་གཟིགས་

KHYO KYI   LU   DI   PHA PA   CHEN RAE ZI
your   body this arya, noble Avalokitesvara

Imagine that my body becomes noble Chenrezi,

སྐུ་མདོག་དཀར་པོ་ཞལ་གཅིག་ཕྱག་བཞི་

KU   DO   KAR PO   ZHAL   CHI   CHA   ZHI
body colour white   face   one   hands four

White in colour with one face, four hands and

ཞབས་གཉིས་སྐྱིལ་ཀྲུང་གི་བཞུགས་པ།

ZHAB   NYI   KHYIL TRUNG   GI   ZHU PA
feet   two   lotus posture   with   sitting

Sitting with both feet in the lotus posture.

ཕྱག་དང་པོ་གཉིས་ཐུགས་ཀར་ཐལ་མོ་སྦྱར་བའི་

CHA   DANG PO   NYI   THU KAR   THAL MO JAR WAI
*hands first   two   heart at   palms held together in the gesture
                                    of prayer*

My first two hands are held with palms joined at the heart and

དབུས་སུ་ནོར་བུ་དགོས་འདོད་ཀུན་འབྱུང་འཛིན་པ།

WU   SU   NOR BU   GOE   DOE   KUN   JUNG   DZIN PA
centre in jewel   need desire all source holding

In their centre is the wish-fulfilling jewel, Source of All Satisfaction.

གཡས་འོག་མས་ཤེལ་ཕྲེང་དང་། གཡོན་འོག་མས་

YAE   OG MAE   SHEL   TRENG   DANG   YON   OG MAE
right lower by crystal rosary   and   left   lower by

My lower right hand holds a crystal rosary and my lower left

པད་དཀར་པོ་ཁ་ཕྱེ་བ་སྙན་གྱི་ཐད་ཀར་འཛིན་པ།

PAD MA	KAR PO	KHA CHE WA	NYEN	GYI THAE KAR	DZIN PA
lotus	*white*	*open*	*ear*	*level with*	*holds*

Holds an open white lotus level with my ear.

སྐུ་ལ་ལོངས་སྤྱོད་རྫོགས་པའི་ཆས་བཅུ་གསུམ་གྱིས་བརྒྱན་པ།

KU	LA	LONG CHO DZO PAI	CHAE	CHU SUM	GYI	GYEN PA
body	*to*	*sambhogakaya*	*dress*	*thirteen*	*by*	*adorned*

My body is bedecked with the thirteen adornments of the sambho-gakaya[21].

For oneself or the one called [   ] who has died, imagine that my body becomes noble Chenrezi, white in colour with one face, four hands and sitting with both feet in the lotus posture. My first two hand are held with palms joined at the heart and in their centre is the wish-fulfilling jewel, Source of All Satisfaction. My lower right hand holds a crystal rosary and your lower left holds a white lotus level with my ear. My body is bedecked with the thirteen adornments of the sambhogakaya.

རང་ངམ།   ཆོས་འདས་ཁྱོད་ཀྱི་སྤྱི་བོའི་ཐད་དུ་ངོ་བོ

RANG NGAM	TSHE DAE	KHO KYI	CHI WOI	THAE DU	NGO WO
I	*or*	*the one who has died*	*your*	*crown of head*	*directly above*	*true*

Directly above the crown of my head or of the one who has died I

རང་གི་རྩ་བའི་བླ་མ་ཡིན་པ་ལ་རྣམ་པ

RANG GI	TSA WAI	LA MA	YIN PA	LA	NAM PA
own	*root*	*guru*	*is*	*with*	*form*

Visualise the following: the essence of my own root guru is in the form of

འཕགས་པ་སྤྱན་རས་གཟིགས་ཞལ་གཅིག་ཕྱག་བཞི་པར་གསལ་བའི

PHA PA	CHEN RAE ZI	ZHAL	CHI	CHA	ZHI PAR	SAL WAI
arya	*Avalokitesvara*	*face*	*one*	*hand*	*four as*	*visualise*

Noble Chenrezi with one face and four hands.

སྤྱི་བོར་མགོན་པོ་འོད་དཔག་ཏུ་མེད་པས་བརྒྱན་པ།

CHI WOR	GON PO	OE PA TU ME	PAE	GYEN PA
crown of head	*benefactor*	*Amitabha*	*by*	*adorned*

The crown of his head is adorned with the benefactor Amitabha.

འཕགས་པའི་གདན་གྱི་པདྨས་ཚངས་པའི་བུ་ག

PHA PAI   DEN   GYI   PAE MAE   TSHANG PAI BU GA
guru   as   seat   of   lotus   brahmaranda, hole at top of head*
Avalokitesvara

*It is the area made by marking a circle four inches above the ears.

Clearly visualise that Chenrezi's lotus cushion completely covers

ནོན་པ་ཞིག་ཏུ་གསལ་བར་གྱུར

NON PA   ZHIG TU   SAL WAR GYUR
cover   as   clearly visualise
completely

The brahmaranda potential opening on the top of my head.

Directly above the crown of my head or of the one who has died I visualise the following: the essence of my own root guru is in the form of noble Chenrezi with one face and four hands. The crown of his head is adorned with the benefactor Amitabha. Clearly visualise that Chenrezi's lotus cushion completely covers the brahmaranda potential opening on the top of my head.

རང་ངམ།   ཚེ་འདས་ཀྱི་ལུས་ཀྱི་དབུས་སུ་

RANG NGAM   TSHE DAE   KYI   LU   KYI   WU   SU
I   or   the one who   of   body   of   centre   in
    has died

For myself or the one who has died, I clearly visualise as follows: in the centre of my body

ཙ་དབུ་མ་ཕྱི་དཀར་ལ

TSA   WU MA   CHI   KAR   LA
channel   avadhuti,   outside   white   with
    central

Is the avadhuti central channel. It is white on the outside and

ནང་རྒྱ་སྐྱེགས་ཀྱི་ཁུ་བ་ལྟར་དམར་པ།

NANG GYA   KYEG   KYI   KHU WA   TAR   MAR PA
inside   lac   of   liquid   as   red
        (like sealing wax)

On the inside it is red like liquid lac.

པདྨའི་འདབ་མ་ལྟར་སྲབ་པ།

PAD MAI   DAB MA   TAR SE PA
lotus   petal   as its thickness, i.e. thin

It is the thickness of a lotus petal.

ཕྱི་ནང་གསལ་སྒྲིབ་མེད་པ།

CHI	NANG	SEL	DRIB ME PA
outside	*inside*	*clear*	*unobscured*

Without and within it is clear and unobscured.

རང་བཞིན་སྒྱུ་ལུས་ཀྱི་རྩ་མ་ཡིན་པ།

RANG ZHIN	GYU	LU	KYI	TSA	MA YIN PA
ordinary	*illusory*	*body*	*of*	*channel*	*is not*

It is not like the nerve channels in my ordinary illusory body.

དཔེར་ན་རག་དུང་མགོ་མཇུག་ལོག་པ་ལྟ་བུ།

PER NA	RA DUNG	GO JUG LOG PA	TA BU
for example	*long straight*	*inverted, i.e. with the*	*similar to*
	brass horn	*mouthpiece downward*	

As an example, it is like an inverted long straight yet tapering post horn.

རྩ་བ་ཕྲ་ལ་ཁ་ཟུམ་ལ་ཁད་ཡོད་པ།   རྩེ་མོ་ཡངས་པ།

TSE WA	TRA	LA	KHA ZUM	LA	KHAE	YOE PA	TSE MO	YANG PA
bottom	*fine*	*as*	*closed*	*as*	*like*	*has*	*top point*	*wide*

The bottom is so fine that it is as if closed. The top end is wide and

སྤྱི་བོ་ཚངས་པའི་བུ་གར་ཁྱབ་པ་ཞིག་གསལ་བར་གྱུར།

CHI WO	TSHANG PAI BU GAR	KHYA PA	SEL WAR GYUR
crown of	*brahmaranda hole*	*to*	*fills*	*visualise clearly*

Fills the area at the crown of my head. I visualise this clearly.

རྩ་དབུ་མ་མར་སྣེ་ཁ་ཟུམ་པ།

TSE	U MA	MAR NE	KHA ZUM PA
channel	*avadhuti*	*lower end*	*close*

The lower end of this central channel is closed.

For myself or the one who has died, I clearly visualise as follows: in the centre of my body is the avadhuti central channel. It is white on the outside and on the inside it is red like liquid lac. It is the thickness of a lotus petal. Without and within it is clear and unobscured. It is not like the nerve channels in my ordinary illusory body. As an example, it is like an inverted long straight yet tapering post horn. The bottom is so fine that it is as if closed. The top end is wide and fills the area at the crown of my head. I visualise this clearly. The lower end of this central channel is closed.

སྙིང་ཁར་པདྨ་འདབ་མ་བརྒྱད་ཀྱི་ལྟེ་བར་

NYING KHAR   **PE MA**   **DAB MA**   **GYAE**   **GYI**   **TE WAR**
heart   *at*   *lotus*   *petal*   *eight*   *of*   *very centre/ at*

At my heart is an eight-petalled lotus at whose centre

རང་གི་རྣམ་པར་ཤེས་པའི་ངོ་བོ་ཐིག་ལེ་དཀར་པོ་

RANG GI   **NAM PAR SHE PAI**   **NGO WO**   **THIG LE**   **KAR PO**
my   *mind, consciousness*   *essence*   *bindu, ball*   *white*

Is a white sphere which is the essence of my consciousness.

བྱ་མ་གསར་གྱི་སྒོང་ང་ལྟར་འཕར་ལ་ཁད་པ།

JA MA   **SAR GYI**   **GO NGA**   **TAR**   **PHAR LA**   **KHE PA**
bird   *new*   *egg*   *as*   *leap, fly*   *trying*

Like an egg from which the chick is about to hatch, it is moving up and down

འཕར་ལ་ཁད་པ།

PHUR LA   **KHE PA**
fly, leap   *trying*

As if it is about to take off.

ཡི་གི་ཧྲཱིཿ ཡིས་མཚན་པ་ཞིག་གསལ་བར་གྱུར།

YI GI HRI   **YI**   **TSHAN PA ZHI**   **SAL WAR GYUR**
letter HRI*   *by, with*   *marked*   *visualise clearly*

*The HRI shows that the sphere, your consciousness, is not different from Chenrezi. It is in your central channel at your heart.

Visualise this sphere as being clearly marked with a letter HRI.

At my heart is an eight-petalled lotus at whose centre is a white sphere which is the essence of my consciousness. Like an egg from which the chick is about to hatch, it is moving up and down as if about to take off. Visualise this sphere as being clearly marked with a letter HRI.

ལང་ལིང་འཕར་བའི་ཟེར་མདངས་ཡར་འཕྲོས་པས༵

LANG LING   **PHAR WAI**   **ZER**   **DANG**   **YAR**   **TROE PAE**
vibrating and   *shimmering*   *ray*   *bright*   *up*   *by radiating*
(It travels up the central channel and out of the crown of your head.)

My consciousness is jumping slightly, ready to go — then it shoots upwards on shimmering rays of light and

སྤྱན་རས་གཟིགས་དབང་ཐུགས་ཀར་ཐིམ་པར་གྱུར༵

CHEN RE ZI WANG   **THU KAR**   **THIM PAR**   **GYUR**
Avalokiteshvara   *into his heart*   *dissolve*   *does*

Merges into the heart mind of Chenrezi.

ཧྲཱིཿ	ཧྲཱིཿ	ཧྲཱིཿ	ཕཊཿ	ཕཊཿ	ཕཊཿ
HIK	**HIK**	**HIK**	**PHAT**	**PHAT**	**PHAT**
Go!	*Go!*	*Go!*	*Cut!*	*Cut!*	*Cut!*

Hik! Hik! Hik! Phat! Phat! Phat!

My consciousness is jumping slightly, ready to go — then it shoots upwards on shimmering rays of light and merges with the heart mind of Chenrezi. Hik! Hik! Hik! Phat! Phat! Phat!

ཕྱགས་རྗེ་ཆེན་པོའི་ཚེ་སྒྲུབ་བཞུགས་སོ།།

Chenrezi Long-Life Practice

བཅོམ་ལྡན་ཚེ་དཔག་མེད་ལ་ཕྱག་འཚལ་ལོ།

Salutation to Victorious Amitayus.

རང་ཉིད་ཕྱགས་རྗེ་ཆེན་པོ་ཡིཿ

RANG NYI   **THU JE CHEN PO**   **YI**
self   *Chenrezi,*   *of*
   great compassion

Arising as Chenrezi,

སྤྱི་གཙུག་པདྨ་ཉི་ཟླའི་གདནཿ

CHI TSU   **PE MA**   **NYI**   **DAI**   **DEN**
crown of my   *lotus*   *sun*   *moon*   *cushions*
my head

On the crown of my head on top of cushions of lotus, sun and moon

ཧྲཱིཿ ལས་འགྲོ་མགོན་ཚེ་དཔག་མེདཿ

HRI   **LAE**   **DRO**   **GON**   **TSHE PA ME**
letter*   *from*   *beings*   *lord,*   *Amitayus, Limitless Life*
   benefactor

* From the letter HRI rays of light rise up as offering to the Buddhas of the ten directions, then the rays return with their blessing and merge into the HRI. Then rays again rise out and strike all the beings in the six realms removing all their sins and sorrows. Then these rays return to the letter HRI which transforms into Amitayus

Is a letter HRI which becomes Amitayus, the benefactor of beings.

དམར་པོ་ཞལ་གཅིག་ཕྱག་གཉིས་པཿ

MAR PO   **ZHAL**   **CHI**   **CHA**   **NYI PA**
red   *face*   *one*   *hand*   *two*

He is red in colour with one face and two hands.

ཕྱག་གཉིས་མཉམ་བཞག་ཚེ་བུམ་བསྣམསཿ

CHA   **NYI**   **NYAM ZHA**   **TSHE BUM**   **NAM**
hands   *two*   *in lap in meditation*   *long-life pot*   *holding*

His two hands are in the meditation gesture in his lap holding the pot of long-life.

ཞབས་གཉིས་རྡོ་རྗེའི་སྐྱིལ་ཀྲུང་བཞུགས༔

ZHAB	NYI	DOR JEI KYIL TRUNG	ZHU
feet	*two*	*the lotus posture*	*sitting*

He sits with his two feet in the lotus posture.

Salutation to Victorious Amitayus. Arising as Chenrezi, on the crown of my head on top of cushions of lotus, sun and moon, is a letter HRI which becomes Amitayus, the benefactor of beings. He is red in colour with one face and two hands. His two hands are in the meditation gesture in his lap holding the pot of long-life. He sits with his two feet in the lotus posture.

ཡུམ་ཆེན་གོས་དཀར་སྐུ་མདོག་དམར༔

YUM	CHEN	GO KAR	KU	DO	MAR
wife	*great*	*Pundarika*	*body*	*colour*	*red*

His wife Gokarmo is red in colour.

ཕྱག་གཡས་ཚེ་དར་ཡབ་ལ་འཁྱུད༔

CHA	YAE	TSHE DAR	YAB	LA	KHYU
hand	*right*	*arrow**	*husband*	*with*	*embrace*

*with five coloured cloths attached to it

She embraces her husband with her right hand which holds a long-life arrow.

གཡོན་པ་ཚེ་བུམ་ཐུགས་ཀར་བསྣམས༔

YON PA	TSE BUM	THU	KAR	NAM
left	*long-life pot*	*heart*	*at*	*holding*

Her left hand holds a pot of long-life at his heart.

ཞབས་གཉིས་ཡབ་ལ་འཁྲིལ་སྦྱོར་མཛད༔

ZHAB	NYI	YAB	LA	TRIL JHOR	DZAE
feet	*two*	*husband*	*to*	*embrace, coupling*	*does*

Her two legs are wrapped around him in union.

བདེ་བ་ཅན་ནས་ཡེ་ཤེས་སེམས༔

DE WA CHEN	NAE	YE SHE SEM
Dewachen, Sukhavati	*from*	*jnanasattvas, pure wisdom forms of Amitayus and Pundarika*

From Dewachen their wisdom forms

སྤྱན་དྲངས་གཉིས་མེད་བརྟན་པར་བཞུགས༔

CHEN DRANG   **NYI ME**   **TEN PAR**   **ZHU**
invite   *merge non-dually*   *steadily*   *stay*

Are invited and they merge and settle without difference.

His wife Gokarmo is red in colour and she embraces her husband with her right hand which holds a long-life arrow. Her left hand holds a pot of long-life at his heart. Her two legs are wrapped around him in union. From Dewachen their wisdom forms are invited and they merge and settle without difference.

ༀ་བཛྲ་ཨ་ཡུ་ཥེ་ས་པ་རི་ཝ་ར

OM   **BENDZA**   **A YU SHE**   **SA PA RI WA RA**
five   *indestructible*   *Amitayus,*   *with your circle of deities*
wisdoms   *emptiness*   *long life*

Om. Indestructible Amitayus and your circle, we offer you

བཛྲ་   ཨཪྒྷཾ་   པཱདྱཾ་   པུཥྤེ་   དྷུཔེ་

BENDZA   **ARGHAM**   **PADYAM**   **PUSHPE**   **DHUPE**
indestructible,   *drinking*   *feet washing*   *flowers*   *incense*
pure   *water*   *water*

Indestructible drinking water, feet-washing water, flowers, incense,

ཨཱལོཀེ་   གནྡྷེ་   ནཻཝིདྱེ་   ཤབྡ་   ཨཱ༔   ཧཱུྃ༔

ALOKE   **GANDHE**   **NEDIDYE**   **SHABDA**   **A**   **HUNG**
lamp   *perfumed*   *food*   *sound*   *emptiness*   *offer*

Lamps, perfumed water, food and sound – please enjoy these offerings of emptiness.

འཇིག་རྟེན་འདྲེན་པའི་གཙོ་བོ་ཚེ་དཔག་མེད༔

JIG TEN   **DREN PAI**   **TSO WO**   **TSHE PA ME**
world   *guides*   *chief*   *Amitayus*
(the buddhas who guide
beings from samsara)

Amitayus the chief of those who guide us from the world,

དུས་མིན་འཆི་བ་མ་ལུས་འཇོམས་མཛད་པའི༔

DU MIN   **CHI WA**   **MA LU**   **JOM**   **DZAE PAI**
untimely   *death*   *without*   *defeat*   *doing*
(before the maximum life
span allowed by one's karma)

You who stop all kinds of untimely death,

མགོན་མེད་སྡུག་བསྔལ་གྱུར་པ་རྣམས་ཀྱི་སྐྱབས༔

GON ME	DU NGAL	GYUR PA NAM	KYI	KYAB
protectors, benefactors	*suffering*	*those who*	*of*	*protector, refuge*

The refuge of those who suffer without a protector,

སངས་རྒྱས་ཚེ་དཔག་མེད་ལ་ཕྱག་འཚལ་བསྟོད༔

SANG GYE	TSHE PA ME	LA	CHA TSHAL	TOE
Buddha	*Amitayus*	*to*	*salutation*	*praise*

Buddha Amitayus, we offer salutation and praise to you.

Amitayus, the chief of those who guide us from the world, you stop all kinds of untimely death and are the refuge of those who suffer without a protector. Buddha Amitayus, we offer salutation and praise to you.

ཨྱོཾ་བཛྲ་ཨ་ཡུ་ཥེ་ཧཱུྃ་བྲྀ་ཎི་ཛཿ༔

OM	BEN DZA	A YU SHE	HUNG BRUM NI DZA
five wisdoms emptiness	*indestructible*	*long life*	(*seed syllables*) [by reciting this]

Om. Indestructible long life. Hung. Bhrum. Ni. Dza —

ཐུགས་ཀའི་ཧཱུྃ་ལས་འོད་ཟེར་འཕྲོས༔

THU KAI	HUNG	LAE	OE ZER	TRO
heart centre	*letter Hung*	*from*	*light rays*	*radiate**

*Again these lights go up as offering to the Buddhas and down to purify all beings.

With this rays of light radiate from the letter Hung in the heart of Amitayus.

འོད་ཟེར་ཡབ་ཀྱི་ཞལ་ནས་འཕོན༔

OE ZER	YAB KYI	ZHAL	NAE	THON
light rays	*husband's*	*mouth*	*from*	*come out*

Light rays stream from his mouth and

ཡུམ་གྱི་ཞལ་དུ་ཞུགས༔

YUM GYI	ZHAL	DU	ZHU
wife's	*mouth*	*in*	*enter*

Enter into his wife's mouth.

སྐུའི་དབྱིབས་རྒྱུད་ཡུམ་གྱི་མཁར་བབས༔

KUI	YIB	GYU	YUM GYI	KHAR	BAB
body's	*shape, form*	*through*	*wife's*	*vagina*	*descends*

Then they descend through her body to her vagina and

དེས་བདག་གི་སྤྱི་གཙུག་ཏུ་བབས་པས༔

DE	DA GI	CHI TSU	TU	BAB	PAE
by that	*my*	*crown of head*	*on*	*descends**	*by which*

*i.e. enter my body through the top of my head

Flow down into me through the top of my head.

Om. Indestructible long life. Hung. Bhrum. Ni. Dza — with this rays of light radiate from the letter Hung in the heart of Amitayus. Light rays stream from his mouth and enter into his wife's mouth. Then they descend through her body to her vagina and flow down into me through the top of my head.

ཚེ་རབས་ཀྱི་སྡིག་པ་ཐམས་ཅད་རྣག་ཁྲག་དང༔

TSHE RAB	KYI	DIG PA	THAM CHE	NAG	TRAG	DANG
all lives	*of*	*sins*	*all*	*puss*	*blood*	*and*

Due to this all the sins that I have ever done in any of my lives

དུད་ཁུའི་ཚུལ་དུ་ནག་འདུ་རུ་རུ་ཕྱིར་འཐོན༔

DUE KHUI	TSHUL	DU	NAG DU RU RU	CHIR	THON
sooty water	*style*	*as*	*very black*	*out*	*come (from my anus)*

Flow out from my body as puss and blood and in the form of very black sooty water and

ཕྱིའི་རྒྱ་མཚོའི་མཐར་སོང་བར་བསམ༔

CHII	GYAM TSOI	THAR	SONG WAR	SAM
outer	*ocean*	*and to*	*gone*	*as*	*believe*

(At the outer most distant edge of the world)

Vanish to the furthest edge of the outer ocean.

བདག་གི་ལུས་བདུད་རྩིས་གང་བར་བསམ༔

DA GI	LU	DU TSI	GANG	WAR	SAM
my	*body*	*liberating elixir*	*full*	*as*	*believe*

Now I am sure that my body is full of liberating elixir.

Due to this all the sins that I have ever done in any of my lives flow out from my body as puss and blood and in the form of very black sooty water and vanish to the farthest edge of the outer ocean. Now I am sure that my body is full of liberating elixir.

ཨོྃ་བཛྲ་ཨཱ་ཡུ་ཥེ་ཧཱུྃ་བྷྲཱུྃ་ནི་ཛཿ

OM	BEN DZA	A YU SHE	HUNG BRUM NI DZA
five wisdoms emptiness	*indestructible*	*long life*	*(seed syllables)*

Om. Indestructible long life. Hung. Bhrum. Ni. Dza.

ཕྱོགས་བཅུའི་སངས་རྒྱས་དང་བྱང་ཆུབ་སེམས་དཔའ་ཐམས་ཅད་ཀྱིས༔

CHO CHUI	SANG GYE	DANG	JANG CHU SEM PA	THAM CHE	KYI
ten directions	*buddhas*	*and*	*bodhisattvas*	*all*	*by*

I imagine that all the Buddhas and Bodhisattvas of the ten directions

ཚེའི་དངོས་གྲུབ་བདག་ལ་གནང་བར་བསམ༔

TSHEI	NGO DRUB	DA LA	NANG WAR	SAM
long life	*siddhi, true attainment*	*me to*	*give as*	*believe, imagine*

Grant me the true attainment of long-life.

ཁམས་གསུམ་སྲིད་གསུམ་

KHAM	SUM	SI	SUM
worlds	*three**	*existences*	*three+*

*desire, form and formless
+men ,gods, and snake gods

I imagine that the lustre and radiance of

ཐམས་ཅད་ཀྱི་ཚེའི་བཀྲག་མདངས་དང༔

THAM CHE	KYI	TSHEI	TRA	DANG	DANG
all	*of*	*lives*	*shining*	*radiance*	*and*

All that lives in the three worlds and three existences, and

འབྱུང་བའི་བཅུད་ཐམས་ཅད་

JUNG WAI	CHU	THAM CHE
elements*	*essence*	*all*

*earth, water, fire, air, space

All the essences of the elements

འོད་ཟེར་གྱི་ཚུལ་དུ་བསྡུས་ནས་

OE ZER	GYI	TSHUL	DU	DUE	NE
light rays	*of*	*method*	*in, with*	*assemble*	*then*

Gather together in the form of light rays

བདག་ལ་ཐིམ་པར་བསམ་ཞིང༔

DA	LA	THIM PAR	SAM ZHING
me	*into*	*melt as*	*believing*

And melt into me.

དེ་ནས་ཚེ་དཔག་མེད་ཡབ་ཡུམ་བདག་ལ་ཐིམ་པར་བསམ༔

DE NE	TSHE PA ME	YAB YUM	DA	LA	THIM PAR	SAM
then	*Amitayus*	*with Pundarika*	*me**	*into*	*melt*	*as believe*

*still in the form of Chenrezi

Then I imagine that Amitayus and his wife merge into me.

*Om. Indestructible long life. Hung. Bhrum. Ni. Dza. I imagine that all
the Buddhas and Bodhisattvas of the ten directions grant me the true
attainment of long-life. I imagine that the lustre and radiance of all that
lives in the three worlds and the three existences, and all the essences
of the elements gather together in the form of light rays and then melt
into me. Then I imagine that Amitayus and his wife also merge into me.*

རེས་སུ་བསྟོ་སྟོན་ལས་བཀ་ཤེས་སྟེ་མཐུན་བྱ་ཚོ༔

[Then dissolve your form as Chenrezi and rest in emptiness for as long as you can.
Then arising in your usual form, recite the general dedication prayer and good luck
verses.]

དགེ་བ་འདི་ཡིས་མྱུར་དུ་བདག

GE WA   DI   YI   NYUR DU   DA
virtue   this   by   quickly   I

By this virtue may I quickly

སྤྱན་རས་གཟིགས་དབང་འགྲུབ་གྱུར་ནས།

CHEN RAE ZI WONG   DRU GYUR   NAE
Chenrezi   accomplish   then

Gain the stage of Chenrezi, and then

འགྲོ་བ་གཅིག་ཀྱང་མ་ལུས་པ།

DRO WA   CHI   KYANG   MA LUE PA
beings   one   even   without exception

All beings without even one exception –

དེ་ཡི་ས་ལ་འགོད་པར་ཤོག

DE YI   SA   LA   GOE PAR   SHO
his,   stage   on   put them   may I
Chenrezi's

May I put them on Chenrezi's stage.

*By this virtue may I quickly gain the stage of Chenrezi. Then may I put
all beings without exception upon that same stage.*

འཇིག་རྟེན་འདྲེན་པའི་གཙོ་བོ་ཚེ་དཔག་མེད༔

JIG TEN   DREN PAI   TSO WO   TSHE PA ME
world   guides   chief   Amitayus
*(the buddhas who guide
beings from samsara)*

Amitayus the chief of those who guide us from the world,

དུས་མིན་འཆི་བ་མ་ལུས་འཇོམས་མཛད་པའི༔

DU MIN	CHI WA	MA LU	JOM	DZAE PAI
untimely	*death*	*without*	*defeat*	*doing*
(before the maximum life				
span allowed by one's karma)				

You who stop all kinds of untimely death,

མགོན་མེད་སྡུག་བསྔལ་གྱུར་པ་རྣམས་ཀྱི་སྐྱབས༔

GON ME	DU NGAL	GYUR PA NAM	KYI	KYAB
protectors,	*suffering*	*those who*	*of*	*protector, refuge*
benefactors				

The refuge of those who suffer without a protector,

སངས་རྒྱས་ཚེ་དཔག་མེད་ཀྱི་བཀྲ་ཤིས་ཤོག༔

SANG GYE	TSHE PA ME	KYI	TRA SHI	SHO
Buddha	*Amitayus*	*of*	*good fortune*	*may*

May there be the good fortune of Buddha Amitayus.

Amitayus, the chief of those who guide us from the world, you stop all kinds of untimely death and are the refuge of those who suffer without a protector. May there be the good fortune of Buddha Amitayus.

སྐྱོན་གྱིས་མ་གོས་སྐུ་མདོག་དཀར༔

KYON	GYI	MA GOE	KU	DO	KAR
fault	*by*	*not affect*	*body*	*colour*	*white*

Not touched by any fault, your body is white,

རྫོགས་སངས་རྒྱས་ཀྱིས་དབུ་ལ་བརྒྱན།

DZO	SANG GYE	KYI	WU	LA	GYEN
perfect	*buddha*	*by*	*head*	*on*	*ornament*
	Amitabha				

With a perfect Buddha ornamenting your head.

ཐུགས་རྗེ་སྤྱན་གྱིས་འགྲོ་ལ་གཟིགས།

THU JE	CHEN	GYE	DRO	LA	ZI
with compassion	*eye*	*by*	*beings*	*to*	*looking*

You look on all beings with the eye of compassion –

སྤྱན་རས་གཟིགས་ཀྱི་བཀྲ་ཤིས་ཤོག།

CHEN RAE ZI	KYI	TRA SHI SHO
Chenrezi,	*of*	*good fortune!*

May we all enjoy the good fortune of Chenrezi!

*Not touched by any fault, your body is white with a perfect buddha
ornamenting your head. You look on all beings with the eye of compassion
– may we all enjoy the good fortune of Chenrezi!*

ས་མ་ཡ་རྒྱ་རྒྱ་རྒྱ༔   Vows. Seal. Seal. Seal.

རྣབ་ཟངས་མཆོད་དམར་པོ་ནས་རིག་འཛིན་ཆེན་པོ་རྒོད་ཀྱི་ལྡེམ་འཕྲུ་ཅན་དངོས་གྲུབ་རྒྱལ་
མཚན་གྱིས་གཏེར་ནས་སྤྱན་དྲངས་པའོ༔

Rig-'Dzin Chen-Po rGod-Kyi lDem-'Phru-Chan dNgos-Grub rGyal-mTshan
took this treasure from the Western Red Copper Treasury.

འཁོར་ལོས་བསྒྱུར་རྒྱལ་རྒྱལ་པོའི་ཕོ་བྲང་དང་༔

KHOR LOE GYUR GYAL	GYAL POI	PHO DRANG	DANG
Rajachakravartin *Universal Monarch*	*king's*	*palace*	*and*

The royal palace of the Universal Monarch, and

རིན་ཆེན་བདུན་དང་བཀྲ་ཤིས་རྫས་བརྒྱད་དང་༔

RIN CHEN	DUN	DANG	TRA SHI DZE	GYE	DANG
precious	*7**	*and*	*auspicious things*	*8#*	*and*

*gold, silver, turquoise, pearl, coral, crystal, lead
mirror, Gi-Wang medicine, curd, Dur-Ba grass, wood apple, a right-whorled conch shell,
vermilion, and white mustard

The seven jewels, and the eight auspicious things, and

ཙི་བཅུད་འབྲུ་ཡི་བཅུད་དང་ཤིང་གི་བཅུད༔

TSI CHU	DRU YI CHU	DANG	SHING GI CHU
fruit, flowers essence	*crops essence*	*and*	*tree's essence*

The essence of fruit, the essence of crops, and the essence of trees:

བཅུད་རྣམས་བསྡུས་ལ་བསྟིམ་ཞིང་སྙིང་པོ་བཟླས༔

CHU NAM	DU LA	TIM ZHING	NYING PO	DA
all essences	*gather together*	*melt into the the torma*	*mantra*	*recite*

All these essences gather together and melt into the torma as the mantras are recited.

བདེ་གཤེགས་རྣམས་དང་རྡོ་རྗེ་སློབ་དཔོན་གྱིས༔

DE SHE		NAM	DANG	DOR JE LOB PON	GYI
sugatas, buddhas		*all*	*and*	*Vajra Acharya Gurus*	*by*

Praying that all Happily Gone and Tantric Gurus will

ཚེ་ཡི་དངོས་གྲུབ་བདུད་རྩིར་བྱིན་གྱིས་བརླབས༔

TSHE YI	NGO DRU	DU TSIR	JIN GYI LAB
long life	*siddhi, true attainment*	*amrita, elixir*	*as bless*

Bless it as the liberating elixir of the true attainment of long life,

གསོལ་བ་གཏབ་ཅིང་འཆི་མེད་བདུད་རྩིར་གྱུར༔

SOL WA DE CHING	CHI ME	DU TSIR	GYUR
praying	*undying*	*amrita*	*becomes*

It becomes the liberating elixir of the deathless.

The Royal palace of the Universal Monarch, and the seven jewels, and the eight auspicious things, and the essence of fruit, the essence of crops, and the essence of trees – all these essences gather together and melt into the torma as the mantras are recited. Praying that all Happily Gone and Tantric Gurus will bless it as the liberating elixir of the true attainment of long life, it becomes the liberating elixir of the deathless.

ཨོཾ་ཨཱཿཧཱུྃ་བཛྲ་གུ་རུ་པདྨ་སིདྡྷི་ཧཱུྃ་ཧཱུྃ་ཧཱུྃ༔

OM	Aa	HUNG	BEN ZA	GU RU
Body	*Speech*	*Mind*	*very strong*	*teacher*

PADMA	SID DHI	HUNG HUNG HUNG
Padmasambhava	*true attainments*	*give us*

Very strong Guru Padmasambhava, having the Three Kayas, grant us true attainments!

ན་ན་ཁ་དྷེ་སིདྡྷི་ཧཱུྃ་ཧཱུྃ་ཧཱུྃ༔

NA NA KHA DHE	SID DHI	HUNG HUNG HUNG
many different	*true attainments*	*give us*

Grant us many different true attainments!

སརྦ་སིདྡྷི་དྷ་ནཾ་མེ་དྷི་ཧྲཱི༔

SAR WA	SID DHI	DHA NAM	ME DHI HRI
all	*true attainments*	*give*	*give*

Grant us all true attainments!

ཨཱཿ་ཡུ་སི་དྷི་ས་མ་ཡ་བསྲུས་བསྲུས༔

Aa YU SID DHI **SA MA YA** **DU** **DU**
life become strong *your vows* *must come! must come!*

Our lives must become strong. Keep your vows. True attainments must come!

Very strong Guru Padmasambhava, having the Three Kayas, grant us true attainments! Grant us many different true attainments! Grant us all true attainments! Our lives must become strong. Keep your vows. True attainments must come!

ཞེས་བརྗོད

[Recite these.]

འཇིག་རྟེན་ཁམས་ཀྱི་ལོངས་སྤྱོད་ལྔ༔

JIG TEN **KHAM** **KYI** **LONG CHO** **NGA**
world *realms* *of* *wealth* *five*
                                         (whatever is pleasing to the senses)

From all the realms of the world everything which pleases the five senses

ཕུབ་ཀྱིས་བསྡུས་ལ་ཚེ་ལ་བསྟིམ་པར་བྱ༔

UB **KYI** **DUE** **LA** **TSHE** **LA** **TIM PA** **JA**
collect *by* *assemble* *then* *life* *in* *melt* *do*
together   *(the long-life blessing articles)*

Gathers together and melts into the life essence.

From all the realms of the world everything which pleases the five senses gathers together and melts into the life essence.

ཞེས་གསུངས་པའི་སྒྲུབ་རྫས་རྣམས་ལ་ཚེ་བཅུད་བསྟིམ་པའི་དམིགས་པ་བྱ།། །།

[Saying that, imagine that the life-essence melts into the practice articles, both what you have on the altar and what you are imagining.]

ཕུན་བསྡུ་ཁར།

[At the end of that practice...]

ཧཱུྃ༔   རིག་འཛིན་ཡོངས་རྫོགས་སྤྱན་འདྲེན་གཤེགས༔

HUNG   **RIG DZIN** **YONG DZO** **CHEN DREN** **SHE**
five wisdoms   *Vidyadharas* *all* *invite* *please come*

Hung.   We invite all you Vidyadharas – please come!

ཕྱི་ནང་གསང་བའི་ཚོགས་མཆོད་འབུལཿ

CHI   NANG   SANG WAI   TSHO CHO   BUL
outer   *inner*   *secret*   *assembled offerings*   *offer*

We offer the outer, inner and secret assembled offerings.

ཉམས་ཆགས་འགལ་འཁྲུལ་མཐོལ་ལོ་བཤགསཿ

NYAM   CHA   GAL   TRUL   THOL LO   SHA
lapses *breaches* *mistakes* *confused* *with hands held* *confess and*
(of vows)   *things*   *in prayer*   *please forgive*

We humbly confess our lapses, breaches, mistakes, confusion, and request forgiveness.

སྐུ་གསུང་ཐུགས་ཡོན་ཕྲིན་ལས་བསྟོདཿ

KU   SUNG   THU   YON   TRIN LAE   TOE
Body   *Speech*   *Mind*   *qualities*   *activities*   *praise*
Nirmanakaya *Sambhogakaya* *Dharmakaya*

We praise your Body, Speech, Mind, Qualities and Activities.

མཆོག་དང་ཐུན་མོང་དངོས་གྲུབ་སྩོལཿ

CHO   DANG   THUN MONG   NGO DRUB   TSOL
supreme *and*   *general*   *siddhis, true*   *please give*
(Buddhahood)   *attainments*

Please grant supreme and general true attainments.

མ་ཧཱ་པཉྩ་ཨ་མྲྀ་ཏ་ཁ་ཧིཿ

MA HA   PAN TSA   A MRI TA   KHA HI
great   *five*   *amrita, liberating* *please eat*
                   elixir

Eat the great five amritas.

མ་ཧཱ་བ་ལིཾ་ཏ་ཁ་ཧིཿ

MA HA   BHA LIN TA   KHA HI
great   *torma*   *eat*

Eat the great sacrifice.

མ་ཧཱ་རཀྟ་ཁ་ཧིཿ

MA HA   RAK TA   KHA HI
great   *blood*   *eat*

Drink the great blood.

མ་ཧཱ་སརྦ་པུ་ཙ་ཁ་ཧིཿ

MA HA   SAR VA   PU TSA   KHA HI
great   *all*   *offerings*   *eat*

Eat all the great offerings.

Hung. We invite all you Vidyadharas – please come! We offer the outer, inner, and secret assembled offerings. We humbly confess our lapses, breaches, mistakes, confusion, and request forgiveness. We praise your Body, Speech, Mind, Qualities and Activities. Please grant supreme and general true attainments. Eat the great five amritas. Eat the great sacrifice. Drink the great blood. Eat the great offerings.

དགེ་བསྔོ། DEDICATION OF MERIT

དགེ་འདིས་བླ་མ་ཁྱེད་འགྲུབ་ནས།

GE	DI	LA MA	KHYE	DRU	NAE
virtue	*by this*	*Guru*	*your*	*practice*	*having*

By this virtue, by doing your practice

འགྲོ་ཀུན་ཉིད་དང་དབྱེར་མེད་ཤོག།

DRO	KUN	NYI	DANG	YER ME	SHO
living beings	*all*	*yourself*	*and*	*inseparable*	*must*

May all beings become inseparable from you, our guru.

འཇིག་རྟེན་བདེ་བའི་དཔལ་ལ་སྤྱོད།

JIG TEN	DE WAI	PAL	LA	CHOE
worldly	*happiness*	*glory*	*with*	*enjoy*

May we all enjoy the rich happiness of this world and have

རིག་འཛིན་བླ་མའི་བཀྲ་ཤིས་ཤོག།

RIG DZIN	LA MAI	TRA SHI	SHO
Vidyadhara	*Guru, of*	*auspicious*	*must be*

The good fortune of our aware Guru.

By this virtue, by doing your practice may all beings become inseparable from you, our guru. May we all enjoy the rich happiness of this world and have the good fortune of our aware Guru.

ཕན་པར་བསམས་པ་ཙམ་གྱིས་ཀྱང་།

PHEN PAR	SAM PA	TSAM	GYI	KYANG
benefit	*think*	*only*	*by*	*even*

When merely the thought of helping others

སངས་རྒྱས་མཆོད་ལས་ཁྱད་འཕགས་ན།

SANG GYE	CHO	LAE	KYE PHA	NA
buddhas	*offering*	*than*	*excellent*	*thus*

Is more excellent than the worship of the Buddhas,

སེམས་ཅན་མ་ལུས་ཐམས་ཅད་ཀྱི།

SEM CHEN   **MA LUE**   **THAM CHE**   **KYI**
sentient beings   *without exception*   *all*   *of*

It is unnecessary even to mention the greatness of striving

བདེ་དོན་བརྩོན་པ་སྨོས་ཅི་དགོས།།

DE DON   **TSON PA**   **MOE**   **CHI**   **GOE**
benefit   *strive*   *say*   *what*   *need*

For the happiness and welfare of all beings without exception.

When merely the thought of helping others is more excellent than the worship of the Buddhas, it is unnecessary even to mention the greatness of striving for the happiness and welfare of all beings without exception.

སྤྱོད་འཇུག་ལས།

Verse from Entering the Way of the Bodhisattva by Shantideva.

Notes

1. When Amitabha's duty in Dewachen is finished Avalokitesvara (Chenrezi) will take over, rescuing those who say his name. And when Chenrezi's service is finished Vajrapani will take over.

2. Manjushri, Vajrapani, Avalokitesvara, Ksitigarbha, Sarvanivaranabhiskumbhi, Akashagarbha, Maitreya, Samantabhadra

3. Everything in this mandala island symbolises the purification of samsara.

4. The five skandha constituents are: form, feeling, perception, association, and consciousness.

5. The eighteen dhatus are: the six sense organs, the six sense objects, and the six sense consciousnesses. The dakinis reside in all aspects of subject and object; they are present everywhere.

6. Padmasambhava stays in our own body, in the constituents, flesh, blood, hair and so on.

7. Secretly, Padmasambhava stays in our own mind as the clarity of happiness and emptiness inseparable.

8. The ball is the presence of the mind in our heart; it is the potential of emptiness.

9. Not at all known to those who wander in the ignorance and suffering of samsara.

10. Without dualistic activity. This is the site and nature of Padmasambhava.

11. Most secretly, there is no more action necessary and so Padmasambhava rests in the natural state.

12. The enlightened mind's implacable form — a wrathful form of Padmasambhava.

13. Moreover, the king is not separate from his realm.

14. This looks like actual physical death, but it means deep meditation that cuts the connection with, and involvement in, the samsaric appearances of this world. In a state unconsciousness of them one can directly travel to Zangdopalri guided by the dakinis and protectors and directly meet and gain teachings and blessings from Padmasambhava himself. This is the ending of one's ordinary existence of bewildered suffering.

15. When I die I want to go to the city of Padmasambhava, and have his circle, the dakinis, play music for my reception to make me happy. But if we don't practise now, how can we practise when we die? Zangdopalri is very near; you can walk there. Imagine that Padmasambhava has been inviting you and he sends people for your reception. Every time you go somewhere think that Zangdopalri is near and you are walking there. This is the first step of Transference (Phowa). In the Nyingmapa tradition many people have had good results with this practice and realised rainbow bodies. You should practise however it is easiest for you and according to your wish. You need faith and the visualisation. But without practice you will not get any result.

16. The five paths on the way to enlightenment are Gyur Lam, Thong Lam, Gom Lam and Thar-Chin-Pai Lam.

17. The ten stages or levels of bodhisattvas: the Joyful, the Immaculate, the Illuminating, the Flaming, the Hard-to-Conquer, the Manifest, the Far-Reaching, the Unmoving, the Excellent Intelligence and the Cloud of Doctrine.

18. The five paths of the causal vehicles: the path of provisions, the path of connection, the path of insight, the path of meditation, and the path of no-more-learning.

19. The four ranks of sages or awareness-holders: the awareness holder of maturation (Namin), the awareness holder of power over the lifespan (Tsewang), the awareness holder of the great seal (Chagchen), the awareness holder of spontaneous presence (Lhundrup).

20. You can change this final line according to your current main practice, replacing Padmasambhava with the name of your meditation deity.

སྣང་བ་མཐའ་ཡས་

NANG WA THA YE
Amitabha
(in Dewachen)

ཆེ་མཆོག་ཧེ་རུ་ཀ་

CHEM CHO HE RU KA
Great excellent Heruka
(in Heruka mandala)

སྤྱན་རས་གཟིགས་དབང་

CHEN RE ZI WONG
Avalokitesvara
(in Potala)

ཨཱརྱ་ཏ་རེ

AR YA TA RE
Tara (in Yulokod)

21. The thirteen adornments of the sambhogakaya are 5 silk garments and 8 jewel ornaments. The individual items vary in different listings.

Dedication Prayer

བསོད་ནམས་འདི་ཡིས་ཐམས་ཅད་གཟིགས་པ་ཉིད།

SO NAM   **DI**   **YI**   **THAM CHE**   **ZI PA**   **NYI**
merit, virtue   *this*   *by*   *all*   *see*   *truly*

By this merit may I become omniscient.

ཐོབ་ནས་ཉེས་པའི་དགྲ་རྣམས་ཕམ་བྱེད་ཅིང་།

THOB   **NAE**   **NYE PAI**   **DRA NAM**   **PHAM JE CHING**
got   *then*   *sinful*   *enemies*   *defeating*

Then, defeating all troublesome enemies,

སྐྱེ་རྒ་ན་འཆིའི་རྦ་ཀློང་འཁྲུགས་པ་ཡི།

KYE   **GA**   **NA**   **CHI**   **BA LONG**   **TRU PA**   **YI**
birth   *old age*   *sickness*   *death*   *tidal wave*   *moving, tossed and tumbled*   *of*

Away from being tossed and tumbled in the tidal wave of birth, old age, sickness and of death,

སྲིད་པའི་མཚོ་ལས་འགྲོ་བ་སྒྲོལ་བར་ཤོག ༎

SI PAI   **TSHO**   **LAE**   **DRO WA**   **DROL WAR**   **SHO**
world's, samsara's   *ocean*   *from*   *beings*   *liberate*   *may I*

May I liberate all beings from the ocean of samsara.

By this merit may I become omniscient. Then defeating all troublesome enemies may I liberate all beings from the ocean of samsara where they are tossed and tumbled by the tidal waves of birth, old age, sickness and death

www.ingramcontent.com/pod-product-compliance
Lightning Source LLC
Chambersburg PA
CBHW040410110426

42812CB00012B/2518